CHILDREN'S DAILY PRAYER

for the School Year 2023–2024

Kara O'Malley

Nihil Obstat
Deacon David Keene, PHD
Chancellor
Archdiocese of Chicago
October 20, 2022

Imprimatur
Most Rev. Robert G. Casey
Vicar General
Archdiocese of Chicago
October 20, 2022

The *Nihil Obstat* and *Imprimatur* are declarations that the material is free from doctrinal or moral error, and thus is granted permission to publish in accordance with c. 827. No legal responsibility is assumed by the grant of this permission. No implication is contained herein that those who have granted the *Nihil Obstat* and *Imprimatur* agree with the content, opinions, or statements expressed.

Scripture quotations are taken from the *New Revised Standard Version Updated Edition* copyright © 2021, National Council of Churches of Christ in the United States of America. Used by permission. All rights reserved worldwide.

Excerpts from the English translation of *The Liturgy of the Hours* © 1973, 1974, 1975, International Commission on English in the Liturgy Corporation (ICEL); excerpts from the English translation of *The Roman Missal* © 2010, ICEL.

Excerpts from the English translation of the *Catechism of the Catholic Church* for the United States of America © 1994; United States Catholic Conference, Inc.—reprinted with the kind permission of *Dicastero per la Comunicazione - Libreria Editrice Vaticana*.

All rights reserved. Blessing prayer for birthdays adapted from *Book of Blessings*, additional blessings for use in the United States, © 1968, United States Conference of Catholic Bishops, Washington, DC. Used with permission.

Many of the concepts and guidelines, as well as various prayer services offered in this book, were originally conceived and developed by Dr. Sofia Cavalletti, Ms. Gianna Gobbi, and their collaborators. Theological underpinnings and many elements of these prayer services were first documented in Cavalletti's foundational books including *The Religious Potential of the Child* and *The Religious Potential of the Child, 6 to 12 Years Old*.

Liturgy Training Publications acknowledges the significant contribution made by Elizabeth McMahon Jeep to the development of *Children's Daily Prayer*. For more than fifteen years, Ms. Jeep worked tirelessly to cultivate this book into the essential prayer resource it is today for children and their parents, as well as for teachers and catechists. We are indebted to her for her authorship and guidance.

CHILDREN'S DAILY PRAYER 2023–2024 © 2023 Archdiocese of Chicago: Liturgy Training Publications, 3949 South Racine Avenue, Chicago, IL 60609; 800-933-1800; fax: 800-933-7094; email: orders@ltp.org; website: www.LTP.org. All rights reserved.

This book was edited by Michaela I. Tudela. Víctor R. Pérez was the production editor, Juan Alberto Castillo was the designer, and Matthew Clark was the production artist.

Cover art by Mikela Smith. Interior art by Paula Wiggins © LTP. Paperclip image by Babich Alexander/Shutterstock.com.

Printed in the United States of America

ISBN: 978-1-61671-696-7

CDP24

CONTENTS

Introduction	v
Instructions for Prayer for the Day and the Week	ix
Reproducible Psalms	xi

ORDINARY TIME, AUTUMN

About the Season	2
Grace before Meals	4
Prayer at Day's End	5
Prayer Service: Beginning of the Year for School Staff	6
Prayer Service: Beginning of the Year for Students	8
Home Prayer: Morning Prayer for Families Departing for the Day	10
Prayer Service: For the Care of Creation on September 1	22
National Day of Service and Remembrance on September 11	32
Home Prayer: Celebrating the Saints, Remembering the Dead	77
Prayer Service: For Thanksgiving	96
Home Prayer: Meal Prayer for Thanksgiving	99
Prayer for the Day and the Week	101–106
Home Prayer: Gathering around an Advent Wreath for Prayer	107

ADVENT

About the Season	110
Grace before Meals	112
Prayer at Day's End	113
Prayer Service: Advent	114
Prayer Service: Solemnity of the Immaculate Conception of Mary	122
Prayer for the Day and the Week	116–136

CHRISTMAS TIME

About the Season	138
Grace before Meals	140
Prayer at Day's End	141
Prayer Service: For Epiphany	147
Prayer for the Day and the Week	142–148

ORDINARY TIME, WINTER

About the Season	150
Grace before Meals	152
Prayer at Day's End	153
Prayer Service: Dr. Martin Luther King Jr.	160
Prayer Service: Week of Prayer for Christian Unity	164
Prayer for the Day and the Week	186

CONTENTS

LENT AND TRIDUUM

About the Season	188
Grace before Meals	190
Prayer at Day's End	191
Home Prayer: Keeping Lent	192
Prayer Service: Ash Wednesday	194
Prayer Service: Solemnity of St. Joseph	224
Home Prayer: Holy Thursday	234
Home Prayer: Good Friday	235
Prayer for the Day and the Week	193–233

EASTER TIME

About the Season	238
Grace before Meals	240
Prayer at Day's End	241
Prayer Service: Easter	242
Prayer Service: To Honor Mary in May	272
Prayer Service: Ascension	282
Prayer Service: Pentecost	290
Prayer for the Day and the Week	244–292

ORDINARY TIME, SUMMER

About the Season	294
Grace before Meals	296
Prayer at Day's End	297
Blessing for Birthdays	333
Prayer Service: Last Day of School	334
Prayer Service: For Sad Days	336
Psalms and Canticles	338
Additional Resources	350
Prayer for the Day and the Week	298–332

The editors appreciate your feedback.
Email: cdp@ltp.org.

INTRODUCTION

UNDERSTANDING THE ORDER OF PRAYER

Children's Daily Prayer is a form of the Liturgy of the Hours, adapted for children. It is based on the Church's tradition of Morning Prayer. A selected psalm is prayed for several weeks at a time. The readings for the daily prayers have been chosen to help children become familiar with significant themes and major stories in Scripture. The Sunday reading is always the Gospel of the day. Reflection questions for silent meditation or group conversation follow the reading.

For schools and homeschooling families, this book provides an order of prayer for each day of the school year (Prayer for the Day). For religious education settings, it provides prayer services for once a week (Prayer for the Week). Not every prayer element in the order of prayer will be useful in every situation. From the elements listed below, you can choose the ones that will be most effective for your group, setting, and time available.

OPENING

This gives the context for the Scripture reading and, when space allows, introduces the saint to be remembered that day. It also indicates when a particular theme or focus will be followed for the week. Sometimes difficult words or concepts in the reading are explained.

SIGN OF THE CROSS

An essential ritual action Catholics use to begin and end prayer. By making the sign of the cross, we place ourselves in the presence of the Father, the Son, and the Holy Spirit. Young children may need to practice making the sign of the cross.

PSALM

Praying the psalm is central to Morning Prayer. You may use the short version on the prayer page or the longer version on the Reproducible Psalms pages.

READING OR GOSPEL

Daily Scripture texts have been carefully selected to help children "walk through the Bible" and become familiar with the great stories and themes of salvation history. By following a story or exploring a theme for several days, the children experience how God has spoken to us through the words of Scripture and also through particular people and events in history. They begin to see how people have cooperated with God in bringing about God's kingdom on earth and to realize their role in this great work. The Prayer for the Week always uses the Sunday Gospel.

FOR SILENT REFLECTION

This is designed to be a time of silence so the children can ponder the Scripture they have heard and experience the value of silence in prayer. You might prefer to use this question at another time when discussing the reading or for journal writing. You may want to substitute your own instruction and questions. Regardless, some silence should be kept after proclaiming the Scripture.

CLOSING PRAYER

This prayer element begins with intercessions and ends with a brief prayer related to the liturgical season. In preparing for daily prayer, children can write the intercessions for the day and include relevant events to school and classroom life, as well as the world. They can also be encouraged to offer their own intentions spontaneously. You may choose to end with the Our Father.

PRAYER SERVICES

Children need to learn that the Church's prayer forms are rich and varied. We have the celebration of the Eucharist and traditional prayers such as the Rosary. We also have a long tradition of other forms of prayer, such as the Liturgy of the Hours, which emphasizes the psalms, or the Liturgy of the Word, which focuses on holy Scripture. Additional prayer services are offered in this book for specific liturgical times, memorials, feasts, or solemnities. (See Contents.) You may prefer to use one of these instead of the Prayer for the Day. Consider using these prayer services when the whole school gathers to celebrate a season. You might add an entrance procession and children and adults can do the ministerial roles.

GRACE BEFORE MEALS AND PRAYER AT DAY'S END

In order to instill in children the habit of prayer, use these prayers before lunch or at the end of the day.

PSALMS AND CANTICLES

Additional psalms and canticles (liturgical songs from the Bible: e.g., the Magnificat) are provided at the end of the book, and you will find many more in your Bible. Substitute them for any of the psalm excerpts in the prayer services or pray them with the children when a different choice better suits what is happening in your classroom community.

HOME PRAYERS

Children enjoy connecting their classroom and home lives. The Home Prayers offer a wonderful catechetical tool and resource for family prayer. You may photocopy these pages to send home.

CREATING A SACRED SPACE AND TIME FOR PRAYER

Children and adults benefit from having a consistent time for prayer. Where possible, it is helpful to the formation of prayer life to have a "sacred space"—that is, a designated place or table with religious objects such as the Bible, a cross, and a beautiful cloth that reflects the color of the liturgical season. The introductions to each liturgical season will offer specific ideas on how to do the following:

1. Use the language in the introduction to help the children understand the character of the time.

2. Look for practical suggestions for how to celebrate the liturgical time in a classroom setting:
   - how to arrange a sacred space within the classroom
   - what colors and objects to use in the sacred space
   - what songs to sing in each liturgical time
   - suggestions for special prayers for that liturgical time and how best to introduce them to children
   - help with adapting ideas from this book to special circumstances, especially for catechists who meet with students once a week.

See more on p. x on how to create a prayer space at home.

HOW CHILDREN PRAY

THE YOUNGEST CHILDREN

Children are natural liturgists and theologians. Young children (until age six) will pray simple but profound acclamations when they are given a real opportunity to hear the Word of God or to experience the language of signs found in our liturgy. Their spontaneous prayers most often reflect their understanding of the Word of God, their thanksgiving for God's goodness, and the joy they receive in

---

TIPS FOR GIVING CHILDREN A GREATER ROLE IN PRAYER

This book is intended to be used by children. It will help them become comfortable as leaders of prayer and will form them in the habit of daily prayer.

1. Ideally daily prayer takes place at the beginning of the day in individual classrooms. Consider inviting the children to work in groups to prepare and lead the prayer in your classroom. The group can take on the roles of leader, psalmist, lector, and perhaps music leader for the *Alleluia*. An intercessor might compose and lead a few petitions and then invite the class to add individual ones.

2. If it is necessary to begin the prayer over the public address system, consider doing only the opening and sign of the cross over the loudspeaker. Then invite the individual classrooms to continue the prayer in their own setting.

3. If you wish to lead the whole prayer over the public address system, consider inviting children from the various grades to do the roles listed in the first paragraph.

4. To help the younger children learn to lead prayer consider inviting older children to lead in the lower grade classrooms as mentioned in item one.

5. Invite your older students to help orient the younger ones to the prayer service. The older ones can help the younger ones practice the readings and compose intercessions so that eventually the younger ones can lead prayer in their own classrooms.

their relationship with Christ. Here are some examples of prayers collected by catechists: "Thank you, Lord, for the light!" (a three-year-old); "Thank you for everything!" (a four-year-old); "I love you!" (a three-year-old); and "I want to take a bath in your light" (a four-year-old). These prayers point to the young child's ability to appreciate the greatest of realities: life in relationship with God. When praying with these "little ones," it is best to proclaim the Scripture (explaining difficult words in advance to help their understanding) and then to ask one or two open-ended questions to help them to reflect on what the passage is saying to them. If you then invite them to say something to Jesus about what they've heard, you may be surprised at what comes out of the mouths of those budding little theologians!

PRAYING WITH OLDER CHILDREN

Older children (ages six to twelve) begin to appreciate the gift of prayer language. We should go slowly and use a light touch, though. When they're younger, give them one beautiful phrase ("Our Father, who art in heaven") that they can begin to appreciate and love. As they grow you can add a second phrase, then a third. But make sure that they understand the words they are using, and encourage them to pray slowly. Older children also enjoy leading prayer and composing their own prayers. If you give them each a small prayer journal and give them time to write in it, they will produce meaningful prayers and little theological drawings (particularly if you give them time to write and draw right after reading Scripture together).

PSALMS

The psalms offer a treasure trove of prayer language. Consider praying with one or two verses at a time. You could write one or two verses onto an unlined index card and display it on your prayer table. You can invite older children to copy them into their prayer journals. But remember to go over each word with the class, asking them to reflect on what the prayer wants to say to God. Children need time to explore the rich implications in their prayer. Also, psalms may be sung or chanted (after all, they were written as songs). Perhaps a parish cantor or choir member would lead a sung version of the psalm. At least the refrain might be sung on one note.

MUSIC IN PRAYER

It is a fact that the songs we sing in church are all prayers, so include singing in your classroom prayer life. What a wonderful difference it makes! Don't be shy, and don't worry about how well you sing. Even if you don't think you have a good voice, children will happily sing with you. So go ahead and make a joyful noise! Children enjoy the chance to lift their voices to God. You may even have a few gifted singers in the class who can help you lead the singing. The best music to use in the classroom is what your parish sings during the Sunday liturgy. You might incorporate the Penitential Act ("Lord Have Mercy, Christ Have Mercy, Lord Have Mercy") in Lent, the refrain of the Gloria in Easter, the Gospel Acclamation (Alleluia), even a chanted Our Father. Any songs, hymns, or chants that your parish sings are good choices. Your parish music director or diocesan director of music can be good resources. Also, in the introductions to each liturgical time, you will find music suggestions.

ART AS PRAYER

Once in a while suggest the children draw a picture after having heard the Scripture reading. Their drawings often reveal their joy and love in ways that language can't always express. Some children are more visual than verbal. Drawing allows them to lengthen and deepen their enjoyment of prayer time. Don't give the children assignments or themes for these "prayer" drawings, and don't offer a lot of fancy art supplies or media. The best, most reverent drawings come from children who are simply invited to draw something that has to do with what they have just heard in the Scripture reading, something to do with the Mass, or anything to do with God. These open-ended suggestions allow the Holy Spirit room to enter into the children's work.

PRAYER CANNOT BE EVALUATED

This book is most often used in school or religious education programs. In these settings, teachers are often required to give children a grade in religion. However, prayer is not class work and teachers and catechists who have any choice in the matter should make certain not to give the children a grade for prayer! Prayer expresses an inner, mysterious reality, for which teachers can provide the environment. Prayer is a person's conversation with God. Consider Jesus' teaching on prayer (Matthew 6:5–13) or take a close look at his parable of the Pharisee and the tax collector (Luke 18:9–14). We don't want the children to pray for the benefit of a grade or praise from the teacher; rather, we want them to pray from their feeling of relationship with a listening God.

JOY

In all you do with the children, feel free to communicate your joy to them, especially your joy in praying. Joy is a great sign of the presence of Christ. If you take pleasure in your students' company, they will understand that they are precious children of God. If you take pleasure in your work, they will understand that work is a beautiful gift. If you listen to them and take their words seriously, you will be incarnating Christ, who so valued children. Perhaps you will be the initial prayer leader and model that role. Something to model is a relaxed attitude when things go wrong (e.g., someone begins the Scripture too early). Try to give simple, clear directions ahead of time and then correct the situation as gently as possible. While you must keep order in your classrooms and an atmosphere of dignity in prayer, don't be afraid of a little silliness at times. Both laughter and tears are signs of the presence of the Holy Spirit.

ABOUT THE AUTHOR

Kara O'Malley has served as a director of Christian formation and director of youth ministry and religious education on the parish level, including direction of parish sacramental preparation. She earned a master's degree in theology from the University of Notre Dame through the Echo Program. She is the author of several LTP publications, including *My Sunday Mass Book, Belonging to God's Family,* and *Celebrating Sundays for Catholic Families*. Kara and her husband, Timothy, are the parents of two young children.

ABOUT THE ARTISTS AND THE ART

The cover art is by illustrator Mikela Smith, who received her BA in painting from the University of Redlands, California, and her MFA from California State Fullerton. Her artistic rendering of children leading prayer and praying together in the classroom captures the spirit and intent of this annual resource. The interior art is by Paula Wiggins, who lives and works in Cincinnati. At the top of the page for each day's prayer, you will find a little picture that reflects the liturgical time. During Ordinary Time in the autumn, a sturdy mustard tree with tiny seeds blowing from it reminds us of the parable of the mustard seed. For Advent we find the familiar Advent wreath. During the short season of Christmas Time, there is a manger scene with sheep and a dove. As we begin counting Ordinary Time, we find an oyster shell with pearls—an image for the parable of the pearl of great price. During Lent, bare branches remind us of this time of living simply, without decoration and distraction, so that we can feel God's presence. During Easter Time, we find the empty tomb in the early dawn of the first Easter. And as we return to Ordinary Time after Pentecost, a beautiful grape vine reminds us of Jesus' parable of the vine and the branches. At the beginning of each new liturgical time, special art accompanies the Grace before Meals and Prayer at Day's End, and you will find appropriate scenes for the various prayer services throughout the year. Finally, notice the harps accompanying the psalms, reminding us that these prayers were originally sung. The incense on the pages of canticles pictures the way we want our prayers to rise to God.

A NOTE ABOUT COPIES

As a purchaser of this book, you have permission to duplicate only the Reproducible Psalms pages, the Grace before Meals and Prayer at Day's End pages, the Prayer Services, and the Home Prayer pages; these copies may be used only with your class or group. The Home Prayer pages may be used only in the students' households. You may not duplicate the psalms or prayers unless you are using them with this book. Other parts of this book may not be duplicated without the permission of Liturgy Training Publications or the copyright holders listed on the acknowledgments page.

INSTRUCTIONS FOR PRAYER FOR THE DAY AND WEEK

FOR THE WHOLE GROUP

All of us participate in the prayer each day by lifting our hearts and voices to God. When the leader begins a Scripture passage by saying, "A reading from the holy Gospel according to . . . ," we respond "Glory to you, O Lord." At the conclusion of the Gospel, we say, "Praise to you, Lord Jesus Christ." At the conclusion of other Scripture readings, we say, "Thanks be to God." We offer our prayers and our intentions to God. When we conclude a prayer we say, "Amen."

Amen means "Yes! I believe it is true!" Let your "Amen" be heard by all.

FOR THE LEADER

1. Find the correct page and read it silently. Parts in bold black type are for everyone. All others are for you alone.

2. Practice reading your part aloud, and pronounce every syllable clearly. The parts marked with ◆ and ✢ are instructions for what to do. Follow the instructions but do not read them or the headings aloud. If you stumble over a word, repeat it until you can say it smoothly.

3. Pause after "A reading from the holy Gospel according to . . . " so the class can respond. Pause again after "The Gospel of the Lord." Remember to allow for silence when the instructions call for it, especially after the Gospel and after reading the questions "For Silent Reflection."

4. Pause after "Let us bring our hopes and needs to God . . . " so that individuals may offer their prayers aloud or in silence. After each petition, the group responds, "Lord, hear our prayer."

5. When you make the sign of the cross, use your right hand and do it slowly and reverently, first touching your forehead ("In the name of the Father"), next just below your chest ("and of the Son"), then your left shoulder ("and of the Holy"), and finally your right shoulder ("Spirit").

6. At prayer time, stand straight and tall in the front of the class. Ask the students to use their reproducible sheet of psalms for reading their part. Read slowly and clearly.

IF THERE ARE TWO LEADERS

One leader reads the Reading or Gospel while the other reads all of the other parts. Practice reading your part(s). Both leaders should stand in front of the class during the entire prayer.

Remember to read very slowly, with a loud, clear voice.

FOR PARENTS

CREATING A SACRED SPACE AT HOME

The Catholic Church designates the home as the domestic church, or "little church," where the seeds of faith begin to take root in a child's heart. The child's relationship with God is essential to their formation and identity, and it all begins in the home. When praying together as a family, it is beneficial to designate a space for prayer as well as establish a consistent time in order to instill a sense of intentionality and regularity. The goal is to instill a permanent structure and place so that praying together becomes a ritualistic and essential part of your day. Here are some suggestions to guide you in creating a sacred space:

- Choose a quiet, distraction-free place in your home, such as a quiet corner or small bedroom. Where your family will gather for prayer should encourage prayerful reflection.
- Furnish your sacred space with a small table, nightstand, or even a shelf that can be dedicated to your prayer, much as an altar is used in church.
- Use a Bible, flowers, candles, and materials such as a colorful cloth to designate the space as sacred and liturgical. Add a cross or crucifix as a focal point for prayer.
- Encourage your children to decorate the space using their own religious artwork or drawings.
- Help your children ready themselves to be still and open to the Word by lighting candles, playing instrumental music at a low volume, or dimming the lights. Allow for a moment of silence before reading the Opening.

ENCOURAGING CHILDREN TO PARTICIPATE IN PRAYER AT HOME

This book is intended to be used by children, not just parents. When children are young, parents have a larger role in creating a sacred space, reading Scripture, and encouraging children's participation. Later, help your children become the leaders in your family prayer. This will encourage them to form a deep commitment and dedication to prayer. Here are some ideas:

- Decide together on a time for your prayer service, whether it is first thing in the morning, after dinnertime, or right before bedtime.
- Add songs or special prayers for special moments in our liturgical year.
- Encourage your children to draw parallels from Sunday Mass to your home prayer service. Take suggestions from your children on creating your sacred space to look more like church, or involve them as leaders, psalmists, readers, music ministers, or intercessors. Allow your children—including the younger ones—to help decorate your sacred space, and participate by reading the Scripture or holding the book as you read.
- Involve your children in writing prayers of intercessions for their needs, the needs of others, and those around the world.

REPRODUCIBLE PSALMS
ORDINARY TIME, AUTUMN

ORDINARY TIME, AUTUMN

Psalm for Sunday, August 20—Friday, September 29

Psalm 66:1–3a, 5, 8, 16–17

LEADER: Make a joyful noise to God, all the earth.

ALL: **Make a joyful noise to God, all the earth.**

LEADER: Make a joyful noise to God, all the earth;
sing the glory of his name;
give to him glorious praise.
Say to God, "How awesome are
your deeds!"

ALL: **Make a joyful noise to God, all the earth.**

Short version: use above only; long version: use above and below.

SIDE A: Come and see what God has done:
he is awesome in his deeds
among mortals.
Bless our God, O peoples,
let the sound of his praise be heard.

SIDE B: Come and hear, all you who fear God,
and I will tell what
he has done for me.
I cried aloud to him,
and he was extolled with my tongue.

ALL: **Make a joyful noise to God, all the earth.**

ORDINARY TIME, AUTUMN

Psalm for Sunday, October 1—Friday, October 27

Psalm 145:2–3, 4–5, 10–11

LEADER: I will praise your name for ever, Lord.

ALL: **I will praise your name for ever, Lord.**

LEADER: Every day I will bless you,
and praise your name forever and ever.
Great is the Lord, and greatly
to be praised;
his greatness is unsearchable.

ALL: **I will praise your name for ever, Lord.**

Short version: use above only; long version: use above and below.

SIDE A: One generation shall laud your works
to another, and shall declare your
mighty acts.
On the glorious splendor of your majesty,
and on your wondrous works,
I will meditate.

SIDE B: All your works shall give thanks to you,
O Lord, and all your faithful shall
bless you.
They shall speak of the glory of your
kingdom, and tell of your power.

ALL: **I will praise your name for ever, Lord.**

REPRODUCIBLE PSALMS
ORDINARY TIME, AUTUMN; ADVENT

ORDINARY TIME, AUTUMN

Psalm for Sunday, November 5—Friday, December 1

Psalm 98:1, 2–3, 3–4

LEADER: The Lord has made known his victory.

ALL: **The Lord has made known his victory.**

LEADER: O sing to the Lord a new song,
    for he has done marvelous things.
His right hand and his holy arm
    have gotten him victory.

ALL: **The Lord has made known his victory.**

Short version: use above only; long version: use above and below.

SIDE A: The Lord has made known his victory;
    he has revealed his vindication in the
        sight of the nations.
He has remembered his steadfast love
    and faithfulness to the house of Israel.

SIDE B: All the ends of the earth have seen the
    victory of our God.
Make a joyful noise to the Lord,
    all the earth;
        break forth into joyous song and
        sing praises.

ALL: **The Lord has made known his victory.**

ADVENT

Psalm for Sunday, December 3—Sunday, December 24

Psalm 85:4a, 8, 10–11, 12–13

LEADER: Restore us again,
    O God of our salvation!

ALL: **Restore us again,
    O God of our salvation!**

LEADER: Let me hear what God the Lord
    will speak,
    for he will speak peace to his people,
    to his faithful, to those who turn to
    him in their hearts.

ALL: **Restore us again,
    O God of our salvation!**

Short version: use above only; long version: use above and below.

SIDE A: Steadfast love and faithfulness will meet;
    righteousness and peace will kiss
        each other.
Faithfulness will spring up from
    the ground,
    and righteousness will look down
    from the sky.

SIDE B: The Lord will give what is good,
    and our land will yield its increase.
Righteousness will go before him
    and will make a path for his steps.

ALL: **Restore us again,
    O God of our salvation!**

REPRODUCIBLE PSALMS
CHRISTMAS TIME; ORDINARY TIME, WINTER

CHRISTMAS TIME

Psalm for Monday, January 1—Sunday, January 7

Psalm 96:1–2a, 2b–3, 5b–6, 11a

LEADER: Let the heavens be glad and the
 earth rejoice!

ALL: **Let the heavens be glad and the
 earth rejoice!**

LEADER: O sing to the LORD a new song;
 sing to the LORD, all the earth.
 Sing to the LORD; bless his name.

ALL: **Let the heavens be glad and the
 earth rejoice!**

Short version: use above only; long version: use above and below.

SIDE A: Tell of his salvation from day to day.
 Declare his glory among the nations,
 his marvelous works among all
 the peoples.

SIDE B: The LORD made the heavens.
 Honor and majesty are before him;
 strength and beauty are in his sanctuary.

ALL: **Let the heavens be glad and the
 earth rejoice!**

ORDINARY TIME, WINTER

Psalm for Monday, January 8—Tuesday, February 13

Psalm 23:1–3a, 3b–4, 5, 6

LEADER: I shall dwell in the house of the LORD my
 whole life long.

ALL: **I shall dwell in the house of the LORD my
 whole life long.**

LEADER: The LORD is my shepherd,
 I shall not want.
 He makes me lie down in
 green pastures;
 he leads me beside still waters;
 he restores my soul.

ALL: **I shall dwell in the house of the LORD my
 whole life long.**

Short version: use above only; long version: use above and below.

SIDE A: He leads me in right paths
 for his name's sake.
 Even though I walk through the
 darkest valley,
 I fear no evil, for you are with me;
 your rod and your staff,
 they comfort me.

SIDE B: You prepare a table before me
 in the presence of my enemies;
 you anoint my head with oil;
 my cup overflows.

ALL: **I shall dwell in the house of the LORD my
 whole life long.**

REPRODUCIBLE PSALMS
LENT; EASTER TIME

LENT

Psalm for Wednesday, February 14—Wednesday, March 27

Psalm 34:4–5, 6–7, 16–17, 18–19

LEADER: The Lord saves the crushed in spirit.

ALL: **The Lord saves the crushed in spirit.**

LEADER: I sought the Lord, and he answered me
and delivered me from all my fears.
Look to him, and be radiant,
so your faces shall never be ashamed.

ALL: **The Lord saves the crushed in spirit.**

Short version: use above only; long version: use above and below.

SIDE A: This poor soul cried and was heard by the Lord
and was saved from every trouble.
The angel of the Lord encamps
around those who fear him and
delivers them.

SIDE B: The face of the Lord is against evildoers,
to cut off the remembrance of them
from the earth.
When the righteous cry for help
the Lord hears
and rescues them from all
their troubles.

ALL: **The Lord saves the crushed in spirit.**

LEADER: The Lord is near to the brokenhearted,
and saves the crushed in spirit.
Many are the afflictions of the righteous,
but the Lord rescues them from
them all.

ALL: **The Lord saves the crushed in spirit.**

EASTER TIME

Psalm for Sunday, March 31—Friday, April 26

Psalm 105:1–2, 3–4, 6–7

LEADER: Let the hearts of those who seek the Lord rejoice.

ALL: **Let the hearts of those who seek the Lord rejoice.**

LEADER: O give thanks to the Lord; call on his name;
make known his deeds among
the peoples.
Sing to him, sing praises to him;
tell of all his wonderful works.

ALL: **Let the hearts of those who seek the Lord rejoice.**

Short version: use above only; long version: use above and below.

SIDE A: Glory in his holy name;
let the hearts of those who seek the
Lord rejoice.
Seek the Lord and his strength;
seek his presence continually.

SIDE B: O offspring of his servant Abraham,
children of Jacob, his chosen ones.
He is the Lord our God;
his judgments are in all the earth.

ALL: **Let the hearts of those who seek the Lord rejoice.**

REPRODUCIBLE PSALMS
EASTER TIME; ORDINARY TIME, SUMMER

EASTER TIME

Psalm for Sunday, April 28—Friday, May 24

Psalm 118:1–2, 4, 22–24, 25–27a

LEADER: The stone that the builders rejected
has become the chief cornerstone.

ALL: **The stone that the builders rejected
has become the chief cornerstone.**

LEADER: O give thanks to the LORD, for he is good;
his steadfast love endures forever!
Let Israel say,
"His steadfast love endures forever."
Let those who fear the LORD say,
"His steadfast love endures forever."

ALL: **The stone that the builders rejected
has become the chief cornerstone.**

Short version: use above only; long version: use above and below.

SIDE A: The stone that the builders rejected
has become the chief cornerstone.
This is the LORD's doing;
it is marvelous in our eyes.
This is the day that the LORD has made;
let us rejoice and be glad in it.

SIDE B: Save us, we beseech you, O LORD!
O LORD, we beseech you,
give us success!
Blessed is the one who comes in the name
of the LORD.
We bless you from the house
of the LORD.
The LORD is God,
and he has given us light.

ALL: **The stone that the builders rejected
has become the chief cornerstone.**

ORDINARY TIME, SUMMER

Psalm for Sunday, May 26—Friday, June 28

Psalm 85:8–9, 10–11, 12–13

LEADER: The LORD speaks of peace to his people.

ALL: **The LORD speaks of peace to his people.**

LEADER: Let me hear what God the LORD
will speak,
for he will speak peace to his people,
to his faithful, to those who turn to
him in their hearts.
Surely his salvation is at hand for those
who fear him,
that his glory may dwell in our land.

ALL: **The LORD speaks of peace to his people.**

Short version: use above only; long version: use above and below.

SIDE A: Steadfast love and faithfulness will meet;
righteousness and peace will kiss
each other.
Faithfulness will spring up from
the ground,
and righteousness will look down
from the sky.

SIDE B: The LORD will give what is good,
and our land will yield its increase.
Righteousness will go before him
and will make a path for his steps.

ALL: **The LORD speaks of peace to his people.**

ORDINARY TIME AUTUMN

SUNDAY, AUGUST 20, 2023 — FRIDAY, DECEMBER 1, 2023

AUTUMN ORDINARY TIME

THE MEANING OF ORDINARY TIME

Times and seasons on our liturgical calendar, in contrast to the secular calendar, are valued in a different, altogether new way. Our Christian calendar even has a different shape! Instead of a rectangle, we draw all the days of a year in a circle. Instead of marking off times according to the weather, we celebrate those great moments when God reveals a great love for us in marvelous and mysterious ways.

Our liturgical calendar has four primary seasons. Advent (the four weeks before Christmas); Christmas Time; Lent (the six weeks before Easter); Easter Time (which extends for fifty days after Easter through Pentecost) but, the longest part of the calendar is called Ordinary Time.

Ordinary Time is thirty-three or thirty-four weeks a year. It is called "Ordinary Time" because the weeks are numbered. The Latin word *ordinalis*, which refers to numbers in a series and stems from the Latin word *ordo*, from which we get the English word *order*. Ordinary Time is therefore "ordered time." Calling it "Ordered Time" reminds us of God's great plan for creation. There was a specific time for the creation of light, planets, water, earth, plants, animals, and humankind. Ordinary Time begins after Christmas, continues until Ash Wednesday when it stops for Lent and Easter, then picks up again after Pentecost Sunday and runs through the summer and autumn until the beginning of Advent. Each Sunday in Ordinary Time has a number and the numbers increase each week.

During autumn Ordinary Time, there are weekly themes for the Scripture readings. Some of the themes help us to understand qualities of our faith: prayer, service and the great commandment to love God and love one another. We will hear about giving God praise by our words and actions. In these weeks, the readings cover a historical spectrum of Scripture.

From the New Testament, we will read parables or stories that Jesus told about God's kingdom. With moral parables in week twenty-four, like the sower, the talents, and the Pharisee and the tax collector, Jesus teaches us about the consequences of our behavior.

From the Old Testament we will read from the Book of Genesis and wonder at the marvelous story of Creation. We will spend two weeks on the story of Abraham our father in faith. God promises Abraham that, despite his childlessness, he would become the father of nations. God establishes this covenant not only between Abraham and himself, but extends it to future generations, including us today. Covenant blessings require total commitment and obedience to the Lord. Time and again, God reaches out to his people in love and friendship. Later, through Moses, God reminds the chosen people that he would be faithful to the covenant and to them, if they would keep faith with him.

For two weeks we will also hear the the story of Joseph, the great-grandson of Abraham. Through his dreams, God showed that he would always provide.

As we near the end of the liturgical year, we will learn more about the role of women in the Bible and celebrate a number of female saints. We close the year by reflecting on who Jesus is: the Messiah, Savior of Israel, Son of Man, Lord of the Sabbath, Teacher and Healer, Good Shepherd, and Christ the King!

PREPARING TO CELEBRATE ORDINARY TIME IN THE CLASSROOM

SACRED SPACE

You want the prayer table or space to be in a place where the children will see it often and perhaps go to it in their free moments. If you can have a separate prayer table it should not be too small, perhaps a coffee-table size. You may wish to buy one or two inexpensive cushions to place before your prayer table so that children will feel invited to sit or kneel there. The essential things for the prayer table are a cross or crucifix (unless one is on the wall), a Bible, a substantial candle and a cloth of liturgical color. Cover the prayer table with a plain green cloth or one that mixes green with other Autumn colors. Large table napkins or placemats work, or remnants from a sewing store. Green, the color of hope and life, is the color of Ordinary Time. If you can, set the Bible on a bookstand. Point out the candle beside the Bible, and remind them that Jesus said, "I am the Light of the world" (John 8:12). You might light the candle, open the Bible, and read that verse to the class. Other objects you might want to include are a simple statue of Mary (September 8), images of angels (Archangels, September 29 and Guardian,

October 2), an image of St. Francis or the children's pets (October 4), a rosary (month of October). Use natural objects, too, such as flowers, dried leaves or small gourds. If there is the space, pictures of loved ones who have died would be appropriate in November.

MOVEMENT AND GESTURE

Consider reverencing the Word of God in the Bible by carrying it in procession. Place a candle ahead of it and perhaps carry wind chimes as it moves through the room. At the prayer space the processors turn and the Bible is raised. The class reverences with a profound bow (a bow from the waist) then the Bible and candle are placed, and the chimes' are silenced. Also consider reverencing the crucifix or the cross near September 14, the Exaltation of the Holy Cross. Take the crucifix from the wall (or use another one) and carry it in procession at the beginning of prayer in a similar manner or take the cross to each child and let them kiss it or hold it or make a head bow before it.

FESTIVITY IN SCHOOL AND HOME

For Ordinary Time in autumn, *Children's Daily Prayer* provides several special prayer services to use in the classroom—or with larger groups such as the whole school—to celebrate the beginning of the school year and to pray for peace (on September 11). The Home Prayer pages can be duplicated for the students to take home and share with their families: Morning Prayer for Families Departing for the Day; Home Prayer for Celebrating the Saints and Remembering the Dead; and a Meal Prayer for Thanksgiving.

SACRED MUSIC

One of the best ways to help the children enter into the special qualities of this or any liturgical time is by teaching them the Sunday music of their parish. Teach the children (or invite the school music teacher, parish music director or a choir member/cantor to do it) how your church sings her "Alleluia!" See what songs and hymns the children know and love. For example, in Ordinary Time, consider "For the Beauty of the Earth" and "Make Me a Channel of Your Peace." Learn and sing just a good refrain. Singing is an integral part of how we pray.

PRAYERS FOR ORDINARY TIME

During this season, take some time to discuss the meaning of the various intercessions of the Our Father with the children in your class. In particular, discuss the kingdom of God—that time of peace and justice proclaimed by and fulfilled in Jesus. Ask what it means for God's kingdom to come. Go through the prayer one intercession at a time asking what each means. Explore with them what Jesus is teaching us about how we should pray: We ask for God's name to be treated as blessed and holy, for the coming of the kingdom of God, for God's will to be accomplished on earth, for our "daily bread," for forgiveness, and for strength in the face of temptation.

A NOTE TO CATECHISTS

Because you meet with your students once a week, you may wish to use the Prayer for the Week pages. These weekly prayer pages contain an excerpt from the Sunday Gospel and will help to prepare the children for Mass. Sometimes, though, you may wish to substitute the Prayer for the Day if it falls on an important solemnity, feast, or memorial of the Church. In this introduction, you will see the suggestions for your prayer space. You may have to set up a prayer space each time you meet with your group. Think in advance about where to place it, have all your materials in one box, and always set it up in the same place.

GRACE BEFORE MEALS
FOR ORDINARY TIME • AUTUMN

LEADER:
Lord, you gift us with your love in so many ways.

ALL: We praise you and thank you!

✚ All make the sign of the cross.

In the name of the Father, and of the Son, and of the Holy Spirit. Amen.

LEADER:
Father, Son, and Spirit,
you bring us joy
through your abundant grace.
As we gather to share this meal,
may we be grateful for the
loving people who prepared it
every step of the way.
We thank all those in lands far from us
and those nearby who
helped grow, nurture, package,
transport, store, and cook our food.
We bless these brothers and sisters
as we bless each other here,
for you created all of us in
your image of goodness and love.
May this meal nourish our bodies
to give you glory and to build your Kingdom.
We ask this through Jesus Christ, our Lord.

ALL: Amen.

✚ All make the sign of the cross.

In the name of the Father, and of the Son, and of the Holy Spirit. Amen.

PRAYER AT DAY'S END
FOR ORDINARY TIME • AUTUMN

LEADER:
God of all wisdom,
we offer back to you
all that we have done today
through the gift of your gentle Spirit.

ALL: For your love is in our hearts!

✚ All make the sign of the cross.

In the name of the Father, and of the Son, and of the Holy Spirit. Amen.

LEADER:
We are grateful for
the signs and wonders of this day,
for the ordinary events and its surprises,
big and small.
We thank you for the
loving people who surround us.
May we continue to reflect your goodness
to others in your name.
We ask this through your beloved Son, Jesus.

ALL: Amen.

✚ All make the sign of the cross.

In the name of the Father, and of the Son, and of the Holy Spirit. Amen.

PRAYER SERVICE
BEGINNING OF THE YEAR FOR SCHOOL STAFF

Seek volunteers to lead this prayer service. You may involve up to seven leaders (as marked below). The fourth leader will need a Bible for the Scripture passage. Choose hymns for the beginning and ending if you wish.

FIRST LEADER:
We gather in Christ's name
to celebrate all of God's children.
Let us ask the Holy Spirit for guidance
as we begin our journey again with them.

◆ Gesture for all to stand.

Together we enter this time of prayer as we make the sign of the cross.

✝ All make the sign of the cross.

In the name of the Father, and of the Son, and of the Holy Spirit. Amen.

SECOND LEADER:
Spirit of God,
enlighten our minds
as we begin another school year, for
these children are gifts of new life.
Draw us closer to all
that is good and true
so that through us
all that they see
is you.
We ask this through Christ our Lord.

Amen.

THIRD LEADER:
Spirit of your Son Jesus,
grant us your wisdom and
integrity each and every day,
for you are the breath of all
that is holy.

Refresh us with ideas that
inspire our youth with your energy
and enthusiasm.
We ask this in Christ's name.

Amen.

♦ Gesture for all to sit.

FOURTH LEADER: Romans 8:31b–35, 37–39
A reading from the Letter of Paul to Romans.

♦ Read the Scripture passage from the Bible.

The Word of the Lord.

♦ All observe silence.

FIFTH LEADER:

♦ Gesture for all to stand.

Let us bring our hopes and needs to God as we pray from the Opening Prayer of our Church leadership as they embarked on the Second Vatican Council. Our response will be: **Guide us with your love.**

For light and strength to know your will,
to make it our own,
and to live it in our lives,
we pray to the Lord.

ALL: Guide us with your love.

For justice for all;
enable us to uphold the rights of others;
do not allow us to be misled by ignorance
or corrupted by fear or favor,
we pray to the Lord.

ALL: Guide us with your love.

Unite us to yourself in the bond of love
and keep us faithful to all that is true,
we pray to the Lord.

ALL: Guide us with your love.

May we temper justice with love,
so that all our discussions and reflections
may be pleasing to you, and earn the reward
promised to good and faithful servants,
we pray to the Lord.

ALL: Guide us with your love.

SIXTH LEADER:
Let us pray as Jesus taught us:
Our Father . . . Amen.

♦ Pause and then say:

Let us offer one another the sign of
Christ's peace.

♦ All offer one another a sign of peace.

SEVENTH LEADER:
Let us pray:
God, our Creator,
your presence through the
Holy Spirit strengthens us
for the days ahead.
Guide us with your patience
and compassion as we
mentor our future leaders in Christ.

Amen.

✢ All make the sign of the cross.

In the name of the Father, and of the Son, and of the Holy Spirit. Amen.

PRAYER SERVICE
BEGINNING OF THE YEAR FOR STUDENTS

This prayer service may be led by the eighth grade students or by older students. The third and fifth leaders will need a Bible for the passages from Matthew and Luke. Take time to help the third and fifth leaders practice the readings. You may wish to sing "This Little Light of Mine" as the opening and closing songs. If the group will sing, prepare someone to lead the songs.

FIRST LEADER:

We are embarking on a journey together
in this brand new school year.
As we look ahead at all that this year
might reveal,
let us remember Jesus,
who will walk beside us every step of the way.

SONG LEADER:

Let us begin by singing the first few verses of our song.

- ◆ Gesture for all to stand, and lead the first few verses of the song.

SECOND LEADER:

- ✚ All make the sign of the cross.

    In the name of the Father, and of the Son, and of the Holy Spirit. Amen.

Let us pray:
God our Creator,
we were made in
your image and likeness.
Help us to be gentle with
ourselves and each other
as we mature this year with your grace.

Guide us in our studies and help us develop
with knowledge and maturity.
We ask this through Christ our Lord.

Amen.

◆ Remain standing and sing Alleluia.

THIRD LEADER: Matthew 5:14–16

A reading from the holy Gospel according
to Matthew.

◆ Read the Gospel passage from the Bible.

The Gospel of the Lord.

◆ All sit and observe silence.

FOURTH LEADER:

◆ Gesture for all to stand.

Let us bring our hopes and needs to God as we
pray, Let your light shine through us.

ALL: Let your light shine through us.

Help us to show honor and respect
to all those who teach and coach us,
we pray to the Lord.

ALL: Let your light shine through us.

Guide us with your counsel, Lord,
when we are frustrated with our studies,
we pray to the Lord.

ALL: Let your light shine through us.

Help us to take care of our
minds and bodies
so that we give you glory in
everything we do,
we pray to the Lord.

ALL: Let your light shine through us.

Help us to remember all that we learn
so that we can apply it to our lives
in the months and years ahead,
we pray to the Lord.

ALL: Let your light shine through us.

FIFTH LEADER: Luke 6:31–36

Let us listen to what Jesus teaches
to his disciples:

A reading from the holy Gospel according
to Luke.

◆ Read the Gospel passage from the Bible.

The Gospel of the Lord.

SIXTH LEADER:

Let us pray:
O God,
we know you are with us on this journey.
Help us to love one another
as you love us.
Guide us with your light of mercy and justice.
May we be considerate with our friends
and respectful of all who lead us.
Help us to learn and grow in your
wisdom throughout this year.
We ask this through Christ our Lord.

Amen.

✣ All make the sign of the cross.

**In the name of the Father, and of the
Son, and of the Holy Spirit. Amen.**

SONG LEADER:

Please join in singing the final verses of our
closing song.

HOME PRAYER
MORNING PRAYER FOR FAMILIES DEPARTING FOR THE DAY

The Catechism of the Catholic Church *calls the family the "domestic church" where children are first introduced to the faith (CCC, 2204 and 2225). A blessing is a prayer that acknowledges and thanks God for the good things in our lives and asks God to be with us. When the household gathers in the morning, perhaps at breakfast, a parent, grandparent, or other adult may lead this blessing.*

The longer prayer can be used on one of the first days of school and other special occasions. At other times, you may just want to bless the child with the sign of the cross on the forehead and a "God bless you" as he or she leaves for school.

✢ All make the sign of the cross.

In the name of the Father, and of the Son, and of the Holy Spirit. Amen.

LEADER:

We each have important things
to do today, and so we ask God's blessing.
We go to school and to work.
We learn and play.
We praise and thank God for each other
and for the love we share.
We ask God to be with those
who are lonely or sick
or without basic needs.
We ask this in Jesus' name.

All: Amen.

LEADER:

Holy God,
giver of all good gifts,
walk with us today,
guide our words and our actions,
and keep us on the path of truth.
Bring us back together in peace
at the end of this day.
We ask this through Christ our Lord.

✢ The leader makes the sign of the cross on one person's forehead saying:

"God bless you and keep you today."

ALL: Amen.

PRAYER FOR THE WEEK
WITH A READING FROM THE GOSPEL FOR **SUNDAY, AUGUST 20, 2023**

OPENING

How do you approach the Lord? Sometimes we might approach the Lord with panic and urgency, like the Canaanite woman in the Gospel today. Sometimes we might be joyful or thankful, sad or regretful. However we approach him, Jesus will be there. He will turn toward us, listen, and respond in love.

✢ All make the sign of the cross.

In the name of the Father, and of the Son, and of the Holy Spirit. Amen.

PSALM
(For a longer psalm, see page xi.)
Psalm 66:1–3a

Make a joyful noise to God, all the earth.

Make a joyful noise to God, all the earth.

Make a joyful noise to God, all the earth;
   sing the glory of his name;
   give to him glorious praise.
Say to God, "How awesome are your deeds!"

Make a joyful noise to God, all the earth.

◆ All stand and sing **Alleluia.**

GOSPEL
Matthew 15:21–28

A reading from the holy Gospel according to Matthew.

Jesus left that place and went away to the district of Tyre and Sidon [SĪ-duhn]. Just then a Canaanite [KAY-nuh-nīt] woman from that region came out and started shouting, "Have mercy on me, Lord, Son of David; my daughter is tormented by a demon." But he did not answer her at all. And his disciples came and urged him, saying, "Send her away, for she keeps shouting after us." He answered, "I was sent only to the lost sheep of the house of Israel." But she came and knelt before him, saying, "Lord, help me." He answered, "It is not fair to take the children's food and throw it to the dogs." She said, "Yes, Lord, yet even the dogs eat the crumbs that fall from their masters' table." Then Jesus answered her, "Woman, great is your faith! Let it be done for you as you wish." And her daughter was healed from that moment.

The Gospel of the Lord.

◆ All sit and observe silence.

FOR SILENT REFLECTION

Think about this silently in your heart. When and how do you turn to Jesus in daily life?

CLOSING PRAYER

Let us pray to God for our needs and the needs of others: our family, neighborhood, and the world. For each need we say, "Lord, hear our prayer."

◆ All may add their own prayers here.

Let us pray: **Our Father . . . Amen.**

Lord Jesus,
give us the heart to turn to you at all times, to
   share our deepest joys and sorrows,
and to continue to know your kindness.
We make this prayer in your name.

Amen.

✢ All make the sign of the cross.

PRAYER FOR
MONDAY, AUGUST 21, 2023

OPENING

Solomon is remembered as the wise king of Israel. His wisdom was a gift from God in answer to his prayer. This week, we will reflect on how and why we pray. Today is the feast of Pope St. Pius X, and his papal motto gives us one reason why: "to restore all things in Christ."

✚ All make the sign of the cross.

In the name of the Father, and of the Son, and of the Holy Spirit. Amen.

PSALM
(For a longer psalm, see page xi.)
Psalm 66:1–3a

Make a joyful noise to God, all the earth.

Make a joyful noise to God, all the earth.

Make a joyful noise to God, all the earth;
   sing the glory of his name;
   give to him glorious praise.
Say to God, "How awesome are your deeds!"

Make a joyful noise to God, all the earth.

READING
2 Chronicles 6:12, 13fg–14b; 7:12ab, 14

A reading from the Second Book of Chronicles.

Then Solomon stood before the altar of the Lord in the presence of the whole assembly of Israel and spread out his hands. Then he knelt on his knees in the presence of the whole assembly of Israel and spread out his hands toward heaven. He said, "O Lord, God of Israel, there is no God like you, in heaven or on earth. Then the Lord appeared to Solomon in the night and said to him, "I have heard your prayer. If my people who are called by my name humble themselves, pray, seek my face, and turn from their wicked ways, then I will hear from heaven and will forgive their sin and heal their land."

The Word of the Lord.

◆ All observe silence.

FOR SILENT REFLECTION

Think about this silently in your heart. How did the Lord respond to Solomon's prayer?

CLOSING PRAYER

Let us pray to God for our needs and the needs of others: our family, neighborhood, and the world. For each need we say, "Lord, hear our prayer."

◆ All may add their own prayers here.

Let us pray: **Our Father . . . Amen.**

O God,
may we turn toward you humbly in prayer
   and seek your face at all times.
Grant us the wisdom to turn to you in times
   of uncertainty,
and the courage to hear your voice.
We ask this through Christ our Lord.

Amen.

✚ All make the sign of the cross.

PRAYER FOR
TUESDAY, AUGUST 22, 2023

OPENING

Keeping the Sabbath is a sign of the covenant of God with his people. Our Catholic understanding of this duty is that we are to be faithful to God in a special way on Sundays, praying the sacrifice of Mass, and not allowing sports, activities, or other obligations to come between us and the love of God in the Eucharist. Sometimes is it is hard to keep this obligation! But in those times, we can turn to the Blessed Mother, who is the perfect example of obedience to God's will. We celebrate Mary's queenship today.

✤ All make the sign of the cross.

In the name of the Father, and of the Son, and of the Holy Spirit. Amen.

PSALM
(For a longer psalm, see page xi.)
Psalm 66:1–3a

Make a joyful noise to God, all the earth.

Make a joyful noise to God, all the earth.

Make a joyful noise to God, all the earth;
   sing the glory of his name;
   give to him glorious praise.
Say to God, "How awesome are your deeds!"

Make a joyful noise to God, all the earth.

READING
Isaiah 56:1–2ace, 6eg, 7–8

A reading from the Book of the prophet Isaiah.

Thus says the Lord: Maintain justice, and do what is right, for soon my salvation will come and my deliverance be revealed. Happy is the mortal who does this, who keeps the Sabbath, and refrains from doing any evil. All who keep the Sabbath and do not profane it and hold fast my covenant—these I will bring to my holy mountain and make them joyful in my house of prayer; their burnt offerings and their sacrifices will be accepted on my altar, for my house shall be called a house of prayer for all peoples. Thus says the Lord God, who gathers the outcasts of Israel: I will gather others to them besides those already gathered.

The Word of the Lord.

◆ All observe silence.

FOR SILENT REFLECTION

Think about this silently in your heart. Do you find it easy or hard to keep the Sabbath holy?

CLOSING PRAYER

Let us pray to God for our needs and the needs of others: our family, neighborhood, and the world. For each need we say, "Lord, hear our prayer."

◆ All may add their own prayers here.

Let us pray: **Our Father . . . Amen.**

Lord,
you have blessed us abundantly
and have given your people many good and
   beautiful gifts.
Help us to be faithful to you
and to return to you in the Eucharist
   every week.
In Jesus' name, we pray.
Amen.

✤ All make the sign of the cross.

PRAYER FOR
WEDNESDAY, AUGUST 23, 2023

OPENING

In his earthly life, Jesus gives us an example of how to pray. He makes time for prayer, even if it involves waking up early. He goes to a quiet place where he can be alone, and he talks to God. We remember St. Rose of Lima today, who prayed every day in a space she built in her backyard. Against her parents' wishes, she refused to marry, and instead devoted her life to prayer and works of charity.

✢ All make the sign of the cross.

In the name of the Father, and of the Son, and of the Holy Spirit. Amen.

PSALM
(For a longer psalm, see page xi.)
Psalm 66:1–3a

Make a joyful noise to God, all the earth.

Make a joyful noise to God, all the earth.

Make a joyful noise to God, all the earth;
    sing the glory of his name;
    give to him glorious praise.
Say to God, "How awesome are your deeds!"

Make a joyful noise to God, all the earth.

◆ All stand and sing **Alleluia.**

GOSPEL
Mark 1:21–22, 35–39

A reading from the holy Gospel according to Mark.

Jesus and the disciples went to Capernaum [kuh-PER-n*m], and when the Sabbath came, Jesus entered the synagogue and taught. They were astounded at his teaching, for he taught them as one having authority and not as the scribes.

In the morning, while it was still very dark, he got up and went out to a deserted place, and there he prayed. And Simon and his companions hunted for him. When they found him, they said to him, "Everyone is searching for you." He answered, "Let us go on to the neighboring towns, so that I may proclaim the message there also, for that is what I came out to do." And he went throughout Galilee [GAL-ih-lee], proclaiming the message in their synagogues and casting out demons.

The Gospel of the Lord.

◆ All sit and observe silence.

FOR SILENT REFLECTION

Think about this silently in your heart. What can you sacrifice in order to make time for prayer?

CLOSING PRAYER

Let us pray to God for our needs and the needs of others: our family, neighborhood, and the world. For each need we say, "Lord, hear our prayer."

◆ All may add their own prayers here.

Let us pray: **Our Father . . . Amen.**

Lord God,
help us to pray more fervently every day,
so that we might grow closer to you.
Through Christ our Lord.

Amen.

✢ All make the sign of the cross.

PRAYER FOR THURSDAY, AUGUST 24, 2023

OPENING

The Lord's Prayer is very familiar to us. But how must it have been to hear the words from Jesus for the first time? The saint we remember today, Bartholomew, was one of the twelve apostles, so he received these words firsthand. How do you think he felt? Maybe he was surprised or challenged by something in this prayer. Maybe he just thought it was hard to remember! In the end, he and the other disciples treated these words of Jesus with reverence and prayed them carefully, just as we are called to do.

✠ All make the sign of the cross.

In the name of the Father, and of the Son, and of the Holy Spirit. Amen.

PSALM
(For a longer psalm, see page xi.)
Psalm 66:1–3a

Make a joyful noise to God, all the earth.

Make a joyful noise to God, all the earth.

Make a joyful noise to God, all the earth;
　sing the glory of his name;
　give to him glorious praise.
Say to God, "How awesome are your deeds!"

Make a joyful noise to God, all the earth.

◆ All stand and sing **Alleluia.**

GOSPEL
Matthew 5:2; 6:9–14

A reading from the holy Gospel according to Matthew.

Jesus began to speak and taught his disciples, saying: "Pray then in this way: Our Father in heaven, may your name be revered as holy. May your kingdom come. May your will be done on earth as it is in heaven. Give us this day our daily bread. And forgive us our debts, as we also have forgiven our debtors. And do not bring us to the time of trial, but rescue us from the evil one. For if you forgive others their trespasses, your heavenly Father will also forgive you."

The Gospel of the Lord.

◆ All sit and observe silence.

FOR SILENT REFLECTION

Think about this silently in your heart. Meditate on the words of the Lord's Prayer. Which part of the prayer would you like to focus on?

CLOSING PRAYER

Let us pray to God for our needs and the needs of others: our family, neighborhood, and the world. For each need we say, "Lord, hear our prayer."

◆ All may add their own prayers here.

Let us pray: **Our Father . . . Amen.**

Dear Jesus,
you gave us the words of your own prayer.
Help us to pray with real intent:
to trust in you and your will, to forgive one
　　another, and to hope in your kingdom.
Who live and reign with God the Father,
in the unity of the Holy Spirit,
God, for ever and ever.

Amen.

✠ All make the sign of the cross.

PRAYER FOR
FRIDAY, AUGUST 25, 2023

OPENING

Today we remember St. Louis of France. He was always mindful of the people of his kingdom: he built cathedrals, churches, libraries, hospitals, and orphanages. He fed the poor, often in person, and during Advent and Lent, all who presented themselves at the palace were given a meal. His life was marked by the words of St. Paul: "seek to do good to one another and to all."

✣ All make the sign of the cross.

In the name of the Father, and of the Son, and of the Holy Spirit. Amen.

PSALM

(For a longer psalm, see page xi.)
Psalm 66:1–3a

Make a joyful noise to God, all the earth.

Make a joyful noise to God, all the earth.

Make a joyful noise to God, all the earth;
   sing the glory of his name;
   give to him glorious praise.
Say to God, "How awesome are your deeds!"

Make a joyful noise to God, all the earth.

READING

1 Thessalonians 5:12a, 14–18, 23–25

A reading from the First Letter of Paul to the Thessalonians.

But we appeal to you, brothers and sisters, and we urge you, brothers and sisters, to admonish the idlers, encourage the fainthearted, help the weak, be patient with all of them. See that none of you repays evil for evil, but always seek to do good to one another and to all. Rejoice always, pray without ceasing, give thanks in all circumstances; for this is the will of God in Christ Jesus for you. May the God of peace himself sanctify you entirely, and may your spirit and soul and body be kept sound and blameless at the coming of our Lord Jesus Christ. The one who calls you is faithful, and he will do this. Brothers and sisters, pray for us.

The Word of the Lord.

◆ All observe silence.

FOR SILENT REFLECTION

Think about this silently in your heart. What does it mean to pray without ceasing?

CLOSING PRAYER

Let us pray to God for our needs and the needs of others: our family, neighborhood, and the world. For each need we say, "Lord, hear our prayer."

◆ All may add their own prayers here.

Let us pray: **Our Father . . . Amen.**

Lord Jesus,
you have led your people to do great things.
May St. Louis of France be a model for us
   to live as you have taught.
Help us to be open to hear your voice,
today and every day.
Who live and reign with God the Father,
in the unity of the Holy Spirit,
God, for ever and ever.

Amen.

✣ All make the sign of the cross.

PRAYER FOR THE WEEK
WITH A READING FROM THE GOSPEL FOR **SUNDAY, AUGUST 27, 2023**

OPENING

Simon's faith prompts Christ to rename him Peter or "rock," but even the faith of the rock is shaken in the shadow of the cross. We all have times of certainty and of doubt in our journey of faith. But we can hold fast to Christ's promise that the powers of death and destruction will not prevail against the Church or the people who are its living stones.

✠ All make the sign of the cross.

In the name of the Father, and of the Son, and of the Holy Spirit. Amen.

PSALM
(For a longer psalm, see page xi.)
Psalm 66:1–3a

Make a joyful noise to God, all the earth.

Make a joyful noise to God, all the earth.

Make a joyful noise to God, all the earth;
   sing the glory of his name;
   give to him glorious praise.
Say to God, "How awesome are your deeds!"

Make a joyful noise to God, all the earth.

◆ All stand and sing **Alleluia.**

GOSPEL
Matthew 16:13–20

A reading from the holy Gospel according to Matthew.

Now when Jesus came into the district of Caesarea Philippi [sez-uh-REE-uh fih-LIP-ī], he asked his disciples, "Who do people say that the Son of Man is?" And they said, "Some say John the Baptist but others Elijah and still others Jeremiah or one of the prophets." He said to them, "But who do you say that I am?" Simon Peter answered, "You are the Messiah, the Son of the living God." And Jesus answered him, "Blessed are you, Simon son of Jonah! For flesh and blood has not revealed this to you but my Father in heaven. And I tell you, you are Peter, and on this rock I will build my church, and the gates of Hades [HAY-deez] will not prevail against it. I will give you the keys of the kingdom of heaven, and whatever you bind on earth will be bound in heaven, and whatever you loose on earth will be loosed in heaven." Then he sternly ordered the disciples not to tell anyone that he was the Messiah.

The Gospel of the Lord.

◆ All sit and observe silence.

FOR SILENT REFLECTION

Think about this silently in your heart. Who do you say that Jesus is?

CLOSING PRAYER

Let us pray to God for our needs and the needs of others: our family, neighborhood, and the world. For each need we say, "Lord, hear our prayer."

◆ All may add their own prayers here.

Let us pray: **Our Father . . . Amen.**

O God,
give us strength to cling to the rock of faith
in good times and bad.
Through Christ our Lord.

Amen.

✠ All make the sign of the cross.

PRAYER FOR
MONDAY, AUGUST 28, 2023

OPENING

Today is the feast day of a great philosopher and Doctor of the Church, St. Augustine. This week, we will hear how Jesus approaches the mysteries of God's kingdom through parables, helping us to know more with each comparison. We learn that the kingdom of God is like a mustard seed: tiny to start, but growing later to become a great tree. The seeds of the kingdom are already within us, ready to take root and grow to astonishing heights. The kingdom of God is for the people of God, and we strive toward it through our whole lives.

✠ All make the sign of the cross.

In the name of the Father, and of the Son, and of the Holy Spirit. Amen.

PSALM
(For a longer psalm, see page xi.)
Psalm 66:1–3a

Make a joyful noise to God, all the earth.

Make a joyful noise to God, all the earth.

Make a joyful noise to God, all the earth;
  sing the glory of his name;
  give to him glorious praise.
Say to God, "How awesome are your deeds!"

Make a joyful noise to God, all the earth.

◆ All stand and sing **Alleluia.**

GOSPEL
Matthew 13:31–32, 34–35

A reading from the holy Gospel according to Matthew.

Jesus put before them another parable: "The kingdom of heaven is like a mustard seed that someone took and sowed in his field; it is the smallest of all the seeds, but when it has grown it is the greatest of shrubs and becomes a tree, so that the birds of the air come and make nests in its branches."

Jesus told the crowds all these things in parables; without a parable he told them nothing. This was to fulfill what had been spoken through the prophet: / "I will open my mouth to speak in parables; / I will proclaim what has been hidden from the foundation." /

The Gospel of the Lord.

◆ All sit and observe silence.

FOR SILENT REFLECTION

Think about this silently in your heart. How can you nurture the seed of the kingdom of God in your life?

CLOSING PRAYER

Let us pray to God for our needs and the needs of others: our family, neighborhood, and the world. For each need we say, "Lord, hear our prayer."

◆ All may add their own prayers here.

Let us pray: **Our Father . . . Amen.**

Lord God,
give us the wisdom to nourish the seeds of
    the kingdom of God that you have
    planted in our hearts.
In Jesus' name we pray.

Amen.

✠ All make the sign of the cross.

PRAYER FOR TUESDAY, AUGUST 29, 2023

OPENING

In today's Gospel, we learn more about the kingdom of God: it is a small amount of yeast that leavens the whole dough and it is a treasure or a pearl that is worth the sum of everything else we own. It is precious and small, and yet it grows quickly when shared with others. It is worth everything, and yet we already have its seeds in our grasp, ready to be nourished and grow. Today, as we remember the death of St. John the Baptist, let us also imitate his work to prepare the way for the Lord and the coming of God's kingdom.

✚ All make the sign of the cross.

In the name of the Father, and of the Son, and of the Holy Spirit. Amen.

PSALM

(For a longer psalm, see page xi.)
Psalm 66:1–3a

Make a joyful noise to God, all the earth.

Make a joyful noise to God, all the earth.

Make a joyful noise to God, all the earth;
   sing the glory of his name;
   give to him glorious praise.
Say to God, "How awesome are your deeds!"

Make a joyful noise to God, all the earth.

◆ All stand and sing **Alleluia.**

GOSPEL

Matthew 13:33, 44–46

A reading from the holy Gospel according to Matthew.

Jesus told them another parable: "The kingdom of heaven is like yeast that a woman took and mixed in with three measures of flour until all of it was leavened.

"The kingdom of heaven is like treasure hidden in a field, which a man found and reburied; then in his joy he goes and sells all that he has and buys that field.

"Again, the kingdom of heaven is like a merchant in search of fine pearls; on finding one pearl of great value, he went and sold all that he had and bought it."

The Gospel of the Lord.

◆ All sit and observe silence.

FOR SILENT REFLECTION

Think about this silently in your heart. How can you help the kingdom of God grow?

CLOSING PRAYER

Let us pray to God for our needs and the needs of others: our family, neighborhood, and the world. For each need we say, "Lord, hear our prayer."

◆ All may add their own prayers here.

Let us pray: **Our Father . . . Amen.**

Heavenly Father,
may we remember our ultimate goal is
   the coming of your kingdom,
a pearl of great price.
May we live every day in service
   of your kingdom.
Through Christ our Lord.

Amen.

✚ All make the sign of the cross.

PRAYER FOR
WEDNESDAY, AUGUST 30, 2023

OPENING

Have you ever planted a seed and waited for it to grow? It can take weeks, or even months, for any sign of growth to appear above the surface of the earth. But even though you cannot see the growth of the plant, it is happening. Today, the mystery of hidden growth is explored. The kingdom of God is silently growing all the time, just like that tiny seed beneath the soil. And just like the seed, it will appear in all bloom and beauty in God's time, though we do not know how.

✚ All make the sign of the cross.

In the name of the Father, and of the Son, and of the Holy Spirit. Amen.

PSALM
(For a longer psalm, see page xi.)
Psalm 66:1–3a

Make a joyful noise to God, all the earth.

Make a joyful noise to God, all the earth.

Make a joyful noise to God, all the earth;
   sing the glory of his name;
   give to him glorious praise.
Say to God, "How awesome are your deeds!"

Make a joyful noise to God, all the earth.

◆ All stand and sing **Alleluia.**

GOSPEL
Mark 4:26–29, 33–34

A reading from the holy Gospel according to Mark.

Jesus said, "The kingdom of God is as if someone would scatter seed on the ground and would sleep and rise night and day, and the seed would sprout and grow, he does not know how. The earth produces of itself first the stalk, then the head, then the full grain in the head. But when the grain is ripe, at once he goes in with his sickle because the harvest has come."

With many such parables he spoke the word to them, as they were able to hear it; he did not speak to them except in parables, but he explained everything in private to his disciples.

The Gospel of the Lord.

◆ All sit and observe silence.

FOR SILENT REFLECTION

Think about this silently in your heart. How is the kingdom of God quietly growing in your heart?

CLOSING PRAYER

Let us pray to God for our needs and the needs of others: our family, neighborhood, and the world. For each need we say, "Lord, hear our prayer."

◆ All may add their own prayers here.

Let us pray: **Our Father . . . Amen.**

O Lord God,
grant us the patience to wait for
   your kingdom,
and to encourage its silent growth in our
   hearts and in our world
through our words and actions.
We pray in your Son Jesus' name.

Amen.

✚ All make the sign of the cross.

PRAYER FOR
THURSDAY, AUGUST 31, 2023

OPENING

We will hear about an odd situation today: all the invited guests will not come to a wedding, so the host instead invites everyone from the street, "both good and bad." How absurd it is for *everyone* invited to refuse to go to a wedding feast! In this parable, the wedding is the kingdom of God. So who are those who have better things to do than to go to God's feast? Why might they be refusing God's invitation?

✢ All make the sign of the cross.

In the name of the Father, and of the Son, and of the Holy Spirit. Amen.

PSALM
(For a longer psalm, see page xii.)
Psalm 66:1–3a

Make a joyful noise to God, all the earth.

Make a joyful noise to God, all the earth.

Make a joyful noise to God, all the earth;
  sing the glory of his name;
  give to him glorious praise.
Say to God, "How awesome are your deeds!"

Make a joyful noise to God, all the earth.

◆ All stand and sing **Alleluia.**

GOSPEL
Matthew 22:1–5, 8–10

A reading from the holy Gospel according to Matthew.

Once more Jesus spoke to them in parables, saying: "The kingdom of heaven may be compared to a king who gave a wedding banquet for his son. He sent his slaves to call those who had been invited to the wedding banquet, but they would not come. Again he sent other slaves, saying, 'Tell those who have been invited: Look, I have prepared my dinner, my oxen and my fat calves have been slaughtered, and everything is ready; come to the wedding banquet.' But they made light of it and went away, one to his farm, another to his business. Then he said to his slaves, 'The wedding is ready, but those invited were not worthy. Go therefore into the main streets, and invite everyone you find to the wedding banquet.' Those slaves went out into the streets and gathered all whom they found, both good and bad, so the wedding hall was filled with guests."

The Gospel of the Lord.

◆ All sit and observe silence.

FOR SILENT REFLECTION

Think about this silently in your heart. How do you answer God's invitations?

CLOSING PRAYER

Let us pray to God for our needs and the needs of others: our family, neighborhood, and the world. For each need we say, "Lord, hear our prayer."

◆ All may add their own prayers here.

Let us pray: **Our Father . . . Amen.**

God our Father,
may we love you above all things
and listen always to your call.
We ask this through Christ our Lord.

Amen.

✢ All make the sign of the cross.

PRAYER SERVICE
FOR THE CARE OF CREATION ON SEPTEMBER 1

In 2015 Pope Francis declared September 1 to be a world-wide day of prayer for the care of creation. His encyclical Laudato Si' (Praised Be) *is subtitled* On Care for Our Common Home. *Using the words of St. Francis, he compares the earth, our common home, to a "sister with whom we share our life and a beautiful mother who opens to embrace us." For this prayer service, divide the class into two groups. This could be girls and boys or another simple division of voices to pray the Canticle of St. Francis. Song suggestions are "All Creatures of Our God and King," "Joyful, Joyful, We Adore Thee," or another hymn that honors creation.*

ALL
O Most High, all-powerful, good Lord God,
to you belong praise, glory,
honor and all blessing.

GROUP I
Be praised, my Lord, for all your creation
and especially for our Brother Sun,
who brings us the day and the light;
he is strong and shines magnificently.
O Lord, we think of you when we look
at him.

GROUP II
Be praised, my Lord, for Sister Moon,
and for the stars
which you have set shining and lovely
in the heavens.

GROUP I
Be praised, my Lord,
for our Brothers Wind and Air
and every kind of weather
by which you, Lord,
uphold life in all your creatures.

GROUP II
Be praised, my Lord, for Sister Water,
who is very useful to us,
and humble and precious and pure.

GROUP I
Be praised, my Lord, for Brother Fire,
through whom you give us light in the darkness:
he is bright and lively and strong.

GROUP II
Be praised, my Lord,
for Sister Earth, our Mother,
who nourishes us and sustains us,
bringing forth
fruits and vegetables of many kinds
and flowers of many colors.

GROUP I
Be praised, my Lord,
for those who forgive for love of you;
and for those
who bear sickness and weakness
in peace and patience
you will grant them a crown.

GROUP II
Be praised, my Lord, for our Sister Death,
whom we must all face.
I praise and bless you, Lord,
and I give thanks to you,
and I will serve you in all humility.

ALL
O Most High, all-powerful, good Lord God,
to you belong praise, glory, honor and all blessing. Amen.

PRAYER FOR
FRIDAY, SEPTEMBER 1, 2023

OPENING

Weddings enact a covenant bond between bride and bridegroom; that is a sign of the covenant between God and his people. Wisdom and prophetic literature (most notably the Song of Songs) have used wedding imagery to help us understand the relationship of God to his people. Jesus continued this tradition in this parable about the coming of the kingdom.

✢ All make the sign of the cross.

In the name of the Father, and of the Son, and of the Holy Spirit. Amen.

PSALM

(For a longer psalm, see page xii.)
Psalm 66:1–3a

Make a joyful noise to God, all the earth.

Make a joyful noise to God, all the earth.

Make a joyful noise to God, all the earth;
  sing the glory of his name;
  give to him glorious praise.
Say to God, "How awesome are your deeds!"

Make a joyful noise to God, all the earth.

◆ All stand and sing **Alleluia**.

GOSPEL

Matthew 25:1–6, 8–10

A reading from the holy Gospel according to Matthew.

Jesus said, "Then the kingdom of heaven will be like this. Ten young women took their lamps and went to meet the bridegroom. Five of them were foolish, and five were wise. When the foolish took their lamps, they took no oil with them, but the wise took flasks of oil with their lamps. As the bridegroom was delayed, all of them became drowsy and slept. But at midnight there was a shout, 'Look! Here is the bridegroom! Come out to meet him.' The foolish said to the wise, 'Give us some of your oil, for our lamps are going out.' But the wise replied, 'No! there will not be enough for you and for us; you had better go to the dealers and buy some for yourselves.' And while they went to buy it, the bridegroom came, and those who were ready went with him into the wedding banquet, and the door was shut."

The Gospel of the Lord.

◆ All sit and observe silence.

FOR SILENT REFLECTION

Think about this silently in your heart. How can you prepare for the bridegroom (Jesus)?

CLOSING PRAYER

Let us pray to God for our needs and the needs of others: our family, neighborhood, and the world. For each need we say, "Lord, hear our prayer."

◆ All may add their own prayers here.

Let us pray: **Our Father . . . Amen.**

Lord Jesus,
we know you are coming,
though we do not know the day or the hour.
Help us to be ready to welcome you.
Who live and reign with God the Father,
in the unity of the Holy Spirit,
God, for ever and ever.

Amen.

✢ All make the sign of the cross.

PRAYER FOR THE WEEK
WITH A READING FROM THE GOSPEL FOR SUNDAY, SEPTEMBER 3, 2023

OPENING

Do we have the strength to take up the sufferings of life, and still follow Jesus? Can we carry this heavy load to the foot of the cross? Can we wait in hope with Jesus on the cross for our pain to be transfigured, glorified, redeemed in the love of God? This is our call as disciples.

✚ All make the sign of the cross.

In the name of the Father, and of the Son, and of the Holy Spirit. Amen.

PSALM
(For a longer psalm, see page xi.)
Psalm 66:1–3a

Make a joyful noise to God, all the earth.

Make a joyful noise to God, all the earth.

Make a joyful noise to God, all the earth;
   sing the glory of his name;
   give to him glorious praise.
Say to God, "How awesome are your deeds!"

Make a joyful noise to God, all the earth.

◆ All stand and sing **Alleluia.**

GOSPEL
matthew 16:21–27

A reading from the holy Gospel according to Matthew.

From that time on, Jesus began to show his disciples that he must go to Jerusalem and undergo great suffering at the hands of the elders and chief priests and scribes and be killed and on the third day be raised. And Peter took him aside and began to rebuke him, saying, "God forbid it, Lord! This must never happen to you." But he turned and said to Peter, "Get behind me, Satan! You are a hindrance to me, for you are setting your mind not on divine things but on human things."

Then Jesus told his disciples, "If any wish to come after me, let them deny themselves and take up their cross and follow me. For those who want to save their life will lose it, and those who lose their life for my sake will find it. For what will it profit them if they gain the whole world but forfeit their life? Or what will they give in return for their life? For the Son of Man is to come with his angels in the glory of his Father, and then he will repay everyone for what has been done."

The Gospel of the Lord.

◆ All sit and observe silence.

FOR SILENT REFLECTION

Think about this silently in your heart. What cross do you carry?

CLOSING PRAYER

Let us pray to God for our needs and the needs of others: our family, neighborhood, and the world. For each need we say, "Lord, hear our prayer."

◆ All may add their own prayers here.

Let us pray: **Our Father . . . Amen.**

Grant us courage, O God,
especially when it is difficult to be faithful.
In Christ's name we pray.

Amen.

✚ All make the sign of the cross.

PRAYER FOR MONDAY, SEPTEMBER 4, 2023

OPENING

Today is Labor Day, a day of reflecting on the dignity of work. This week we will reflect on God's Great Commandment. Today's Scripture text makes up part of the Shema, a Jewish prayer said during evening and morning prayer. The Shema contains a profession of faith in God and reliance on him alone. Like the ancient Israelites, we too are invited to respond to God's grace and mercy with love, obedience, and faithfulness.

✢ All make the sign of the cross.

In the name of the Father, and of the Son, and of the Holy Spirit. Amen.

PSALM

(For a longer psalm, see page xi.)
Psalm 66:1–3a

Make a joyful noise to God, all the earth.

Make a joyful noise to God, all the earth.

Make a joyful noise to God, all the earth;
 sing the glory of his name;
 give to him glorious praise.
Say to God, "How awesome are your deeds!"

Make a joyful noise to God, all the earth.

READING

Deuteronomy 5:1a; 6:1, 3, 5–9

A reading from the Book of Deuteronomy.

Moses convened all Israel, and said to them: Now this is the commandment—the statutes and the ordinances—that the Lord your God charged me to teach you to observe in the land that you are about to cross into and occupy. Hear therefore, O Israel, and observe them diligently, so that it may go well with you, and so that you may multiply greatly in a land flowing with milk and honey, as the Lord, the God of your ancestors, has promised you. You shall love the Lord your God with all your heart and with all your soul and with all your might. Keep these words that I am commanding you today in your heart. Recite them to your children and talk about them when you are at home and when you are away, when you lie down and when you rise. Bind them as a sign on your hand, fix them as an emblem on your forehead, and write them on the doorposts of your house and on your gates.

The Word of the Lord.

◆ All observe silence.

FOR SILENT REFLECTION

Think about this silently in your heart. How do you commit yourself to God?

CLOSING PRAYER

Let us pray to God for our needs and the needs of others: our family, neighborhood, and the world. For each need we say, "Lord, hear our prayer."

◆ All may add their own prayers here.

Let us pray: **Our Father . . . Amen.**

God our Father,
we praise you and love you.
Help us to keep your commandments.
In Christ's name we pray.

Amen.

✢ All make the sign of the cross.

PRAYER FOR
TUESDAY, SEPTEMBER 5, 2023

OPENING

The Pharisees [FAYR-uh-seez] tried to trick Jesus by making him choose the "greatest" of God's commandments. Instead, Jesus linked the all-consuming, all-giving love for God with a love of neighbor that is just as fervent. These two loves are just one in the end—it is not possible to have one without the other. Indeed all the law and all the prophets (that is to say, all of faith) hang upon this love.

✚ All make the sign of the cross.

In the name of the Father, and of the Son, and of the Holy Spirit. Amen.

PSALM
(For a longer psalm, see page xi.)
Psalm 66:1–3a

Make a joyful noise to God, all the earth.

Make a joyful noise to God, all the earth.

Make a joyful noise to God, all the earth;
   sing the glory of his name;
   give to him glorious praise.
Say to God, "How awesome are your deeds!"

Make a joyful noise to God, all the earth.

◆ All stand and sing **Alleluia.**

GOSPEL
Matthew 22:34–40

A reading from the holy Gospel according to Matthew.

When the Pharisees [FAYR-uh-seez] heard that Jesus had silenced the Sadducees [SAD-yoo-seez], they gathered together, and one of them, an expert in the law, asked him a question to test him. "Teacher, which commandment in the law is the greatest?" He said to him, "'You shall love the Lord your God with all your heart and with all your soul and with all your mind.' This is the greatest and first commandment. And a second is like it: 'You shall love your neighbor as yourself.' On these two commandments hang all the Law and the Prophets."

The Gospel of the Lord.

◆ All sit and observe silence.

FOR SILENT REFLECTION

Think about this silently in your heart. How can you love God better? How can you love others better?

CLOSING PRAYER

Let us pray to God for our needs and the needs of others: our family, neighborhood, and the world. For each need we say, "Lord, hear our prayer."

◆ All may add their own prayers here.

Let us pray: **Our Father . . . Amen.**

Kind and loving God,
Jesus reminds us that loving you
   and one another
is the way to do good in this world.
Help us to love perfectly, as Jesus loved.
We ask this in the name of your Son,
Jesus Christ our Lord.

Amen.

✚ All make the sign of the cross.

PRAYER FOR WEDNESDAY, SEPTEMBER 6, 2023

OPENING

Over the next two days, we will hear the Parable of the Good Samaritan. When a Jewish religious leader questioned Jesus about who his neighbor is, Jesus responded with this parable. Note that the priest and the Levite are religious leaders.

✢ All make the sign of the cross.

In the name of the Father, and of the Son, and of the Holy Spirit. Amen.

PSALM

(For a longer psalm, see page xi.)
Psalm 66:1–3a

Make a joyful noise to God, all the earth.

Make a joyful noise to God, all the earth.

Make a joyful noise to God, all the earth;
 sing the glory of his name;
 give to him glorious praise.
Say to God, "How awesome are your deeds!"

Make a joyful noise to God, all the earth.

◆ All stand and sing **Alleluia.**

GOSPEL

Luke 10:25–26b, 27, 29, 30–32

A reading from the holy Gospel according to Luke.

An expert in the law stood up to test Jesus. "Teacher," he said, "what must I do to inherit eternal life?" He said to him, "What is written in the law? What do you read there?" He answered, "You shall love the Lord your God with all your heart and with all your soul and with all your strength and with all your mind and your neighbor as yourself." But wanting to vindicate himself, he asked Jesus, "And who is my neighbor?" Jesus replied, "A man was going down from Jerusalem to Jericho [JAYR-ih-koh], and fell into the hands of robbers, who stripped him, beat him, and took off, leaving him half dead. Now by chance a priest was going down that road, and when he saw him he passed by on the other side. So likewise a Levite [LEE-vīt], when he came to the place and saw him, passed by on the other side."

The Gospel of the Lord.

◆ All sit and observe silence.

FOR SILENT REFLECTION

Think about this silently in your heart. Who is your neighbor? Who do you need to learn to love?

CLOSING PRAYER

Let us pray to God for our needs and the needs of others: our family, neighborhood, and the world. For each need we say, "Lord, hear our prayer."

◆ All may add their own prayers here.

Let us pray: **Our Father . . . Amen.**

Lord Jesus,
your heart is full of love for your people.
Teach each of us to truly see our neighbor
 and love them as you do.
Who live and reign with God the Father,
in the unity of the Holy Spirit,
God, for ever and ever.

Amen.

✢ All make the sign of the cross.

PRAYER FOR
THURSDAY, SEPTEMBER 7, 2023

OPENING

We continue the Parable of the Good Samaritan. Usually when we hear this story, we might picture ourselves as one of the passerby (ideally the Samaritan who stops to help). But consider what it would be like to be the wounded traveler. How would you feel if everyone passed by without helping you? Would you be surprised when an enemy helped you? In this parable, we learn how to love like God, the ultimate Good Samaritan, to pour out love and care for others without counting the cost.

✠ All make the sign of the cross.

In the name of the Father, and of the Son, and of the Holy Spirit. Amen.

PSALM
(For a longer psalm, see page xi.)
Psalm 66:1–3a

Make a joyful noise to God, all the earth.

Make a joyful noise to God, all the earth.

Make a joyful noise to God, all the earth;
   sing the glory of his name;
   give to him glorious praise.
Say to God, "How awesome are your deeds!"

Make a joyful noise to God, all the earth.

◆ All stand and sing **Alleluia**.

GOSPEL
Luke 10:33–37

A reading from the holy Gospel according to Luke.

Jesus said: "But a Samaritan [suh-MAYR-uh-tuhn] while traveling came near him and when he saw him he was moved with compassion. He went to him and bandaged his wounds, treating them with oil and wine. Then he put him on his own animal, brought him to an inn, and took care of him. The next day he took out two denarii [dih-NAHR-ee-ī], gave them to the innkeeper, and said, 'Take care of him, and when I come back I will repay you whatever more you spend.' Which of these three, do you think, was a neighbor to the man who fell into the hands of the robbers?" He said, "The one who showed him mercy." Jesus said to him, "Go and do likewise."

The Gospel of the Lord.

◆ All sit and observe silence.

FOR SILENT REFLECTION

Think about this silently in your heart. How can you be a Good Samaritan?

CLOSING PRAYER

Let us pray to God for our needs and the needs of others: our family, neighborhood, and the world. For each need we say, "Lord, hear our prayer."

◆ All may add their own prayers here.

Let us pray: **Our Father . . . Amen.**

Lord God,
give us the gifts of courage and compassion,
so we may treat everyone with the same
care and love that you give us.
May we reflect today on whom we can help,
those we know and do not know.
Through Jesus Christ our Lord.

Amen.

✠ All make the sign of the cross.

PRAYER FOR
FRIDAY, SEPTEMBER 8, 2023

OPENING

Today we celebrate the Blessed Mother's birthday. In Mary's birth, we see the dawning of salvation, which Jesus brings about in all fullness. Mary was conceived without sin, and is a sign of hope for us all. In Mary, we can hope to achieve the good work Jesus charges us with in today's reading: to offer words of grace and truth, to be kind, tenderhearted, forgiving. To be imitators of God.

✚ All make the sign of the cross.

In the name of the Father, and of the Son, and of the Holy Spirit. Amen.

PSALM
(For a longer psalm, see page xi.)
Psalm 66:1–3a

Make a joyful noise to God, all the earth.

Make a joyful noise to God, all the earth.

Make a joyful noise to God, all the earth;
   sing the glory of his name;
   give to him glorious praise.
Say to God, "How awesome are your deeds!"

Make a joyful noise to God, all the earth.

READING
Ephesians 4:25, 29, 31–32; 5:1–2

A reading from the Letter of Paul to the Ephesians [ee-FEE-zhuhnz].

So then, putting away falsehood, let each of you speak the truth with your neighbor, for we are members of one another. Let no evil talk come out of your mouths but only what is good for building up, as there is need, so that your words may give grace to those who hear. Put away from you all bitterness and wrath and anger and wrangling and slander, together with all malice. Be kind to one another, tenderhearted, forgiving one another, as God in Christ has forgiven you.

Therefore be imitators of God, as beloved children, and walk in love, as Christ loved us and gave himself up for us, a fragrant offering and sacrifice to God.

The Word of the Lord.

◆ All observe silence.

FOR SILENT REFLECTION

Think about this silently in your heart. Do you need to put aside falsehood, anger or slander? How can you live in love as Jesus taught us?

CLOSING PRAYER

Let us pray to God for our needs and the needs of others: our family, neighborhood, and the world. For each need we say, "Lord, hear our prayer."

◆ All may add their own prayers here.

Let us pray: **Our Father . . . Amen.**

O God,
we ask for the strength to encourage
   one another in the faith.
Help us to forgive those who hurt us,
and rid our hearts of anger and pain.
Lead us to your mercy and guide us
   with your grace.
In Christ's name we pray.

Amen.

✚ All make the sign of the cross.

PRAYER FOR THE WEEK
WITH A READING FROM THE GOSPEL FOR **SUNDAY, SEPTEMBER 10, 2023**

OPENING

It is tempting to share every insult and injury with friends and on social media and put the offender "on blast." But Jesus offers a way that is rooted in charity, holding the offender accountable, but not condemning and judging. Jesus' way leaves open the door for repentance, forgiveness, and God's grace.

✝ All make the sign of the cross.

In the name of the Father, and of the Son, and of the Holy Spirit. Amen.

PSALM
(For a longer psalm, see page xi.)
Psalm 66:1–3a

Make a joyful noise to God, all the earth.

Make a joyful noise to God, all the earth.

Make a joyful noise to God, all the earth;
 sing the glory of his name;
 give to him glorious praise.
Say to God, "How awesome are your deeds!"

Make a joyful noise to God, all the earth.

◆ All stand and sing **Alleluia**.

GOSPEL
Matthew 18:15–20

A reading from the holy Gospel according to Matthew.

Jesus said, "If your brother or sister sins against you, go and point out the fault when the two of you are alone. If you are listened to, you have regained that one. But if you are not listened to, take one or two others along with you, so that every word may be confirmed by the evidence of two or three witnesses. If the person refuses to listen to them, tell it to the church, and if the offender refuses to listen even to the church, let such a one be to you as a gentile [JEN-tīl] and a tax collector. Truly I tell you, whatever you bind on earth will be bound in heaven, and whatever you loose on earth will be loosed in heaven. Again, truly I tell you, if two of you agree on earth about anything you ask, it will be done for you by my Father in heaven. For where two or three are gathered in my name, I am there among them."

The Gospel of the Lord.

◆ All sit and observe silence.

FOR SILENT REFLECTION

Think about this silently in your heart. How can you show grace to those who offend you?

CLOSING PRAYER

Let us pray to God for our needs and the needs of others: our family, neighborhood, and the world. For each need we say, "Lord, hear our prayer."

◆ All may add their own prayers here.

Let us pray: **Our Father . . . Amen.**

Gracious God,
create in us a generous spirit,
so we may forgive others as often as you
 forgive us.
We ask this through Christ our Lord.

Amen.

✝ All make the sign of the cross.

PRAYER FOR MONDAY, SEPTEMBER 11, 2023

OPENING

We know, as Jesus' followers did, that a strong foundation will make for a strong building, capable of withstanding storms. We are called to build our lives on the strong foundation of faith, on the rock of our hope in God, through sickness and pain, discord and separation, violence and war. This week we will reflect on how we can build on this foundation to both hear and do God's will.

✢ All make the sign of the cross.

In the name of the Father, and of the Son, and of the Holy Spirit. Amen.

PSALM

(For a longer psalm, see page xi.)
Psalm 66:1–3a

Make a joyful noise to God, all the earth.

Make a joyful noise to God, all the earth.

Make a joyful noise to God, all the earth;
　sing the glory of his name;
　give to him glorious praise.
Say to God, "How awesome are your deeds!"

Make a joyful noise to God, all the earth.

◆ All stand and sing **Alleluia.**

GOSPEL

Matthew 7:24–29

A reading from the holy Gospel according to Matthew.

Jesus said, "Everyone, then, who hears these words of mine and acts on them will be like a wise man who built his house on rock. The rain fell, the floods came, and the winds blew and beat on that house, but it did not fall because it had been founded on rock. And everyone who hears these words of mine and does not act on them will be like a foolish man who built his house on sand. The rain fell, and the floods came, and the winds blew and beat against that house, and it fell—and great was its fall!" Now when Jesus had finished saying these words, the crowds were astounded at his teaching, for he taught them as one having authority and not as their scribes.

The Gospel of the Lord.

◆ All sit and observe silence.

FOR SILENT REFLECTION

Think about this silently in your heart. What foundation have you built your life on?

CLOSING PRAYER

Let us pray to God for our needs and the needs of others: our family, neighborhood, and the world. For each need we say, "Lord, hear our prayer."

◆ All may add their own prayers here.

Let us pray: **Our Father . . . Amen.**

Heavenly Father,
deliver your people from pain and suffering,
especially those who currently suffer
under the sword of violence and degradation.
In Jesus' name, we pray.

Amen.

✢ All make the sign of the cross.

PRAYER SERVICE
NATIONAL DAY OF SERVICE AND REMEMBRANCE ON SEPTEMBER 11

Prepare six leaders for this service. The second leader will need a Bible for the Scripture and may need help practicing for the reading. You may begin by singing "Healer of Our Every Ill," or "This Is My Song," or perhaps begin in silence with a simple tolling of a hand bell.

FIRST LEADER:
May the grace and peace of our Lord Jesus Christ be with us, now and for ever.

Amen.

Let us pray:
Lord Jesus Christ,
we remember all those who died
on that September day in 2001,
people of different faiths and
backgrounds and ways of life.
We turn to you now, Lord of all,
to give us the courage to be peacemakers
and servants to all people in the world.

Amen.

◆ All stand and sing **Alleluia**.

SECOND LEADER: Luke 6:36–37
A reading from the holy Gospel according to Luke.

◆ Read the Gospel passage from the Bible.

The Gospel of the Lord.

THIRD LEADER:
Let us pause and pray in silence for all those who have died in wars and other conflicts around the world.

◆ Allow a minute of silence.

FOURTH LEADER:
We recall the beautiful prayer of peace of St. Francis of Assisi:

Lord, make me an instrument of your peace;
where there is hatred, let me sow love;
where there is injury, pardon;
where there is doubt, faith;
where there is despair, hope;
where there is darkness, light;
and where there is sadness, joy.
Grant that I may not so much seek
to be consoled as to console;
to be understood as to understand;
to be loved as to love;
for it is in giving that we receive,
it is in pardoning that we are pardoned,
and it is in dying that we are born to eternal life.

Amen.

FIFTH LEADER:
Now let us offer to one another a sign of Christ's peace:

◆ All offer one another a sign of peace.

SIXTH LEADER:
And may the Lord bless us,

✜ All make the sign of the cross.

protect us from all evil,
and bring us to everlasting life.

Amen.

PRAYER FOR TUESDAY, SEPTEMBER 12, 2023

OPENING

The Letter of James is full of practical guidance on discipleship. In today's passage, we are first told to slow down and listen for the Word of God, for we cannot do God's work if we are not open to hear God's voice. But after you hear, says James, do not forget to *do* something!

✚ All make the sign of the cross.

In the name of the Father, and of the Son, and of the Holy Spirit. Amen.

PSALM
(For a longer psalm, see page xi.)
Psalm 66:1–3a

Make a joyful noise to God, all the earth.

Make a joyful noise to God, all the earth.

Make a joyful noise to God, all the earth;
  sing the glory of his name;
  give to him glorious praise.
Say to God, "How awesome are your deeds!"

Make a joyful noise to God, all the earth.

READING
James 1:19–20, 22–25

A reading from the Letter of James.

You must understand this, my beloved brothers and sisters: let everyone be quick to listen, slow to speak, slow to anger, for human anger does not produce God's righteousness. But be doers of the word and not merely hearers who deceive themselves. For if any are hearers of the word and not doers, they are like those who look at themselves in a mirror; for they look at themselves and, on going away, immediately forget what they were like. But those who look into the perfect law, the law of liberty, and persevere, being not hearers who forget but doers who act—they will be blessed in their doing.

The Word of the Lord.

◆ All observe silence.

FOR SILENT REFLECTION

Think about this silently in your heart. Why is it important to act on God's Word?

CLOSING PRAYER

Let us pray to God for our needs and the needs of others: our family, neighborhood, and the world. For each need we say, "Lord, hear our prayer."

◆ All may add their own prayers here.

Let us pray: **Our Father . . . Amen.**

God our Father,
give us ears to hear your word.
Change our hearts that we might put your
     word into action.
Help us to be faithful disciples.
In Christ's name we pray.

Amen.

✚ All make the sign of the cross.

PRAYER FOR WEDNESDAY, SEPTEMBER 13, 2023

OPENING

St. John Chrysostom [KRIS-ihs-t*m or krihs-IS-t*m] was an early Church Father, and the archbishop of Constantinople. He was well known for his preaching (his name means "golden-mouthed"). St. John condemned the abuses of both church and political leaders of his time, and insisted that the wealthy must share their abundance with the poor. He was an astute hearer of the law, but he was also a doer, facing personal attacks and criticism as he sought to accompany words with action. Are you willing, like St. John, to be a doer of the work of God?

✚ All make the sign of the cross.

In the name of the Father, and of the Son, and of the Holy Spirit. Amen.

PSALM

(For a longer psalm, see page xi.)
Psalm 66:1–3a

Make a joyful noise to God, all the earth.

Make a joyful noise to God, all the earth.

Make a joyful noise to God, all the earth;
  sing the glory of his name;
  give to him glorious praise.
Say to God, "How awesome are your deeds!"

Make a joyful noise to God, all the earth.

READING

Romans 2:13–16

A reading from the Letter of Paul to the Romans.

For it is not the hearers of the law who are righteous in God's sight but the doers of the law who will be justified. When gentiles [JEN-tils], who do not possess the law, by nature do what the law requires, these, though not having the law, are a law to themselves. They show that what the law requires is written on their hearts, as their own conscience also bears witness, and their conflicting thoughts will accuse or perhaps excuse them on the day when, according to my gospel, God through Christ Jesus judges the secret thoughts of all.

The Word of the Lord.

◆ All observe silence.

FOR SILENT REFLECTION

Think about this silently in your heart. How has the law been written on your heart? How does this affect your actions?

CLOSING PRAYER

Let us pray to God for our needs and the needs of others: our family, neighborhood, and the world. For each need we say, "Lord, hear our prayer."

◆ All may add their own prayers here.

Let us pray: **Our Father . . . Amen.**

God our Father,
like St. John Chrysostom before us,
help us to be both hearers and doers
    of your law.
We ask this through Christ our Lord.

Amen.

✚ All make the sign of the cross.

PRAYER FOR
THURSDAY, SEPTEMBER 14, 2023

OPENING

Today is the Feast of the Exaltation of the Holy Cross. The cross in the ancient world was a symbol of death and dishonor, a method of punishment reserved for the worst offenders. Jesus, through his death and resurrection, turned the cross from a sign of death to a sign of redemption and new life. We display this cross as a sign that we are a people transformed in its shadow. It is a reminder to live up to Christ's promise: to cause no harm in great and small matters and to follow God's law of love.

✢ All make the sign of the cross.

In the name of the Father, and of the Son, and of the Holy Spirit. Amen.

PSALM
(For a longer psalm, see page xi.)
Psalm 66:1–3a

Make a joyful noise to God, all the earth.

Make a joyful noise to God, all the earth.

Make a joyful noise to God, all the earth;
 sing the glory of his name;
 give to him glorious praise.
Say to God, "How awesome are your deeds!"

Make a joyful noise to God, all the earth.

READING
Sirach 5:10–15a

A reading from the Book of Sirach [SEER-ak].

Stand firm in what you know, and let your speech be consistent. Be quick to hear, and utter a reply patiently. If you understand, answer your neighbor, but if not, put your hand over your mouth. Honor and dishonor come from speaking, and the tongue of mortals may be their downfall. Do not be called double-tongued and do not lay traps with your tongue, for shame comes to the thief and severe condemnation to the double-tongued. In great and small matters cause no harm.

The Word of the Lord.

◆ All observe silence.

FOR SILENT REFLECTION

Think about this silently in your heart. Have you ever hurt anyone with your words? How can you listen and speak more thoughtfully today?

CLOSING PRAYER

Let us pray to God for our needs and the needs of others: our family, neighborhood, and the world. For each need we say, "Lord, hear our prayer."

◆ All may add their own prayers here.

Let us pray: **Our Father . . . Amen.**

Lord Jesus,
by your holy cross you have redeemed
 the world.
Give us the courage to follow that cross
and live as a people made new in you.
Who live and reign with God the Father,
in the unity of the Holy Spirit,
God, for ever and ever.

Amen.

✢ All make the sign of the cross.

PRAYER FOR
FRIDAY, SEPTEMBER 15, 2023

OPENING

In the parable of the sheep and the goats, the righteous have done acts of service for others, seeking not to be praised for their goodness or to achieve their salvation, but to help the person before them. Each day, we are given the opportunity to do good for others. Today is the feast of Our Lady of Sorrows, and we remember the deep pain Mary bore. Yet, through all her sorrows, Mary did not fail to do good for others. May we too leave no good undone.

✣ All make the sign of the cross.

In the name of the Father, and of the Son, and of the Holy Spirit. Amen.

PSALM
(For a longer psalm, see page xi.)
Psalm 66:1–3a

Make a joyful noise to God, all the earth.

Make a joyful noise to God, all the earth.

Make a joyful noise to God, all the earth;
   sing the glory of his name;
   give to him glorious praise.
Say to God, "How awesome are your deeds!"

Make a joyful noise to God, all the earth.

◆ All stand and sing **Alleluia.**

GOSPEL
Matthew 25:34–37, 40

A reading from the holy Gospel according to Matthew.

The king will say to those at his right hand, "Come, you that are blessed by my Father, inherit the kingdom prepared for you from the foundation of the world, for I was hungry and you gave me food, I was thirsty and you gave me something to drink, I was a stranger and you welcomed me, I was naked and you gave me clothing, I was sick and you took care of me, I was in prison and you visited me." Then the righteous will answer him, "Lord, when was it that we saw you hungry and gave you food or thirsty and gave you something to drink?" And the king will answer them, "Truly I tell you, just as you did it to one of the least of these brothers and sisters of mine, you did it to me."

The Gospel of the Lord.

◆ All sit and observe silence.

FOR SILENT REFLECTION

Think about this silently in your heart. When was your last opportunity to do good? When have you left good undone?

CLOSING PRAYER

Let us pray to God for our needs and the needs of others: our family, neighborhood, and the world. For each need we say, "Lord, hear our prayer."

◆ All may add their own prayers here.

Let us pray: **Our Father . . . Amen.**

Lord God,
open our eyes that we may see the needs
   of those around us.
Open our ears so we can hear those
   who need help.
Open our hearts that we may serve others.
We ask this in Jesus' name.

Amen.

✣ All make the sign of the cross.

PRAYER FOR THE WEEK

WITH A READING FROM THE GOSPEL FOR **SUNDAY, SEPTEMBER 17, 2023**

OPENING

Forgiveness is hard. Wounds of speech and deed are often deep and difficult to heal. Despite these wounds, Jesus calls us to forgive not once or twice, but seventy-seven times. And in the deepest, most painful times and places, the love that we pour out is forgiveness, even if we have to do it seventy-seven times.

✠ *All make the sign of the cross.*

In the name of the Father, and of the Son, and of the Holy Spirit. Amen.

PSALM

(For a longer psalm, see page xi.)
Psalm 66:1–3a

Make a joyful noise to God, all the earth.

Make a joyful noise to God, all the earth.

Make a joyful noise to God, all the earth;
  sing the glory of his name;
  give to him glorious praise.
Say to God, "How awesome are your deeds!"

Make a joyful noise to God, all the earth.

◆ *All stand and sing* **Alleluia.**

GOSPEL

Matthew 18:21acd, 22–24b, 25–27

A reading from the holy Gospel according to Matthew.

Then Peter came and said to Jesus, "Lord, how often should I forgive? As many as seven times?" Jesus said to him, "Not seven times, but, I tell you, seventy-seven times. For this reason the kingdom of heaven may be compared to a king who wished to settle accounts with his slaves. One who owed him ten thousand talents was brought to him, and, as he could not pay, his lord ordered him to be sold, together with his wife and children and all his possessions and payment to be made. So the slave fell on his knees before him, saying, 'Have patience with me, and I will pay you everything.' And out of pity for him, the lord of that slave released him and forgave him the debt."

The Gospel of the Lord.

◆ *All sit and observe silence.*

FOR SILENT REFLECTION

Think about this silently in your heart. When have you struggled to forgive? Why?

CLOSING PRAYER

Let us pray to God for our needs and the needs of others: our family, neighborhood, and the world. For each need we say, "Lord, hear our prayer."

◆ *All may add their own prayers here.*

Let us pray: **Our Father . . . Amen.**

Lord Jesus,
you forgave those who betrayed you
as you suffered on the cross.
Give us your own merciful heart
so that we too might forgive those
  who hurt us.
Who live and reign with God the Father,
in the unity of the Holy Spirit,
God, for ever and ever.

Amen.

✠ *All make the sign of the cross.*

PRAYER FOR
MONDAY, SEPTEMBER 18, 2023

OPENING

Our focus this week will be on the parables of Jesus. Today we hear about God the Sower, who has been scattering seeds of faith in you. These seeds may take a variety of forms: attending Mass, family prayer, your religion classes, a teacher who listens when you're overwhelmed, a friend giving you a hug on a rough day. These seeds of God's love are abundantly scattered throughout our days, though we do not always notice them.

✢ *All make the sign of the cross.*

In the name of the Father, and of the Son, and of the Holy Spirit. Amen.

PSALM
(For a longer psalm, see page xi.)
Psalm 66:1–3a

Make a joyful noise to God, all the earth.

Make a joyful noise to God, all the earth.

Make a joyful noise to God, all the earth;
   sing the glory of his name;
   give to him glorious praise.
Say to God, "How awesome are your deeds!"

Make a joyful noise to God, all the earth.

◆ *All stand and sing* **Alleluia.**

GOSPEL
Matthew 13:2–9

A reading from the holy Gospel according to Matthew.

Such great crowds gathered around him that Jesus got into a boat and sat there, while the whole crowd stood on the beach. And he told them many things in parables, saying: "Listen! A sower went out to sow. And as he sowed, some seeds fell on the path, and the birds came and ate them up. Other seeds fell on rocky ground, where they did not have much soil, and they sprang up quickly, since they had no depth of soil. But when the sun rose, they were scorched, and since they had no root, they withered away. Other seeds fell among thorns, and the thorns grew up and choked them. Other seeds fell on good soil and brought forth grain, some a hundredfold, some sixty, some thirty. If you have ears, hear!"

The Gospel of the Lord.

◆ *All sit and observe silence.*

FOR SILENT REFLECTION

Think about this silently in your heart. How can you make your life fertile ground for God's grace to flourish and grow?

CLOSING PRAYER

Let us pray to God for our needs and the needs of others: our family, neighborhood, and the world. For each need we say, "Lord, hear our prayer."

◆ *All may add their own prayers here.*

Let us pray: **Our Father . . . Amen.**

Father,
you shower grace upon us every day.
We pray that your love may take root
   in our lives,
to be shared with others.
In Jesus' name we pray.

Amen.

✢ *All make the sign of the cross.*

PRAYER FOR TUESDAY, SEPTEMBER 19, 2023

OPENING

The corporal works of mercy give us a model for how we should treat others: as if they were Christ in disguise. They are called corporal because they refer to physical needs (of the body or *corpus*). Our call as Christians is to feed and give drink, to clothe those in need, to welcome the refugee or downtrodden, to protect and care for the sick, to remember and care for the prisoner. To truly see and care for those who are easiest to ignore.

✚ All make the sign of the cross.

In the name of the Father, and of the Son, and of the Holy Spirit. Amen.

PSALM
(For a longer psalm, see page xi.)
Psalm 66:1–3a

Make a joyful noise to God, all the earth.

Make a joyful noise to God, all the earth.

Make a joyful noise to God, all the earth;
   sing the glory of his name;
   give to him glorious praise.
Say to God, "How awesome are your deeds!"

Make a joyful noise to God, all the earth.

◆ All stand and sing **Alleluia**.

GOSPEL
Matthew 25:34–36

A reading from the holy Gospel according to Matthew.

The king will say to those at his right hand, "Come, you that are blessed by my Father, inherit the kingdom prepared for you from the foundation of the world, for I was hungry and you gave me food, I was thirsty and you gave me something to drink, I was a stranger and you welcomed me, I was naked and you gave me clothing, I was sick and you took care of me, I was in prison and you visited me."

The Gospel of the Lord.

◆ All sit and observe silence.

FOR SILENT REFLECTION

Think about this silently in your heart. What work of mercy can you do this week?

CLOSING PRAYER

Let us pray to God for our needs and the needs of others: our family, neighborhood, and the world. For each need we say, "Lord, hear our prayer."

◆ All may add their own prayers here.

Let us pray: **Our Father . . . Amen.**

Lord God,
give us eyes to see and ears to hear the cries of our brothers and sisters who suffer.
May we give out of our abundance to those
   who are in need.
We ask this through Christ our Lord.

Amen.

✚ All make the sign of the cross.

PRAYER FOR WEDNESDAY, SEPTEMBER 20, 2023

OPENING

In today's parable, the master trusts his servants to do his work, and he gives them what they need for that work. Our Master, God, has trusted each of us to do his work on this earth. Like the varying amount of talents given to the servants, we have each been given very different gifts, talents, abilities, and resources to accomplish our work. Today's saints, St. Andrew Kim Tae-gŏn, Paul Chŏng Ha-sang, and the Korean martyrs shared their gifts of faith even as they faced persecution. God gives all of us the same mission: to use our gifts to love others.

✚ All make the sign of the cross.

In the name of the Father, and of the Son, and of the Holy Spirit. Amen.

PSALM
(For a longer psalm, see page xi.)
Psalm 66:1–3a

Make a joyful noise to God, all the earth.

Make a joyful noise to God, all the earth.

Make a joyful noise to God, all the earth;
 sing the glory of his name;
 give to him glorious praise.
Say to God, "How awesome are your deeds!"

Make a joyful noise to God, all the earth.

◆ All stand and sing **Alleluia**.

GOSPEL
Matthew 25:14–15, 19–21

A reading from the holy Gospel according to Matthew.

Jesus said, "For it is as if a man, going on a journey, summoned his slaves and entrusted his property to them; to one he gave five talents, to another two, to another one, to each according to his ability. Then he went away. After a long time the master of those slaves came and settled accounts with them. Then the one who had received the five talents came forward, bringing five more talents, saying, 'Master, you handed over to me five talents; see, I have made five more talents.' His master said to him, 'Well done, good and trustworthy slave; you have been trustworthy in a few things; I will put you in charge of many things; enter into the joy of your master.'"

The Gospel of the Lord.

◆ All sit and observe silence.

FOR SILENT REFLECTION

Think about this silently in your heart. What gifts has God given you to do his work?

CLOSING PRAYER

Let us pray to God for our needs and the needs of others: our family, neighborhood, and the world. For each need we say, "Lord, hear our prayer."

◆ All may add their own prayers here.

Let us pray: **Our Father . . . Amen.**

Father,
you have given each of us many good gifts.
Give us the wisdom to use them in love.
In Jesus' name we pray.

Amen.

✚ All make the sign of the cross.

PRAYER FOR
THURSDAY, SEPTEMBER 21, 2023

OPENING

Tax collectors of Jesus' time worked with the Romans and were considered traitors by their fellow Jews. In contrast, Pharisees strictly followed the law and were devout in practice. Those listening to Jesus would expect the Pharisee to be the favored one. Listen for who goes home justified. Today we honor St. Matthew, who was a tax collector before he met Jesus. He was so fully converted toward God that he wrote one of the Gospels to share the Good News with others.

✣ All make the sign of the cross.

In the name of the Father, and of the Son, and of the Holy Spirit. Amen.

PSALM
(For a longer psalm, see page xi.)
Psalm 66:1–3a

Make a joyful noise to God, all the earth.

Make a joyful noise to God, all the earth.

Make a joyful noise to God, all the earth;
  sing the glory of his name;
  give to him glorious praise.
Say to God, "How awesome are your deeds!"

Make a joyful noise to God, all the earth.

◆ All stand and sing **Alleluia.**

GOSPEL
Luke 18:9–14

A reading from the holy Gospel according to Luke.

He also told this parable to some who trusted in themselves that they were righteous and regarded others with contempt: "Two men went up to the temple to pray, one a Pharisee and the other a tax collector. The Pharisee, standing by himself, was praying thus, 'God, I thank you that I am not like other people: thieves, rogues, adulterers, or even like this tax collector. I fast twice a week; I give a tenth of all my income.' But the tax collector, standing far off, would not even lift up his eyes to heaven but was beating his breast and saying, 'God, be merciful to me, a sinner!' I tell you, this man went down to his home justified rather than the other, for all who exalt themselves will be humbled, but all who humble themselves will be exalted."

The Gospel of the Lord.

◆ All sit and observe silence.

FOR SILENT REFLECTION

Think about this silently in your heart. Do you compare yourself to others? Why?

CLOSING PRAYER

Let us pray to God for our needs and the needs of others: our family, neighborhood, and the world. For each need we say, "Lord, hear our prayer."

◆ All may add their own prayers here.

Let us pray: **Our Father . . . Amen.**

O God,
teach us to be kind and humble
and banish all self-importance.
Through Christ our Lord.

Amen.

✣ All make the sign of the cross.

PRAYER FOR
FRIDAY, SEPTEMBER 22, 2023

OPENING

We have the very human urge to store and stockpile for a rainy day. But God asks us different questions: have you given enough love? Enough joy? Enough comfort? Enough mercy? Have you shared enough of your abundance with those in need? We are called not to stockpile our wealth, but to give it away.

✢ All make the sign of the cross.

In the name of the Father, and of the Son, and of the Holy Spirit. Amen.

PSALM
(For a longer psalm, see page xi.)
Psalm 66:1–3a

Make a joyful noise to God, all the earth.

Make a joyful noise to God, all the earth.

Make a joyful noise to God, all the earth;
   sing the glory of his name;
   give to him glorious praise.
Say to God, "How awesome are your deeds!"

Make a joyful noise to God, all the earth.

◆ All stand and sing **Alleluia.**

GOSPEL
Luke 12:16–21

A reading from the holy Gospel according to Luke.

Jesus told his disciples a parable: "The land of a rich man produced abundantly. And he thought to himself, 'What should I do, for I have no place to store my crops?' Then he said, 'I will do this: I will pull down my barns and build larger ones, and there I will store all my grain and my goods. And I will say to my soul, Soul, you have ample goods laid up for many years; relax, eat, drink, be merry.' But God said to him, 'You fool! This very night your life is being demanded of you. And the things you have prepared, whose will they be?' So it is with those who store up treasures for themselves but are not rich toward God."

The Gospel of the Lord.

◆ All sit and observe silence.

FOR SILENT REFLECTION

Think about this silently in your heart. What do you stockpile? How can you give more?

CLOSING PRAYER

Let us pray to God for our needs and the needs of others: our family, neighborhood, and the world. For each need we say, "Lord, hear our prayer."

◆ All may add their own prayers here.

Let us pray: **Our Father . . . Amen.**

Loving God,
you have given us so many gifts.
May we use our talent and treasure
   to serve others,
especially the ignored and forgotten.
Through Christ our Lord.

Amen.

✢ All make the sign of the cross.

PRAYER FOR THE WEEK
WITH A READING FROM THE GOSPEL FOR **SUNDAY, SEPTEMBER 24, 2023**

OPENING

In today's parable, Jesus paints what we might view as unfair: workers all get paid the same amount regardless of how much work they have done. Yet this, he tells us, is the kingdom of God—a place where love triumphs over fairness.

✛ All make the sign of the cross.

In the name of the Father, and of the Son, and of the Holy Spirit. Amen.

PSALM
(For a longer psalm, see page xi.)
Psalm 66:1–3a

Make a joyful noise to God, all the earth.

Make a joyful noise to God, all the earth.

Make a joyful noise to God, all the earth;
   sing the glory of his name;
   give to him glorious praise.
Say to God, "How awesome are your deeds!"

Make a joyful noise to God, all the earth.

◆ All stand and sing **Alleluia.**

GOSPEL
Matthew 20:1–2, 6a, 7c–8, 10, 11b–13, 15b

A reading from the holy Gospel according to Matthew.

"The kingdom of heaven is like a landowner who went out early in the morning to hire laborers for his vineyard. After agreeing with the laborers for a denarius for the day, he sent them into his vineyard. And about five o'clock he went out and found others standing around, and he said to them, 'You also go into the vineyard.' When evening came, the owner of the vineyard said to his manager, 'Call the laborers and give them their pay, beginning with the last and then going to the first.' Now when the first came, they thought they would receive more; but each of them also received a denarius. They grumbled against the landowner, saying, 'These last worked only one hour, and you have made them equal to us who have borne the burden of the day and the scorching heat.' But he replied to one of them, 'Friend, I am doing you no wrong; did you not agree with me for a denarius? Are you envious because I am generous?'"

The Gospel of the Lord.

◆ All sit and observe silence.

FOR SILENT REFLECTION

Think about this silently in your heart. How might I orient my view of fairness through God's eyes?

CLOSING PRAYER

Let us pray to God for our needs and the needs of others: our family, neighborhood, and the world. For each need we say, "Lord, hear our prayer."

◆ All may add their own prayers here.

Let us pray: **Our Father . . . Amen.**

O God,
teach us to love with your notion of justice
   and mercy.
We ask this through Christ our Lord.

Amen.

✛ All make the sign of the cross.

PRAYER FOR
MONDAY, SEPTEMBER 25, 2023

OPENING

This week we will be reflecting on the creation of the world. In today's reading, God is portrayed as a potter, making man (in Hebrew, *adam*) from the clay of the ground (in Hebrew, *adama*). Then God breathed life into this man. The Hebrew word that is translated here as "breath" is *ruah*. Elsewhere it is translated as "wind" or "spirit." God formed this Adam from the earth and breathed his own spirit into him. Breath also brought about new life in the spirit after the resurrection. When Jesus appeared to his disciples in the upper room "he breathed on them and said to them, 'Receive the holy Spirit'" (John 20:22).

✚ All make the sign of the cross.

In the name of the Father, and of the Son, and of the Holy Spirit. Amen.

PSALM
(For a longer psalm, see page xi.)
Psalm 66:1–3a

Make a joyful noise to God, all the earth.

Make a joyful noise to God, all the earth.

Make a joyful noise to God, all the earth;
 sing the glory of his name;
 give to him glorious praise.
Say to God, "How awesome are your deeds!"

Make a joyful noise to God, all the earth.

READING
Genesis 2:4–7

A reading from the Book of Genesis.

These are the generations of the heavens and the earth when they were created. In the day that the LORD God made the earth and the heavens, when no plant of the field was yet in the earth and no vegetation of the field had yet sprung up—for the LORD God had not caused it to rain upon the earth, and there was no one to till the ground, but a stream would rise from the earth and water the whole face of the ground—then the LORD God formed man from the dust of the ground and breathed into his nostrils the breath of life; and the man became a living being.

The Word of the Lord.

◆ All observe silence.

FOR SILENT REFLECTION

Think about this silently in your heart. How has God breathed his life into me?

CLOSING PRAYER

Let us pray to God for our needs and the needs of others: our family, neighborhood, and the world. For each need we say, "Lord, hear our prayer."

◆ All may add their own prayers here.

Let us pray: **Our Father . . . Amen.**

Father in heaven,
you have made us out of dust
and breathed your spirit into us.
Thank you for the gift of life,
for creating and forming us in your image.
Help us to honor our covenant with you,
and serve you every day.
Through Christ our Lord.

Amen.

✚ All make the sign of the cross.

PRAYER FOR TUESDAY, SEPTEMBER 26, 2023

OPENING

God created the earth and the sky, the land and the sea, birds and animals, fish and plants, even humans—all out of love. We remember the land he created as a garden, beautiful and lush, full of every good thing. We call it paradise, because it was a place without envy or greed, anger or violence, a place even without death. This paradise is the dream God has for creation—the dream he also has for each of us. It is a world of goodness, beauty, truth, and love. Today we celebrate the feast day of Sts. Cosmas and Damian, twin brothers who lived during the late third century. They were known for treating and curing the ill. Listen for their names during the First Eucharistic Prayer at Mass.

✢ All make the sign of the cross.

In the name of the Father, and of the Son, and of the Holy Spirit. Amen.

PSALM
(For a longer psalm, see page xi.)
Psalm 66:1–3a

Make a joyful noise to God, all the earth.

Make a joyful noise to God, all the earth.

Make a joyful noise to God, all the earth;
   sing the glory of his name;
   give to him glorious praise.
Say to God, "How awesome are your deeds!"

Make a joyful noise to God, all the earth.

READING
Genesis 2:8–11a, 13–14

A reading from the Book of Genesis.

And the LORD God planted a garden in Eden, in the east, and there he put the man whom he had formed. Out of the ground the LORD God made to grow every tree that is pleasant to the sight and good for food, the tree of life also in the midst of the garden, and the tree of the knowledge of good and evil. A river flows out of Eden to water the garden, and from there it divides and becomes four branches. The name of the first is Pishon. The name of the second river is Gihon; it is the one that flows around the whole land of Cush [KOOSH]. The name of the third river is Tigris, which flows east of Assyria. And the fourth river is the Euphrates [yoo-FRAY-teez].

The Word of the Lord.

◆ All observe silence.

FOR SILENT REFLECTION

Think about this silently in your heart. Imagine the paradise God created.

CLOSING PRAYER

Let us pray to God for our needs and the needs of others: our family, neighborhood, and the world. For each need we say, "Lord, hear our prayer."

◆ All may add their own prayers here.

Let us pray: **Our Father . . . Amen.**

God of all creation,
you give us everything that is good.
We praise and thank you in Jesus' name.

Amen.

✢ All make the sign of the cross.

PRAYER FOR
WEDNESDAY, SEPTEMBER 27, 2023

OPENING

The man God created was a caretaker, and the garden belonged to God. Do we always take care of God's creation? Today we remember St. Vincent de Paul, who dedicated his life and ministry to caring for the poor and forgotten of society. Like St. Vincent, we are called not to hoard the gifts of God's creation, but to share them generously and with great love.

✣ All make the sign of the cross.

In the name of the Father, and of the Son, and of the Holy Spirit. Amen.

PSALM
(For a longer psalm, see page xi.)
Psalm 66:1–3a

Make a joyful noise to God, all the earth.

Make a joyful noise to God, all the earth.

Make a joyful noise to God, all the earth;
   sing the glory of his name;
   give to him glorious praise.
Say to God, "How awesome are your deeds!"

Make a joyful noise to God, all the earth.

READING
Genesis 2:15, 18–20

A reading from the Book of Genesis.

The LORD God took the man and put him in the garden of Eden to till it and keep it. Then the LORD God said, "It is not good that the man should be alone; I will make him a helper as his partner." So out of the ground the LORD God formed every animal of the field and every bird of the air and brought them to the man to see what he would call them, and whatever the man called every living creature, that was its name. The man gave names to all cattle and to the birds of the air and to every animal of the field, but for the man there was not found a helper as his partner.

The Word of the Lord.

◆ All observe silence.

FOR SILENT REFLECTION

Think about this silently in your heart. How can you be a better caretaker of God's creation?

CLOSING PRAYER

Let us pray to God for our needs and the needs of others: our family, neighborhood, and the world. For each need we say, "Lord, hear our prayer."

◆ All may add their own prayers here.

Let us pray: **Our Father . . . Amen.**

Creator God,
give us the wisdom to take care of your
   beautiful creation:
this earth, with its bounty of life,
and all of the wonderful creatures
   that reside in it.
Through Christ our Lord.

Amen.

✣ All make the sign of the cross.

PRAYER FOR
THURSDAY, SEPTEMBER 28, 2023

OPENING

God desired to give the man a "helper" in his work, a companion made not of the ground but of his very flesh, someone with whom he could have a supportive and loving relationship. Humans were created to live in relationship, to love and nurture others and to be loved in return. All the saints have had friends and companions that strengthened them in their call to holiness. Today we remember St. Lorenzo Ruiz and his companions, who were martyred in Japan in the seventeenth century. Before their death, they were brutally tortured, but it is said that they were strengthened by each other, and in the end, they refused to recant their faith.

✢ All make the sign of the cross.

In the name of the Father, and of the Son, and of the Holy Spirit. Amen.

PSALM

(For a longer psalm, see page xi.)
Psalm 66:1–3a

Make a joyful noise to God, all the earth.

Make a joyful noise to God, all the earth.

Make a joyful noise to God, all the earth;
　sing the glory of his name;
　give to him glorious praise.
Say to God, "How awesome are your deeds!"

Make a joyful noise to God, all the earth.

READING

Genesis 2:21–24

A reading from the Book of Genesis.

So the Lord God caused a deep sleep to fall upon the man, and he slept; then he took one of his ribs and closed up its place with flesh. And the rib that the Lord God had taken from the man he made into a woman and brought her to the man. Then the man said, "This at last is bone of my bones and flesh of my flesh; this one shall be called Woman, for out of Man this one was taken." Therefore a man leaves his father and his mother and clings to his wife, and they become one flesh.

The Word of the Lord.

◆ All observe silence.

FOR SILENT REFLECTION

Think about this silently in your heart. Who are the companions in your life who help you stay strong in faith?

CLOSING PRAYER

Let us pray to God for our needs and the needs of others: our family, neighborhood, and the world. For each need we say, "Lord, hear our prayer."

◆ All may add their own prayers here.

Let us pray: **Our Father . . . Amen.**

Lord,
you have made us to love one another.
Strengthen our relationships
that they might bear the fruit of your love,
　mercy, and holiness.
In your Son's name, we pray.

Amen.

✢ All make the sign of the cross.

PRAYER FOR
FRIDAY, SEPTEMBER 29, 2023

OPENING

God made humans in his image. He gave us strength and a mind for thinking. He gave us all the senses to engage with his creation. He showed us good and evil. We respond simply to this marvelous gift by praising his holy name and proclaiming his goodness. Today, on the feast of the archangels Michael, Gabriel, and Raphael, we remember the angels, who were also created by God and given many amazing gifts.

✚ All make the sign of the cross.

> In the name of the Father, and of the Son, and of the Holy Spirit. Amen.

PSALM

(For a longer psalm, see page xi.)
Psalm 66:1–3a

Make a joyful noise to God, all the earth.

Make a joyful noise to God, all the earth.

Make a joyful noise to God, all the earth;
 sing the glory of his name;
 give to him glorious praise.
Say to God, "How awesome are your deeds!"

Make a joyful noise to God, all the earth.

READING
Sirach 16:24, 26a, 27a, 29; 17:1a, 3, 6–7, 9–10, 13

A reading from the Book of Sirach [SEER-ak].

Listen to me, my child, and acquire knowledge, and pay close attention to my words. When the Lord created his works from the beginning, he arranged his works in an eternal order. Then the Lord looked upon the earth and filled it with his good things.

The Lord created human beings out of earth. God endowed them with strength like his own and made them in his own image. Discretion and tongue and eyes, ears and a mind for thinking God gave them. He filled them with knowledge and understanding and showed them good and evil. And they will praise God's holy name, to proclaim the grandeur of his works. Their eyes saw God's glorious majesty, and their ears heard the glory of God's voice.

The Word of the Lord.

◆ All observe silence.

FOR SILENT REFLECTION

Think about this silently in your heart. Ponder on the truth that you were made in God's image. What does that mean to you?

CLOSING PRAYER

Let us pray to God for our needs and the needs of others: our family, neighborhood, and the world. For each need we say, "Lord, hear our prayer."

◆ All may add their own prayers here.

Let us pray: **Our Father . . . Amen.**

Holy God,
heaven and earth are full of your glory!
 Hosanna in the highest!
May we keep your Word
in our minds and hearts
throughout our day.
We ask this in the name of your Son our Lord Jesus Christ.

Amen.

✚ All make the sign of the cross.

PRAYER FOR THE WEEK
WITH A READING FROM THE GOSPEL FOR **SUNDAY, OCTOBER 1, 2023**

OPENING

What does it mean to praise God? Jesus doesn't want his disciples to be Christians in name only, but to truly live their faith. We are called not only to praise God with our words, prayers, and songs, but also with our actions. Today's Gospel is a reminder that actions speak louder than words.

✦ All make the sign of the cross.

In the name of the Father, and of the Son, and of the Holy Spirit. Amen.

PSALM
(For a longer psalm, see page xi.)
Psalm 145:2–3

I will praise your name for ever, Lord.

I will praise your name for ever, Lord.

Every day I will bless you
 and praise your name forever and ever.
Great is the Lord and greatly to be praised;
 his greatness is unsearchable.

I will praise your name for ever, Lord.

◆ All stand and sing **Alleluia**.

GOSPEL
Matthew 21:28–32

A reading from the holy Gospel according to Matthew.

Jesus said, "What do you think? A man had two sons; he went to the first and said, 'Son, go and work in the vineyard today.' He answered, 'I will not,' but later he changed his mind and went. The father went to the second and said the same, and he answered, 'I go, sir,' but he did not go. Which of the two did the will of his father?" The disciples said, "The first." Jesus said to them, "Truly I tell you, the tax collectors and the prostitutes are going into the kingdom of God ahead of you. For John came to you in the way of righteousness, and you did not believe him, but the tax collectors and the prostitutes believed him, and even after you saw it you did not change your minds and believe him."

The Gospel of the Lord.

◆ All sit and observe silence.

FOR SILENT REFLECTION

Think about this silently in your heart. How do you praise God in thought, word, or action?

CLOSING PRAYER

Let us pray to God for our needs and the needs of others: our family, neighborhood, and the world. For each need we say, "Lord, hear our prayer."

◆ All may add their own prayers here.

Let us pray: **Our Father . . . Amen.**

Heavenly Father,
we adore you and we praise you.
Make us into your hands and feet
to do your will on earth.
We ask this through Christ our Lord.

Amen.

✦ All make the sign of the cross.

PRAYER FOR
MONDAY, OCTOBER 2, 2023

OPENING

This week we are going to reflect on what it means to praise God. The first book of Chronicles highlights the work of King David, especially regarding the Ark of the Covenant being brought to Jerusalem and preparing for the construction and establishment of the temple. Today we hear the organization of the tribe of Levi into ministers whose job is "to invoke, to thank, and to praise the Lord." All of us are likewise called to this work every time we gather at Mass, when we join together with all those assembled, with the faithful worldwide, and even with the saints and angels, to praise the Lord.

✦ All make the sign of the cross.

In the name of the Father, and of the Son, and of the Holy Spirit. Amen.

PSALM

(For a longer psalm, see page xi.)
Psalm 145:2–3

I will praise your name for ever, Lord.

I will praise your name for ever, Lord.

Every day I will bless you
　and praise your name forever and ever.
Great is the Lord and greatly to be praised;
　his greatness is unsearchable.

I will praise your name for ever, Lord.

READING

1 Chronicles 16:4–5ab, 6–10

A reading from the First Book of Chronicles.

David appointed certain of the Levites [LEE-vīts] as ministers before the ark of the Lord, to invoke, to thank, and to praise the Lord, the God of Israel. Asaph [AY-saf] was the chief. Asaph was to sound the cymbals, and the priests Benaiah and Jahaziel were to blow trumpets regularly before the ark of the covenant of God.

Then on that day David first appointed the singing of praises to the Lord by Asaph and his kindred. O give thanks to the Lord, call on his name, make known his deeds among the peoples. Sing to him, sing praises to him; tell of all his wonderful works. Glory in his holy name; let the hearts of those who seek the Lord rejoice.

The Word of the Lord.

◆ All observe silence.

FOR SILENT REFLECTION

Think about this silently in your heart. Do you join in with all the faithful to praise and thank God during Mass?

CLOSING PRAYER

Let us pray to God for our needs and the needs of others: our family, neighborhood, and the world. For each need we say, "Lord, hear our prayer."

◆ All may add their own prayers here.

Let us pray: **Our Father . . . Amen.**

Lord God,
you have given us voices, words, and songs.
Help us to use them to praise and thank you.
In Jesus' name, we pray.

Amen.

✦ All make the sign of the cross.

PRAYER FOR TUESDAY, OCTOBER 3, 2023

OPENING

The sense of smell is linked with our sense of taste. It can warn us of danger or provide comfort. Today's wisdom from the Book of Sirach invites us to scatter a fragrance "like incense"; in other words, a holy fragrance. To invite people into the presence of God in subtle or unknown ways, simply by the way we live our lives. The saints give us an example of the many ways that we can scatter this holy fragrance to bless the Lord and to put forth blossoms everywhere we go.

✤ All make the sign of the cross.

In the name of the Father, and of the Son, and of the Holy Spirit. Amen.

PSALM

(For a longer psalm, see page xi.)
Psalm 145:2–3

I will praise your name for ever, Lord.

I will praise your name for ever, Lord.

Every day I will bless you
   and praise your name forever and ever.
Great is the Lord and greatly to be praised;
   his greatness is unsearchable.

I will praise your name for ever, Lord.

READING
Sirach 39:13a, 14–16a, 32–33, 35

A reading from the Book of Sirach [SEER-ak].

Listen to me, my faithful children. Send out fragrance like incense and put forth blossoms like a lily. Raise your voice and sing a hymn of praise; bless the Lord for all his works. Ascribe majesty to his name and give thanks to him with praise, with songs on your lips and with harps; this is what you shall say in thanksgiving: "All the works of the Lord are very good." So from the beginning I have been steadfast and have thought it out and left it in writing: All the works of the Lord are good, and he will supply every need in its time. So now sing praise with all your heart and voice, and bless the name of the Lord.

The Word of the Lord.

◆ All observe silence.

FOR SILENT REFLECTION

Think about this silently in your heart. How can you spread the holy fragrance of God?

CLOSING PRAYER

Let us pray to God for our needs and the needs of others: our family, neighborhood, and the world. For each need we say, "Lord, hear our prayer."

◆ All may add their own prayers here.

Let us pray: **Our Father . . . Amen.**

Lord Jesus,
you lived a holy life and praised God
      without ceasing.
Help us to follow you so that our lives may
      bear good fruit.
Who live and reign with God the Father,
in the unity of the Holy Spirit,
God, for ever and ever.

Amen.

✤ All make the sign of the cross.

PRAYER FOR
WEDNESDAY, OCTOBER 4, 2023

OPENING

Reacting to the abuses of religious practice, Jesus was angry when he drove the money-changers out of the temple. Similarly, St. Francis of Assisi, whom we celebrate today, was also concerned with reforming the Church of his time. St. Francis' whole life became focused on renewing the embodied experience of Christian life in service to the poor, forgotten, voiceless, and abandoned. He served as a noticeable antidote to the excesses of both Church and society.

✚ All make the sign of the cross.

> **In the name of the Father, and of the Son, and of the Holy Spirit. Amen.**

PSALM
(For a longer psalm, see page xi.)
Psalm 145:2–3

I will praise your name for ever, LORD.

I will praise your name for ever, LORD.

Every day I will bless you
  and praise your name forever and ever.
Great is the LORD and greatly to be praised;
  his greatness is unsearchable.

I will praise your name for ever, LORD.

◆ All stand and sing **Alleluia**.

GOSPEL
Matthew 21:12a, 13ab, 14–16

A reading from the holy Gospel according to Matthew.

Then Jesus entered the temple and drove out all who were selling and buying in the temple. He said to them, "It is written, 'My house shall be called a house of prayer.'" The blind and the lame came to him in the temple, and he cured them. But when the chief priests and the scribes saw the amazing things that he did and heard the children crying out in the temple and saying, "Hosanna to the Son of David," they became angry and said to him, "Do you hear what these are saying?" Jesus said to them, "Yes; have you never read, 'Out of the mouths of infants and nursing babies you have prepared praise for yourself'?"

The Gospel of the Lord.

◆ All sit and observe silence.

FOR SILENT REFLECTION

Think about this silently in your heart. How are you called to serve God and the Church?

CLOSING PRAYER

Let us pray to God for our needs and the needs of others: our family, neighborhood, and the world. For each need we say, "Lord, hear our prayer."

◆ All may add their own prayers here.

Let us pray: **Our Father . . . Amen.**

Lord,
make each of us an instrument of peace,
like your servant, St. Francis.
May we dedicate ourselves to the service
of you and your people.
Through Christ our Lord.

Amen.

✚ All make the sign of the cross.

PRAYER FOR
THURSDAY, OCTOBER 5, 2023

OPENING

Today, we remember St. Faustina, born to a poor Polish family in the early twentieth century. St. Faustina had visions of Jesus, who revealed to her the image of Divine Mercy and told her to inscribe "Jesus, I trust in you" on the image. Do you trust in Jesus? As we hear in today's reading, he is in everything, visible and invisible. We breathe him in, shelter him in our hearts, and marvel at his beauty in the created world. He is closer to us than parents or friends.

✢ All make the sign of the cross.

In the name of the Father, and of the Son, and of the Holy Spirit. Amen.

PSALM

(For a longer psalm, see page xi.)
Psalm 145:2–3

I will praise your name for ever, Lord.

I will praise your name for ever, Lord.

Every day I will bless you
  and praise your name forever and ever.
Great is the Lord and greatly to be praised;
  his greatness is unsearchable.

I will praise your name for ever, Lord.

READING

Colossians 1:15–20

A reading from the Letter to the Colossians.

Christ is the image of the invisible God, the firstborn of all creation, for in him all things in heaven and on earth were created, things visible and invisible, whether thrones or dominions or rulers or powers—all things have been created through him and for him. He himself is before all things, and in him all things hold together. He is the head of the body, the church; he is the beginning, the firstborn from the dead, so that he might come to have first place in everything. For in him all the fullness of God was pleased to dwell, and through him God was pleased to reconcile to himself all things, whether on earth or in heaven, by making peace through the blood of his cross.

The Word of the Lord.

◆ All observe silence.

FOR SILENT REFLECTION

Think about this silently in your heart. How has Jesus come to you in your life?

CLOSING PRAYER

Let us pray to God for our needs and the needs of others: our family, neighborhood, and the world. For each need we say, "Lord, hear our prayer."

◆ All may add their own prayers here.

Let us pray: **Our Father . . . Amen.**

Lord Jesus,
we trust in you.
Lead us in all that we do
and give us wisdom to follow you.
Who live and reign with God the Father,
in the unity of the Holy Spirit,
God, for ever and ever.

Amen.

✢ All make the sign of the cross.

PRAYER FOR
FRIDAY, OCTOBER 6, 2023

OPENING

You might not realize just how much you praise God. Every time we pray or sing or shout "alleluia" we are praising God! The word comes from Hebrew *hallel* ("praise") and *Yah* (the shortened form of "Yahweh," the name for God). So as we sing "Hallelujah" we are singing "praise God!" St. Bruno, whose feast day we celebrate today, lived in the eleventh century. He wrote commentaries on the Psalms and on the letters of St. Paul.

✚ All make the sign of the cross.

In the name of the Father, and of the Son, and of the Holy Spirit. Amen.

PSALM
(For a longer psalm, see page xi.)
Psalm 145:2–3

I will praise your name for ever, Lord.

I will praise your name for ever, Lord.

Every day I will bless you
  and praise your name forever and ever.
Great is the Lord and greatly to be praised;
  his greatness is unsearchable.

I will praise your name for ever, Lord.

READING
Revelation 19:1–2a, 3ab, 4–5abc, 6–7a

A reading from the Book of Revelation.

After this I heard what seemed to be the loud voice of a great multitude in heaven, saying, "Hallelujah! Salvation and glory and power to our God, for his judgments are true and just." Once more they said, "Hallelujah!" And the twenty-four elders and the four living creatures fell down and worshiped God who is seated on the throne, saying, "Amen. Hallelujah!" And from the throne came a voice saying, "Praise our God, all you his servants." Then I heard what seemed to be the voice of a great multitude, like the sound of many waters and like the sound of mighty thunderpeals, crying out, "Hallelujah! For the Lord God the Almighty reigns. Let us rejoice and exult and give him the glory."

The Word of the Lord.

◆ All observe silence.

FOR SILENT REFLECTION

Think about this silently in your heart. How do you praise God when you pray?

CLOSING PRAYER

Let us pray to God for our needs and the needs of others: our family, neighborhood, and the world. For each need we say, "Lord, hear our prayer."

◆ All may add their own prayers here.

Let us pray: **Our Father . . . Amen.**

O Lord Almighty,
we praise you for your majesty
and for your goodness!
Hallelujah!
May we be reflections of your love and truth
to others in everything we say and do.
Through Christ our Lord.

Amen.

✚ All make the sign of the cross.

PRAYER FOR THE WEEK
WITH A READING FROM THE GOSPEL FOR **SUNDAY, OCTOBER 8, 2023**

OPENING

God created humans to be the stewards of his creation, just as the tenants in today's reading were entrusted with land to care for. Like the owner, God sent many faithful servants, starting with Abraham, to the people of Israel to remind them of the call they had received. Let us open our hearts to God's voice, that the fruits of the kingdom might grow through our lives.

✚ All make the sign of the cross.

In the name of the Father, and of the Son, and of the Holy Spirit. Amen.

PSALM
(For a longer psalm, see page xi.)
Psalm 145:2–3

I will praise your name for ever, Lord.

I will praise your name for ever, Lord.

Every day I will bless you
  and praise your name forever and ever.
Great is the Lord and greatly to be praised;
  his greatness is unsearchable.

I will praise your name for ever, Lord.

◆ All stand and sing **Alleluia.**

GOSPEL Matthew 21:33b, 33f, 34–35, 37a, 38, 39c–41a, 41c–42a, 43

A reading from the holy Gospel according to Matthew.

Jesus said to his disciples, "There was a landowner who planted a vineyard. Then he leased it to tenants. When the harvest time had come, he sent his slaves to the tenants to collect his produce. But the tenants seized his slaves and beat one, killed another, and stoned another. Then he sent his son to them, saying, 'They will respect my son.' But when the tenants saw the son, they said to themselves, 'This is the heir; come, let us kill him and get his inheritance.' So they killed him. Now when the owner of the vineyard comes, what will he do to those tenants?" They said to him, "He will lease the vineyard to other tenants who will give him the produce at the harvest time." Jesus said to them, "Therefore I tell you, the kingdom of God will be taken away from you and given to a people that produces its fruits."

The Gospel of the Lord.

◆ All sit and observe silence.

FOR SILENT REFLECTION

Think about this silently in your heart. How can you be attentive to God's call in your life?

CLOSING PRAYER

Let us pray to God for our needs and the needs of others: our family, neighborhood, and the world. For each need we say, "Lord, hear our prayer."

◆ All may add their own prayers here.

Let us pray: **Our Father . . . Amen.**

Father in heaven,
open our hearts to your message
and your messengers.
May our works give glory to you.
Through Christ our Lord.

Amen.

✚ All make the sign of the cross.

PRAYER FOR
MONDAY, OCTOBER 9, 2023

OPENING

For the next two weeks, we will hear the story of Abram. Abram and his wife Sarai are old and barren, a metaphor for hopelessness. But God has the power to change things, for Abram and Sarai, and for all of us. Today we remember St. John Leonardi, an Italian priest who formed the Confraternity of Christian Doctrine, an organization that today serves the religious education of children.

✚ All make the sign of the cross.

In the name of the Father, and of the Son, and of the Holy Spirit. Amen.

PSALM

(For a longer psalm, see page xi.)
Psalm 145:2–3

I will praise your name for ever, LORD.

I will praise your name for ever, LORD.

Every day I will bless you
 and praise your name forever and ever.
Great is the LORD and greatly to be praised;
 his greatness is unsearchable.

I will praise your name for ever, LORD.

READING

Genesis 11:27–29c, 30–32

A reading from the Book of Genesis.

Now these are the descendants of Terah [TER-uh]. Terah was the father of Abram, Nahor [NAY-hohr], and Haran [HAYR-uhn], and Haran was the father of Lot. Haran died before his father Terah in the land of his birth, in Ur [oor] of the Chaldeans [kal-DEE-uhnz]. Abram and Nahor took wives; the name of Abram's wife was Sarai [SAYR-ī], and the name of Nahor's wife was Milcah. Now Sarai was barren; she had no child. Terah took his son Abram and his grandson Lot son of Haran and his daughter-in-law Sarai, his son Abram's wife, and they went out together from Ur of the Chaldeans to go into the land of Canaan [KAY-n*n], but when they came to Haran, they settled there. The days of Terah were two hundred five years; and Terah died in Haran.

The Word of the Lord.

◆ All observe silence.

FOR SILENT REFLECTION

Think about this silently in your heart. How are you called to be holy?

CLOSING PRAYER

Let us pray to God for our needs and the needs of others: our family, neighborhood, and the world. For each need we say, "Lord, hear our prayer."

◆ All may add their own prayers here.

Let us pray: **Our Father . . . Amen.**

Lord,
give us the courage to follow you
and to trust your plan for us.
We pray in the name of Jesus Christ
 our Lord.

Amen.

✚ All make the sign of the cross.

PRAYER FOR TUESDAY, OCTOBER 10, 2023

OPENING

Today we hear of God's great promise to Abram that he would make of him "a great nation." What an amazing leap of faith Abram took in response to God's call! Abram was coming from a place of hopelessness, but he heard God's voice, and he believed his promises. At seventy-five years old, he moved his family far away from everything they had known and began a new life. Sometimes God calls us to do hard things.

✚ All make the sign of the cross.

In the name of the Father, and of the Son, and of the Holy Spirit. Amen.

PSALM

(For a longer psalm, see page xi.)
Psalm 145:2–3

I will praise your name for ever, Lord.

I will praise your name for ever, Lord.

Every day I will bless you
  and praise your name forever and ever.
Great is the Lord and greatly to be praised;
  his greatness is unsearchable.

I will praise your name for ever, Lord.

READING

Genesis 12:1–4a, 4c–5c

A reading from the Book of Genesis.

Now the Lord said to Abram, "Go from your country and your kindred and your father's house to the land that I will show you. I will make of you a great nation, and I will bless you and make your name great, so that you will be a blessing. I will bless those who bless you, and the one who curses you I will curse, and in you all the families of the earth shall be blessed."

So Abram went, as the Lord had told him. Abram was seventy-five years old when he departed from Haran. Abram took his wife Sarai [SAYR-ī] and his brother's son Lot and all the possessions that they had gathered and the persons whom they had acquired in Haran [HAYR-uhn], and they set forth to go to the land of Canaan [KAY-n*n].

The Word of the Lord.

◆ All observe silence.

FOR SILENT REFLECTION

Think about this silently in your heart. May we respond to God's will as faithfully and joyfully as Abram did.

CLOSING PRAYER

Let us pray to God for our needs and the needs of others: our family, neighborhood, and the world. For each need we say, "Lord, hear our prayer."

◆ All may add their own prayers here.

Let us pray: **Our Father . . . Amen.**

Loving Father in heaven,
you have promised us every good thing
  in your Son, Jesus Christ.
Give us the faith to believe your promises
  and to do your will.
Through Christ our Lord.

Amen.

✚ All make the sign of the cross.

PRAYER FOR
WEDNESDAY, OCTOBER 11, 2023

OPENING

Pope St. John XXIII, whom we remember today, was born at the end of the nineteenth century and became one of the most influential popes of the twentieth. Pope St. John XXIII convened the Second Vatican Council with the goals of bringing renewed enthusiasm, knowledge, and joy to the entire Christian people, and renewed unity of all Christians. "The Good Pope" wanted all of God's people to live together in love and friendship, to remember the familial bond we share, the bond that can be traced back to the promise God made to Abram.

✚ All make the sign of the cross.

In the name of the Father, and of the Son, and of the Holy Spirit. Amen.

PSALM
(For a longer psalm, see page xi.)
Psalm 145:2–3

I will praise your name for ever, Lord.

I will praise your name for ever, Lord.

Every day I will bless you
   and praise your name forever and ever.
Great is the Lord and greatly to be praised;
   his greatness is unsearchable.

I will praise your name for ever, Lord.

READING
Genesis 13:5–6a, 11, 14–16, 18b, d

A reading from the Book of Genesis.

Now Lot, who went with Abram, also had flocks and herds and tents, and the land could not support both of them living together. So Lot chose for himself all the plain of the Jordan, and Lot journeyed eastward, and they separated from each other. The Lord said to Abram, after Lot had separated from him, "Raise your eyes now, and look from the place where you are, northward and southward and eastward and westward, for all the land that you see I will give to you and to your offspring forever. I will make your offspring like the dust of the earth, so that if one can count the dust of the earth, your offspring also can be counted." So Abram settled by the oaks of Mamre [MAM-ree], and there he built an altar to the Lord.

The Word of the Lord.

◆ All observe silence.

FOR SILENT REFLECTION

Think about this silently in your heart. What is your inheritance from God? What has he given you?

CLOSING PRAYER

Let us pray to God for our needs and the needs of others: our family, neighborhood, and the world. For each need we say, "Lord, hear our prayer."

◆ All may add their own prayers here.

Let us pray: **Our Father . . . Amen.**

O Lord,
may we each be a spark of light,
   a core of love,
ever to grow in communion with God.
Through Christ our Lord.
Amen.

✚ All make the sign of the cross.

PRAYER FOR
THURSDAY, OCTOBER 12, 2023

OPENING

After rescuing his nephew Lot, as well as Lot's entire household (who had been taken captive as a casualty of warring kings), Abram refused any reward for his action, other than a blessing from the priest Melchizedek [mehl-KEEZ-uh-dehk]. Abram would not let anyone except God enrich him, recognizing that this and every victory belonged to God, not to him or his ability. Such humility before the Lord is difficult—it is human nature to desire to be recognized and rewarded for our achievements. Abram teaches us another way: one of true thankfulness and praise to the one who has given all.

✢ All make the sign of the cross.

In the name of the Father, and of the Son, and of the Holy Spirit. Amen.

PSALM

(For a longer psalm, see page xi.)
Psalm 145:2–3

I will praise your name for ever, LORD.

I will praise your name for ever, LORD.

Every day I will bless you
  and praise your name forever and ever.
Great is the LORD and greatly to be praised;
  his greatness is unsearchable.

I will praise your name for ever, LORD.

READING
Genesis 14:14a, 14d, 16b-c, 18–19a, 21–23a, 24b

A reading from the Book of Genesis.

When Abram heard that his nephew Lot had been taken captive, he led forth his trained men, and went in pursuit. He brought back his nephew with his goods and women and the people. And King Melchizedek [mehl-KEEZ-uh-dehk] of Salem brought out bread and wine; he was priest of God Most High. He blessed Abram. Then the king of Sodom said to Abram, "Give me the persons, but take the goods for yourself." But Abram said, "I have sworn to God Most High, maker of heaven and earth, that I would not take a thread or a sandal strap or anything that is yours. I will take nothing but what the young men have eaten and the share of the men who went with me."

The Word of the Lord.

◆ All observe silence.

FOR SILENT REFLECTION

Think about this silently in your heart. Do you thank God for the blessings in your life?

CLOSING PRAYER

Let us pray to God for our needs and the needs of others: our family, neighborhood, and the world. For each need we say, "Lord, hear our prayer."

◆ All may add their own prayers here.

Let us pray: **Our Father . . . Amen.**

Lord God,
we thank you for all the good you have
  accomplished through us.
Help us to be open to your work in our lives.
Through Christ our Lord.

Amen.

✢ All make the sign of the cross.

PRAYER FOR
FRIDAY, OCTOBER 13, 2023

OPENING

In today's reading, God made a covenant with Abraham. We have heard of covenants before, most notably the covenant God made with Abraham's ancestor Noah. God extended this covenant in a new way, promising Abraham that, despite his childlessness, he would be "fruitful," the father of nations. Most importantly to us, God promised that this covenant was established not only between Abraham and God, but extended to future generations. We heirs of Abraham also share in the promise God made to him.

✣ All make the sign of the cross.

In the name of the Father, and of the Son, and of the Holy Spirit. Amen.

PSALM

(For a longer psalm, see page xi.)
Psalm 145:2–3

I will praise your name for ever, LORD.

I will praise your name for ever, LORD.

Every day I will bless you
   and praise your name forever and ever.
Great is the LORD and greatly to be praised;
   his greatness is unsearchable.

I will praise your name for ever, LORD.

READING

Genesis 17:1–5a, 6–7

A reading from the Book of Genesis.

When Abram was ninety-nine years old, the LORD appeared to Abram and said to him, "I am God Almighty; walk before me, and be blameless. And I will make my covenant between me and you and will make you exceedingly numerous." Then Abram fell on his face, and God said to him, "As for me, this is my covenant with you: You shall be the ancestor of a multitude of nations. No longer shall your name be Abram, but your name shall be Abraham. I will make you exceedingly fruitful, and I will make nations of you, and kings shall come from you. I will establish my covenant between me and you and your offspring after you throughout their generations, for an everlasting covenant, to be God to you and to your offspring after you."

The Word of the Lord.

◆ All observe silence.

FOR SILENT REFLECTION

Think about this silently in your heart. Why do you think God changed Abram's name when he established the covenant with him?

CLOSING PRAYER

Let us pray to God for our needs and the needs of others: our family, neighborhood, and the world. For each need we say, "Lord, hear our prayer."

◆ All may add their own prayers here.

Let us pray: **Our Father . . . Amen.**

Dear God,
you are the source of all blessing
   and goodness.
Grant us faith like that of our father in faith,
   Abraham.
Through Christ our Lord.

Amen.

✣ All make the sign of the cross.

PRAYER FOR THE WEEK
WITH A READING FROM THE GOSPEL FOR **SUNDAY, OCTOBER 15, 2023**

OPENING

Like the king in today's Gospel, God sends out countless invitations: friends who want you to join them in a new activity, a teacher encouraging you, or a parent recognizing an act of kindness toward sibling or neighbor. Each of these moments are invitations from God, challenging us to stretch beyond the comfortable, to live into the amazing life he has dreamed for each of us.

✢ All make the sign of the cross.

In the name of the Father, and of the Son, and of the Holy Spirit. Amen.

PSALM
(For a longer psalm, see page xi.)
Psalm 145:2–3

I will praise your name for ever, Lord.

I will praise your name for ever, Lord.

Every day I will bless you
 and praise your name forever and ever.
Great is the Lord and greatly to be praised;
 his greatness is unsearchable.

I will praise your name for ever, Lord.

◆ All stand and sing **Alleluia.**

GOSPEL
Matthew 22:1–5, 8–10

A reading from the holy Gospel according to Matthew.

Once more Jesus spoke to the disciples in parables, saying: "The kingdom of heaven may be compared to a king who gave a wedding banquet for his son. He sent his slaves to call those who had been invited to the wedding banquet, but they would not come. Again he sent other slaves, saying, 'Tell those who have been invited: Look, I have prepared my dinner, my oxen and my fat calves have been slaughtered, and everything is ready; come to the wedding banquet.' But they made light of it and went away, one to his farm, another to his business. Then the king said to his slaves, 'The wedding is ready, but those invited were not worthy. Go therefore into the main streets, and invite everyone you find to the wedding banquet.' Those slaves went out into the streets and gathered all whom they found, both good and bad, so the wedding hall was filled with guests."

The Gospel of the Lord.

◆ All sit and observe silence.

FOR SILENT REFLECTION

Think about this silently in your heart. What does this parable tell you about God?

CLOSING PRAYER

Let us pray to God for our needs and the needs of others: our family, neighborhood, and the world. For each need we say, "Lord, hear our prayer."

◆ All may add their own prayers here.

Let us pray: **Our Father . . . Amen.**

Gracious God,
you welcome us to your heavenly banquet,
where we may celebrate your love and mercy.
Through Christ our Lord.

Amen.

✢ All make the sign of the cross.

PRAYER FOR
MONDAY, OCTOBER 16, 2023

OPENING

St. Margaret Mary Alacoque (1647–1690) was a French nun and mystic who received a vision of the Sacred Heart of Jesus, and the revelation that she could transform the coldness of others through love. This same love took flesh as Abraham tenderly cared for the Lord, who appeared in three visitors to his tent. Abraham's hospitality encompassed washing feet, preparing food, and serving the guests—actions that are repeated in the New Testament as a sign of love for others and God.

✣ All make the sign of the cross.

In the name of the Father, and of the Son, and of the Holy Spirit. Amen.

PSALM
(For a longer psalm, see page xi.)
Psalm 145:2–3

I will praise your name for ever, Lord.

I will praise your name for ever, Lord.

Every day I will bless you
   and praise your name forever and ever.
Great is the Lord and greatly to be praised;
   his greatness is unsearchable.

I will praise your name for ever, Lord.

READING
Genesis 18:1, 2a, 4, 6–8b, 9, 10b, 11a

A reading from the Book of Genesis.

The Lord appeared to Abraham by the oaks of Mamre [MAM-ree], as he sat at the entrance of his tent in the heat of the day. Abraham looked up and saw three men standing near him. He said, "Let a little water be brought, and wash your feet, and rest yourselves under the tree." And Abraham hastened into the tent to Sarah and said, "Make ready quickly three measures of choice flour, knead it, and make cakes." Abraham ran to the herd and took a calf, tender and good, and gave it to the servant, who hastened to prepare it. Then he took curds and milk and the calf that he had prepared and set it before them. They said to him, "Where is your wife Sarah?" And he said, "There, in the tent." Then one said, "Your wife Sarah shall have a son." Now Abraham and Sarah were old, advanced in age.

The Word of the Lord.

◆ All observe silence.

FOR SILENT REFLECTION

Think about this silently in your heart. To whom should we show hospitality?

CLOSING PRAYER

Let us pray to God for our needs and the needs of others: our family, neighborhood, and the world. For each need we say, "Lord, hear our prayer."

◆ All may add their own prayers here.

Let us pray: **Our Father . . . Amen.**

Lord God,
may we always open our door
   to the stranger, the hungry,
   and those in need.
May our hearts be full of love and generosity
   for all we meet.
Through Christ our Lord.

Amen.

✣ All make the sign of the cross.

PRAYER FOR TUESDAY, OCTOBER 17, 2023

OPENING

Our faith values intercessory prayer: we call on one another, on Mary and the saints, for assistance when we are troubled. Abraham's humble dialogue with God revealed that the Lord hears and responds to these prayers. We remember today St. Ignatius of Antioch, a second-century bishop, who was martyred in the Circus Maximus in Rome.

✚ All make the sign of the cross.

In the name of the Father, and of the Son, and of the Holy Spirit. Amen.

PSALM

(For a longer psalm, see page xi.)
Psalm 145:2–3

I will praise your name for ever, Lord.

I will praise your name for ever, Lord.

Every day I will bless you
  and praise your name forever and ever.
Great is the Lord and greatly to be praised;
  his greatness is unsearchable.

I will praise your name for ever, Lord.

READING

Genesis 18:20, 23–24a, 24c, 26, 29, 30b, 32b-c

A reading from the Book of Genesis.

The Lord said, "How great is the outcry against Sodom [SOD-uhm] and Gomorrah [guh-MOHR-ah] and how very grave their sin!" Then Abraham came near and said, "Will you indeed sweep away the righteous with the wicked? Suppose there are fifty righteous within the city; will you not forgive it for the fifty righteous who are in it?" And the Lord said, "If I find at Sodom fifty righteous in the city, I will forgive the whole place for their sake." Again Abraham spoke to the Lord, "Suppose forty are found there." The Lord answered, "For the sake of forty I will not do it." "Suppose thirty are found there." He answered, "I will not do it, if I find thirty there." "Suppose ten are found there." He answered, "For the sake of ten I will not destroy it."

The Word of the Lord.

◆ All observe silence.

FOR SILENT REFLECTION

Think about this silently in your heart. Think of who might need your intercessory prayer right now.

CLOSING PRAYER

Let us pray to God for our needs and the needs of others: our family, neighborhood, and the world. For each need we say, "Lord, hear our prayer."

◆ All may add their own prayers here.

Let us pray: **Our Father . . . Amen.**

O Lord,
remember your faithful people in distress
and bring them your peace.
Give us the courage you gave St. Ignatius,
who bravely faced his death rather than
  deny you.
Through Christ our Lord.

Amen.

✚ All make the sign of the cross.

PRAYER FOR WEDNESDAY, OCTOBER 18, 2023

OPENING

In the sacrifice of Isaac, we see a magnificent example of faith in God. Abraham trusts the Lord so much that he is willing to sacrifice his own beloved and long-awaited son. We are called to trust God even when life is most difficult. Today is the feast of St. Luke, the author of the Gospel of Luke and Acts of the Apostles. His accounts encompass themes of prayer, the Holy Spirit, and mercy, all of which depict the author as a compassionate, spiritual man.

✢ All make the sign of the cross.

In the name of the Father, and of the Son, and of the Holy Spirit. Amen.

PSALM

(For a longer psalm, see page xi.)
Psalm 145:2–3

I will praise your name for ever, Lord.

I will praise your name for ever, Lord.

Every day I will bless you
    and praise your name forever and ever.
Great is the Lord and greatly to be praised;
    his greatness is unsearchable.

I will praise your name for ever, Lord.

READING

Genesis 22:1a, 2–3, 5, 7a, 7c–8a

A reading from the Book of Genesis.

God tested Abraham. He said, "Take your son, your only son Isaac, whom you love, and go to the land of Moriah and offer him there as a burnt offering on one of the mountains that I shall show you." So Abraham rose early in the morning, saddled his donkey, and took two of his young men with him and his son Isaac; he cut the wood for the burnt offering and set out and went to the place in the distance that God had shown him. Then Abraham said to his young men, "Stay here with the donkey; the boy and I will go over there; we will worship, and then we will come back to you." Isaac said to his father Abraham, "Father, the fire and the wood are here, but where is the lamb for a burnt offering?" Abraham said, "God himself will provide the lamb for a burnt offering, my son."

The Word of the Lord.

◆ All observe silence.

FOR SILENT REFLECTION

Think about this silently in your heart. What are you willing to give up for God?

CLOSING PRAYER

Let us pray to God for our needs and the needs of others: our family, neighborhood, and the world. For each need we say, "Lord, hear our prayer."

◆ All may add their own prayers here.

Let us pray: **Our Father . . . Amen.**

Heavenly Father,
bless us with the faith and trust of Abraham.
May the Holy Spirit help us understand and
    live God's Word.
Through Christ our Lord.

Amen.

✢ All make the sign of the cross.

PRAYER FOR
THURSDAY, OCTOBER 19, 2023

OPENING

In Abraham's time, the firstborn son belonged to God, so God asking him for this sacrifice was not the most surprising part of the story (though certainly tragic after Abraham and Sarai had waited so long for a child!). The surprise is in the second part of God's action: staying Abraham's hand and sparing the child. Today we remember the seventeenth-century Jesuit missionaries Isaac Jogues [Ī-zik johgz] and John de Brébeuf [BRAY-buhf] and their companions, who evangelized the native peoples of North America.

✢ All make the sign of the cross.

In the name of the Father, and of the Son, and of the Holy Spirit. Amen.

PSALM
(For a longer psalm, see page xi.)
Psalm 145:2–3

I will praise your name for ever, Lord.

I will praise your name for ever, Lord.

Every day I will bless you
  and praise your name forever and ever.
Great is the Lord and greatly to be praised;
  his greatness is unsearchable.

I will praise your name for ever, Lord.

READING
Genesis 22:9b, 11a, 12–13, 15, 17a

A reading from the Book of Genesis.

Abraham built an altar there and laid the wood in order. He bound his son Isaac and laid him on the altar on top of the wood. But the angel of the Lord called to him from heaven, and said, "Abraham, do not lay your hand on the boy or do anything to him, for now I know that you fear God, since you have not withheld your son, your only son, from me." And Abraham looked up and saw a ram, caught in a thicket by its horns. Abraham went and took the ram and offered it up as a burnt offering instead of his son. The angel of the Lord called to Abraham a second time from heaven, "I will indeed bless you, and I will make your offspring as numerous as the stars of heaven and as the sand on the seashore."

The Word of the Lord.

◆ All observe silence.

FOR SILENT REFLECTION

Think about this silently in your heart. Bring anything you are worried or anxious about to God.

CLOSING PRAYER

Let us pray to God for our needs and the needs of others: our family, neighborhood, and the world. For each need we say, "Lord, hear our prayer."

◆ All may add their own prayers here.

Let us pray: **Our Father . . . Amen.**

Loving God,
you call us to obedience,
to give ourselves wholeheartedly
  to your purposes.
Help us to trust you in all things.
We ask this through Christ our Lord.

Amen.

✢ All make the sign of the cross.

PRAYER FOR
FRIDAY, OCTOBER 20, 2023

OPENING

St. Paul of the Cross (1694–1775) was a former soldier who developed a devotion to the passion of Christ, and formed the Passionist order. Today, we will hear the conclusion of Abraham's remarkable story. God keeps the covenant promise he made to him after he dies of old age. Note that numbers in the Bible have symbolic rather than literal meaning. God's promise extends all the way to us today.

✢ All make the sign of the cross.

In the name of the Father, and of the Son, and of the Holy Spirit. Amen.

PSALM

(For a longer psalm, see page xi.)
Psalm 145:2–3

I will praise your name for ever, Lord.

I will praise your name for ever, Lord.

Every day I will bless you
  and praise your name forever and ever.
Great is the Lord and greatly to be praised;
  his greatness is unsearchable.

I will praise your name for ever, Lord.

READING

Genesis 25:7–11

A reading from the Book of Genesis.

This is the length of Abraham's life, one hundred seventy-five years. Abraham breathed his last and died in a good old age, old and full of years, and was gathered to his people. His sons Isaac and Ishmael [ISH-may-uhl] buried him in the cave of Machpelah [mak-PEE-luh], in the field of Ephron son of Zohar the Hittite [HIT-tīt], east of Mamre [MAM-ree], the field that Abraham purchased from the Hittites. There Abraham was buried with his wife Sarah. After the death of Abraham, God blessed his son Isaac. And Isaac settled at Beer-lahai-roi.

The Word of the Lord.

◆ All observe silence.

FOR SILENT REFLECTION

Think about this silently in your heart. What does God's promise to Abraham mean to you?

CLOSING PRAYER

Let us pray to God for our needs and the needs of others: our family, neighborhood, and the world. For each need we say, "Lord, hear our prayer."

◆ All may add their own prayers here.

Let us pray: **Our Father . . . Amen.**

Lord God,
you promised Abraham, our father in faith,
that your blessing would be on
  his descendants.
Bless your holy people gathered today
and help us to live in faith, hope, and love
as we journey closer to you.
Through Christ our Lord.

Amen.

✢ All make the sign of the cross.

PRAYER FOR THE WEEK
WITH A READING FROM THE GOSPEL FOR SUNDAY, OCTOBER 22, 2023

OPENING

The Jews of Jesus' time paid taxes using coins that bore the image of the emperor they belonged to. But what (or who) belongs to God? In baptism, Jesus was stamped on our heart and soul. Today we are called, like those Jewish authorities who questioned Jesus, to give God what belongs to him—namely, our whole selves. For as a people made in the image of God, we bear his stamp.

✚ All make the sign of the cross.

In the name of the Father, and of the Son, and of the Holy Spirit. Amen.

PSALM
(For a longer psalm, see page xi.)
Psalm 145:2–3

I will praise your name for ever, Lord.

I will praise your name for ever, Lord.

Every day I will bless you
   and praise your name forever and ever.
Great is the Lord and greatly to be praised;
   his greatness is unsearchable.

I will praise your name for ever, Lord.

◆ All stand and sing **Alleluia.**

GOSPEL
Matthew 22:15, 17–21

A reading from the holy Gospel according to Matthew.

The Pharisees went and plotted to entrap Jesus in what he said. "Tell us, then, what you think. Is it lawful to pay taxes to Caesar, or not?" But Jesus, aware of their malice, said, "Why are you putting me to the test, you hypocrites? Show me the coin used for the tax." And they brought him a denarius [dih-NAHR-ee-uhs]. Then he said to them, "Whose head is this and whose title?" They answered, "Caesar's." Then he said to them, "Give therefore to Caesar the things that are the Caesar's, and to God the things that are God's."

The Gospel of the Lord.

◆ All sit and observe silence.

FOR SILENT REFLECTION

Think about this silently in your heart. How can you give God what belongs to him?

CLOSING PRAYER

Let us pray to God for our needs and the needs of others: our family, neighborhood, and the world. For each need we say, "Lord, hear our prayer."

◆ All may add their own prayers here.

Let us pray: **Our Father . . . Amen.**

Good and loving Father,
thank you for all you have given us.
Help us to be thoughtful and wise
    in all we say and do.
Through Christ our Lord.

Amen.

✚ All make the sign of the cross.

PRAYER FOR
MONDAY, OCTOBER 23, 2023

OPENING

A covenant is a sacred commitment. In a covenant, both parties pledge themselves to one another. God committed himself not to just one person, but to a people, for better or worse. He kept his promise. Though Abraham died, God gave his blessing to Isaac in turn, and renewed the promises he made to Abraham. St. John of Capistrano (1386–1456), whose feast day is today, was so optimistic that he was able to tackle problems of his day with confidence and a deep faith in Christ.

✚ All make the sign of the cross.

In the name of the Father, and of the Son, and of the Holy Spirit. Amen.

PSALM
(For a longer psalm, see page xi.)
Psalm 145:2–3

I will praise your name for ever, Lord.

I will praise your name for ever, Lord.

Every day I will bless you
 and praise your name forever and ever.
Great is the Lord and greatly to be praised;
 his greatness is unsearchable.

I will praise your name for ever, Lord.

READING
Genesis 26:2, 3b-c, 3e–5, 25

A reading from the Book of Genesis.

The Lord appeared to Isaac and said, "Do not go down to Egypt; settle in the land that I shall show you. I will be with you and will bless you. I will fulfill the oath that I swore to your father Abraham. I will make your offspring as numerous as the stars of heaven and will give to your offspring all these lands, and all the nations of the earth shall gain blessing for themselves through your offspring, because Abraham obeyed my voice and kept my charge, my commandments, my statutes, and my laws." So Isaac built an altar there, called on the name of the Lord, and pitched his tent there. And there Isaac's servants dug a well.

The Word of the Lord.

◆ All observe silence.

FOR SILENT REFLECTION

Think about this silently in your heart. How might you show that you believe in God's promises?

CLOSING PRAYER

Let us pray to God for our needs and the needs of others: our family, neighborhood, and the world. For each need we say, "Lord, hear our prayer."

◆ All may add their own prayers here.

Let us pray: **Our Father . . . Amen.**

Lord God,
may we bring your blessing to all nations
 on earth.
May we keep your commandments, statutes,
 and laws,
for we trust that you are with us always.
Through Christ our Lord.

Amen.

✚ All make the sign of the cross.

PRAYER FOR
TUESDAY, OCTOBER 24, 2023

OPENING

Today is the feast day of St. Anthony Mary Claret (1807–1870). As a child, St. Anthony and his family prayed the Rosary together and went to church, which fostered his deep love and devotion to Jesus and Mary. In God's blessing to Jacob, he changed his name to Israel, meaning "prince of God." When God changes a name, this signifies a new call in life. Jacob was called to turn around from the deceitful twin who stole a blessing from his elder brother, to the patriarch of Israel, the Father of a mighty nation.

✚ All make the sign of the cross.

In the name of the Father, and of the Son, and of the Holy Spirit. Amen.

PSALM
(For a longer psalm, see page xi.)
Psalm 145:2–3

I will praise your name for ever, Lord.

I will praise your name for ever, Lord.

Every day I will bless you
   and praise your name forever and ever.
Great is the Lord and greatly to be praised;
   his greatness is unsearchable.

I will praise your name for ever, Lord.

READING
Genesis 35:9–12, 14–15

A reading from the Book of Genesis.

God appeared to Jacob again when he came from Paddan-aram, and he blessed him. God said to him, "Your name is Jacob; no longer shall you be called Jacob, but Israel shall be your name." So he was called Israel. God said to him, "I am God Almighty: be fruitful and multiply; a nation and a company of nations shall come from you, and kings shall spring from you. The land that I gave to Abraham and Isaac I will give to you, and I will give the land to your offspring after you." Jacob set up a pillar in the place where God had spoken with him, a pillar of stone, and he poured out a drink offering on it and poured oil on it. So Jacob called the place where God had spoken with him Bethel.

The Word of the Lord.

◆ All observe silence.

FOR SILENT REFLECTION

Think about this silently in your heart. Do you think of going to church as a way to offer thanks and gratitude to God?

CLOSING PRAYER

Let us pray to God for our needs and the needs of others: our family, neighborhood, and the world. For each need we say, "Lord, hear our prayer."

◆ All may add their own prayers here.

Let us pray: **Our Father . . . Amen.**

Gracious God,
thank you for your ever-lasting promise
      to your people.
Help us to turn away from sin and follow you
      more closely.
We ask this through Christ our Lord.

Amen.

✚ All make the sign of the cross.

PRAYER FOR
WEDNESDAY, OCTOBER 25, 2023

OPENING

By the time of Moses, the tribes of Israel had scattered far from one another and from the promised land, but God renewed the covenant he had made with their ancestors. He delivered them out of slavery in Egypt in a dramatic fashion, but even after these events, the faith of the people wavered as they found themselves on a long journey in the desert. Through Moses, God reminded them that he would be faithful to the covenant and to them, if they would keep faith with him. However, the chosen people struggled to keep God's commandments.

✠ All make the sign of the cross.

In the name of the Father, and of the Son, and of the Holy Spirit. Amen.

PSALM
(For a longer psalm, see page xi.)
Psalm 145:2–3

I will praise your name for ever, Lord.

I will praise your name for ever, Lord.

Every day I will bless you
    and praise your name forever and ever.
Great is the Lord and greatly to be praised;
    his greatness is unsearchable.

I will praise your name for ever, Lord.

READING
Exodus 19:1, 3c–5a, 7–8

A reading from the Book of Exodus.

On the third new moon after the Israelites had gone out of the land of Egypt, they came into the wilderness of Sinai. The Lord called to Moses from the mountain, saying, "Thus you shall say to the house of Jacob and tell the Israelites: 'You have seen what I did to the Egyptians, and how I bore you on eagles' wings and brought you to myself. Now therefore, if you obey my voice and keep my covenant, you shall be my treasured possession out of all the peoples.'" So Moses went, summoned the elders of the people, and set before them all these words that the Lord had commanded him. The people all answered as one, "Everything that the Lord has spoken we will do." Moses reported the words of the people to the Lord.

The Word of the Lord.

◆ All observe silence.

FOR SILENT REFLECTION

Think about this silently in your heart. Which of God's commandments do you need more help to keep?

CLOSING PRAYER

Let us pray to God for our needs and the needs of others: our family, neighborhood, and the world. For each need we say, "Lord, hear our prayer."

◆ All may add their own prayers here.

Let us pray: **Our Father . . . Amen.**

Dear God our Father,
thank you for your unfailing faith and love,
even when our faith falters.
Give us the courage to follow you
even when the way is not easy.
In Jesus' name we pray.

Amen.

✠ All make the sign of the cross.

PRAYER FOR
THURSDAY, OCTOBER 26, 2023

OPENING

Many of the prophets spoke of a new covenant. In Jeremiah, we hear that the new covenant will last forever, will be written on human hearts, and will give everyone true knowledge of God. We believe that this new covenant was begun in the life, death, and resurrection of Jesus Christ. In him, we find the fullness of knowledge of God; we find God in the heart of our humanity. And in the ascension of Christ, we know that humanity sits at the right hand of God eternally. Through this covenant, God has blessed every aspect of our existence.

✣ All make the sign of the cross.

> **In the name of the Father, and of the Son, and of the Holy Spirit. Amen.**

PSALM
(For a longer psalm, see page xi.)
Psalm 145:2–3

I will praise your name for ever, Lord.

I will praise your name for ever, Lord.

Every day I will bless you
   and praise your name forever and ever.
Great is the Lord and greatly to be praised;
   his greatness is unsearchable.

I will praise your name for ever, Lord.

READING
Jeremiah 31:31, 33b–34

A reading from the Book of the prophet Jeremiah.

The days are surely coming, says the Lord, when I will make a new covenant with the house of Israel and the house of Judah. I will put my law within them, and I will write it on their hearts, and I will be their God, and they shall be my people. No longer shall they teach one another or say to each other, "Know the Lord," for they shall all know me, from the least of them to the greatest, says the Lord, for I will forgive their iniquity and remember their sin no more.

The Word of the Lord.

◆ All observe silence.

FOR SILENT REFLECTION

Think about this silently in your heart. How does God write his commandments on your heart?

CLOSING PRAYER

Let us pray to God for our needs and the needs of others: our family, neighborhood, and the world. For each need we say, "Lord, hear our prayer."

◆ All may add their own prayers here.

Let us pray: **Our Father . . . Amen.**

Heavenly Father,
we thank you for your faithfulness and the
   promises you have given your people.
We thank you for your Son, who died
   for our sins and rose again.
Help us to uphold our own promises to you.
In Christ's name we pray.

Amen.

✣ All make the sign of the cross.

PRAYER FOR
FRIDAY, OCTOBER 27, 2023

OPENING

The Eucharist, as Jesus tells us, is a sign of the new covenant that actually *brings that covenant into existence*. Each time we eat and drink the Body and Blood of Christ, we renew this covenant. God gives us the gracious gift of himself, of his love, spirit, and holiness. In return, we give our whole selves away in service to God and his people. We receive the Body of Christ to become Christ's body in the world.

✠ All make the sign of the cross.

In the name of the Father, and of the Son, and of the Holy Spirit. Amen.

PSALM
(For a longer psalm, see page xi.)
Psalm 145:2–3

I will praise your name for ever, Lord.

I will praise your name for ever, Lord.

Every day I will bless you
   and praise your name forever and ever.
Great is the Lord and greatly to be praised;
   his greatness is unsearchable.

I will praise your name for ever, Lord.

◆ All stand and sing **Alleluia.**

GOSPEL
Matthew 26:17a, 19–20, 26–29

A reading from the holy Gospel according to Matthew.

On the first day of Unleavened Bread the disciples did as Jesus had directed them, and they prepared the Passover meal. When it was evening, Jesus took his place with the twelve disciples. While they were eating, Jesus took a loaf of bread, and after blessing it he broke it, gave it to the disciples, and said, "Take, eat; this is my body." Then he took a cup, and after giving thanks he gave it to them, saying, "Drink from it, all of you, for this is my blood of the covenant, which is poured out for many for the forgiveness of sins. I tell you, I will never again drink of this fruit of the vine until that day when I drink it new with you in my Father's kingdom."

The Gospel of the Lord.

◆ All sit and observe silence.

FOR SILENT REFLECTION

Think about this silently in your heart. How are you Christ's body for others?

CLOSING PRAYER

Let us pray to God for our needs and the needs of others: our family, neighborhood, and the world. For each need we say, "Lord, hear our prayer."

◆ All may add their own prayers here.

Let us pray: **Our Father . . . Amen.**

Lord Jesus,
thank you for the gift of yourself
      in the new covenant.
Help me to live faithfully and to love others
      as you do.
Who live and reign with God the Father,
in the unity of the Holy Spirit,
God, for ever and ever.

Amen.

✠ All make the sign of the cross.

PRAYER FOR THE WEEK
WITH A READING FROM THE GOSPEL FOR **SUNDAY, OCTOBER 29, 2023**

OPENING

The Jewish leaders were not pleased that Jesus was gaining such a large following, and they tried to trick him by asking him to choose a commandment that was the greatest. Jesus instead put together two great commandments into one, so that loving God and loving your neighbor as yourself could be seen as two sides of the same coin. God is Love. You cannot truly love God without also showing love for the least of his people. But when we love others, we draw nearer to God and the divine love expressed in the Trinity.

✢ All make the sign of the cross.

In the name of the Father, and of the Son, and of the Holy Spirit. Amen.

PSALM
(For a longer psalm, see page xii.)
Psalm 145:2–3

I will praise your name for ever, Lord.

I will praise your name for ever, Lord.

Every day I will bless you
 and praise your name forever and ever.
Great is the Lord and greatly to be praised;
 his greatness is unsearchable.

I will praise your name for ever, Lord.

◆ All stand and sing **Alleluia.**

GOSPEL
Matthew 22:34–40

A reading from the holy Gospel according to Matthew.

When the Pharisees [FAYR-uh-seez] heard that he had silenced the Sadducees [SAD-yoo-seez], they gathered together, and one of them, an expert in the law, asked him a question to test him. "Teacher, which commandment in the law is the greatest?" He said to him, "'You shall love the Lord your God with all your heart and with all your soul and with all your mind.' This is the greatest and first commandment. And a second is like it: 'You shall love your neighbor as yourself.' On these two commandments hang all the Law and the Prophets."

The Gospel of the Lord.

◆ All sit and observe silence.

FOR SILENT REFLECTION

Think about this silently in your heart. How can you better love your neighbor? Is there someone you struggle to love?

CLOSING PRAYER

Let us pray to God for our needs and the needs of others: our family, neighborhood, and the world. For each need we say, "Lord, hear our prayer."

◆ All may add their own prayers here.

Let us pray: **Our Father . . . Amen.**

Loving God,
you have filled our lives with your love,
that we might also love others abundantly.
Give us the grace to live lives of love.
Through Christ our Lord.

Amen.

✢ All make the sign of the cross.

PRAYER FOR
MONDAY, OCTOBER 30, 2023

OPENING

This week we will hear about the life of Joseph, beloved son of Jacob. Today's reading is a story of jealousy. Jacob favored Joseph over his other eleven sons, and his brothers "hated him." Joseph fanned the flames of their hatred by sharing dreams (later revealed to be prophetic) that suggested he would rule over them. This was a family in conflict. But God still chose this messed-up family, full of pride and jealousy, to be his chosen people.

✚ All make the sign of the cross.

In the name of the Father, and of the Son, and of the Holy Spirit. Amen.

PSALM

(For a longer psalm, see page xii.)
Psalm 145:2–3

I will praise your name for ever, LORD.

I will praise your name for ever, LORD.

Every day I will bless you
   and praise your name forever and ever.
Great is the LORD and greatly to be praised;
   his greatness is unsearchable.

I will praise your name for ever, LORD.

READING

Genesis 37:3–4b, 5–8

A reading from the Book of Genesis.

Now Israel loved Joseph more than any other of his children because he was the son of his old age, and he had made him an ornamented robe. But when his brothers saw that their father loved Joseph more than all his brothers, they hated him. Once Joseph had a dream, and when he told it to his brothers, they hated him even more. He said to them, "Listen to this dream that I dreamed. There we were, binding sheaves in the field. Suddenly my sheaf rose and stood upright; then your sheaves gathered around it and bowed down to my sheaf." His brothers said to him, "Are you indeed to reign over us? Are you indeed to have dominion over us?" So they hated him even more because of his dreams and his words.

The Word of the Lord.

◆ All observe silence.

FOR SILENT REFLECTION

Think about this silently in your heart. How does God come to be with you, even in the messy parts of your life?

CLOSING PRAYER

Let us pray to God for our needs and the needs of others: our family, neighborhood, and the world. For each need we say, "Lord, hear our prayer."

◆ All may add their own prayers here.

Let us pray: **Our Father . . . Amen.**

Lord,
you call your people from every time,
   place and situation.
May we hear your call and respond with
   loving hearts.
Through Christ our Lord.

Amen.

✚ All make the sign of the cross.

PRAYER FOR
TUESDAY, OCTOBER 31, 2023

OPENING

Both Jacob and Joseph seemed unaware of the brothers' resentment, which grew until the brothers plotted to kill Joseph. Jealousy is a powerful emotion and it can be hard to overcome. In this case, it led to siblings kidnapping and selling their own brother. For us, it probably takes a less extreme form, but it is still harmful to both us and those we envy. The antidote to this kind of jealousy is good will, to consciously desire the flourishing of the other with all your might.

✙ All make the sign of the cross.

In the name of the Father, and of the Son, and of the Holy Spirit. Amen.

PSALM
(For a longer psalm, see page xii.)
Psalm 145:2–3

I will praise your name for ever, Lord.

I will praise your name for ever, Lord.

Every day I will bless you
   and praise your name forever and ever.
Great is the Lord and greatly to be praised;
   his greatness is unsearchable.

I will praise your name for ever, Lord.

READING
Genesis 37:14a-b, 17e–18a, 19–20, 23b, 24a, 25a-b, 26a-b, 27a, 28b-d

A reading from the Book of Genesis.

Jacob said to Joseph, "Go now, see if it is well with your brothers and with the flock." So Joseph went after his brothers and found them at Dothan. They saw him from a distance, and said to one another, "Here comes this dreamer. Come now, let us kill him and throw him into one of the pits; then we shall say that a wild animal has devoured him, and we shall see what will become of his dreams." So they stripped Joseph of his robe, and they took him and threw him into a pit. Then they sat down to eat, and looking up they saw a caravan of Ishmaelites [ISH-may-uh-līˉtz] on their way to Egypt. Then Judah said to his brothers, "What profit is there if we kill our brother? Let us sell him to the Ishmaelites." They drew Joseph out of the pit, and sold him to the Ishmaelites for twenty pieces of silver.

The Word of the Lord.

◆ All observe silence.

FOR SILENT REFLECTION

Think about this silently in your heart. Have you ever struggled with jealousy?

CLOSING PRAYER

Let us pray to God for our needs and the needs of others: our family, neighborhood, and the world. For each need we say, "Lord, hear our prayer."

◆ All may add their own prayers here.

Let us pray: **Our Father . . . Amen.**

Everlasting Father,
help us to be holy.
Replace the cruelty within our heart
with your peace, love, and gentle kindness.
Through Christ our Lord.

Amen.

✙ All make the sign of the cross.

PRAYER FOR
WEDNESDAY, NOVEMBER 1, 2023

OPENING

Today is the feast of All Saints, a day when we remember the special, ordinary people who lived lives of holiness and now live in God. We know and celebrate the names of some of these saints, but many of them are unknown. This is our feast of hope: that the daily ways in which we show love, our humility and sacrifices, the mercy we bestow, the peace we create, even the pains we endure, bring us closer and closer to eternal life with God.

✢ *All make the sign of the cross.*

In the name of the Father, and of the Son, and of the Holy Spirit. Amen.

PSALM

(For a longer psalm, see page xii.)
Psalm 145:2–3

I will praise your name for ever, Lord.

I will praise your name for ever, Lord.

Every day I will bless you
   and praise your name forever and ever.
Great is the Lord and greatly to be praised;
   his greatness is unsearchable.

I will praise your name for ever, Lord.

◆ *All stand and sing* **Alleluia.**

GOSPEL
Matthew 5:2–12A

A reading from the holy Gospel according to Matthew.

Then Jesus began to speak and taught the crowds, saying: "Blessed are the poor in spirit, for theirs is the kingdom of heaven. Blessed are those who mourn, for they will be comforted. Blessed are the meek, for they will inherit the earth. Blessed are those who hunger and thirst for righteousness, for they will be filled. Blessed are the merciful, for they will receive mercy. Blessed are the pure in heart, for they will see God. Blessed are the peacemakers, for they will be called children of God. Blessed are those who are persecuted for the sake of righteousness, for theirs is the kingdom of heaven. Blessed are you when people revile you and persecute you and utter all kinds of evil against you falsely on my account. Rejoice and be glad, for your reward is great in heaven."

The Gospel of the Lord.

◆ *All sit and observe silence.*

FOR SILENT REFLECTION

Think about this silently in your heart. What qualities in the saints do you most admire?

CLOSING PRAYER

Let us pray to God for our needs and the needs of others: our family, neighborhood, and the world. For each need we say, "Lord, hear our prayer."

◆ *All may add their own prayers here.*

Let us pray: **Our Father . . . Amen.**

Heavenly Father,
you have inspired your saints to live
   holy lives; teach us to live in faith.
Through Christ our Lord.

Amen.

✢ *All make the sign of the cross.*

HOME PRAYER
CELEBRATING THE SAINTS, REMEMBERING THE DEAD

Find the reading (1 Thessalonians 4:13–18) in your Bible, ask for a volunteer to read it, and encourage the reader to practice reading it a few times. Then gather the household in one room. You may want to light a candle to create an even more prayerful environment.

LEADER:
Saints live among us today as well as with Christ in heaven. These heroes of our faith persevere in troubled times as they follow the path of Jesus. Their unselfish actions, as well as their talents, skills, and virtuous living inspire us as they pray for us.

✦ All make the sign of the cross.

ALL: In the name of the Father, and of the Son, and of the Holy Spirit. Amen.

LEADER: *Psalm 112: 1–6*
Let us pray the psalm response:
Happy are those who fear the LORD.

ALL: Happy are those who fear the LORD.

LEADER:
Praise the LORD!
  Happy are those who fear the LORD,
    who greatly delight in his commandments.
Their descendants will be mighty in the land;
  the generation of the upright will
    be blessed.

ALL: Happy are those who fear the LORD.

LEADER:
Wealth and riches are in their houses,
  and their righteousness endures forever.
They rise in the darkness as a light for the
    upright;
  they are gracious, merciful, and righteous.

ALL: Happy are those who fear the LORD.

LEADER: *1 Thessalonians 4:13–18*
A reading from the First Letter of Paul to the Thessalonians.

◆ Read the Scripture passage from the Bible.

The Word of the Lord.

◆ All observe a brief silence.

LEADER:
And now let us remember family members and friends who have died:

◆ The leader begins, then pauses so others may add names too.

LEADER:
Lord God,
we ask you to bring these and all
those who have gone before us
into your beloved presence.

◆ Leader pauses, then continues.

Jesus, our Savior,
you are the Source of all life.
We are grateful for our leaders in faith,
as well as our family members and friends
who are with you now in heaven.
Their goodness reveals your holy truth.
Help us to honor your Spirit within us in
everything we do.
We ask this in your name.

ALL: Amen.

✦ All make the sign of the cross.

PRAYER FOR
THURSDAY, NOVEMBER 2, 2023

OPENING

Joseph's interpretation of his own dreams is now the source of his salvation. His explanation of Pharaoh's dream allowed the Egyptians to prepare for the upcoming famine, and led to Joseph himself ascending from slave to second in command in Egypt. Today is the feast of All Souls, when we remember and pray for the souls of the faithful departed and hope that they might enter into eternal life with God. We profess our belief that in death, life is changed but not ended.

✣ All make the sign of the cross.

In the name of the Father, and of the Son, and of the Holy Spirit. Amen.

PSALM

(For a longer psalm, see page xii.)
Psalm 145:2–3

I will praise your name for ever, Lord.

I will praise your name for ever, Lord.

Every day I will bless you
   and praise your name forever and ever.
Great is the Lord and greatly to be praised;
   his greatness is unsearchable.

I will praise your name for ever, Lord.

READING

Genesis 41:5–7a, 8b-d, 14a, 15a, 15c, 29a, 30a, 33, 34b, 36a

A reading from the Book of Genesis.

Pharaoh [FAYR-oh] dreamed: seven ears of grain, plump and good, were growing on one stalk. Then seven ears, thin and blighted, sprouted after them. The thin ears swallowed up the seven plump and full ears. In the morning Pharoah called for all the magicians of Egypt and all its wise men. Pharaoh told them his dreams, but there was no one who could interpret them. Pharaoh sent for Joseph and said, "I have heard it said of you that when you hear a dream you can interpret it." Joseph said, "There will come seven years of great plenty. After them will arise seven years of famine. Therefore let Pharaoh select a man who is discerning and wise and set him over the land of Egypt. Take one-fifth of the produce of the land during the seven plenteous years. That food shall be a reserve for the land against the seven years of famine."

The Word of the Lord.

◆ All observe silence.

FOR SILENT REFLECTION

Think about this silently in your heart. What gifts has God given you?

CLOSING PRAYER

Let us pray to God for our needs and the needs of others: our family, neighborhood, and the world. For each need we say, "Lord, hear our prayer."

◆ All may add their own prayers here.

Let us pray: **Our Father . . . Amen.**

Lord God,
let us be comforted by memories of our
   beloved dead,
and may they now dwell with you in eternity.
We ask this through Jesus Christ our Lord.

Amen.

✣ All make the sign of the cross.

PRAYER FOR FRIDAY, NOVEMBER 3, 2023

OPENING

Joseph's prophetic voice allowed the Egyptians to prepare for a devastating famine, and even as every other country suffered, the Egyptians had food. Joseph trusted his gift, and Pharaoh trusted Joseph's prophecy. St. Martin de Porres (1579–1639), was the son of an indigenous woman and a Spanish man in Lima, Peru, in the late sixteenth century. He is the patron saint of social justice and race relations. St. Martin suffered racism in his life, but he channeled those experiences towards helping others with compassion and empathy.

✦ All make the sign of the cross.

In the name of the Father, and of the Son, and of the Holy Spirit. Amen.

PSALM

(For a longer psalm, see page xii.)
Psalm 145:2–3

I will praise your name for ever, Lord.

I will praise your name for ever, Lord.

Every day I will bless you
  and praise your name forever and ever.
Great is the Lord and greatly to be praised;
  his greatness is unsearchable.

I will praise your name for ever, Lord.

READING

Genesis 41:39–40, 47–48a, 53–54, 57a

A reading from the Book of Genesis.

So Pharaoh said to Joseph, "Since God has shown you all this, there is no one so discerning and wise as you. You shall be over my house, and all my people shall order themselves as you command; only with regard to the throne will I be greater than you." During the seven plenteous years the earth produced abundantly. Joseph gathered up all the food of the seven years when there was plenty and stored up food in the cities. The seven years of plenty that prevailed came to an end, and the seven years of famine began to come, just as Joseph had said. There was famine in every country, but throughout the land of Egypt there was bread. Moreover all the world came to Joseph in Egypt to buy grain.

The Word of the Lord.

◆ All observe silence.

FOR SILENT REFLECTION

Think about this silently in your heart. How often do you quietly listen for what God is telling you?

CLOSING PRAYER

Let us pray to God for our needs and the needs of others: our family, neighborhood, and the world. For each need we say, "Lord, hear our prayer."

◆ All may add their own prayers here.

Let us pray: **Our Father . . . Amen.**

God our Father,
give us the courage to live a life of such
  prophetic faith, hope, and love
that it brings others closer to you.
Through Christ our Lord.

Amen.

✦ All make the sign of the cross.

PRAYER FOR THE WEEK
WITH A READING FROM THE GOSPEL FOR **SUNDAY, NOVEMBER 5, 2023**

OPENING

One of the pope's official titles is "Servant of the Servants of God." The pope, though a spiritual father for all those in communion with Rome, is nonetheless expected to lead not through majesty or might, but through service. So we too are called to take positions of authority and use them as a means to serve others, and to humble ourselves in service of God.

✠ All make the sign of the cross.

In the name of the Father, and of the Son, and of the Holy Spirit. Amen.

PSALM
(For a longer psalm, see page xii.)
Psalm 98:1

The Lord has made known his victory.

The Lord has made known his victory.

O sing to the Lord a new song,
  for he has done marvelous things.
His right hand and his holy arm
  have gotten him victory.

The Lord has made known his victory.

◆ All stand and sing **Alleluia.**

GOSPEL
Matthew 23:1–4, 6, 7b–8, 11–12

A reading from the holy Gospel according to Matthew.

Then Jesus said to the crowds and to his disciples, "The scribes and the Pharisees sit on Moses's seat; therefore, do whatever they teach you and follow it, but do not do as they do, for they do not practice what they teach. They tie up heavy burdens, hard to bear, and lay them on the shoulders of others, but they themselves are unwilling to lift a finger to move them. They love to have the place of honor at banquets and the best seats in the synagogues and to have people call them rabbi. But you are not to be called rabbi, for you have one teacher, and you are all brothers and sisters. The greatest among you will be your servant. All who exalt themselves will be humbled, and all who humble themselves will be exalted."

The Gospel of the Lord.

◆ All sit and observe silence.

FOR SILENT REFLECTION

Think about this silently in your heart. How can you serve others this week?

CLOSING PRAYER

Let us pray to God for our needs and the needs of others: our family, neighborhood, and the world. For each need we say, "Lord, hear our prayer."

◆ All may add their own prayers here.

Let us pray: **Our Father . . . Amen.**

Almighty God,
you cast down the mighty from their thrones
    and lift up the lowly.
Let our hearts always imitate your humility,
so that we may live in service to you
    and others.
Through Christ our Lord.
Amen.

✠ All make the sign of the cross.

PRAYER FOR MONDAY, NOVEMBER 6, 2023

OPENING

Joseph's brothers came to Egypt to buy grain in the midst of the famine. Joseph recognized them, but they did not recognize him. Though Joseph treated them as spies and had them imprisoned, the brothers accepted this injustice as punishment for their treatment of Joseph. All of us are guilty of hurting others when we are unkind. But God is merciful: we can seek forgiveness with true repentance and humility.

✢ All make the sign of the cross.

In the name of the Father, and of the Son, and of the Holy Spirit. Amen.

PSALM

(For a longer psalm, see page xii.)
Psalm 98:1

The Lord has made known his victory.

The Lord has made known his victory.

O sing to the Lord a new song,
  for he has done marvelous things.
His right hand and his holy arm
  have gotten him victory.

The Lord has made known his victory.

READING
Genesis 42:1a-b, 2b–4, 6a, 7a-b, 8b, 9b, 17, 21a-b, 23a, 24a, 25a

A reading from the Book of Genesis.

When Jacob learned that there was grain in Egypt, he said to his sons, "Go down and buy grain for us there, that we may live and not die." So ten of Joseph's brothers went down to buy grain in Egypt. But Jacob did not send Joseph's brother Benjamin, for he feared that harm might come to him. Now Joseph was governor over the land. When Joseph saw his brothers, he recognized them, but he treated them like strangers and spoke harshly. They did not recognize him. Joseph said to them, "You are spies." And he put them all together in prison for three days. They said to one another, "Alas, we are paying the penalty for what we did to our brother." They did not know that Joseph understood them. He turned away from them and wept. Joseph then gave orders to fill their bags with grain.

The Word of the Lord.

◆ All observe silence.

FOR SILENT REFLECTION

Think about this silently in your heart. Have you hurt someone recently? How can you make amends?

CLOSING PRAYER

Let us pray to God for our needs and the needs of others: our family, neighborhood, and the world. For each need we say, "Lord, hear our prayer."

◆ All may add their own prayers here.

Let us pray: **Our Father . . . Amen.**

Father of mercy,
fill us with your love that we might humbly
  repent of our sins,
and make amends when we have done harm
  to another.
Through Christ our Lord.

Amen.

✢ All make the sign of the cross.

PRAYER FOR
TUESDAY, NOVEMBER 7, 2023

OPENING

Have you ever been surprised by something you thought would never happen? Joseph, though in a position of power, is still overcome with emotion at seeing his youngest, beloved brother. After such a cruel and dramatic separation, he must have thought he would never see his family again. And yet, here he found himself, in a position not only to see them, but to serve them. Joseph, like Jesus, shows us that a leader is not jealous, cruel, or demanding, but merciful, forgiving, and loving.

✢ All make the sign of the cross.

In the name of the Father, and of the Son, and of the Holy Spirit. Amen.

PSALM
(For a longer psalm, see page xii.)
Psalm 98:1

The Lord has made known his victory.

The Lord has made known his victory.

O sing to the Lord a new song,
　for he has done marvelous things.
His right hand and his holy arm
　have gotten him victory.

The Lord has made known his victory.

READING
Genesis 42:29a; 43:2–3, 15c-d, 29a-c, 30–31, 34c

A reading from the Book of Genesis.

Joseph's brothers came to their father Jacob in the land of Canaan [KAY-n*n]. And when they had eaten up the grain they had brought from Egypt, their father said to them, "Go again; buy us a little more food." But Judah said to him, "The man solemnly warned us, saying, 'You shall not see my face unless your brother Benjamin is with you.'" Then they went on their way down to Egypt and stood before Joseph. Then Joseph looked up and saw his brother Benjamin, his mother's son, and said, "Is this your youngest brother?" With that, Joseph hurried out, because he was overcome with affection for his brother, and he was about to weep. So he went into a private room and wept there. Then he washed his face and came out, and controlling himself he said, "Serve the meal." So they drank and were merry with him.

The Word of the Lord.

◆ All observe silence.

FOR SILENT REFLECTION

Think about this silently in your heart. How can you show mercy to someone in your life?

CLOSING PRAYER

Let us pray to God for our needs and the needs of others: our family, neighborhood, and the world. For each need we say, "Lord, hear our prayer."

◆ All may add their own prayers here.

Let us pray: **Our Father . . . Amen.**

Holy Lord,
you are kind and merciful.
Teach us the way of mercy that we might live
　in peace and love.
We ask this through Christ our Lord.

Amen.

✢ All make the sign of the cross.

PRAYER FOR WEDNESDAY, NOVEMBER 8, 2023

OPENING

Joseph decided to test his brothers, to be sure that their hearts had changed after their mistreatment of him. When the planted cup was found in Benjamin's sack, the brothers "tore their clothes." This is a sign that they will shoulder the blame for their brother. The brothers were tested, as many of us are, by circumstances beyond their control. Their reaction was not to blame others but to humbly seek mercy.

✢ All make the sign of the cross.

In the name of the Father, and of the Son, and of the Holy Spirit. Amen.

PSALM

(For a longer psalm, see page xii.)
Psalm 98:1

The Lord has made known his victory.

The Lord has made known his victory.

O sing to the Lord a new song,
   for he has done marvelous things.
His right hand and his holy arm
   have gotten him victory.

The Lord has made known his victory.

READING
Genesis 44:1a-b, 2a-c, 3–4c, 4e, 6a, 10c-d, 12–13a

A reading from the Book of Genesis.

Joseph commanded the steward of his house, "Fill the men's sacks with food. Put my cup, the silver cup, in the top of the sack of the youngest." As soon as the morning was light, the men were sent away with their donkeys. When they had gone only a short distance from the city, Joseph said to his steward, "Go, overtake them, say to them, 'Why have you stolen my silver cup?'" When the steward overtook them, he said, "He with whom the cup is found shall become my lord's slave, but the rest of you shall go free." The steward searched, beginning with the eldest and ending with the youngest; and the cup was found in Benjamin's sack. At this the brothers tore their clothes. Then each one loaded his donkey, and they returned to the city.

The Word of the Lord.

◆ All observe silence.

FOR SILENT REFLECTION

Think about this silently in your heart. Do you ask for God's mercy?

CLOSING PRAYER

Let us pray to God for our needs and the needs of others: our family, neighborhood, and the world. For each need we say, "Lord, hear our prayer."

◆ All may add their own prayers here.

Let us pray: **Our Father . . . Amen.**

Dear God our Father,
we cannot understand all your ways.
Strengthen our faith so that we may always
   hold fast to you,
especially in times of trial.
We ask this through Christ our Lord.

Amen.

✢ All make the sign of the cross.

PRAYER FOR
THURSDAY, NOVEMBER 9, 2023

OPENING

Today we celebrate the Dedication of the Lateran Basilica in Rome. It is the cathedral of the bishop of Rome, the pope. The Lateran Basilica is our "mother church." As we conclude the story of Joseph, Joseph reveals himself to his brothers, but only after they have revealed themselves to be humbled, contrite, and ready to sacrifice in order to save their brother, Benjamin. They were not trying to appear virtuous to gain acclaim or favor; they had become virtuous. Their repentance of their sins against Joseph brought about a complete change of heart.

✢ All make the sign of the cross.

In the name of the Father, and of the Son, and of the Holy Spirit. Amen.

PSALM
(For a longer psalm, see page xii.)
Psalm 98:1

The LORD has made known his victory.

The LORD has made known his victory.

O sing to the Lord a new song,
 for he has done marvelous things.
His right hand and his holy arm
 have gotten him victory.

The LORD has made known his victory.

READING
Genesis 44:14a, 14c, 18a, 19b, 20b–20e; 45:3a-b, 3d-e, 7, 9, 11a, 15

A reading from the Book of Genesis. Judah and his brothers came to Joseph's house. They fell to the ground before him. Then Judah said, "O my lord, have you a father or a brother? We have a father, an old man, and a young brother, the child of his old age. His brother Joseph is dead." Joseph said to his brothers, "I am Joseph." But his brothers could not answer him, so dismayed were they at his presence. Joseph said, "God sent me before you to preserve for you a remnant on earth and to keep alive for you many survivors. Hurry and go up to my father and say to him, 'Thus says your son Joseph, God has made me lord of all Egypt; come down to me; do not delay. I will provide for you there.'" And he kissed all his brothers and wept upon them, and after that his brothers talked with him.

The Word of the Lord.

◆ All observe silence.

FOR SILENT REFLECTION

Think about this silently in your heart. How do you choose love and service in your daily life?

CLOSING PRAYER

Let us pray to God for our needs and the needs of others: our family, neighborhood, and the world. For each need we say, "Lord, hear our prayer."

◆ All may add their own prayers here.

Let us pray: **Our Father . . . Amen.**

God our Father,
you helped the brothers repent.
Teach us to do the same, in Christ's name.

Amen.

✢ All make the sign of the cross.

PRAYER FOR
FRIDAY, NOVEMBER 10, 2023

OPENING

Through this winding story of Joseph, the great hand of God's providence came to bear as Israel's entire household (the nation of Israel) settled in the best part of Egypt. Today, we remember Pope St. Leo the Great, a fifth-century pope. During this time, the faithful were besieged by heresies about the mysteries of Christ and the Church. Pope Leo strengthened and illuminated the faithful through his powerful sermons and strong faith.

✢ All make the sign of the cross.

In the name of the Father, and of the Son, and of the Holy Spirit. Amen.

PSALM
(For a longer psalm, see page xii.)
Psalm 98:1

The Lord has made known his victory.

The Lord has made known his victory.

O sing to the Lord a new song,
   for he has done marvelous things.
His right hand and his holy arm
   have gotten him victory.

The Lord has made known his victory.

READING
Genesis 46:5–6b, 28b–30; 47:11

A reading from the Book of Genesis.

Jacob set out from Beer-sheba, and the sons of Israel carried their father Jacob, their little ones, and their wives in the wagons that Pharaoh [FAYR-oh] had sent to carry him. They also took their livestock and the goods that they had acquired in the land of Canaan [KAY-n*n]. When they came to the land of Goshen [GOH-shuhn], Joseph made ready his chariot and went up to meet his father Israel in Goshen. He presented himself to him, fell on his neck, and wept on his neck a good while. Israel said to Joseph, "I can die now, having seen for myself that you are still alive." Joseph settled his father and his brothers and granted them a holding in the land of Egypt, in the best part of the land, in the land of Rameses, as Pharaoh had instructed.

The Word of the Lord.

◆ All observe silence.

FOR SILENT REFLECTION

Think about this silently in your heart. How has God's providence worked in your life?

CLOSING PRAYER

Let us pray to God for our needs and the needs of others: our family, neighborhood, and the world. For each need we say, "Lord, hear our prayer."

◆ All may add their own prayers here.

Let us pray: **Our Father . . . Amen.**

Heavenly Father,
we rejoice as you unfold
   your plan of salvation.
May we reflect your goodness,
and remain faithful to your covenant.
Through Christ our Lord.

Amen.

✢ All make the sign of the cross.

PRAYER FOR THE WEEK

WITH A READING FROM THE GOSPEL FOR **SUNDAY, NOVEMBER 12, 2023**

OPENING

We are entering into the last weeks of the liturgical year. The Gospel readings during this time are intended to prepare us for the end of the world. At this time of year, as the days grow shorter and darker, we are reminded not to procrastinate, but to behave as if we might meet the Lord at any moment.

✛ All make the sign of the cross.

In the name of the Father, and of the Son, and of the Holy Spirit. Amen.

PSALM

(For a longer psalm, see page xii.)
Psalm 98:1

The L ORD has made known his victory.

The L ORD has made known his victory.

O sing to the Lord a new song,
 for he has done marvelous things.
His right hand and his holy arm
 have gotten him victory.

The L ORD has made known his victory.

◆ All stand and sing **Alleluia.**

GOSPEL

Matthew 25:2–6, 8–10

A reading from the holy Gospel according to Matthew.

Jesus said, "Five young women were foolish, and five were wise. When the foolish took their lamps, they took no oil with them, but the wise took flasks of oil with their lamps. As the bridegroom was delayed, all of them became drowsy and slept. But at midnight there was a shout, 'Look! Here is the bridegroom! Come out to meet him.' The foolish said to the wise, 'Give us some of your oil, for our lamps are going out.' But the wise replied, 'No! there will not be enough for you and for us; you had better go to the dealers and buy some for yourselves.' And while they went to buy it, the bridegroom came, and those who were ready went with him into the wedding banquet, and the door was shut."

The Gospel of the Lord.

◆ All sit and observe silence.

FOR SILENT REFLECTION

Think about this silently in your heart. If Jesus were to come to you today, would he find you prepared?

CLOSING PRAYER

Let us pray to God for our needs and the needs of others: our family, neighborhood, and the world. For each need we say, "Lord, hear our prayer."

◆ All may add their own prayers here.

Let us pray: **Our Father . . . Amen.**

Lord Jesus,
help us to prepare for your coming
 as the wise bridesmaids did,
that we might greet you joyfully.
Who live and reign with God the Father,
in the unity of the Holy Spirit,
God, for ever and ever.

Amen.

✛ All make the sign of the cross.

PRAYER FOR MONDAY, NOVEMBER 13, 2023

OPENING

This week, we will look at the role of women in the Bible. King Josiah was presented with a long-lost book (believed to be the Book of Deuteronomy). He sent the book to the prophetess Huldah for interpretation. We do not know why Huldah was chosen, but she was truly given the gift of prophecy, and she spoke words of blessing to Josiah. We will also celebrate some female saints this week. Today is the feast of St. Frances Xavier Cabrini, the first American saint. She founded institutions for the poor, the abandoned, the uneducated, and the sick in the late nineteenth century.

✚ All make the sign of the cross.

In the name of the Father, and of the Son, and of the Holy Spirit. Amen.

PSALM

(For a longer psalm, see page xii.)
Psalm 98:1

The Lord has made known his victory.

The Lord has made known his victory.

O sing to the Lord a new song,
   for he has done marvelous things.
His right hand and his holy arm
   have gotten him victory.

The Lord has made known his victory.

READING

2 Chronicles 34:21a-b, 22a, d, 23a, 26d-e, 27a-b, 27d–28a, c

A reading from the Second Book of Chronicles.

King Josiah said, "Go, inquire of the Lord for me and for those who are left in Israel and in Judah, concerning the words of the book that has been found."

So Hilkiah [hil-Kī-uh] and those whom the king had sent went to the prophet Huldah, and spoke to her to that effect. She declared to them, "Thus says the Lord, the God of Israel: Regarding the words that you have heard, because your heart was penitent and you humbled yourself before God when you heard his words against this place and its inhabitants, and you have humbled yourself before me, I also have heard you, says the Lord. I will gather you to your ancestors and you shall be gathered to your grave in peace." They took the message back to the king.

The Word of the Lord.

◆ All observe silence.

FOR SILENT REFLECTION

Think about this silently in your heart. How does God call you to speak his Word?

CLOSING PRAYER

Let us pray to God for our needs and the needs of others: our family, neighborhood, and the world. For each need we say, "Lord, hear our prayer."

◆ All may add their own prayers here.

Let us pray: **Our Father . . . Amen.**

We praise and bless you, O God,
for the good women in our Church
   and in our lives.
Through Christ our Lord.

Amen.

✚ All make the sign of the cross.

PRAYER FOR
TUESDAY, NOVEMBER 14, 2023

OPENING

Miriam is described as the sister of Moses and Aaron, and equal to them. After the dramatic crossing of the Red Sea, she was called a prophet. She then took to song and interpreted the events that just occurred, in order to give God the sole credit and praise for the salvation of this people. At other points in the Bible, Miriam was regarded as the savior of Moses when he was an infant, an intercessor between God and the people of Israel, and an advocate on behalf of this people.

✚ All make the sign of the cross.

In the name of the Father, and of the Son, and of the Holy Spirit. Amen.

PSALM
(For a longer psalm, see page xii.)
Psalm 98:1

The LORD has made known his victory.

The LORD has made known his victory.

O sing to the Lord a new song,
   for he has done marvelous things.
His right hand and his holy arm
   have gotten him victory.

The LORD has made known his victory.

READING
Exodus 15:1–2, 13, 18, 20–21

A reading from the Book of Exodus [EK-suh-duhs].

Then Moses and the Israelites sang this song to the LORD: "I will sing to the LORD, for he has triumphed gloriously; horse and rider he has thrown into the sea. The LORD is my strength and my might, and he has become my salvation; this is my God, and I will praise him; my father's God, and I will exalt him. In your steadfast love you led the people whom you redeemed; you guided them by your strength to your holy abode. The LORD will reign forever and ever."

Then the prophet Miriam, Aaron's sister, took a tambourine in her hand, and all the women went out after her with tambourines and with dancing. And Miriam sang to them: "Sing to the LORD, for he has triumphed gloriously; horse and rider he has thrown into the sea."

The Word of the Lord.

◆ All observe silence.

FOR SILENT REFLECTION

Think about this silently in your heart. What qualities does a true leader in faith have?

CLOSING PRAYER

Let us pray to God for our needs and the needs of others: our family, neighborhood, and the world. For each need we say, "Lord, hear our prayer."

◆ All may add their own prayers here.

Let us pray: **Our Father . . . Amen.**

Lord,
like your servant Miriam,
help us to lead others closer to you,
and to praise your name always.
Through Christ our Lord.

Amen.

✚ All make the sign of the cross.

PRAYER FOR WEDNESDAY, NOVEMBER 15, 2023

OPENING

The story of the sinful woman highlights the immense power of forgiveness: changing the heart of the forgiven, producing abundant love, and initiating acts of service. Today's saint, Albert the Great, is the patron of scientists and philosophers. He said, "It is by the path of love, which is charity, that God draws near to man and man to God."

✠ All make the sign of the cross.

In the name of the Father, and of the Son, and of the Holy Spirit. Amen.

PSALM
(For a longer psalm, see page xii.)
Psalm 98:1

The LORD has made known his victory.

The LORD has made known his victory.

O sing to the Lord a new song,
　for he has done marvelous things.
His right hand and his holy arm
　have gotten him victory.

The LORD has made known his victory.

◆ All stand and sing **Alleluia**.

GOSPEL
Luke 7:36–37b, 37d–39, 48, 50

A reading from the holy Gospel according to Luke.

One of the Pharisees [FAYR-uh-seez] asked Jesus to eat with him, and when he went into the Pharisee's house he reclined to dine. And a woman in the city who was a sinner, brought an alabaster jar of ointment. She stood behind him at his feet, weeping, and began to bathe his feet with her tears and to dry them with her hair, kissing his feet and anointing them with the ointment. Now when the Pharisee who had invited him saw it, he said to himself, "If this man were a prophet, he would have known who and what kind of woman this is who is touching him, that she is a sinner." Then Jesus said to her, "Your sins are forgiven. Your faith has saved you; go in peace."

The Gospel of the Lord.

◆ All sit and observe silence.

FOR SILENT REFLECTION

Think about this silently in your heart. How can you act with great love?

CLOSING PRAYER

Let us pray to God for our needs and the needs of others: our family, neighborhood, and the world. For each need we say, "Lord, hear our prayer."

◆ All may add their own prayers here.

Let us pray: **Our Father . . . Amen.**

Almighty God,
may we serve you with all our hearts
and know your forgiveness in our lives.
We ask this through Christ our Lord,
who shows us his boundless mercy.

Amen.

✠ All make the sign of the cross.

PRAYER FOR THURSDAY, NOVEMBER 16, 2023

OPENING

The Gospels agree that the first witnesses to the resurrection were women. They were models of faith, standing vigil at the foot of the cross when the apostles were scattered by fear and guilt. In that day of despair, the women still came to Jesus' tomb to lovingly anoint his body and perform the burial rites. Today we remember two more great women, St. Margaret of Scotland, a queen, and St. Gertrude of Germany, a nun. They lived very different lives, but both were examples of faith in Jesus.

✢ All make the sign of the cross.

In the name of the Father, and of the Son, and of the Holy Spirit. Amen.

PSALM
(For a longer psalm, see page xii.)
Psalm 98:1

The Lord has made known his victory.

The Lord has made known his victory.

O sing to the Lord a new song,
   for he has done marvelous things.
His right hand and his holy arm
   have gotten him victory.

The Lord has made known his victory.

◆ All stand and sing **Alleluia.**

GOSPEL
Luke 24:2–3, 4b–5b, 5d–e, 6a, 7–10

A reading from the holy Gospel according to Luke.

The women found the stone rolled away from the tomb, but when they went in they did not find the body. Suddenly two men in dazzling clothes stood beside them. The women were terrified and bowed their faces to the ground, but the men said to them, "He is not here but has risen. Remember how he told you that the Son of Man must be handed over to the hands of sinners and be crucified and on the third day rise again." Then they remembered his words, and returning from the tomb they told all this to the eleven and to all the rest. Now it was Mary Magdalene, Joanna, Mary the mother of James, and the other women with them who told this to the apostles.

The Gospel of the Lord.

◆ All sit and observe silence.

FOR SILENT REFLECTION

Think about this silently in your heart. How do you show faith in God, even when you might feel disheartened?

CLOSING PRAYER

Let us pray to God for our needs and the needs of others: our family, neighborhood, and the world. For each need we say, "Lord, hear our prayer."

◆ All may add their own prayers here.

Let us pray: **Our Father . . . Amen.**

God our Father,
your Son died for our sins and rose again
      on the third day.
We make our prayer of thanks in his name.
Amen.

✢ All make the sign of the cross.

PRAYER FOR FRIDAY, NOVEMBER 17, 2023

OPENING

In the Acts of the Apostles and in the epistles, we see the important role of women in the early Church. At the end of Paul's letter to the Romans, he included a long list of greetings, which emphasized the unity of the one holy Church. Paul makes it clear that this faith is for everyone: man or woman, Jew or Gentile, of all nationalities and social strata. Today's saint, Elizabeth of Hungary, was an example of faith and humility. Though she was the daughter of a king, she chose to serve the poor.

✦ All make the sign of the cross.

In the name of the Father, and of the Son, and of the Holy Spirit. Amen.

PSALM
(For a longer psalm, see page xii.)
Psalm 98:1

The Lord has made known his victory.

The Lord has made known his victory.

O sing to the Lord a new song,
   for he has done marvelous things.
His right hand and his holy arm
   have gotten him victory.

The Lord has made known his victory.

READING
Romans 16:1–2ac, 3–4a, 5a, 6–7, 12, 16b

A reading from the Letter of Paul to the Romans.

I commend to you our sister Phoebe, a deacon of the church at Cenchreae [SEN-kruh-ee], so that you may welcome her in the Lord, as is fitting for the saints, for she has been a benefactor of many and of myself as well. Greet Prisca and Aquila [AK-wih-luh], my coworkers in Christ Jesus, who risked their necks for my life. Greet also the church in their house. Greet Mary, who has worked very hard for **you.** Greet Andronicus [an-DRAHN-uh-kuhs] and Junia, my fellow Israelites who were in prison with me; they are prominent among the apostles, and they were in Christ before I was. Greet those workers in the Lord, Tryphaena [tray-FI-nuh] and Tryphosa [tri-FO-suh]. Greet the beloved Persis, who has worked hard in the Lord. All the churches of Christ greet you.

The Word of the Lord.

◆ All observe silence.

FOR SILENT REFLECTION

Think about this silently in your heart. How do you show others that you are a Christian?

CLOSING PRAYER

Let us pray to God for our needs and the needs of others: our family, neighborhood, and the world. For each need we say, "Lord, hear our prayer."

◆ All may add their own prayers here.

Let us pray: **Our Father . . . Amen.**

O God,
we pray for our Church leaders.
May the Holy Spirit guide them to
lead us with wisdom and with courage.
Through Jesus Christ our Lord.

Amen.

✦ All make the sign of the cross.

PRAYER FOR THE WEEK

WITH A READING FROM THE GOSPEL FOR SUNDAY, NOVEMBER 19, 2023

OPENING

We are continuing to reflect on how we can prepare to meet God. In the parable of the talents, Jesus reminded his followers that it was not enough to be given gifts; they had to be used. God has scattered his blessings among us, and trusts each of us to use our gifts to build the kingdom of God.

✚ All make the sign of the cross.

In the name of the Father, and of the Son, and of the Holy Spirit. Amen.

PSALM
(For a longer psalm, see page xii.)
Psalm 98:1

The LORD has made known his victory.

The LORD has made known his victory.

O sing to the Lord a new song,
  for he has done marvelous things.
His right hand and his holy arm
  have gotten him victory.

The LORD has made known his victory.

◆ All stand and sing **Alleluia.**

GOSPEL
Matthew 25:14–15, 19–21

A reading from the holy Gospel according to Matthew.

Jesus said, "For it is as if a man, going on a journey, summoned his slaves and entrusted his property to them; to one he gave five talents, to another two, to another one, to each according to his ability. Then he went away. After a long time the master of those slaves came and settled accounts with them. Then the one who had received the five talents came forward, bringing five more talents, saying, 'Master, you handed over to me five talents; see, I have made five more talents.' His master said to him, 'Well done, good and trustworthy slave; you have been trustworthy in a few things, I will put you in charge of many things; enter into the joy of your master.'"

The Gospel of the Lord.

◆ All sit and observe silence.

FOR SILENT REFLECTION

Think about this silently in your heart. What do you do with the gifts God has given to you?

CLOSING PRAYER

Let us pray to God for our needs and the needs of others: our family, neighborhood, and the world. For each need we say, "Lord, hear our prayer."

◆ All may add their own prayers here.

Let us pray: **Our Father . . . Amen.**

God our Father,
we thank you for entrusting your people
  to do your work here on earth,
to share the good news of the Gospel.
We pray in Christ's name.

Amen.

✚ All make the sign of the cross.

PRAYER FOR MONDAY, NOVEMBER 20, 2023

OPENING

This week we will reflect on Jesus' true identity. At the beginning of his Gospel, Matthew emphasizes that Jesus is the long-awaited Messiah of Israel, presenting a genealogy that connected him to the great forefathers of salvation history: David and Abraham. David was the signifier of his royal claim in the nation of Israel; Abraham recalled the universal scope of Jesus' mission as the Father of all nations.

✠ All make the sign of the cross.

In the name of the Father, and of the Son, and of the Holy Spirit. Amen.

PSALM
(For a longer psalm, see page xii.)
Psalm 98:1

The Lord has made known his victory.

The Lord has made known his victory.

O sing to the Lord a new song,
  for he has done marvelous things.
His right hand and his holy arm
  have gotten him victory.

The Lord has made known his victory.

◆ All stand and sing **Alleluia.**

GOSPEL
Matthew 1:1–2, 5c–6a, 12a, 15bc–17

A reading from the holy Gospel according to Matthew.

An account of the genealogy of Jesus the Messiah, the son of David, the son of Abraham. Abraham was the father of Isaac, and Isaac the father of Jacob, and Jacob the father of Judah and his brothers. And Obed the father of Jesse, and Jesse the father of King David. And after the deportation to Babylon: Eleazar [el-ee-AY-zehr] the father of Matthan [MATH-uhn], and Matthan the father of Jacob, and Jacob the father of Joseph the husband of Mary, who bore Jesus, who is called the Messiah. So all the generations from Abraham to David are fourteen generations; and from David to the deportation to Babylon, fourteen generations; and from the deportation to Babylon to the Messiah, fourteen generations.

The Gospel of the Lord.

◆ All sit and observe silence.

FOR SILENT REFLECTION

Think about this silently in your heart. Why is it important to know Jesus' lineage?

CLOSING PRAYER

Let us pray to God for our needs and the needs of others: our family, neighborhood, and the world. For each need we say, "Lord, hear our prayer."

◆ All may add their own prayers here.

Let us pray: **Our Father . . . Amen.**

Lord Jesus,
you are the Messiah, the Holy One of God.
Save us from the snares of sin, and lead us
  to be holy in your name.
Who live and reign with God the Father,
in the unity of the Holy Spirit,
God, for ever and ever.

Amen.

✠ All make the sign of the cross.

PRAYER FOR
TUESDAY, NOVEMBER 21, 2023

OPENING

Today we remember the Presentation of the Blessed Virgin Mary. When she was about three or four years old, Mary, the mother of Jesus, was also presented in the temple, where her life was offered to God. Today's Gospel will take us to the scene of crucifixion. To claim Jesus was the King of the Jews was a crime against the emperor and King Herod, enraging the Jews and Romans alike.

✤ All make the sign of the cross.

In the name of the Father, and of the Son, and of the Holy Spirit. Amen.

PSALM
(For a longer psalm, see page xii.)
Psalm 98:1

The Lord has made known his victory.

The Lord has made known his victory.

O sing to the Lord a new song,
  for he has done marvelous things.
His right hand and his holy arm
  have gotten him victory.

The Lord has made known his victory.

◆ All stand and sing **Alleluia.**

GOSPEL
Matthew 27:11, 27a, 28–29, 31c, 33, 35a, 37

A reading from the holy Gospel according to Matthew.

Now Jesus stood before the governor, and the governor asked him, "Are you the king of the Jews?" Jesus said, "You say so."

Then the soldiers of the governor took Jesus into the governor's headquarters. They stripped him and put a scarlet robe on him, and after twisting some thorns into a crown they put it on his head. They put a reed in his right hand and knelt before him and mocked him, saying, "Hail, King of the Jews!" Then they led him away to crucify him. They came to a place called Golgotha [GAWL-guh-thuh] (which means Place of a Skull), and when they had crucified him, over his head they put the charge against him, which read, "This is Jesus, the King of the Jews."

The Gospel of the Lord.

◆ All sit and observe silence.

FOR SILENT REFLECTION

Think about this silently in your heart. Jesus rules our hearts and minds.

CLOSING PRAYER

Let us pray to God for our needs and the needs of others: our family, neighborhood, and the world. For each need we say, "Lord, hear our prayer."

◆ All may add their own prayers here.

Let us pray: **Our Father . . . Amen.**

Loving God,
thank you for your Son Jesus,
king of heaven and earth, our redeemer.
In his name we pray.

Amen.

✤ All make the sign of the cross.

PRAYER FOR WEDNESDAY, NOVEMBER 22, 2023

OPENING

It must have been very strange for John the Baptist, himself an important prophet, to see the Spirit of the Lord descend on his cousin, Jesus. But John did not turn away in disbelief—he trusted the revelation he had been given and he shared it with others. This is the heart of the Gospel: to see, to trust, and to share the Good News. Today is the feast of St. Cecilia, an early Roman martyr and patron saint of musicians.

✢ All make the sign of the cross.

In the name of the Father, and of the Son, and of the Holy Spirit. Amen.

PSALM
(For a longer psalm, see page xii.)
Psalm 98:1

The LORD has made known his victory.

The LORD has made known his victory.

O sing to the Lord a new song,
  for he has done marvelous things.
His right hand and his holy arm
  have gotten him victory.

The LORD has made known his victory.

◆ All stand and sing **Alleluia.**

GOSPEL
John 1:29, 32–34

A reading from the holy Gospel according to John.

The next day John the Baptist saw Jesus coming toward him and declared, "Here is the Lamb of God who takes away the sin of the world! I saw the Spirit descending from heaven like a dove, and it remained on him. I myself did not know him, but the one who sent me to baptize with water said to me, 'He on whom you see the Spirit descend and remain is the one who baptizes with the Holy Spirit.' And I myself have seen and have testified that this is the Chosen One."

The Gospel of the Lord.

◆ All sit and observe silence.

FOR SILENT REFLECTION

Think about this silently in your heart. How has God revealed himself to you?

CLOSING PRAYER

Let us pray to God for our needs and the needs of others: our family, neighborhood, and the world. For each need we say, "Lord, hear our prayer."

◆ All may add their own prayers here.

Let us pray: **Our Father . . . Amen.**

Lamb of God,
we sing your praises!
Grant us the eyes to see you,
the heart to know you,
and the hands to do your work.
Who live and reign with God the Father,
  in the unity of the Holy Spirit,
God, for ever and ever.

Amen.

✢ All make the sign of the cross.

PRAYER SERVICE FOR THANKSGIVING

Prepare seven leaders for this service. The fourth leader will need a Bible to read the Gospel passage and may need help finding and practicing the reading. You may want to begin by singing "One Bread, One Body," and end with "Table of Plenty." If the group will sing, prepare a song leader.

FIRST LEADER:

✚ All make the sign of the cross.

> **In the name of the Father, and of the Son, and of the Holy Spirit. Amen.**

Let us pray:

Almighty God,
you bless us every day with the
signs and wonders of your creation.
We thank you for the fresh air,
trees, stars, and planets, as well as
all the animals and creatures that live on
    land and in the sea.
We are grateful that you have entrusted us
with care of your environment.

SECOND LEADER: Psalm 136:1–9

Our refrain is: For his steadfast love endures forever.

ALL: For his steadfast love endures forever.

LEADER: O give thanks to the LORD, for he is good,

ALL: For his steadfast love endures forever;

LEADER: Who alone does great wonders,

ALL: For his steadfast love endures forever;

LEADER: Who by understanding made the heavens,

ALL: For his steadfast love endures forever;

LEADER: Who spread out the earth on the waters,

ALL: For his steadfast love endures forever;

LEADER: Who made the great lights,

ALL: For his steadfast love endures forever;

LEADER: The sun to rule over the day,

ALL: For his steadfast love endures forever;

LEADER: The moon and stars to rule over the night,

ALL: For his steadfast love endures forever.

THIRD LEADER:
Creator God,
your presence is with us
today and always.
We are grateful for the
gift of your Son Jesus,
who lived and walked among us,
and whose Spirit fills our hearts
with gratitude and joy.

ALL: Amen.

FOURTH LEADER: 1 John 4:7–16
A reading from the first Letter of John.

◆ Read the Scripture passage from the Bible.

The Word of the Lord.

FIFTH LEADER: Psalm 100:1–5
Our refrain is: Make a joyful noise to the Lord.

ALL: Make a joyful noise to the Lord.

LEADER: Make a joyful noise to the Lord, all the earth,
Worship the Lord with gladness;
Come into his presence with singing.

ALL: Make a joyful noise to the Lord.

LEADER: Know that the Lord is God.
It is he that made us, and we are his;
We are his people, and the sheep of his pasture.

ALL: Make a joyful noise to the Lord.

LEADER: Enter his gates with thanksgiving, and his courts with praise.
Give thanks to him, bless his name.

ALL: Make a joyful noise to the Lord.

SIXTH LEADER:
Loving God,
we thank you for all that you
provide for us.
We are grateful for all the loved ones
in our lives now,
and those who have gone before us.
You nurture us in so many ways.
May we always remember to praise you
and love others as you love us.
We ask this through Christ our Lord.

SEVENTH LEADER:
May the love of God,

✛ All make the sign of the cross.

Father, Son, and Holy Spirit,
always surround us in faith,
now and forever.

ALL: Amen.

PRAYER FOR
THURSDAY, NOVEMBER 23, 2023

OPENING

Jesus' life, death, resurrection, and ascension were the fulfillment of God's work of creation. In Jesus, we have been given the promise of divinity, that we too can live in God's love forever. Not only is today Thanksgiving Day in the US, but it is also the feast day of Sts. Clement, who was pope from the year 90 to his death in 100, and Columban, an Irish missionary who established a monastery in Bobbio (d. 615). Blessed Miguel Agustín Pro's last cry was "¡Viva Cristo Rey!" (Long live Christ the King!) when he was martyred in 1927.

✢ All make the sign of the cross.

In the name of the Father, and of the Son, and of the Holy Spirit. Amen.

PSALM
(For a longer psalm, see page xii.)
Psalm 98:1

The Lord has made known his victory.

The Lord has made known his victory.

O sing to the Lord a new song,
  for he has done marvelous things.
His right hand and his holy arm
  have gotten him victory.

The Lord has made known his victory.

◆ All stand and sing **Alleluia**.

GOSPEL
John 4:31–35, 37–38

A reading from the holy Gospel according to John.

Meanwhile the disciples were urging Jesus, "Rabbi, eat something." But he said to them, "I have food to eat that you do not know about." So the disciples said to one another, "Surely no one has brought him something to eat?" Jesus said to them, "My food is to do the will of him who sent me and to complete his work. Do you not say, 'Four months more, then comes the harvest'? But I tell you, look around you, and see how the fields are ripe for harvesting. For here the saying holds true, 'One sows and another reaps.' I sent you to reap that for which you did not labor. Others have labored, and you have entered into their labor."

The Gospel of the Lord.

◆ All sit and observe silence.

FOR SILENT REFLECTION

Think about this silently in your heart. What are you thankful to God for?

CLOSING PRAYER

Let us pray to God for our needs and the needs of others: our family, neighborhood, and the world. For each need we say, "Lord, hear our prayer."

◆ All may add their own prayers here.

Let us pray: **Our Father . . . Amen.**

Loving God,
may we never forget to show gratitude
  in prayer
and do acts of kindness.
Through Christ our Lord.

Amen.

HOME PRAYER
MEAL PRAYER FOR THANKSGIVING

Find the reading (John 15:12–17) in your Bible, ask for a volunteer to read the Scripture passage, and encourage the reader to practice reading it a few times. If practical, light candles for your Thanksgiving table. You may wish to begin with a simple song of thanksgiving or a favorite "Alleluia." Then an older child or an adult reads the leader parts.

LEADER:
Almighty God,
look at the abundance here before us!
It fills us with joy and gratitude.
Let us begin our prayer with the
    sign of the cross.

✢ All make the sign of the cross.

In the name of the Father, and of the Son, and of the Holy Spirit. Amen.

◆ All stand and sing **Alleluia.**

READER: John 15:12–17
A reading from the holy Gospel according to John.

◆ Read the Gospel passage from the Bible.

The Gospel of the Lord.

◆ All sit and observe silence.

LEADER:
We come to this table,
grateful for the delicious meal we're about
    to share,
as well as the family and friends who
surround us here.
Let us pray:
Heavenly Father,
we thank you for the love and friendship
that envelops us today.
Help us to nurture one another
with your peace and serenity in the
midst of our busy lives.
We thank all those who helped prepare
    this meal.
We are mindful of people in our
    community and
in other regions who may not have enough to
    eat today.
May we appreciate all that you provide for us
    now, and
we look forward to our heavenly banquet
    with you.
We ask this through our Lord Jesus Christ,
your Son, who lives and reigns with you
in the unity of the Holy Spirit, one God,
    for ever and ever.

ALL: Amen.

✢ All make the sign of the cross.

PRAYER FOR FRIDAY, NOVEMBER 24, 2023

OPENING

In Jesus' earthly life, we find the ultimate example of how to live in God. He has revealed to us exactly what it means to be human, and touched our humanity with divinity. Through his example we have learned to pray earnestly, to follow the sacred traditions, to act justly and with love. We have learned to practice with our whole lives the self-sacrificing love that he has shared with us.

✢ All make the sign of the cross.

In the name of the Father, and of the Son, and of the Holy Spirit. Amen.

PSALM

(For a longer psalm, see page xii.)
Psalm 98:1

The Lord has made known his victory.

The Lord has made known his victory.

O sing to the Lord a new song,
  for he has done marvelous things.
His right hand and his holy arm
  have gotten him victory.

The Lord has made known his victory.

◆ All stand and sing **Alleluia.**

GOSPEL

Matthew 23:1–6ac, 7b–8, 10

A reading from the holy Gospel according to Matthew.

Then Jesus said to the crowds and to his disciples, "The scribes and the Pharisees sit on Moses's seat; therefore, do whatever they teach you and follow it; but do not do as they do, for they do not practice what they teach. They tie up heavy burdens, hard to bear, and lay them on the shoulders of others, but they themselves are unwilling to lift a finger to move them. They love to have the place of honor at banquets and the best seats in the synagogues, and to have people call them rabbi. But you are not to be called rabbi, for you have one teacher, and you are all brothers and sisters. Nor are you to be called instructors, for you have one instructor, the Messiah."

The Gospel of the Lord.

◆ All sit and observe silence.

FOR SILENT REFLECTION

Think about this silently in your heart. How do you follow the example of Jesus?

CLOSING PRAYER

Let us pray to God for our needs and the needs of others: our family, neighborhood, and the world. For each need we say, "Lord, hear our prayer."

◆ All may add their own prayers here.

Let us pray: **Our Father . . . Amen.**

Lord Jesus,
you teach us all is good, beautiful, and holy.
Help us to be worthy of the love you have
    bestowed on us.
Who live and reign with God the Father,
    in the unity of the Holy Spirit,
God, for ever and ever.

Amen.

✢ All make the sign of the cross.

PRAYER FOR THE WEEK
WITH A READING FROM THE GOSPEL FOR **SUNDAY, NOVEMBER 26, 2023**

OPENING

This Sunday ends the liturgical year. We celebrate Our Lord Jesus Christ, King of the Universe, but our reading does not involve much majesty. Instead, we hear Christ explain exactly what kind of king he is. To inherit this kingdom, we are called to do him homage by caring for least among us.

✢ All make the sign of the cross.

In the name of the Father, and of the Son, and of the Holy Spirit. Amen.

PSALM
(For a longer psalm, see page xii.)
Psalm 98:1

The L%%ORD%% has made known his victory.

The L%%ORD%% has made known his victory.

O sing to the Lord a new song,
   for he has done marvelous things.
His right hand and his holy arm
   have gotten him victory.

The L%%ORD%% has made known his victory.

◆ All stand and sing **Alleluia.**

GOSPEL
Matthew 25:34b–38, 40

A reading from the holy Gospel according to Matthew.

Jesus said, "Come, you that are blessed by my Father, inherit the kingdom prepared for you from the foundation of the world, for I was hungry and you gave me food, I was thirsty and you gave me something to drink, I was a stranger and you welcomed me, I was naked and you gave me clothing, I was sick and you took care of me, I was in prison and you visited me." Then the righteous will answer him, "Lord, when was it that we saw you hungry and gave you food or thirsty and gave you something to drink? And when was it that we saw you a stranger and welcomed you or naked and gave you clothing?" And the king will answer them, "Truly I tell you, just as you did it to one of the least of these brothers and sisters of mine, you did it to me."

The Gospel of the Lord.

◆ All sit and observe silence.

FOR SILENT REFLECTION

Think about this silently in your heart. How have you seen Jesus in another person?

CLOSING PRAYER

Let us pray to God for our needs and the needs of others: our family, neighborhood, and the world. For each need we say, "Lord, hear our prayer."

◆ All may add their own prayers here.

Let us pray: **Our Father . . . Amen.**

O Prince of Peace,
you rule over our hearts with love, justice,
   and mercy.
May your kingdom come on earth.
Who live and reign with God the Father
in the unity of the Holy Spirit,
God, for ever and ever.

Amen.

✢ All make the sign of the cross.

PRAYER FOR MONDAY, NOVEMBER 27, 2023

OPENING

This week, we will be reflecting on the kingship of Christ. Earthly leaders in today's reading do not act with justice and righteousness. The Lord, true shepherd and king, will attend to those who scatter the flock instead of nurturing the people of God, and will raise up new leaders to shepherd them. God is the true King: he cares for his people and raises virtuous leaders.

✚ All make the sign of the cross.

In the name of the Father, and of the Son, and of the Holy Spirit. Amen.

PSALM

(For a longer psalm, see page xii.)
Psalm 98:1

The LORD has made known his victory.

The LORD has made known his victory.

O sing to the Lord a new song,
   for he has done marvelous things.
His right hand and his holy arm
   have gotten him victory.

The LORD has made known his victory.

READING

Jeremiah 22:2b–3ab; 23:2acdfg, 3ab, 4abe

A reading from the Book of the prophet Jeremiah.

Hear the word of the LORD, O king of Judah sitting on the throne of David—you, and your servants, and your people who enter these gates. Thus says the LORD: Act with justice and righteousness.

Therefore thus says the LORD, concerning the shepherds who shepherd my people: It is you who have scattered my flock. So I will attend to you for your evil doings. Then I myself will gather the remnant of my flock out of all the lands where I have driven them, and I will bring them back to their fold. I will raise up shepherds over them who will shepherd them, and they shall not fear any longer, says the LORD.

The Word of the Lord.

◆ All observe silence.

FOR SILENT REFLECTION

Think about this silently in your heart. Have you ever led others? What kind of leader are you?

CLOSING PRAYER

Let us pray to God for our needs and the needs of others: our family, neighborhood, and the world. For each need we say, "Lord, hear our prayer."

◆ All may add their own prayers here.

Let us pray: **Our Father . . . Amen.**

Lord God,
you rule with mercy and compassion.
Teach us to follow you as we lead others.
Through Christ our Lord.

Amen.

✚ All make the sign of the cross.

PRAYER FOR
TUESDAY, NOVEMBER 28, 2023

OPENING

The prophet Zechariah described the day of the Lord, the end times, as a day of light. On that day, there will be no frost or snow, and no night, only light. For Christ the King is also the Light of the World. We live in his light even now, but imperfectly, in a world marred by sin and suffering. But the day will come when we see clearly the glory of God. Our hope is in the Lord.

✦ All make the sign of the cross.

In the name of the Father, and of the Son, and of the Holy Spirit. Amen.

PSALM

(For a longer psalm, see page xii.)
Psalm 98:1

The LORD has made known his victory.

The LORD has made known his victory.

O sing to the Lord a new song,
  for he has done marvelous things.
His right hand and his holy arm
  have gotten him victory.

The LORD has made known his victory.

READING

Zechariah 14:1a, 5d, 6–9, 20ab

A reading from the Book of the prophet Zechariah [zek-uh-RĪ-uh].

See, a day is coming for the LORD. Then the LORD my God will come. On that day there shall not be either cold or frost. And there shall be continuous day (it is known to the LORD), not day and not night, for at evening time there shall be light. On that day living water shall flow out from Jerusalem, half of it to the eastern sea and half of it to the western sea; it shall continue in summer as in winter. And the LORD will become king over all the earth; on that day the LORD will be one and his name one. On that day there shall be inscribed on the bells of the horses, "Holy to the LORD."

The Word of the Lord.

◆ All observe silence.

FOR SILENT REFLECTION

Think about this silently in your heart. What does it mean to hope in the Lord?

CLOSING PRAYER

Let us pray to God for our needs and the needs of others: our family, neighborhood, and the world. For each need we say, "Lord, hear our prayer."

◆ All may add their own prayers here.

Let us pray: **Our Father . . . Amen.**

Lord God,
you are all in all.
Give us your grace that we might live in you
    and hope in your eternal promise.
In Christ's name we pray.

Amen.

✦ All make the sign of the cross.

PRAYER FOR
WEDNESDAY, NOVEMBER 29, 2023

OPENING

At the time of Jesus' birth, the Magi from the east followed a strange star, believing themselves to be seeking a king. But King Herod knew nothing of a new king of the Jews. The kingship of Christ was hidden in the baby's smallness and helplessness. The Magi recognized the king they were seeking, even in his smallness, and bowed down to him.

✚ All make the sign of the cross.

In the name of the Father, and of the Son, and of the Holy Spirit. Amen.

PSALM
(For a longer psalm, see page xii.)
Psalm 98:1

The Lord has made known his victory.

The Lord has made known his victory.

O sing to the Lord a new song,
  for he has done marvelous things.
His right hand and his holy arm
  have gotten him victory.

The Lord has made known his victory.

◆ All stand and sing **Alleluia.**

GOSPEL
Matthew 2:1ac–3a, 4–5ab, 9b–11c

A reading from the holy Gospel according to Matthew.

In the time of King Herod, magi from the east came to Jerusalem, asking, "Where is the child who has been born king of the Jews? For we observed his star in the east and have come to pay him homage." When King Herod heard this, he inquired of them where the Messiah was to be born. They told him, "In Bethlehem of Judea." They set out; and there, ahead of them, went the star that they had seen in the east, until it stopped over the place where the child was. When they saw that the star had stopped, they were overwhelmed with joy. They saw the child with Mary his mother, and they knelt down and paid him homage.

The Gospel of the Lord.

◆ All sit and observe silence.

FOR SILENT REFLECTION

Think about this silently in your heart. When you genuflect, you are giving homage to God. It is a gesture that acknowledges that God is great and deserves praise and worship.

CLOSING PRAYER

Let us pray to God for our needs and the needs of others: our family, neighborhood, and the world. For each need we say, "Lord, hear our prayer."

◆ All may add their own prayers here.

Let us pray: **Our Father . . . Amen.**

O God,
we offer humble thanks to our
    Lord and Savior.
May we share the good news of salvation
    with all we meet.
Through Christ our Lord.

Amen.

✚ All make the sign of the cross.

PRAYER FOR THURSDAY, NOVEMBER 30, 2023

OPENING

In today's reading, Peter proclaimed to the fledgling Church that the kingship of Christ is a promise that has been fulfilled. The Messiah, longed for by generations, is Jesus the crucified one, uncorrupted by death. Jesus was not what the people of Israel expected in their Savior. Today is the feast of St. Andrew the Apostle, who was the brother of St. Peter and one of the first disciples that Jesus called, according to the Gospels of Matthew and of Luke.

✢ All make the sign of the cross.

In the name of the Father, and of the Son, and of the Holy Spirit. Amen.

PSALM
(For a longer psalm, see page xii.)
Psalm 98:1

The LORD has made known his victory.

The LORD has made known his victory.

O sing to the Lord a new song,
   for he has done marvelous things.
His right hand and his holy arm
   have gotten him victory.

The LORD has made known his victory.

READING
Acts 2:14a-c, 29–33a, 32, 36

A reading from the Acts of the Apostles.

But Peter, standing with the eleven, raised his voice and addressed them. "Fellow Israelites, I may say to you confidently of our ancestor David that he both died and was buried, and his tomb is with us to this day. Since he was a prophet, he knew that God had sworn with an oath to him that God would put one of his descendants on his throne. Foreseeing this, David spoke of the resurrection of the Messiah. This Jesus God raised up, and of that all of us are witnesses. Therefore let the entire house of Israel know with certainty that God has made him both Lord and Messiah, this Jesus whom you crucified."

The Word of the Lord.

◆ All observe silence.

FOR SILENT REFLECTION

Think about this silently in your heart. Would you have believed Jesus was the Messiah if you lived during the time he was on earth?

CLOSING PRAYER

Let us pray to God for our needs and the needs of others: our family, neighborhood, and the world. For each need we say, "Lord, hear our prayer."

◆ All may add their own prayers here.

Let us pray: **Our Father . . . Amen.**

Lord Jesus,
give us the faith of your disciples,
who saw and believed
   what you had told them,
and proclaimed you King of
   Heaven and Earth.
Who live and reign with God the Father,
   in the unity of the Holy Spirit,
God, for ever and ever.

Amen.

✢ All make the sign of the cross.

PRAYER FOR
FRIDAY, DECEMBER 1, 2023

OPENING

St. Paul exhorts Timothy to keep faith until the reign of Christ the King. We also should strive to pursue righteousness, godliness, faith, love, endurance, and gentleness. We call these qualities *virtues*. The catechism tells us that a virtue is a "habitual and firm disposition to do the good. It allows the person not only to perform good acts, but to give the best of himself. . . . He pursues the good and chooses it in concrete actions" (CCC, 1803).

✚ All make the sign of the cross.

> **In the name of the Father, and of the Son, and of the Holy Spirit. Amen.**

PSALM

(For a longer psalm, see page xii.)
Psalm 98:1

The LORD has made known his victory.

The LORD has made known his victory.

O sing to the Lord a new song,
  for he has done marvelous things.
His right hand and his holy arm
  have gotten him victory.

The LORD has made known his victory.

READING

1 Timothy 6:11abhi, 12a, 13ac, 14–16

A reading from the First Letter of Paul to Timothy.

But as for you, man of God, pursue righteousness, godliness, faith, love, endurance, gentleness. Fight the good fight of the faith. In the presence of God, who gives life to all things, and of Christ Jesus, I charge you to keep the commandment without spot or blame until the manifestation of our Lord Jesus Christ, which he will bring about at the right time—he who is the blessed and only Sovereign, the King of kings and Lord of lords. It is he alone who has immortality and dwells in unapproachable light, whom no one has ever seen or can see; to him be honor and eternal dominion. Amen.

The Word of the Lord.

◆ All observe silence.

FOR SILENT REFLECTION

Think about this silently in your heart. How do you live a virtuous life?

CLOSING PRAYER

Let us pray to God for our needs and the needs of others: our family, neighborhood, and the world. For each need we say, "Lord, hear our prayer."

◆ All may add their own prayers here.

Let us pray: **Our Father . . . Amen.**

Heavenly Father,
you are all that is good and loving.
Help us to pursue the good
  with all our being.
Through Christ our Lord.

Amen.

✚ All make the sign of the cross.

HOME PRAYER
GATHERING AROUND AN ADVENT WREATH FOR PRAYER

Saturday evening before the First Sunday of Advent, gather the household around the wreath. Point out that the wreath is circular, with no beginning or end, like God's love. Explain that there are four candles, one for each Sunday of Advent. The third candle is rose because on the third Sunday we celebrate the joy of waiting for Christmas.

Use this service the first time you light your wreath and then on the following three Sundays when you light each new candle after the Psalm Response.

During the first week of Advent, light the first violet candle. During the second week of Advent, light two violet candles. For the third week, light two violet candles and one rose candle. During the final week of Advent, light all four candles. For your weekday celebration, simply light the candle(s), read one verse from Isaiah 40:1–5 and 9–11 (choose a different verse each time), and then say grace.

Before you begin, find the reading (John 1:1–5) in your Bible, ask a volunteer to read it, and encourage the reader to practice reading it a few times.

You may wish to begin with a simple Advent song, such as "O Come, O Come, Emmanuel," or "Soon and Very Soon." Then an older child or adult reads the leader parts.

LEADER:

Since ancient times, people have marked the passage of time with the light of the sun. In this holy season of Advent, we observe the passage of time through the light of this wreath, for each candle represents another week closer to the radiance of the newborn Son Jesus. Our anticipation for his glorious arrival can teach us much about patience as well as sharing the flame of our faith. So let us begin our time of prayer with the Sign of the Cross:

✢ All make the sign of the cross.

ALL: In the name of the Father, and of the Son, and of the Holy Spirit. Amen.

◆ Light the candle(s). Then all stand and sing **Alleluia**.

READER: John 1:1–5

A reading from the holy Gospel according to John.

◆ Read the Gospel passage from the Bible.

The Gospel of the Lord.

◆ All sit and observe silence.

LEADER:

God our Creator,
bless us as we gather around this
    Advent wreath,
ever anxious for the arrival of your Son, Jesus.
Renew us with your patience and
the light of your promise.
Help us to prepare our hearts
so that we are open to
your coming into our lives.
We ask this through Jesus Christ, our Lord.

ALL: Amen.

✢ All make the sign of the cross.

ADVENT

SUNDAY, DECEMBER 3, 2023 — SUNDAY, DECEMBER 24, 2023

ADVENT

THE MEANING OF ADVENT

"A shoot shall come out from the stump of Jesse, and a branch shall grow out of his roots" (Isaiah 11:1).

Jesse was the father of King David, a great leader of the Jewish people. But then Jesse's descendants became weak and scattered. The Jewish people no longer had a strong ruler and they suffered many periods of darkness, misery, and despair. The people of Israel had become like a great tree cut down to its stump. Yet God did not forsake the people. God, Israel's faithful protector, promised to make a new plant sprout. The people waited and prayed and hoped for many years, knowing God would keep this promise. We too are a people to whom God has made a solemn promise.

Advent is our time of waiting in "devout and joyful expectation" (*General Norms for the Liturgical Year*, 39) for the celebration of Christ's Incarnation and also for his Second Coming. We prepare as we wait by giving a little more to the poor and taking stock of our souls, as well as baking cookies and thinking about gifts for those we love. We wait, as did our spiritual ancestors, to celebrate the nativity of the Messiah. The first Sunday of Advent is also when the Church begins her new calendar year.

We begin our Advent with a week of Scriptures called the Messianic Prophecies. The prophets foretell where Jesus would be born and who his mother would be. They also predict Jesus' triumphant entry into Jerusalem on a donkey, his title of Good Shepherd, and that he will suffer. In the second and third week of our waiting we hear encouraging words that the Messiah would be the Light that breaks the darkness of injustice and brings peace. We'll hear the call of John the Baptist to "Prepare the Way of the Lord" (Luke 3:4).

PREPARING TO CELEBRATE ADVENT IN THE CLASSROOM

SACRED SPACE

During Advent create a mood of anticipation in the classroom. Use purples and violets on the bulletin boards instead of red and green since we are an Advent people. You can place the empty manger from a Christmas Nativity scene on your classroom prayer table. Slowly add elements like straw and animals and, in the last week, the Holy Family and shepherds. You might wait to add the star and the Magi after Christmas vacation, but it is not necessary.

You can also use an Advent wreath, which has a circular candleholder usually decorated with pine branches. It has four candles: three violet and one rose-colored (but you can use all violet or even white). When you first introduce the wreath to your class, wonder together with the children about why it's circular, why use pine boughs, why four candles. Children will often come up with beautiful answers to these questions: the wreath is round because God's love has no beginning and no end; the pine branches never lose their leaves or color just as God's love for us can never die; and the four candles represent the four Sundays of Advent, the four points of the compass, the four branches of the cross, the four Gospels, and so on. Explain that each day you will light one candle for each week in Advent; when all the candles are lit, then Christmas will be right around the corner! The children may be curious about the rose-colored candle. Explain that it is the third one that we light, for the third Sunday in Advent, which is called Gaudete [gow-DAY-tay] (Latin for "rejoice") because our wait is almost over!

MOVEMENT AND GESTURE

Children of all ages love solemn processions. Consider organizing an Advent procession. After sharing some of the material in "The Meaning of Advent" with them, explain that Advent has a new color, violet. Suggest to the children that you have a procession to change the color of your prayer tablecloth. You will want to speak with the children about processions they have participated in or have seen in church. Explain that a procession is a prayerful way to walk, and stress the importance of silence (or singing along if you plan to sing). You'll need children to place the Bible, Advent wreath, and other elements after the cloth is laid and, finally, someone to light the first candle. If you are not singing the procession could be accompanied by a wind chime.

FESTIVITY IN SCHOOL AND HOME

There are two wonderful feasts to celebrate in Advent, St. Nicholas (you may wish to hand out candy canes or "gold" chocolate coins) on December 6, and on December 13, St. Lucy (you may wish hand out cookies and hot chocolate). You might celebrate them in the week even if their day comes on a Saturday or Sunday. Please consider saving your celebration of Christmas until true Christmas time *after* December 25. The time of Advent is a great spiritual gift that helps us grow in the beautiful theological virtue of hope. Also, if you wait until you return from Christmas break to celebrate the great Christmas feast of Epiphany, the children will have settled down and may be more able to listen to the glad tidings of great joy.

In this book you will find special prayer services that may be used in the classroom or with a larger group. One is a service for Advent, pages 114–115, which could be used at any time; the other is for the Solemnity of the Immaculate Conception of the Blessed Virgin Mary on December 8, pages 122–123.

SACRED MUSIC

Discover which songs your parish will be singing during Advent. Sometimes the setting for the sung parts of the Mass will change with the liturgical time. Other Advent songs that children love include "The King of Glory Comes," "People Look East," and "O Come, O Come, Emmanuel."

PRAYERS FOR ADVENT

A wonderful prayer to become acquainted with during Advent is Mary's prayer of praise, the *Magnificat* (Luke 1:46–55). All those who pray the Liturgy of the Hours recite this beautiful prayer each evening to remember Mary's joy as she prayed to God, the Mighty One. It has been set to various tunes and may be sung such as the Taize "Magnificat" (canon).

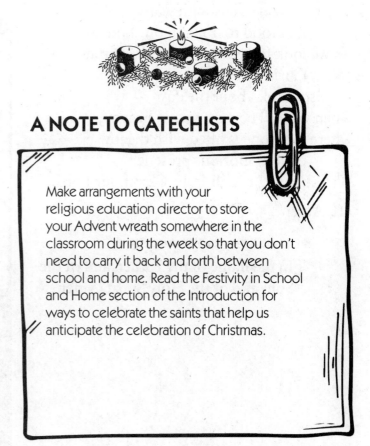

A NOTE TO CATECHISTS

Make arrangements with your religious education director to store your Advent wreath somewhere in the classroom during the week so that you don't need to carry it back and forth between school and home. Read the Festivity in School and Home section of the Introduction for ways to celebrate the saints that help us anticipate the celebration of Christmas.

GRACE BEFORE MEALS
ADVENT

LEADER:
Let the clouds rain down the Just One,
and the earth bring forth a Savior.

✠ All make the sign of the cross.

In the name of the Father, and of the Son, and of the Holy Spirit. Amen.

LEADER:
Lord God,
you provide for us in so many ways.
You have given us the earth,
    full of so much goodness.
You have blessed us with water to drink
    and food to nourish our bodies.
As we look forward to your gift of the
    Christ child,
we also think about the day
when we will be with you in heaven,
where everyone is filled with the joy
    of your glorious presence.
We ask this through Jesus Christ our Lord.

ALL: Amen.

✠ All make the sign of the cross.

In the name of the Father, and of the Son, and of the Holy Spirit. Amen.

PRAYER AT DAY'S END
ADVENT

LEADER:
O Wisdom of our God Most High,
guiding creation with power and love,
come to teach us the path of knowledge!

✢ All make the sign of the cross.

In the name of the Father, and of the Son, and of the Holy Spirit. Amen.

LEADER:
Holy God,
we thank you for this day
with all of its adventures, big and small.
May our days continue to be filled
with the light of your Son, our Lord,
your gift to us,
who shows us the way of
patience and forgiveness and love.
We ask this in his name.

ALL: Amen.

✢ All make the sign of the cross.

In the name of the Father, and of the Son, and of the Holy Spirit. Amen.

PRAYER SERVICE
ADVENT

Prepare a leader, reader, intercessor, and (if possible) a music leader for the service. Go over the intercessions with the class, and mention they are based on some Old Testament titles for Jesus we call the O Antiphons. Practice singing the refrain to "O Come, O Come Emmanuel" as the response, if possible. Place an Advent wreath on the table with a Bible and a purple cloth. Place the reading into the Bible and mark it with a ribbon or book mark. Review the reading with the reader and note that some verses are omitted. Decide who will light and extinguish the candles on the wreath. You might sing "Soon and Very Soon" at the end of the service.

LEADER:

◆ Gesture for all to stand.

✠ All make the sign of the cross.

In the name of the Father, and of the Son, and of the Holy Spirit. Amen.

LEADER:
Let us pray:
O God of wonder,
as we are busy preparing for Christmas
help us prepare our hearts for Jesus.
We are grateful for your simple words
    of hope
and the gift of new life in the Christ child.
May we follow the true light of Jesus
that shines for all people
through the darkness of sin and sorrow.
We ask this through Christ our Lord.

ALL: Amen.

◆ Gesture for all to sit. An adult lights the appropriate number of candles on the Advent wreath. Allow a moment of silence to enjoy the beauty of the lit wreath. (For a discussion of the significance of the Advent wreath and a prayer for blessing it, see Preparing to Celebrate Advent in the Classroom, the section on Sacred Space on page 110.)

LEADER: Isaiah 40:5a, 11
Let us pray the Psalm Response:

The glory of the Lord shall be revealed.

ALL: The glory of the Lord shall be revealed.

LEADER:
He will feed his flock like a shepherd;
   he will gather the lambs in his arms,
and carry them in his bosom,
   and gently lead the mother sheep.

ALL: The glory of the Lord shall be revealed.

READER: Isaiah 11:1–10
A reading from the Book of the prophet Isaiah.

◆ Read the Scripture passage from a Bible.

The Word of the Lord.

◆ All observe silence.

INTERCESSOR:
O come, Emmanuel, free people who are held captive by racism, prejudice, and bullying. We sing:

ALL: "Rejoice! Rejoice! Emmanuel shall come to you, O Israel."

O come, Wisdom. Teach us how to be good to one another. We sing (say):

O come, Lord. Rule our hearts and minds in goodness. We sing (say):

O come, Shoot of Jesse's Stem. Forgive us our sins. We sing (say):

O come, Key of David. Open heaven for us. We sing (say):

O come, Dayspring. Replace the darkness of sin. We sing (say):

O come, Desire of Nations. Unite all the world's people. We sing (say):

LEADER:
Come quickly, Lord Jesus,
and guide us in God's way
of peace and justice.
Fill us with your gentle love
as we look forward to celebrating Christmas
with our family and friends.
You are our light and joy!

✢ All make the sign of the cross.

In the name of the Father, and of the Son and of the Holy Spirit.

◆ After the service an adult extinguishes the candles on the Advent wreath.

PRAYER FOR THE WEEK
WITH A READING FROM THE GOSPEL FOR **SUNDAY, DECEMBER 3, 2023**

OPENING

This Advent consider how you might "keep awake" to the presence of the Lord. Two thousand years ago, God did not come in a chariot of fire or a rainbow cloud or clap of thunder. He came in an infant child, born to a poor family and a conquered people. The Lord comes in surprising ways to each of us: can you stay awake to meet him?

✣ All make the sign of the cross.

In the name of the Father, and of the Son, and of the Holy Spirit. Amen.

PSALM
(For a longer psalm, see page xii.)
Psalm 85:8

Restore us again, O God of our salvation!

Restore us again, O God of our salvation!

Let me hear what God the LORD will speak,
   for he will speak peace to his people,
to his faithful, to those who turn to him in
   their hearts.

Restore us again, O God of our salvation!

◆ All stand and sing **Alleluia.**

GOSPEL
Mark 13:33–37

A reading from the holy Gospel according to Mark.

Beware, keep alert, for you do not know when the time will come. It is like a man going on a journey, when he leaves home and puts his slaves in charge, each with his work, and commands the doorkeeper to be on the watch. Therefore, keep awake, for you do not know when the master of the house will come, in the evening or at midnight or at cockcrow or at dawn, or else he may find you asleep when he comes suddenly. And what I say to you I say to all: Keep awake.

The Gospel of the Lord.

◆ All sit and observe silence.

FOR SILENT REFLECTION

Think about this silently in your heart. What are some ways you can stay awake for the Lord this Advent?

CLOSING PRAYER

Let us pray to God for our needs and the needs of others: our family, neighborhood, and the world. For each need we say, "Lord, hear our prayer."

◆ All may add their own prayers here.

Let us pray: **Our Father . . . Amen.**

Lord Jesus,
you have come to save your people.
Help us to see you and know you when you
      come again.
Who live and reign with God the Father,
in the unity of the Holy Spirit,
God, for ever and ever.

Amen.

✣ All make the sign of the cross.

PRAYER FOR MONDAY, DECEMBER 4, 2023

OPENING

The Messiah will be born of the line of David in the town of Bethlehem. He will be a ruler, but also a shepherd. He will be the "one of peace." Hearing these words of the prophet Micah from almost three thousand years ago, do they describe Jesus Christ? However, his friends and neighbors expected something else of a messiah—certainly not this poor, simple man who grew up in Nazareth. Today, we remember St. John Damascene (676–749), a prolific defender of the Christian faith, poet, and theologian of the Eastern Church.

✠ All make the sign of the cross.

In the name of the Father, and of the Son, and of the Holy Spirit. Amen.

PSALM
(For a longer psalm, see page xii.)
Psalm 85:8

Restore us again, O God of our salvation!

Restore us again, O God of our salvation!

Let me hear what God the LORD will speak,
for he will speak peace to his people,
to his faithful, to those who turn to him in their hearts.

Restore us again, O God of our salvation!

READING
Micah 1:2a; 5:1–2, 4–5a

A reading from the Book of the prophet Micah [Mī-kuh].

Hear, you peoples, all of you. Now you are walled around with a wall; siege is laid against us; with a rod they strike the ruler of Israel upon the cheek.

But you, O Bethlehem of Ephrathah [EF-ruh-thuh], who are one of the little clans of Judah, from you shall come forth for me one who is to rule in Israel, whose origin is from of old, from ancient days. And he shall stand and feed his flock in the strength of the LORD, in the majesty of the name of the LORD his God. And they shall live secure, for now he shall be great to the ends of the earth, and he shall be the one of peace.

The Word of the Lord.

◆ All observe silence.

FOR SILENT REFLECTION

Think about this silently in your heart. Why do you think Jesus' friends and neighbors found it hard to see him as the Messiah?

CLOSING PRAYER

Let us pray to God for our needs and the needs of others: our family, neighborhood, and the world. For each need we say, "Lord, hear our prayer."

◆ All may add their own prayers here.

Let us pray: **Our Father . . . Amen.**

Lord Jesus,
you came to save your people.
Help us to see your face in all those we meet.
Who live and reign with God the Father,
in the unity of the Holy Spirit,
God, for ever and ever.

Amen.

✠ All make the sign of the cross.

PRAYER FOR
TUESDAY, DECEMBER 5, 2023

OPENING

In today's reading, King Ahaz, of the line of David, was besieged and worried he would lose his authority. Isaiah gave him a sign that his house would continue to reign: a young woman will bear a son named Immanuel. Jesus is the sign and fulfillment of the promise made to the people of Israel. He truly is Immanuel, "God-with-us."

✢ All make the sign of the cross.

In the name of the Father, and of the Son, and of the Holy Spirit. Amen.

PSALM
(For a longer psalm, see page xii.)
Psalm 85:8

Restore us again, O God of our salvation!

Restore us again, O God of our salvation!

Let me hear what God the LORD will speak,
   for he will speak peace to his people,
to his faithful, to those who turn to him in
   their hearts.

Restore us again, O God of our salvation!

READING
Isaiah 7:3, 4A, C, 10–14

A reading from the Book of the prophet Isaiah.

Then the LORD said to Isaiah, "Go out to meet Ahaz [AY-haz], you and your son Shear-jashub [SHEE-uhr-jay-shuhb], at the end of the conduit of the upper pool on the highway to the fuller's field, and say to him: Take heed, be quiet, do not fear, because of the fierce anger of Rezin and Aram and the son of Remaliah."

Again the LORD spoke to Ahaz, saying, "Ask a sign of the LORD your God; let it be deep as Sheol or high as heaven." But Ahaz said, "I will not ask, and I will not put the LORD to the test." Then Isaiah said, "Hear then, O house of David! Is it too little for you to weary mortals, that you weary my God also? Therefore the Lord himself will give you a sign. Look, the young woman is with child and shall bear a son, and shall name him Immanuel."

The Word of the Lord.

◆ All observe silence.

FOR SILENT REFLECTION

Think about this silently in your heart. How is God with you?

CLOSING PRAYER

Let us pray to God for our needs and the needs of others: our family, neighborhood, and the world. For each need we say, "Lord, hear our prayer."

◆ All may add their own prayers here.

Let us pray: **Our Father . . . Amen.**

Lord Jesus,
you brought heaven to earth when you were
   born in Bethlehem.
Help us to see your divine presence
   in the world,
in our neighbors and in our own hearts.
Who live and reign with God the Father,
in the unity of the Holy Spirit,
God, for ever and ever.

Amen.

✢ All make the sign of the cross.

PRAYER FOR WEDNESDAY, DECEMBER 6, 2023

OPENING

In the ancient Near East, *shepherd* was a common title for kings and deities. The prophet Ezekiel promised the people of Israel that they would be given a new shepherd: one who would give them good food and rest, bring back the lost, heal the injured, and strengthen the weak. Jesus, the Good Shepherd, is the fulfillment of this prophecy. Today is the feast of St. Nicholas, himself a shepherd (bishop) of the people of Myra.

✢ All make the sign of the cross.

In the name of the Father, and of the Son, and of the Holy Spirit. Amen.

PSALM
(For a longer psalm, see page xii.)
Psalm 85:8

Restore us again, O God of our salvation!

Restore us again, O God of our salvation!

Let me hear what God the Lord will speak,
   for he will speak peace to his people,
to his faithful, to those who turn to him in
   their hearts.

Restore us again, O God of our salvation!

READING
Ezekiel 34:11, 12c, 14–16

A reading from the Book of the prophet Ezekiel.

For thus says the Lord God: I myself will search for my sheep and will sort them out. I will rescue them from all the places to which they have been scattered on a day of clouds and thick darkness. I will feed them with good pasture, and the mountain heights of Israel shall be their pasture; there they shall lie down in good grazing land, and they shall feed on rich pasture on the mountains of Israel. I myself will be the shepherd of my sheep, and I will make them lie down, says the Lord God. I will seek the lost, and I will bring back the strays, and I will bind up the injured, and I will strengthen the weak, but the fat and the strong I will destroy. I will feed them with justice.

The Word of the Lord.

◆ All observe silence.

FOR SILENT REFLECTION

Think about this silently in your heart. St. Nicholas showed his gratitude for God's gifts by giving to others. What gifts can you share with those in need?

CLOSING PRAYER

Let us pray to God for our needs and the needs of others: our family, neighborhood, and the world. For each need we say, "Lord, hear our prayer."

◆ All may add their own prayers here.

Let us pray: **Our Father . . . Amen.**

Father,
give us your heart of love
that we might give out of our abundance
      as your servant Nicholas did.
We pray in Christ's name.

Amen.

✢ All make the sign of the cross.

PRAYER FOR THURSDAY, DECEMBER 7, 2023

OPENING

Today we remember St. Ambrose (c. 340–397), bishop of Milan. Ambrose helped the poor and encouraged others to do so, too. He stripped expensive finery from the bishop's household and proclaimed that rulers must obey the laws of God. In today's reading, Zechariah prophesied that the Messiah would come not with armies, but in humility, riding on a donkey.

✤ All make the sign of the cross.

In the name of the Father, and of the Son, and of the Holy Spirit. Amen.

PSALM
(For a longer psalm, see page xii.)
Psalm 85:8

Restore us again, O God of our salvation!

Restore us again, O God of our salvation!

Let me hear what God the LORD will speak,
 for he will speak peace to his people,
to his faithful, to those who turn to him in
 their hearts.

Restore us again, O God of our salvation!

READING
Zechariah 9:9–11, 16–17a

A reading from the Book of the prophet Zechariah [zek-uh-Rī-uh].

Rejoice greatly, O daughter Zion! Shout aloud, O daughter Jerusalem! See, your king comes to you; triumphant and victorious is he, humble and riding on a donkey, on a colt, the foal of a donkey. He will cut off the chariot from Ephraim [EE-fray-ihm] and the war-horse from Jerusalem; and the battle-bow shall be cut off, and he shall command peace to the nations; his dominion shall be from sea to sea and from the River to the ends of the earth. As for you also, because of the blood of my covenant with you, I will set your prisoners free from the waterless pit. On that day the LORD their God will save them, for they are the flock of his people, for like the jewels of a crown they shall shine on his land. For what goodness and beauty are his!

The Word of the Lord.

◆ All observe silence.

FOR SILENT REFLECTION

Think about this silently in your heart. What does it mean to be humble? In what ways was Jesus humble?

CLOSING PRAYER

Let us pray to God for our needs and the needs of others: our family, neighborhood, and the world. For each need we say, "Lord, hear our prayer."

◆ All may add their own prayers here.

Let us pray: **Our Father . . . Amen.**

Lord Jesus,
you come in power and humility.
Teach us to live life for others as you did.
Who live and reign with God the Father,
in the unity of the Holy Spirit,
God, for ever and ever.

Amen.

✤ All make the sign of the cross.

PRAYER FOR
FRIDAY, DECEMBER 8, 2023

OPENING

We believe that Jesus was the fulfilment of the "Suffering Servant" prophecy: one who was wounded for our transgressions, and who took the punishment that made us whole. Today is the Solemnity of the Immaculate Conception of the Blessed Virgin Mary. Mary was free from original sin from the moment of her conception. Thus both Mary and Jesus point to the ultimate destiny of humanity: to be full of God's grace and free of sin. Mary, under the title of the Immaculate Conception, is the principal patroness of the United States.

✚ All make the sign of the cross.

In the name of the Father, and of the Son, and of the Holy Spirit. Amen.

PSALM
(For a longer psalm, see page xii.)
Psalm 85:8

Restore us again, O God of our salvation!

Restore us again, O God of our salvation!

Let me hear what God the Lord will speak,
    for he will speak peace to his people,
to his faithful, to those who turn to him in
    their hearts.

Restore us again, O God of our salvation!

READING
Isaiah 53:3ac, 4–5, 9

A reading from the Book of the prophet Isaiah.

He was despised and rejected by others; a man of suffering and acquainted with infirmity, and we held him of no account. Surely he has borne our infirmities and carried our diseases, yet we accounted him stricken, struck down by God, and afflicted. But he was wounded for our transgressions, crushed for our iniquities; upon him was the punishment that made us whole, and by his bruises we are healed. They made his grave with the wicked and his tomb with the rich, although he had done no violence, and there was no deceit in his mouth.

The Word of the Lord.

◆ All observe silence.

FOR SILENT REFLECTION

Think about this silently in your heart. How is Mary, who came into the world without sin, a model for us?

CLOSING PRAYER

Let us pray to God for our needs and the needs of others: our family, neighborhood, and the world. For each need we say, "Lord, hear our prayer."

◆ All may add their own prayers here.

Let us pray: **Our Father . . . Amen.**

Lord Jesus,
you took on the sin of all humanity
    on the cross.
May we be deserving of the sacrifice you
    made to give us new life.
Who live and reign with God the Father,
in the unity of the Holy Spirit,
God, for ever and ever.

Amen.

✚ All make the sign of the cross.

PRAYER SERVICE
SOLEMNITY OF THE IMMACULATE CONCEPTION OF MARY

Prepare six leaders for this service. The third leader will need a Bible for the passages from Luke. Help the third leader practice the readings. You may wish to sing "Sing of Mary" as the opening song. If the group will sing, prepare someone to lead it.

FIRST LEADER:

We remember Mary, the Mother of Jesus, on this special day. We celebrate her Immaculate Conception and believe she was conceived with God's special grace in her mother's womb so that one day she would bear Jesus, her Son, our Lord and Savior. She was filled with God's grace and the guidance of the Holy Spirit as she continually followed God's will. She nurtured Jesus in her womb, guided her Son in his youth, and stood by him in his ministry, even through his death and Resurrection. She is the patroness of the United States because of her constant courage. Let us begin our prayer service in her honor by singing the opening song.

SONG LEADER:

- Gesture for all to stand, and lead the first few verses of the song.

SECOND LEADER:

+ All make the sign of the cross.

   In the name of the Father, and of the Son, and of the Holy Spirit. Amen.

Let us pray:
Almighty Father,
you gave Mary special grace
when she was conceived
in her mother's womb.
You chose for her a unique role
to bring salvation to the world.
She is a sign of hope

because of her courage to say yes to you,
every moment of her life.
We pray with her to your Son Jesus,
our Lord and Savior,
in union with the Holy Spirit.

Amen.

◆ Remain standing and sing Alleluia.

THIRD LEADER: Luke 1:26–38
A reading from the holy Gospel according
to Luke.

◆ Read the Gospel passage from the Bible.

The Gospel of the Lord.

◆ All sit and observe silence.

FOURTH LEADER:

◆ Gesture for all to stand.

Let us bring our hopes and needs to God as
we pray, "Lord, hear our prayer."

For the courage to say, "yes" to God
as Mary did throughout her life,
we pray to the Lord.

For all who are struggling with
tough decisions in life,
may they look to Mary as
a true friend on their journey,
we pray to the Lord.

For all married people,
may they continue to be an example
of the love and devotion that
Mary and Joseph shared,
we pray to the Lord.

For all mothers
and those who nurture others,
help us to respect and protect life
from conception until natural death,
we pray to the Lord.

For those throughout the world
who are suffering from
hunger, lack of shelter, or disease,
and for those who have died,
may we have the compassion of Mary
to give us hope and the promise
of new life through Jesus,
we pray to the Lord.

FIFTH LEADER:
Let us pray the Hail Mary:

ALL: Hail Mary, full of grace . . .

◆ Pause, and then say:

Let us offer one another the sign of
Christ's peace.

◆ All offer one another a sign of peace.

SIXTH LEADER:
Let us pray Mary's special prayer,
the Magnificat:
"My soul magnifies the Lord,
 and my spirit rejoices in God my Savior,
for he has looked with favor on the lowliness
    of his servant.
  Surely, from now on all generations will
    call me blessed;
for the Mighty One has done great things
    for me,
and holy is his name."

✢ All make the sign of the cross.

**In the name of the Father, and of the
Son, and of the Holy Spirit. Amen.**

PRAYER FOR THE WEEK
WITH A READING FROM THE GOSPEL FOR **SUNDAY, DECEMBER 10, 2023**

OPENING

John, a well-known prophet in his time, saw his work as a signpost leading not to his glory, but to that of the true Messiah. He urged his followers to repent and prepare for the coming of the Lord. He prepared many hearts to receive Jesus. Have you known any prophets who have prepared your heart for Jesus?

✚ All make the sign of the cross.

In the name of the Father, and of the Son, and of the Holy Spirit. Amen.

PSALM
(For a longer psalm, see page xii.)
Psalm 85:8

Restore us again, O God of our salvation!

Restore us again, O God of our salvation!

Let me hear what God the Lord will speak,
   for he will speak peace to his people,
to his faithful, to those who turn to him in
   their hearts.

Restore us again, O God of our salvation!

◆ All stand and sing **Alleluia.**

GOSPEL
Mark 1:1–5

A reading from the holy Gospel according to Mark.

The beginning of the good news of Jesus Christ. As it is written in the prophet Isaiah, "See, I am sending my messenger ahead of you, who will prepare your way, the voice of one crying out in the wilderness: 'Prepare the way of the Lord; make his paths straight,'" so John the baptizer appeared in the wilderness, proclaiming a baptism of repentance for the forgiveness of sins. And the whole Judean region and all the people of Jerusalem were going out to him and were baptized by him in the River Jordan, confessing their sins.

The Gospel of the Lord.

◆ All sit and observe silence.

FOR SILENT REFLECTION

Think about this silently in your heart. How can you be a prophet for others?

CLOSING PRAYER

Let us pray to God for our needs and the needs of others: our family, neighborhood, and the world. For each need we say, "Lord, hear our prayer."

◆ All may add their own prayers here.

Let us pray: **Our Father . . . Amen.**

Lord Jesus,
John prepared a way for you.
Help us to prepare the way this Advent that
   we might welcome you into our hearts.
May we ask for forgiveness when we have
   done wrong,
and forgive others who have wronged us.
Who live and reign with God the Father,
in the unity of the Holy Spirit,
God, for ever and ever.

Amen.

✚ All make the sign of the cross.

PRAYER FOR MONDAY, DECEMBER 11, 2023

OPENING

Have you ever been in a dark room and struggled to find your way? You might be able to see by some dim light, but it can be disorienting to try to navigate around, with unknown perils lurking at every step. Today's reading from Isaiah compares waiting for the Lord to wandering in the dark. We might be able to see well enough to stumble forward, but with no true clarity. We are a people waiting for the light of the world to dawn, once and for all. St. Damasus I, whose feast day we celebrate today, defended the faith during a turbulent time in Church history.

✢ All make the sign of the cross.

In the name of the Father, and of the Son, and of the Holy Spirit. Amen.

PSALM
(For a longer psalm, see page xii.)
Psalm 85:8

Restore us again, O God of our salvation!

Restore us again, O God of our salvation!

Let me hear what God the Lord will speak,
 for he will speak peace to his people,
to his faithful, to those who turn to him in
 their hearts.

Restore us again, O God of our salvation!

READING
Isaiah 59:9–12a

A reading from the Book of the prophet Isaiah.

Therefore justice is far from us, and deliverance does not reach us; we wait for light, but there is only darkness; and for brightness, but we walk in gloom. We grope like the blind along a wall, groping like those who have no eyes; we stumble at noon as in the twilight, among the vigorous as though we were dead. We all growl like bears; like doves we moan mournfully. We wait for justice, but there is none; for salvation, but it is far from us. For our transgressions before you are many, and our sins testify against us.

The Word of the Lord.

◆ All observe silence.

FOR SILENT REFLECTION

Think about this silently in your heart. How does Jesus transform darkness into light?

CLOSING PRAYER

Let us pray to God for our needs and the needs of others: our family, neighborhood, and the world. For each need we say, "Lord, hear our prayer."

◆ All may add their own prayers here.

Let us pray: **Our Father . . . Amen.**

Lord,
you are the light that shines in the darkness,
and your people wait for your light
 in a time of darkness.
Give us the faith to hope in you.
Who live and reign with God the Father,
in the unity of the Holy Spirit,
God, for ever and ever.

Amen.

✢ All make the sign of the cross.

PRAYER FOR
TUESDAY, DECEMBER 12, 2023

OPENING

Today is the Feast of Our Lady of Guadalupe, when Our Lady appeared to a poor, indigenous Mexican man, Juan Diego, as a native woman dressed like an Aztec princess. She sent him to the bishop of Mexico to ask for a chapel in her honor. The bishop wanted a sign from God, and so Mary provided roses for Juan Diego to carry back in his *tilma* (cloak). When Juan Diego released the roses in front of the bishop, the tilma bore the image of Mary. Though he was burdened by the bishop's doubt, Juan Diego did not give up, and eventually his faith became a light for a whole nation of believers. Like Juan Diego, we each carry a flame of faith that we are called to share and spread until the light of Christ shines on all of us once and for all.

✢ All make the sign of the cross.

In the name of the Father, and of the Son, and of the Holy Spirit. Amen.

PSALM
(For a longer psalm, see page xii.)
Psalm 85:8

Restore us again, O God of our salvation!

Restore us again, O God of our salvation!

Let me hear what God the LORD will speak,
　for he will speak peace to his people,
to his faithful, to those who turn to him in
　their hearts.

Restore us again, O God of our salvation!

READING
Isaiah 60:1–4a, 5A

A reading from the Book of the prophet Isaiah.

Arise, shine, for your light has come, and the glory of the LORD has risen upon you. For darkness shall cover the earth and thick darkness the peoples, but the LORD will arise upon you, and his glory will appear over you. Nations shall come to your light and kings to the brightness of your dawn. Lift up your eyes and look around. Then you shall see and be radiant; your heart shall thrill and rejoice.

The Word of the Lord.

◆ All observe silence.

FOR SILENT REFLECTION

Think about this silently in your heart. How do you nurture the flame of faith?

CLOSING PRAYER

Let us pray to God for our needs and the needs of others: our family, neighborhood, and the world. For each need we say, "Lord, hear our prayer."

◆ All may add their own prayers here.

Let us pray: **Our Father . . . Amen.**

Lord God,
you have entrusted each of us
with the flame of faith.
Help us to nurture it that our faith might
　spread and grow.
Through Christ our Lord.

Amen.

✢ All make the sign of the cross.

PRAYER FOR WEDNESDAY, DECEMBER 13, 2023

OPENING

As Christians, we believe the Messiah has come and will come again. We have been given gifts by the Holy Spirit to help in this time of waiting: wisdom, understanding, counsel, fortitude, knowledge, and fear of the Lord. Given by the Holy Spirit in the sacraments, they help us to act with the grace of God. If we nurture these gifts and rely on them, we will grow ever closer to God, even as we wait for him to come again. Today is the feast of St. Lucy, whose name means "light." Her feast day has traditionally been a celebration of hope and light at the darkest time of year.

✣ All make the sign of the cross.

In the name of the Father, and of the Son, and of the Holy Spirit. Amen.

PSALM
(For a longer psalm, see page xii.)
Psalm 85:8

Restore us again, O God of our salvation!

Restore us again, O God of our salvation!

Let me hear what God the Lord will speak,
   for he will speak peace to his people,
to his faithful, to those who turn to him in
   their hearts.

Restore us again, O God of our salvation!

READING
Isaiah 11:1–3a, 5, 10

A reading from the Book of the prophet Isaiah.

A shoot shall come out from the stump of Jesse, and a branch shall grow out of his roots. The spirit of the Lord shall rest on him, the spirit of wisdom and understanding, the spirit of counsel and might, the spirit of knowledge and the fear of the Lord. His delight shall be in the fear of the Lord. Righteousness shall be the belt around his waist, and faithfulness the belt around his loins.

On that day the root of Jesse shall stand as a signal to the peoples; the nations shall inquire of him, and his dwelling shall be glorious.

The Word of the Lord.

◆ All observe silence.

FOR SILENT REFLECTION

Think about this silently in your heart. How do the gifts of the Holy Spirit bring you closer to God?

CLOSING PRAYER

Let us pray to God for our needs and the needs of others: our family, neighborhood, and the world. For each need we say, "Lord, hear our prayer."

◆ All may add their own prayers here.

Let us pray: **Our Father . . . Amen.**

Lord Jesus,
you are the Messiah,
sent to bring salvation to your people.
We await you in faith, hope, and love.
Who live and reign with God the Father,
in the unity of the Holy Spirit,
God, for ever and ever.

Amen.

✣ All make the sign of the cross.

PRAYER FOR
THURSDAY, DECEMBER 14, 2023

OPENING

Isaiah prophesied a kind of paradise, where even predators are at peace with their prey, where the most vulnerable (the child) becomes the leader. This is the "holy mountain" of the Lord, a place of profound peace. It is what we all await. St. John of the Cross (1542–1591), whose feast day we celebrate today, was a Carmelite who followed the teachings of Teresa of Avila and sought to reform the Church. In doing so, he was persecuted and imprisoned, experiencing acute depression and loneliness, what he called "the dark night of the soul." Yet through it all, he hoped in the Lord.

✙ All make the sign of the cross.

In the name of the Father, and of the Son, and of the Holy Spirit. Amen.

PSALM
(For a longer psalm, see page xii.)
Psalm 85:8

Restore us again, O God of our salvation!

Restore us again, O God of our salvation!

Let me hear what God the LORD will speak,
　for he will speak peace to his people,
to his faithful, to those who turn to him in
　their hearts.

Restore us again, O God of our salvation!

READING
Isaiah 11:6–9

A reading from the Book of the prophet Isaiah.

The wolf shall live with the lamb; the leopard shall lie down with the kid; the calf and the lion will feed together, and a little child shall lead them. The cow and the bear shall graze; their young shall lie down together; and the lion shall eat straw like the ox. The nursing child shall play over the hole of the asp, and the weaned child shall put its hand on the adder's den. They will not hurt or destroy on all my holy mountain, for the earth will be full of the knowledge of the LORD as the waters cover the sea.

The Word of the Lord.

◆ All observe silence.

FOR SILENT REFLECTION

Think about this silently in your heart. How can I make peace today?

CLOSING PRAYER

Let us pray to God for our needs and the needs of others: our family, neighborhood, and the world. For each need we say, "Lord, hear our prayer."

◆ All may add their own prayers here.

Let us pray: **Our Father . . . Amen.**

O Jesus our Lord,
we wait for you,
even when we feel loneliness and grief.
May we remember your promises
　in times of trial.
Who live and reign with God the Father,
in the unity of the Holy Spirit,
God, for ever and ever.

Amen.

✙ All make the sign of the cross.

PRAYER FOR FRIDAY, DECEMBER 15, 2023

OPENING

We wait for the Lord in an uneasy time, when war and violence, injustice and hate, suffering and death still exist in the world. We wait for and hope in the coming of the Messiah who will bring justice, righteousness, quiet, and trust. The kingdom of God is quiet and lovely: the advent of love, of peace, of comfort, of home.

✙ All make the sign of the cross.

In the name of the Father, and of the Son, and of the Holy Spirit. Amen.

PSALM

(For a longer psalm, see page xii.)
Psalm 85:8

Restore us again, O God of our salvation!

Restore us again, O God of our salvation!

Let me hear what God the LORD will speak,
 for he will speak peace to his people,
to his faithful, to those who turn to him in
 their hearts.

Restore us again, O God of our salvation!

READING

Isaiah 32:1, 16–18

A reading from the Book of the prophet Isaiah.

See, a king will reign in righteousness, and princes will rule with justice.

Then justice will dwell in the wilderness and righteousness abide in the fruitful field. The effect of righteousness will be peace, and the result of righteousness, quietness and trust forever. My people will abide in a peaceful habitation, in secure dwellings, and in quiet resting places.

The Word of the Lord.

◆ All observe silence.

FOR SILENT REFLECTION

Think about this silently in your heart. Use this quiet moment to rest in God's presence.

CLOSING PRAYER

Let us pray to God for our needs and the needs of others: our family, neighborhood, and the world. For each need we say, "Lord, hear our prayer."

◆ All may add their own prayers here.

Let us pray: **Our Father . . . Amen.**

O Lord,
you have prepared a place for each of us,
that we might live in you eternally.
All glory and honor to you, Emmanuel!
Who live and reign with God the Father,
in the unity of the Holy Spirit,
God, for ever and ever.

Amen.

✙ All make the sign of the cross.

PRAYER FOR THE WEEK
WITH A READING FROM THE GOSPEL FOR **SUNDAY, DECEMBER 17, 2023**

OPENING

Would you have followed John the Baptist if you were by the river Jordan? With the benefit of 2,000 years, it can be hard for us to appreciate just how difficult it was for people to trust in John's authority. John was questioned and persecuted, but he never wavered from his work of preparing the way for the true Messiah. And his wait and preparation bore fruit: he was blessed to baptize the Lord, Jesus Christ.

✚ All make the sign of the cross.

In the name of the Father, and of the Son, and of the Holy Spirit. Amen.

PSALM
(For a longer psalm, see page xii.)
Psalm 85:8

Restore us again, O God of our salvation!

Restore us again, O God of our salvation!

Let me hear what God the LORD will speak,
  for he will speak peace to his people,
to his faithful, to those who turn to him in their hearts.

Restore us again, O God of our salvation!

◆ All stand and sing **Alleluia.**

GOSPEL
John 1:6, 19, 23–27

A reading from the holy Gospel according to John.

There was a man sent from God whose name was John. This the testimony given by John when the Jews sent priests and Levites [LEE-vīts] from Jerusalem to ask him, "Who are you?" He said, "I am the voice of one crying out in the wilderness, 'Make straight the way of the Lord,'" as the prophet Isaiah said. Now they had been sent from the Pharisees [FAYR-uh-seez]. They asked him, "Why then are you baptizing if you are neither the Messiah, nor Elijah, nor the prophet?" John answered them, "I baptize with water. Among you stands one whom you do not know, the one who is coming after me; I am not worthy to untie the strap of his sandal."

The Gospel of the Lord.

◆ All sit and observe silence.

FOR SILENT REFLECTION

Think about this silently in your heart. How can you prepare the way for the Lord in your heart this Advent?

CLOSING PRAYER

Let us pray to God for our needs and the needs of others: our family, neighborhood, and the world. For each need we say, "Lord, hear our prayer."

◆ All may add their own prayers here.

Let us pray: **Our Father . . . Amen.**

Heavenly Father,
help us to be as steadfast in faith
    as your servant John,
as we wait for your Son to come in glory.
We pray in his name.

Amen.

✚ All make the sign of the cross.

PRAYER FOR MONDAY, DECEMBER 18, 2023

OPENING

The opening of today's reading from Isaiah seems like a contradiction: "do not fear" but also "[God] will come with vengeance," and then "He will come and save you." We are reminded again that God's justice is inescapable. But the righteous have nothing to fear, and will in fact be saved from the injustice and suffering that mar human existence. Are you among the righteous? How can you live more kindly, more justly, more patiently, more lovingly?

✢ All make the sign of the cross.

In the name of the Father, and of the Son, and of the Holy Spirit. Amen.

PSALM
(For a longer psalm, see page xii.)
Psalm 85:8

Restore us again, O God of our salvation!

Restore us again, O God of our salvation!

Let me hear what God the LORD will speak,
  for he will speak peace to his people,
to his faithful, to those who turn to him in
  their hearts.

Restore us again, O God of our salvation!

READING
Isaiah 35:4–6

A reading from the Book of the prophet Isaiah.

Say to those who are of a fearful heart, "Be strong, do not fear! Here is your God. He will come with vengeance, with terrible recompense. He will come and save you." Then the eyes of the blind shall be opened, and the ears of the deaf shall be opened; then the lame shall leap like a deer, and the tongue of the speechless sing for joy. For waters shall break forth in the wilderness and streams in the desert.

The Word of the Lord.

◆ All observe silence.

FOR SILENT REFLECTION

Think about this silently in your heart. What are three things I can do this week to love others better?

CLOSING PRAYER

Let us pray to God for our needs and the needs of others: our family, neighborhood, and the world. For each need we say, "Lord, hear our prayer."

◆ All may add their own prayers here.

Let us pray: **Our Father . . . Amen.**

Lord,
you are the source of all that is good.
Help us to follow you
and live lives of virtue, honor, and love.
Through Christ our Lord.

Amen.

✢ All make the sign of the cross.

PRAYER FOR
TUESDAY, DECEMBER 19, 2023

OPENING

Isaiah proclaims that the Lord will come with might, scattering our enemies. But he will also come with tenderness and care, feeding his flock and gathering them lovingly in his arms. Our God is mighty and awesome, but also as loving and gentle as a parent embracing each of us. As people of faith, we hope for the eternal embrace of God, the time when God will be all in all.

✢ All make the sign of the cross.

In the name of the Father, and of the Son, and of the Holy Spirit. Amen.

PSALM
(For a longer psalm, see page xii.)
Psalm 85:8

Restore us again, O God of our salvation!

Restore us again, O God of our salvation!

Let me hear what God the LORD will speak,
  for he will speak peace to his people,
to his faithful, to those who turn to him in
  their hearts.

Restore us again, O God of our salvation!

READING
Isaiah 40:9–11

A reading from the Book of the prophet Isaiah.

Get you up to a high mountain, O Zion, herald of good news; lift up your voice with strength, O Jerusalem, herald of good news, lift it up, do not fear; say to the cities of Judah, "Here is your God!" See, the Lord GOD comes with might, and his arm rules for him; his reward is with him and his recompense before him. He will feed his flock like a shepherd; he will gather the lambs in his arms, and carry them in his bosom and gently lead the mother sheep.

The Word of the Lord.

◆ All observe silence.

FOR SILENT REFLECTION

Think about this silently in your heart. What do you hope for?

CLOSING PRAYER

Let us pray to God for our needs and the needs of others: our family, neighborhood, and the world. For each need we say, "Lord, hear our prayer."

◆ All may add their own prayers here.

Let us pray: **Our Father . . . Amen.**

O Good Shepherd,
we are a people of hope.
Give us faith and love to sustain us
until we can meet you face to face.
Who live and reign with God the Father,
in the unity of the Holy Spirit,
God, for ever and ever.

Amen.

✢ All make the sign of the cross.

PRAYER FOR WEDNESDAY, DECEMBER 20, 2023

OPENING

"Awake, awake!" Isaiah cries out to the Lord. We echo his cry. Awake, Lord, and save those suffering from disease. Awake, Lord, and end the wars that plague our earth. Awake, Lord, and strike hatred from human hearts. Awake, Lord, and give food to the hungry and drink to the thirsty. Awake, awake! Our God hears our prayers. But do we hear the cries of our neighbors? Can we awaken to the needs of others? How can we be God's hands, feet, heart for the world as we wait for him to come again? Can we feed the hungry, comfort the sick, give refuge to the persecuted, make peace, and truly love all those we meet?

✛ All make the sign of the cross.

In the name of the Father, and of the Son, and of the Holy Spirit. Amen.

PSALM

(For a longer psalm, see page xii.)
Psalm 85:8

Restore us again, O God of our salvation!

Restore us again, O God of our salvation!

Let me hear what God the LORD will speak,
   for he will speak peace to his people,
to his faithful, to those who turn to him in
   their hearts.

Restore us again, O God of our salvation!

READING

Isaiah 51:9a–b, 10–11

A reading from the Book of the prophet Isaiah.

Awake, awake, put on strength, O arm of the LORD! Awake, as in days of old, the generations of long ago! Was it not you who dried up the sea, the waters of the great deep; who made the depths of the sea a way for the redeemed to cross over? So the ransomed of the LORD shall return and come to Zion with rejoicing; everlasting joy shall be upon their heads; they shall obtain joy and gladness, and sorrow and sighing shall flee away.

The Word of the Lord.

◆ All observe silence.

FOR SILENT REFLECTION

Think about this silently in your heart. How can you be attentive to the needs of those in your community?

CLOSING PRAYER

Let us pray to God for our needs and the needs of others: our family, neighborhood, and the world. For each need we say, "Lord, hear our prayer."

◆ All may add their own prayers here.

Let us pray: **Our Father . . . Amen.**

Faithful God,
you led the Israelites to freedom.
Your Son freed us from sin and death.
Help us to awaken to your presence
   in our world and in our lives,
as we wait in hope for Christ's return.
In his name we pray.

Amen.

✛ All make the sign of the cross.

PRAYER FOR THURSDAY, DECEMBER 21, 2023

OPENING

On that first Christmas night, the glory of the Lord shone upon the humble stable in Bethlehem. It amazed the shepherds. It led the Magi. In this Advent season, we too are waiting to see the glory of the Lord, to have it revealed once and for all. We are preparing our hearts and our lives to receive that glory. Today we remember St. Peter Canisius [kuh-NEE-see-uhs] of the Netherlands (1521–97). St. Peter was a Jesuit and a popular preacher. He wrote one of the first catechisms, which is used to help leaders teach about God.

✦ All make the sign of the cross.

In the name of the Father, and of the Son, and of the Holy Spirit. Amen.

PSALM

(For a longer psalm, see page xii.)
Psalm 85:8

Restore us again, O God of our salvation!

Restore us again, O God of our salvation!

Let me hear what God the LORD will speak,
  for he will speak peace to his people,
to his faithful, to those who turn to him in
  their hearts.

Restore us again, O God of our salvation!

READING

Isaiah 40:3–5a

A reading from the Book of the prophet Isaiah.

A voice cries out: "In the wilderness prepare the way of the LORD; make straight in the desert a highway for our God. Every valley shall be lifted up, and every mountain and hill be made low; the uneven ground shall become level, and the rough places a plain. Then the glory of the LORD shall be revealed, and all flesh shall see it together, for the mouth of the LORD has spoken."

The Word of the Lord.

◆ All observe silence.

FOR SILENT REFLECTION

Think about this silently in your heart. How does the glory of the Lord shine through your life?

CLOSING PRAYER

Let us pray to God for our needs and the needs of others: our family, neighborhood, and the world. For each need we say, "Lord, hear our prayer."

◆ All may add their own prayers here.

Let us pray: **Our Father . . . Amen.**

Dear God,
your light has brightened the way
for your saints throughout history.
Help us to share that light
until the fullness of your glory
    at last is revealed.
Through Christ our Lord.

Amen.

✦ All make the sign of the cross.

PRAYER FOR FRIDAY, DECEMBER 22, 2023

OPENING

We are in the final days of preparation for the Lord's coming at Christmas. The Messiah was born in a stable; he was a helpless baby, fully dependent on the care of others. Where do we encounter him today? He is in the vulnerable and the small, the persecuted, the powerless. He is in each one of us as well: in each person made in his image and likeness. Let us treat our family, friends, neighbors, strangers, and ourselves with care. During this season of hope, may we see God in one another.

◆ All make the sign of the cross.

In the name of the Father, and of the Son, and of the Holy Spirit. Amen.

PSALM

(For a longer psalm, see page xii.)
Psalm 85:8

Restore us again, O God of our salvation!

Restore us again, O God of our salvation!

Let me hear what God the LORD will speak,
  for he will speak peace to his people,
to his faithful, to those who turn to him in
  their hearts.

Restore us again, O God of our salvation!

◆ All stand and sing **Alleluia.**

GOSPEL

Mark 1:1–4

A reading from the holy Gospel according to Mark.

The beginning of the good news of Jesus Christ. As it is written in the prophet Isaiah, "See, I am sending my messenger ahead of you, who will prepare your way, the voice of one crying out in the wilderness: 'Prepare the way of the Lord; make his paths straight,'" so John the baptizer appeared in the wilderness, proclaiming a baptism of repentance for the forgiveness of sins.

The Gospel of the Lord.

◆ All sit and observe silence.

FOR SILENT REFLECTION

Think about this silently in your heart. How have you prepared for the coming of Jesus?

CLOSING PRAYER

Let us pray to God for our needs and the needs of others: our family, neighborhood, and the world. For each need we say, "Lord, hear our prayer."

◆ All may add their own prayers here.

Let us pray: **Our Father . . . Amen.**

Almighty God,
help us to recognize you in each person
    we meet today,
and give us your heart to love and care for
    each of them.
We ask this through Christ our Lord.

Amen.

◆ All make the sign of the cross.

PRAYER FOR THE WEEK
WITH A READING FROM THE GOSPEL FOR SUNDAY, DECEMBER 24, 2023

OPENING

Mary was perplexed by the words of the angel. Yet she said yes to God's extraordinary plan; she said yes to God and welcomed him into her life. It is when we welcome Jesus into our hearts that we can truly be "God-bearers" like Mary, people who manifest the love of God through our lives.

✦ All make the sign of the cross.

In the name of the Father, and of the Son, and of the Holy Spirit. Amen.

PSALM
(For a longer psalm, see page xii.)
Psalm 85:8

Restore us again, O God of our salvation!

Restore us again, O God of our salvation!

Let me hear what God the Lord will speak,
　for he will speak peace to his people,
to his faithful, to those who turn to him in
　their hearts.

Restore us again, O God of our salvation!

◆ All stand and sing **Alleluia.**

GOSPEL
Luke 1:26–32

A reading from the holy Gospel according to Luke.

In the sixth month the angel Gabriel was sent by God to a town in Galilee called Nazareth, to a virgin engaged to a man whose name was Joseph, of the house of David. The virgin's name was Mary. And he came to her and said, "Greetings, favored one! The Lord is with you." But she was much perplexed by his words and pondered what sort of greeting this might be. The angel said to her, "Do not be afraid, Mary, for you have found favor with God. And now, you will conceive in your womb and bear a son, and you will name him Jesus. He will be great and will be called the Son of the Most High, and the Lord God will give to him the throne of his ancestor David."

The Gospel of the Lord.

◆ All sit and observe silence.

FOR SILENT REFLECTION

Think about this silently in your heart. Have you ever been perplexed by what God calls you to do? Pray that you may always have a willing and open heart to listen.

CLOSING PRAYER

Let us pray to God for our needs and the needs of others: our family, neighborhood, and the world. For each need we say, "Lord, hear our prayer."

◆ All may add their own prayers here.

Let us pray: **Our Father . . . Amen.**

Lord God,
Mary trusted in your plan for her,
even when she felt afraid or confused.
Give us the grace to echo her yes
and truly do your will on earth.
Through Christ our Lord.

Amen.

✦ All make the sign of the cross.

CHRISTMAS TIME

SUNDAY, JANUARY 1, 2024 — SUNDAY, JANUARY 7, 2024

2023–2024 CHRISTMAS

THE MEANING OF CHRISTMAS

"For a child has been born for us,
    a son given to us;
authority rests upon his shoulders;
    and he is named
Wonderful Counselor, Mighty God,
    Everlasting Father, Prince of Peace."

(Isaiah 9:6)

God keeps the great promise of the gift of Jesus! Of course, God amazes us with other gifts we never could have imagined or asked for. The earth is filled with God's gifts. Think of the solid ground that supports us, gravity that keeps us from floating away, the atmosphere that provides oxygen for breathing and a shield to protect us from the heat of the sun, and water that keeps our cells healthy. We need so many things just to stay alive. And yet the earth contains much more than is necessary to keep us going. Within the earth, precious metals and gems delight us with their shine. Seashells and spider webs amaze us with their geometry. Roses and lilacs fill the air with perfume. Peacocks and pinecones and pecans add to the world's great fascination. And every day our friends and family share new ways to love. What a world we have been given!

But God wants to give us something even more precious: a share in God's very own life. So Immanuel, God-with-us, came to us in Bethlehem. God, who was there before the universe, who was the Word that spoke the world into existence, gave himself to us as an infant who could do nothing for itself. This gift has changed everything. God's heart is opened for us. Out of the tree stump of despair, God has brought a flowering branch.

Our Scriptures are full of epiphanies or manifestations; that is, events that clearly show people that this baby, Jesus, is the promised Messiah. We will stand in front of the manger in Bethlehem this week and gaze in wonder with Mary, Joseph, the angels, the shepherds, and the Magi as we realize this holy child, Jesus, is our God.

PREPARING TO CELEBRATE CHRISTMAS IN THE CLASSROOM

SACRED SPACE

Replace the Advent wreath with a new, white pillar candle and change the purple cloth to a white one. You might add some gold tinsel or a gold cloth. Place the star and the Magi in the Nativity scene.

MOVEMENT AND GESTURE

If you have older students, they light and hold congregational candles (thin tapers) during the Epiphany Prayer Service.

FESTIVITY IN SCHOOL AND HOME

The prayer service for Epiphany on page 147 provides a beautiful and prayerful way to celebrate the arrival of the Magi in Bethlehem.

SACRED MUSIC

Christmas Time is a time of music! Many beautiful carols, including "Joy to the World," "Angels We Have Heard on High," "O Come, All Ye Faithful," and "We Three Kings" can be sung with the children. You may even wish to organize a caroling party and go door to door through your school.

PRAYERS FOR CHRISTMAS

The opening verses of the Gospel according to St. John contain some of the most beautiful poetry in the world: "In the beginning was the Word, and the Word was with God, and the Word was God. He was in the beginning with God. All things came into being through him, and without him not one thing came into being. What has come into being in him was life, and the life was the light of all people. The light shines in the darkness, and the darkness did not overcome it" (John 1:1–5).

These verses beautifully express the mystery of the Incarnation, the mystery of God becoming a human being to be close to us. You might want to spend some time during religion class reading this beautiful hymn line by line. Ask the children whom St. John means when he speaks about the "Word of God." See what they say when you ask them how "all things came into being" through Christ when we know Jesus was born after the creation of the world. How can one person be the "light of all people"? What kind of light do people need? What do the children think St. John means when he says, "the darkness did not overcome" the Light of the World?

A NOTE TO CATECHISTS

See whether you can share a Christmas Nativity scene with the teacher who shares your classroom. Or take your students on a "field trip" to the church and let them pray in front of the parish Nativity scene! Perhaps families could share their Nativity sets, or pieces from them. This is especially wonderful if you have a variety of nationalities and ethnic groups among your children.

GRACE BEFORE MEALS

CHRISTMAS TIME

LEADER:
"For a child has been born for us,"

ALL: "a son given to us."

✚ All make the sign of the cross.

In the name of the Father, and of the Son, and of the Holy Spirit. Amen.

LEADER:
Heavenly Father,
may the food we are about to share
help to nourish our bodies and minds,
just as you nurture us always
with the gift of your Son
and your everlasting Spirit.
May we be a living sign of the
presence of Jesus,
who is hope for the world.
We ask this through Christ our Lord.

ALL: Amen.

✚ All make the sign of the cross.

In the name of the Father, and of the Son, and of the Holy Spirit. Amen.

PRAYER AT DAY'S END
CHRISTMAS TIME

LEADER:
Sing to the Lord a new song,

ALL: for he has done wondrous deeds!

✛ All make the sign of the cross.

In the name of the Father, and of the Son, and of the Holy Spirit. Amen.

LEADER:
Heavenly Father,
the gift of your Son
gives us so much joy!
We thank you for this day,
filled with wonder and small adventures.
May we always remember that you
are the source of all goodness
as we praise the miracle of Jesus,
whom you sent to us
to lead the way back to you.
We ask this through Christ our Lord
and Savior.

ALL: Amen.

✛ All make the sign of the cross.

In the name of the Father, and of the Son, and of the Holy Spirit. Amen.

PRAYER FOR
MONDAY, JANUARY 1, 2024

OPENING

As we usher in the new year, we honor Mary, the Mother of God. Mary was not amazed like the others to hear the story of the shepherds, but was full of quiet joy. She "treasured all those words," like any new mother doting on her miraculous baby. But she also "pondered them in her heart"; the same heart that would be pierced by a sword. Mary's life, like ours, would not be free of pain, but she would face the cross with faith and courage, loving her son without end.

✣ All make the sign of the cross.

In the name of the Father, and of the Son, and of the Holy Spirit. Amen.

PSALM
(For a longer psalm, see page xiii.)
Psalm 96:1–2A

Let the heavens be glad and the earth rejoice!

Let the heavens be glad and the earth rejoice!

O sing to the Lord a new song;
   sing to the Lord, all the earth.
Sing to the Lord; bless his name.

Let the heavens be glad and the earth rejoice!

◆ All stand and sing **Alleluia.**

GOSPEL
Luke 2:16–21

A reading from the holy Gospel according to Luke.

So they went with haste and found Mary and Joseph and the child lying in the manger. When they saw this, they made known what had been told them about this child; and all who heard it were amazed at what the shepherds told them, and Mary treasured all these words and pondered them in her heart. The shepherds returned, glorifying and praising God for all they had heard and seen, as it had been told them.

When the eighth day came, it was time to circumcise the child, and he was called Jesus, the name given by the angel before he was conceived in the womb.

The Gospel of the Lord.

◆ All sit and observe silence.

FOR SILENT REFLECTION

Think about this silently in your heart. What do you admire about Mary? How can you grow to be more like her in faith?

CLOSING PRAYER

Let us pray to God for our needs and the needs of others: our family, neighborhood, and the world. For each need we say, "Lord, hear our prayer."

◆ All may add their own prayers here.

Let us pray: **Our Father . . . Amen.**

Holy Mary, Mother of God,
you brought forth the Light of the World.
May we have the courage to also bring
   Christ's light into the world today.
We ask your intercession
   in the name of your Son,
   Jesus Christ our Lord.

Amen.

✣ All make the sign of the cross.

PRAYER FOR
TUESDAY, JANUARY 2, 2024

OPENING

Today we honor St. Basil the Great and St. Gregory of Nazianzen, both early Church Fathers and prolific preachers and writers. Both were outspoken about God's love for the poor, which is emphasized in the Gospel today. The glory of God shines around the shepherds of the field, poor and lowly of stature. They are the first to receive the good news of Christ's birth.

◆ All make the sign of the cross.

In the name of the Father, and of the Son, and of the Holy Spirit. Amen.

PSALM
(For a longer psalm, see page xiii.)
Psalm 96:1–2A

Let the heavens be glad and the earth rejoice!

Let the heavens be glad and the earth rejoice!

O sing to the Lord a new song;
   sing to the Lord, all the earth.
Sing to the Lord; bless his name.

Let the heavens be glad and the earth rejoice!

◆ All stand and sing **Alleluia.**

GOSPEL
Luke 2:8–14

A reading from the holy Gospel according to Luke.

Now in that same region there were shepherds living in the fields, keeping watch over their flock by night. Then an angel of the Lord stood before them, and the glory of the Lord shone around them, and they were terrified. But the angel said to them, "Do not be afraid, for see, I am bringing you good news of great joy for all the people: to you is born this day in the city of David a Savior, who is the Messiah, the Lord. This will be a sign for you: you will find a child wrapped in bands of cloth and lying in a manger." And suddenly there was with the angel a multitude of the heavenly host, praising God and saying, "Glory to God in the highest heaven, and on earth peace among those whom he favors!"

The Gospel of the Lord.

◆ All sit and observe silence.

FOR SILENT REFLECTION

Think about this silently in your heart. Remember those in need in your community. How can you help them?

CLOSING PRAYER

Let us pray to God for our needs and the needs of others: our family, neighborhood, and the world. For each need we say, "Lord, hear our prayer."

◆ All may add their own prayers here.

Let us pray: **Our Father . . . Amen.**

Dear Lord,
you chose the shepherds
   to receive your glory.
Help us to see the poor and forgotten
   with your eyes.
Through Christ our Lord.

Amen.

✦ All make the sign of the cross.

PRAYER FOR
WEDNESDAY, JANUARY 3, 2024

OPENING

After receiving the angels' message, the shepherds set out for Bethlehem to find the child Jesus. After they met him, they "returned, glorifying and praising God." They returned to their normal life routine, but they had been changed by the encounter with God. So we, too, are changed by our encounters with God in the world, in one another, and especially in the Eucharist. Today is the Feast of the Most Holy Name of Jesus, when we remember "the name that is above every other name" (Philippians 2:9).

✢ All make the sign of the cross.

In the name of the Father, and of the Son, and of the Holy Spirit. Amen.

PSALM
(For a longer psalm, see page xiii.)
Psalm 96:1–2A

Let the heavens be glad and the earth rejoice!

Let the heavens be glad and the earth rejoice!

O sing to the Lord a new song;
   sing to the Lord, all the earth.
Sing to the Lord; bless his name.

Let the heavens be glad and the earth rejoice!

◆ All stand and sing **Alleluia.**

GOSPEL
Luke 2:15–20

A reading from the holy Gospel according to Luke.

When the angels had left them and gone into heaven, the shepherds said to one another, "Let us go now to Bethlehem and see this thing that has taken place, which the Lord has made known to us." So they went with haste and found Mary and Joseph and the child lying in the manger. When they saw this, they made known what had been told them about this child, and all who heard it were amazed at what the shepherds told them, and Mary treasured all these words and pondered them in her heart. The shepherds returned, glorifying and praising God for all they had heard and seen, as it had been told them.

The Gospel of the Lord.

◆ All sit and observe silence.

FOR SILENT REFLECTION

Think about this silently in your heart. How have you been changed through encounters with God?

CLOSING PRAYER

Let us pray to God for our needs and the needs of others: our family, neighborhood, and the world. For each need we say, "Lord, hear our prayer."

◆ All may add their own prayers here.

Let us pray: **Our Father . . . Amen.**

Father in heaven,
you bless us with your presence always.
May we know you
and have the courage to be open
to your work in our lives.
In Jesus Christ's name we pray.

Amen.

✢ All make the sign of the cross.

PRAYER FOR THURSDAY, JANUARY 4, 2024

OPENING

Simeon waited his whole life to see the Messiah, and in his faith he recognized him in the baby who was brought to the temple for dedication. Simeon's words at this encounter, called the Canticle of Simeon, have been chanted in Night Prayer. Today, we remember St. Elizabeth Ann Seton (1774–1821), an ordinary wife, mother, and teacher. She spent her life in love and service to others. She is the patron saint of Catholic schools.

✠ *All make the sign of the cross.*

In the name of the Father, and of the Son, and of the Holy Spirit. Amen.

PSALM

(For a longer psalm, see page xiii.)
Psalm 96:1–2A

Let the heavens be glad and the earth rejoice!

Let the heavens be glad and the earth rejoice!

O sing to the LORD a new song;
 sing to the LORD, all the earth.
Sing to the LORD; bless his name.

Let the heavens be glad and the earth rejoice!

◆ *All stand and sing* **Alleluia.**

GOSPEL

Luke 2:22b, 25a–b, 26–29a, 30–32

A reading from the holy Gospel according to Luke.

Mary and Joseph brought Jesus up to Jerusalem to present him to the Lord. Now there was a man in Jerusalem whose name was Simeon; this man was righteous and devout. It had been revealed to him by the Holy Spirit that he would not see death before he had seen the Lord's Messiah. Guided by the Spirit, Simeon came into the temple, and when the parents brought in the child Jesus to do for him what was customary under the law, Simeon took him in his arms and praised God, saying, "Master, now you are dismissing your servant in peace, for my eyes have seen your salvation, which you have prepared in the presence of all peoples, a light for revelation to the gentiles and for glory to your people Israel."

The Gospel of the Lord.

◆ *All sit and observe silence.*

FOR SILENT REFLECTION

Think about this silently in your heart. How do you live out your faith every day?

CLOSING PRAYER

Let us pray to God for our needs and the needs of others: our family, neighborhood, and the world. For each need we say, "Lord, hear our prayer."

◆ *All may add their own prayers here.*

Let us pray: **Our Father . . . Amen.**

Almighty God,
Mary and Joseph presented Jesus to you.
May your Son free our hearts from sin
and bring us into your holy presence.
We ask this through Christ our Lord.

Amen.

✠ *All make the sign of the cross.*

PRAYER FOR
FRIDAY, JANUARY 5, 2024

OPENING

The Holy Family were refugees forced to flee their homeland, a plight all too many people face today. How may we stand with the migrants in our world today? We continue to commemorate Catholic schools by honoring St. John Neumann (1811–1860). He was a bishop in Philadelphia who founded the first Catholic school system in the United States.

✚ All make the sign of the cross.

In the name of the Father, and of the Son, and of the Holy Spirit. Amen.

PSALM

(For a longer psalm, see page xiii.)
Psalm 96:1–2A

Let the heavens be glad and the earth rejoice!

Let the heavens be glad and the earth rejoice!

O sing to the Lord a new song;
　sing to the Lord, all the earth.
Sing to the Lord; bless his name.

Let the heavens be glad and the earth rejoice!

◆ All stand and sing **Alleluia.**

GOSPEL

Matthew 2:13–14ac, 15a, 19–21ac, 23a

A reading from the holy Gospel according to Matthew.

Now after the Magi had left, an angel of the Lord appeared to Joseph in a dream and said, "Get up, take the child and his mother, and flee to Egypt, and remain there until I tell you, for Herod is about to search for the child, to destroy him." Then Joseph got up, and went to Egypt, and remained there until the death of Herod.

When Herod died, an angel of the Lord suddenly appeared in a dream to Joseph in Egypt and said, "Get up, take the child and his mother, and go to the land of Israel, for those who were seeking the child's life are dead." Then Joseph got up, and went to the land of Israel. There he made his home in a town called Nazareth.

The Gospel of the Lord.

◆ All sit and observe silence.

FOR SILENT REFLECTION

Think about this silently in your heart. How might it feel to have to leave your homeland and start anew somewhere else?

CLOSING PRAYER

Let us pray to God for our needs and the needs of others: our family, neighborhood, and the world. For each need we say, "Lord, hear our prayer."

◆ All may add their own prayers here.

Let us pray: **Our Father . . . Amen.**

Faithful God,
you care for all those who are threatened by
　　　war or violence.
Help us to welcome the migrant and refugee.
Through Christ our Lord.

Amen.

✚ All make the sign of the cross.

PRAYER SERVICE FOR EPIPHANY

Prepare a leader, two readers, and three processors for this service. Perhaps someone can serve as the music leader for the songs and the "Alleluia." The class may need the words to the songs on a sheet of paper. The Gospel should be marked with ribbon or a book marker in the Bible. Place the Nativity scene, Bible, and candle prominently. Put the shepherds away, and place the Wise Men a short distance away, but within easy reach of the processors. This service suggests two songs.

MUSIC LEADER:
Our gathering song is "Joy to the World."

LEADER:

✤ All make the sign of the cross.

In the name of the Father and of the Son and of the Holy Spirit. Amen.

Let us pray:
We bless you and thank you, O God,
because, like the Wise men,
we understand the glory
of your gift of Jesus,
who is the Light of the World.

ALL: Amen.

◆ Gesture for all to sit.

READER 1: Psalm 148:1–2, 3–4, 9–10, 11–12, 13
Our refrain is: Praise the Lord!

ALL: Praise the Lord!

Praise the Lord from the heavens
  Praise him in the heights!

Praise him, all his angels;
  Praise him, all his host!

ALL: Praise the Lord!

Kings of the earth and all peoples,
  Princes and ruler of the earth!

Young men and women alike,
  Old and young together!

ALL: Praise the Lord!

◆ After a short silence the second lector moves to the Bible and gestures for all to stand and sing Alleluia.

READER 2: Matthew 2:9b–12
A reading from the holy Gospel according to Matthew.

◆ Read the Gospel passage from the Bible.

The Gospel of the Lord.

◆ All sit silently.

In silence, and one at a time, the processors bring the Wise Men forward and place them in the Nativity Scene.

MUSIC LEADER:
Let us stand and sing "We Three Kings."

LEADER:
Let us pray:
Most powerful Creator God,
everything that breathes
gives you glory.
Inspire us just as you did
the Wise Men
to see your glory in the Christ child.
We ask this in Jesus' name.

ALL: Amen.

PRAYER FOR THE WEEK
WITH A READING FROM THE GOSPEL FOR **SUNDAY, JANUARY 7, 2024**

OPENING

Today is the feast of the Epiphany. An *epiphany* is "a sudden manifestation or perception of the essential nature or meaning of something." The Magi sought the newborn king among rulers but found him in the vulnerable body of an infant. This could not be what they expected. It was an epiphany: a moment of understanding the essential nature of kingship, of power, of God. And they were overwhelmed with joy.

✢ All make the sign of the cross.

In the name of the Father, and of the Son, and of the Holy Spirit. Amen.

PSALM
(For a longer psalm, see page xiii.)
Psalm 96:1–2A

Let the heavens be glad and the earth rejoice!

Let the heavens be glad and the earth rejoice!

O sing to the Lord a new song;
  sing to the Lord, all the earth.
Sing to the Lord; bless his name.

Let the heavens be glad and the earth rejoice!

◆ All stand and sing **Alleluia.**

GOSPEL
Matthew 2:1–2, 8ab, 9bc, 10–11ab

A reading from the holy Gospel according to Matthew.

In the time of King Herod, after Jesus was born in Bethlehem of Judea, magi from the east came to Jerusalem, asking, "Where is the child who has been born king of the Jews? For we observed his star in the east, and have come to pay him homage." Then King Herod sent them to Bethlehem, saying, "Go and search diligently for the child." They set out, and there, ahead of them, went the star that they had seen in the east, until it stopped over the place where the child was. When they saw that the star had stopped, they were overwhelmed with joy. On entering the house, they saw the child with Mary his mother, and they knelt down and paid him homage.

The Gospel of the Lord.

◆ All sit and observe silence.

FOR SILENT REFLECTION

Think about this silently in your heart. The three Wise Men were overwhelmed with joy at seeing Jesus. Have you ever been overwhelmed with joy at seeing someone?

CLOSING PRAYER

Let us pray to God for our needs and the needs of others: our family, neighborhood, and the world. For each need we say, "Lord, hear our prayer."

◆ All may add their own prayers here.

Let us pray: **Our Father . . . Amen.**

Glory to you, O God!
By the light of a single star,
you guided all to the Light of the World.
May we live in harmony with one another.
We ask this through Christ our Lord.

Amen.

✢ All make the sign of the cross.

ORDINARY TIME WINTER

MONDAY, JANUARY 8, 2024 — TUESDAY, FEBRUARY 13, 2024

WINTER ORDINARY TIME

THE MEANING OF ORDINARY TIME

We've just celebrated the two great seasons of Advent and Christmas and now move back into Ordinary Time. Our seasons celebrate certain aspects of what we call Christ's "paschal mystery." For example, during the four weeks of Advent we focused on preparing to celebrate Christ's first coming in the incarnation and preparing for Christ's Second Coming at the parousia [par-oo-SEE-u]. The several weeks of Christmas focus on the wonder and joy of that first reality of God-with-us in Jesus. Now we move into the beginning of this year's ordered—that is, counted—Sundays of Ordinary Time. Each celebrates the paschal mystery in its entirety: Christ has died and is risen and will come again. Winter Ordinary Time is usually quite short, lasting only a few weeks.

The Prayers for the Week will reflect the Sunday Gospels, but during the week we will again "walk through the Bible." In week one we'll hear about Jesus' early years with the great stories of the presentation in the temple (an epiphany for Simeon and Anna), the finding in the temple, and Jesus' baptism. We end the week with Jesus' instruction to the apostles and to us to go out and proclaim the Gospel, the "good news." Week two examines the theme of rejoicing—what it means to rejoice in the works of the Lord. Week three looks at the transfiguration of Jesus by introducing Elijah and Moses in the Old Testament, relating St. Luke's story of the transfiguration and its implications for Jesus. As we move toward Lent, we hear Scriptures that point to the sacrament of confirmation; to the Body of Christ and the varied ways we live out the same call to holiness; and stories of Jesus' healing miracles.

PREPARING TO CELEBRATE ORDINARY TIME IN THE CLASSROOM

You will need to replace your white cloth with a green one, now that it is Ordinary Time again. Plan another procession with your students if they respond well to them. Otherwise, you might ask them if they have any ideas about how to change the cloths with care and dignity. You might be surprised at the depth of their suggestions.

SACRED SPACE

Place a clear bowl with water in the prayer space for the first week to honor the baptism of Jesus and our own.

A plain vase with a bunch of bare branches would be appropriate, or a potted plant. A spider plant or an ivy will withstand long weekends without too much attention. Give its care and watering to your students. Make a job chart and allow them to take turns watering the plant. Watching the plant grow will provide a concrete sign of the growth that can take place in our hearts during this liturgical season.

MOVEMENT AND GESTURE

Integrate the bowl of water into the daily prayer by bringing the bowl to the children or having them go to the bowl to make the sign of the cross. You might get holy water from the parish church but using tap water is also fine. Water is intrinsically holy. If the water becomes dirty it should be used to water plants or poured into the earth because it is holy by God's creation and by our use. See the suggestions for February 2, the Presentation of the Lord, below.

FESTIVITY IN SCHOOL AND HOME

From January 18 through 25, the Church joins with our Protestant brothers and sisters in the Week of Prayer for Christian Unity. A special prayer service, which may be used anytime during the week, is provided on page 164.

On February 2 we celebrate the feast of the Presentation of the Lord, also known as Candlemas. This is a beautiful feast to celebrate with children. If your school does not attend Mass that day, you might use the Scriptures from Monday and Tuesday of the first week of Ordinary Time. Before you begin prayer that day, dim the classroom lights and light a candle. Help the student proclaiming the Scripture to practice so that it can be done well, and allow time for the class to ponder the story together. If the children are old enough they might light and hold congregational candles (tapers) during the Gospel. (See more, under Prayers for Ordinary Time and A Note to Catechists.)

SACRED MUSIC

This would be the perfect time to learn how to sing one of the psalms. Psalm 27 ("The Lord Is My Light and My Salvation") and Psalm 23 ("The Lord Is My Shepherd") are two beautiful psalms that have many different musical settings. Children might also enjoy "This Little Light of Mine" and "I Want to Walk as a Child of the Light." Invite children to share favorite spiritual songs from their ethnic backgrounds and try singing songs from other countries ("We are Marching in the Light," "Pan de Vida," the round "Shalom Chevarim"). Also, don't forget to sing Alleluia often during these days. When Lent arrives, we will have to wait a long time before Easter when we can sing it again. The best Alleluia to sing is the one your parish uses before the Sunday Gospel.

PRAYERS FOR ORDINARY TIME

A tradition from the Liturgy of the Hours is to pray the *Canticle of Simeon* before going to bed. This is the prayer of the elderly man Simeon, who met the Holy Family in the Temple of Jerusalem when Mary and Joseph brought Jesus there as a baby. God had promised Simeon he would not die before he saw the Messiah. Simeon took the child Jesus in his arms and said this prayer:

"Master, now you are dismissing your servant
    in peace,
    according to your word;
for my eyes have seen your salvation,
    which you have prepared in the presence
        of all peoples,
    a light for revelation to the Gentiles
        and for glory to your people Israel."
            (Luke 2:29–32)

Introduce this prayer on February 2, the feast of the Presentation of the Lord. You may want to ask the children about certain key words in the prayer. Possible "wondering" questions could include: Why does Simeon call himself God's "servant"? Does the word "servant" recall anything that Mary once said? How did Simeon know that Jesus was a special baby? How is this small baby a "light" and a "glory"?

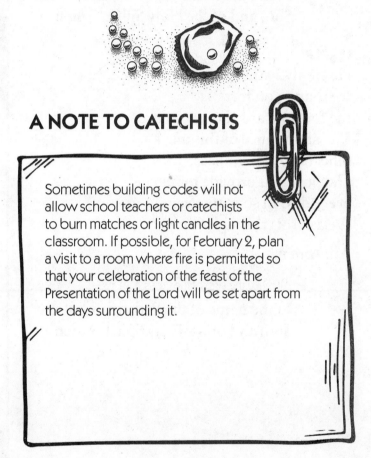

A NOTE TO CATECHISTS

Sometimes building codes will not allow school teachers or catechists to burn matches or light candles in the classroom. If possible, for February 2, plan a visit to a room where fire is permitted so that your celebration of the feast of the Presentation of the Lord will be set apart from the days surrounding it.

GRACE BEFORE MEALS
ORDINARY TIME • WINTER

LEADER:
Who is this King of glory?

ALL: The Lord, strong and mighty.

✢ All make the sign of the cross.

In the name of the Father, and of the Son, and of the Holy Spirit. Amen.

LEADER:
Heavenly Father,
we thank you for
the food we are about to share.
The abundance of this meal
reflects your goodness,
and how you provide for us
every day, in so many ways.
We ask this through Christ our Lord.

All: Amen.

✢ All make the sign of the cross.

In the name of the Father, and of the Son, and of the Holy Spirit. Amen.

PRAYER AT DAY'S END
ORDINARY TIME • WINTER

LEADER:
Your word is a light to my feet,

ALL: and a light to my path.

✢ All make the sign of the cross.

In the name of the Father, and of the Son, and of the Holy Spirit. Amen.

LEADER:
Heavenly Father,
thank you for this day of learning.
As we make our way home or
to other activities,
help us turn to you
for guidance in everything we do.
Keep us safe as we respond
to your Word in our hearts
as we meet with family and friends.
We ask this through Christ our Lord.

All: Amen.

✢ All make the sign of the cross.

In the name of the Father, and of the Son, and of the Holy Spirit. Amen.

153

PRAYER FOR
MONDAY, JANUARY 8, 2024

OPENING

Today is the Feast of the Baptism of the Lord. On that day by the Jordan River, the three Persons of the Trinity were shown at the same time. Through baptism, each of us has been brought into the love and fellowship of the Trinity, blessed by the Holy Spirit and called beloved of the Father.

✚ All make the sign of the cross.

In the name of the Father, and of the Son, and of the Holy Spirit. Amen.

PSALM
(For a longer psalm, see page xiii.)
Psalm 23:1–3a

I shall dwell in the house of the LORD my whole life long.

I shall dwell in the house of the LORD my whole life long.

The LORD is my shepherd; I shall not want.
    He makes me lie down in green pastures;
he leads me beside still waters;
    he restores my soul.

I shall dwell in the house of the LORD my whole life long.

◆ All stand and sing **Alleluia.**

GOSPEL
Mark 1:7–11

A reading from the holy Gospel according to Mark.

John the Baptist proclaimed, "The one who is more powerful than I is coming after me; I am not worthy to stoop down and untie the strap of his sandals. I have baptized you with water, but he will baptize you with the Holy Spirit."

In those days Jesus came from Nazareth of Galilee and was baptized by John in the Jordan. And just as he was coming up out of the water, he saw the heavens torn apart and the Spirit descending like a dove upon him. And a voice came from the heavens, "You are my Son, the Beloved; with you I am well pleased."

The Gospel of the Lord.

◆ All sit and observe silence.

FOR SILENT REFLECTION

Think about this silently in your heart. What do you remember or what have you been told about your own baptism?

CLOSING PRAYER

Let us pray to God for our needs and the needs of others: our family, neighborhood, and the world. For each need we say, "Lord, hear our prayer."

◆ All may add their own prayers here.

Let us pray: **Our Father . . . Amen.**

God our Father,
thank you for your great love
and for caring for us as your
    sons and daughters.
May our baptisms remind us to live good and
    holy lives.
Through Christ our Lord.

Amen.

✚ All make the sign of the cross.

PRAYER FOR TUESDAY, JANUARY 9, 2024

OPENING

When the infant Jesus was presented, an old prophetess named Anna was in the Temple. She spent her whole life there, worshipping day and night. She recognized the infant Jesus as the savior of his people, and spoke about him to others. We are called to the same faith as Anna: to recognize Jesus in our lives, and to speak about him to others. We are called to spread the good news of his redemption.

◆ All make the sign of the cross.

In the name of the Father, and of the Son, and of the Holy Spirit. Amen.

PSALM

(For a longer psalm, see page xiii.)
Psalm 23:1–3a

I shall dwell in the house of the LORD my whole life long.

I shall dwell in the house of the LORD my whole life long.

The LORD is my shepherd; I shall not want.
  He makes me lie down in green pastures;
he leads me beside still waters;
  he restores my soul.

I shall dwell in the house of the LORD my whole life long.

◆ All stand and sing **Alleluia.**

GOSPEL
Luke 2:36–38

A reading from the holy Gospel according to Luke.

In the temple, there was also a prophet, Anna the daughter of Phanuel [FAN-yoo-ehl], of the tribe of Asher. She was of a great age, having lived with her husband seven years after her marriage, then as a widow to the age of eighty-four. She never left the temple but worshiped there with fasting and prayer night and day. At that moment she came and began to praise God and to speak about the child to all who were looking for the redemption of Jerusalem.

The Gospel of the Lord.

◆ All sit and observe silence.

FOR SILENT REFLECTION

Think about this silently in your heart. How do you recognize Jesus in your life?

CLOSING PRAYER

Let us pray to God for our needs and the needs of others: our family, neighborhood, and the world. For each need we say, "Lord, hear our prayer."

◆ All may add their own prayers here.

Let us pray: **Our Father . . . Amen.**

Lord Jesus,
Anna saw you in the Temple
and knew your saving power.
Give us the eyes of faith so that we too might
    see as clearly.
Who live and reign with God the Father,
in the unity of the Holy Spirit,
God, for ever and ever.

Amen.

◆ All make the sign of the cross.

PRAYER FOR WEDNESDAY, JANUARY 10, 2024

OPENING

Imagine how Mary and Joseph felt as they searched for their lost young son. They found him in the temple after three days—three days of feeling worried and terrified. Mary will, years later, face another agonizing three-day vigil of loss. However, the hope of the resurrection, of God's eternal love, shines through the darkness.

✛ *All make the sign of the cross.*

In the name of the Father, and of the Son, and of the Holy Spirit. Amen.

PSALM

(For a longer psalm, see page xiii.)
Psalm 23:1–3a

I shall dwell in the house of the LORD my whole life long.

I shall dwell in the house of the LORD my whole life long.

The LORD is my shepherd; I shall not want.
　He makes me lie down in green pastures;
he leads me beside still waters;
　he restores my soul.

I shall dwell in the house of the LORD my whole life long.

◆ *All stand and sing* **Alleluia.**

GOSPEL

Luke 2:41–47

A reading from the holy Gospel according to Luke.

Now every year Jesus' parents went to Jerusalem for the festival of the Passover. And when he was twelve years old, they went up as usual for the festival. When the festival was ended and they started to return, the boy Jesus stayed behind in Jerusalem, but his parents were unaware of this. Assuming that he was in the group of travelers, they went a day's journey. Then they started to look for him among their relatives and friends. When they did not find him, they returned to Jerusalem to search for him. After three days they found Jesus in the temple, sitting among the teachers, listening to them and asking them questions. And all who heard him were amazed at his understanding and his answers.

The Gospel of the Lord.

◆ *All sit and observe silence.*

FOR SILENT REFLECTION

Think about this silently in your heart. How did you overcome feelings of loss or sadness?

CLOSING PRAYER

Let us pray to God for our needs and the needs of others: our family, neighborhood, and the world. For each need we say, "Lord, hear our prayer."

◆ *All may add their own prayers here.*

Let us pray: **Our Father . . . Amen.**

Lord God,
be with us in times of terror and loss,
and give us strength to keep searching
　　for the light.
Through Christ our Lord.
Amen.

✛ *All make the sign of the cross.*

PRAYER FOR THURSDAY, JANUARY 11, 2024

OPENING

In today's passage from the Acts of the Apostles, we hear Peter preaching that those who hear his call and do his will are his people. It was radical to preach the notion that all nations—not just the people of Israel—were invited to hear God's call. Jesus found his place with the lost and forgotten, the poor, the outcasts. He brought them hope and healing. As members of Christ's Body, we are called to do the same.

✚ All make the sign of the cross.

In the name of the Father, and of the Son, and of the Holy Spirit. Amen.

PSALM

(For a longer psalm, see page xiii.)
Psalm 23:1–3a

I shall dwell in the house of the LORD my whole life long.

I shall dwell in the house of the LORD my whole life long.

The LORD is my shepherd; I shall not want.
   He makes me lie down in green pastures;
he leads me beside still waters;
   he restores my soul.

I shall dwell in the house of the LORD my whole life long.

READING

Acts 10:34–38

A reading from the Acts of the Apostles.

Then Peter began to speak to them: "I truly understand that God shows no partiality, but in every people anyone who fears him and practices righteousness is acceptable to him. You know the message he sent to the people of Israel, preaching peace by Jesus Christ—he is Lord of all. That message spread throughout Judea, beginning in Galilee after the baptism that John announced: how God anointed Jesus of Nazareth with the Holy Spirit and with power; how he went about doing good and healing all who were oppressed by the devil, for God was with him.

The Word of the Lord.

◆ All observe silence.

FOR SILENT REFLECTION

Think about this silently in your heart. Is there someone who needs to feel hope? How can you bring light to someone this week?

CLOSING PRAYER

Let us pray to God for our needs and the needs of others: our family, neighborhood, and the world. For each need we say, "Lord, hear our prayer."

◆ All may add their own prayers here.

Let us pray: **Our Father . . . Amen.**

Lord Jesus,
you came to bring life to the world.
Help us to share the light of hope with
      all those in need.
In your name, we pray.
Amen.

✚ All make the sign of the cross.

PRAYER FOR
FRIDAY, JANUARY 12, 2024

OPENING

In the Ascension, Jesus was taken body and soul to the Father. Our humanity, the glorified human body of Christ, is seated at the right hand of the Father. And all of us, sharing that humanity for generations past and yet to come, now live as Christ's body on earth, as his hands and feet and voice to proclaim his good news and do his work in the world.

✢ All make the sign of the cross.

In the name of the Father, and of the Son, and of the Holy Spirit. Amen.

PSALM
(For a longer psalm, see page xiii.)
Psalm 23:1–3a

I shall dwell in the house of the Lord my whole life long.

I shall dwell in the house of the Lord my whole life long.

The Lord is my shepherd; I shall not want.
　He makes me lie down in green pastures;
he leads me beside still waters;
　he restores my soul.

I shall dwell in the house of the Lord my whole life long.

◆ All stand and sing **Alleluia.**

GOSPEL
Mark 16:14a, 15–16a, 17, 19, 20

A reading from the holy Gospel according to Mark.

Later Jesus appeared to the eleven themselves as they were sitting at the table. And he said to them, "Go into all the world and proclaim the good news to the whole creation. The one who believes and is baptized will be saved. And these signs will accompany those who believe: by using my name they will cast out demons; they will speak in new tongues."

So then the Lord Jesus, after he had spoken to them, was taken up into heaven and sat down at the right hand of God. And they went out and proclaimed the good news everywhere, while the Lord worked with them and confirmed the message by the signs that accompanied it.

The Gospel of the Lord.

◆ All sit and observe silence.

FOR SILENT REFLECTION

Think about this silently in your heart. Share something about Jesus with someone else today.

CLOSING PRAYER

Let us pray to God for our needs and the needs of others: our family, neighborhood, and the world. For each need we say, "Lord, hear our prayer."

◆ All may add their own prayers here.

Let us pray: **Our Father . . . Amen.**

Lord Jesus,
help us to do your work and
　speak your words every day.
Who live and reign with God the Father,
in the unity of the Holy Spirit,
God for ever and ever.

Amen.

✢ All make the sign of the cross.

PRAYER FOR THE WEEK
WITH A READING FROM THE GOSPEL FOR **SUNDAY, JANUARY 14, 2024**

OPENING

What are you looking for? All believers must grapple with this question throughout life. As we move into Ordinary Time, we have an opportunity to grow in our faith. We learn more about Jesus' life and teachings. Listen as we hear about Jesus' first disciples.

✣ All make the sign of the cross.

In the name of the Father, and of the Son, and of the Holy Spirit. Amen.

PSALM
(For a longer psalm, see page xiii.)
Psalm 23:1–3a

I shall dwell in the house of the LORD my whole life long.

I shall dwell in the house of the LORD my whole life long.

The LORD is my shepherd; I shall not want.
    He makes me lie down in green pastures;
he leads me beside still waters;
    he restores my soul.

I shall dwell in the house of the LORD my whole life long.

◆ All stand and sing **Alleluia.**

GOSPEL
John 1:35–38c, 40–42

A reading from the holy Gospel according to John.

John was standing with two of his disciples, and as he watched Jesus walk by he exclaimed, "Look, here is the Lamb of God!" The two disciples heard him say this, and they followed Jesus. When Jesus turned and saw them following, he said to them, "What are you looking for?" They said to him, "Rabbi" [RAB-ī] (which translated means Teacher). One of the two who heard John speak and followed him was Andrew, Simon Peter's brother. He first found his brother Simon and said to him, "We have found the Messiah" [meh-SĪ-uh] (which is translated Anointed). He brought Simon to Jesus, who looked at him and said, "You are Simon son of John. You are to be called Cephas" [SEE-fuhs] (which is translated Peter).

The Gospel of the Lord.

◆ All sit and observe silence.

FOR SILENT REFLECTION

Think about this silently in your heart. What are you looking for?

CLOSING PRAYER

Let us pray to God for our needs and the needs of others: our family, neighborhood, and the world. For each need we say, "Lord, hear our prayer."

◆ All may add their own prayers here.

Let us pray: **Our Father . . . Amen.**

Christ Jesus,
may we joyfully answer your call
    to follow you.
Who live and reign with God the Father,
in the unity of the Holy Spirit,
God for ever and ever.

Amen.

✣ All make the sign of the cross.

PRAYER SERVICE
DR. MARTIN LUTHER KING JR.

Place an image of Martin Luther King in the sacred space. Prepare a leader, four readers, and a song leader. If possible, sing the refrain of "Let Justice Roll Like a River," or some other suitable song. Be sure to keep some silence where it's indicated. Since the Scriptures are abridged, copy them and put them in the Bible marked with ribbons. Put the MLK quotes in a binder.

LEADER:

◆ Gesture for all to stand.

✚ All make the sign of the cross.

In the name of the Father, and of the Son, and of the Holy Spirit. Amen

LEADER:
We remember and celebrate
Dr. Martin Luther King,
who worked for the just treatment
of African Americans.
Even though he received many death threats,
he spoke out courageously
and taught us how to make changes
through non-violent protest.

◆ Gesture for all to sit.

READER 1
From Dr. King's "I Have a Dream" Speech:
"I have a dream that my four little
children will one day live in a nation
where they will not be judged
by the color of their skin,
but by the content of their character."

◆ Observe some silence.

READER 2
A quote from Dr. King's book *Strength to Love*:
"Returning hate for hate multiplies hate, adding deeper darkness to a night already devoid of stars. Darkness cannot drive out darkness; only light can do that. Hate cannot drive out hate; only love can do that."

◆ Observe some silence.

READER 3 Colossians 3:12, 14–15a
A reading from St. Paul's Letter to
the Colossians.

As God's chosen ones, holy and beloved, clothe yourselves with compassion, kindness, humility, meekness, and patience. Above all, clothe yourselves with love, which binds everything together in perfect harmony. And let the peace of Christ rule in your hearts.

The Word of the Lord.

◆ Observe some silence.

LEADER:

◆ Gesture for all to stand.

LEADER:
Let us pray.
O God of justice and love,
give us the courage
to challenge injustice wherever we see it.
Help us be open to all your children
and not let race, religion,
or anything else divide us.
We ask this in Jesus' name.

ALL: Amen

✚ All make the sign of the cross.

In the name of the Father, and of the Son, and of the Holy Spirit. Amen.

◆ All stand to sing the song.

PRAYER FOR TUESDAY, JANUARY 16, 2024

OPENING

This week, we will reflect on what it means to rejoice in the works of the Lord. In today's reading, we hear about Solomon succeeding King David to the throne. Like his ancestor Jacob before him, Solomon was not the oldest son, and yet he received the blessing and the inheritance. And after he was anointed king, the people followed him and rejoiced.

✚ *All make the sign of the cross.*

In the name of the Father, and of the Son, and of the Holy Spirit. Amen.

PSALM

(For a longer psalm, see page xiii.)
Psalm 23:1–3a

I shall dwell in the house of the Lord my whole life long.

I shall dwell in the house of the Lord my whole life long.

The Lord is my shepherd; I shall not want.
  He makes me lie down in green pastures;
he leads me beside still waters;
  he restores my soul.

I shall dwell in the house of the Lord my whole life long.

READING

1 Kings 1:1, 32acd, 33, 38ae, 39ac, 40

A reading from the First Book of Kings.

King David was old and advanced in years, and although they covered him with clothes, he could not get warm. King David said, "Summon to me the priest Zadok [ZAY-dok], [and] the prophet Nathan." The king said to them, "Take with you the servants of your lord and have my son Solomon ride on my own mule and bring him down to Gihon." So the priest Zadok went down and had Solomon ride on King David's mule. There the priest Zadok took the horn of oil from the tent and anointed Solomon. And all the people said, "Long live King Solomon!" And all the people went up following him, playing on pipes and rejoicing with great joy, so that the earth quaked at their noise.

The Word of the Lord.

◆ *All observe silence.*

FOR SILENT REFLECTION

Think about this silently in your heart. How has God blessed you? How can you show your joy?

CLOSING PRAYER

Let us pray to God for our needs and the needs of others: our family, neighborhood, and the world. For each need we say, "Lord, hear our prayer."

◆ *All may add their own prayers here.*

Let us pray: **Our Father . . . Amen.**

God our Father,
we rejoice in the many blessings you have
  showered upon us,
and give you thanks!
Through Jesus Christ our Lord.

Amen.

✚ *All make the sign of the cross.*

PRAYER FOR WEDNESDAY, JANUARY 17, 2024

OPENING

In the first year of his reign, King Hezekiah [hehz-eh-Kī-uh] went to great pains to restore the unity of the Passover feast, and with it, the unity of the kingdom of Israel, which had splintered following the death of Solomon. Today's saint is Anthony of Egypt, a monk who left his solitary life to fight for the unity of faith and worship in the midst of the Arian controversy which divided the fourth-century Church.

✢ All make the sign of the cross.

In the name of the Father, and of the Son, and of the Holy Spirit. Amen.

PSALM
(For a longer psalm, see page xiii.)
Psalm 23:1–3a

I shall dwell in the house of the LORD my whole life long.

I shall dwell in the house of the LORD my whole life long.

The LORD is my shepherd; I shall not want.
    He makes me lie down in green pastures;
he leads me beside still waters;
    he restores my soul.

I shall dwell in the house of the LORD my whole life long.

READING
2 Chronicles 30:1acd, 13a, 21, 25

A reading from the First Book of Kings.

King Hezekiah [hehz-eh-Kī-uh] sent word to all Israel and Judah that they should come to the house of the LORD at Jerusalem, to keep the Passover to the LORD the God of Israel. Many people came together in Jerusalem to keep the Festival of Unleavened Bread in the second month. The people of Israel who were present at Jerusalem kept the Festival of Unleavened Bread seven days with great gladness, and the Levites [LEE-vīts] and the priests praised the LORD day by day, accompanied by loud instruments for the LORD. The whole assembly of Judah, the priests and the Levites, and the whole assembly that came out of Israel, and the resident aliens who came out of the land of Israel, and the resident aliens who lived in Judah rejoiced.

The Word of the Lord.

◆ All observe silence.

FOR SILENT REFLECTION

Think about this silently in your heart. Why did the Israelites rejoice in today's reading?

CLOSING PRAYER

Let us pray to God for our needs and the needs of others: our family, neighborhood, and the world. For each need we say, "Lord, hear our prayer."

◆ All may add their own prayers here.

Let us pray: **Our Father . . . Amen.**

Lord God,
we rejoice in our unity
and beg you to preserve your people in peace.
We pray in Christ's name.

Amen.

✢ All make the sign of the cross.

PRAYER FOR
THURSDAY, JANUARY 18, 2024

OPENING

The world tells us to live in ways that oppose the Beatitudes. Some of life's goals are to pursue security and happiness. But Jesus tells us that this is a false security and true happiness comes from God. Build your life on God, rejoice, and be glad!

✚ All make the sign of the cross.

In the name of the Father, and of the Son, and of the Holy Spirit. Amen.

PSALM

(For a longer psalm, see page xiii.)
Psalm 23:1–3a

I shall dwell in the house of the Lord my whole life long.

I shall dwell in the house of the Lord my whole life long.

The Lord is my shepherd; I shall not want.
 He makes me lie down in green pastures;
he leads me beside still waters;
 he restores my soul.

I shall dwell in the house of the Lord my whole life long.

◆ All stand and sing **Alleluia.**

GOSPEL

Matthew 5:2–12a

A reading from the holy Gospel according to Matthew.

Jesus began to speak and taught them, saying: "Blessed are the poor in spirit, for theirs is the kingdom of heaven. Blessed are those who mourn, for they will be comforted. Blessed are the meek, for they will inherit the earth. Blessed are those who hunger and thirst for righteousness, for they will be filled. Blessed are the merciful, for they will receive mercy. Blessed are the pure in heart, for they will see God. Blessed are the peacemakers, for they will be called children of God. Blessed are those who are persecuted for the sake of righteousness, for theirs is the kingdom of heaven. Blessed are you when people revile you and persecute you and utter all kinds of evil against you falsely on my account. Rejoice and be glad, for your reward is great in heaven."

The Gospel of the Lord.

◆ All sit and observe silence.

FOR SILENT REFLECTION

Think about this silently in your heart. How is your life built on God?

CLOSING PRAYER

Let us pray to God for our needs and the needs of others: our family, neighborhood, and the world. For each need we say, "Lord, hear our prayer."

◆ All may add their own prayers here.

Let us pray: **Our Father . . . Amen.**

Father in heaven,
thank you for teaching us the right ways
and to orient our lives toward living
 the Beatitudes.
We pray in Christ's name.

Amen.

✚ All make the sign of the cross.

PRAYER SERVICE
WEEK OF PRAYER FOR CHRISTIAN UNITY

Prepare four leaders and a song leader for this service. The second leader will need a Bible to read the Scripture passage and may need help finding and practicing it.

FIRST LEADER:
May the peace of Christ, who unites brothers and sisters around the world in his name, be with us, now and for ever.

ALL: Amen.

◆ All make the sign of the cross.

Let us pray:
Almighty God,
Creator of all wisdom,
you have made each of us
in your image
to reflect your many gifts.
We have been blessed through the waters of Baptism,
to join with all Christians in the loving power of
Father, Son, and Spirit.
Send your Spirit to guide us
as we seek your truth
and become united with Jesus
as our leader in faith.
We ask this through Christ our Lord.

ALL: Amen.

◆ All stand and sing **Alleluia**.

SECOND LEADER: John 15:12–17
A reading from the holy Gospel according to John.

◆ Read the Gospel passage from the Bible.

The Gospel of the Lord.

Let us pause and pray in silence for peace and unity among all Christians.

◆ Observe a time of silence.

THIRD LEADER:
Lord God,
you have made yourself known
to all the nations.
We declare your handiwork through
acts of peace and social justice
that assist all in need.
Guide us with your ways of peace.
Give us the courage to seek solutions
that benefit all
and that serve people
to build dignity and respect
for one another.
We ask this through Christ our Lord.

ALL: Amen.

FOURTH LEADER:
Now let us offer to one another a sign of Christ's peace.

◆ All offer one another a sign of peace.

And may the Lord bless us,

◆ All make the sign of the cross.

protect us from all evil,
and bring us to everlasting life.

ALL: Amen.

PRAYER FOR FRIDAY, JANUARY 19, 2024

OPENING

It is impossible to be happy forever. We will all experience times of sadness, of confusion, of pain, of fear, even of boredom. However, joy is the current that runs under the surface of the Christian life. Joy is the right of our baptism. Even though we may grieve and suffer pain, we can still rejoice, because the Lord is with us. The Lord hears our cries. The Lord feels our pain. The Lord will give us peace.

✦ All make the sign of the cross.

In the name of the Father, and of the Son, and of the Holy Spirit. Amen.

PSALM

(For a longer psalm, see page xiii.)
Psalm 23:1–3a

I shall dwell in the house of the LORD my whole life long.

I shall dwell in the house of the LORD my whole life long.

The LORD is my shepherd; I shall not want.
   He makes me lie down in green pastures;
he leads me beside still waters;
   he restores my soul.

I shall dwell in the house of the LORD my whole life long.

READING

Philippians 3:17, 20; 4:4–7

A reading from the Letter to the Philippians [fih-LIP-ee-uhnz].

Brothers and sisters, join in imitating me, and observe those who live according to the example you have in us. But our citizenship is in heaven, and it is from there that we are expecting a Savior, the Lord Jesus Christ. Rejoice in the Lord always; again I will say, Rejoice. Let your gentleness be known to everyone. The Lord is near. Do not be anxious about anything, but in everything by prayer and supplication with thanksgiving let your requests be made known to God. And the peace of God, which surpasses all understanding, will guard your hearts and your minds in Christ Jesus.

The Word of the Lord.

◆ All observe silence.

FOR SILENT REFLECTION

Think about this silently in your heart. What is the difference between happiness and joy?

CLOSING PRAYER

Let us pray to God for our needs and the needs of others: our family, neighborhood, and the world. For each need we say, "Lord, hear our prayer."

◆ All may add their own prayers here.

Let us pray: **Our Father . . . Amen.**

Lord God,
we rejoice in your love
and wait for the day when we might
   live in you forever!
Through Christ our Lord.

Amen.

✦ All make the sign of the cross.

PRAYER FOR THE WEEK
WITH A READING FROM THE GOSPEL FOR **SUNDAY, JANUARY 21, 2024**

OPENING

After hearing Jesus' call, four men immediately followed him. They left their livelihood, their families, and their whole life without hesitation. The invitation to us may not be as clear as the one in today's Gospel, but it is there.

✠ All make the sign of the cross.

In the name of the Father, and of the Son, and of the Holy Spirit. Amen.

PSALM

(For a longer psalm, see page xiii.)
Psalm 23:1–3a

I shall dwell in the house of the LORD my whole life long.

I shall dwell in the house of the LORD my whole life long.

The LORD is my shepherd; I shall not want.
   He makes me lie down in green pastures;
he leads me beside still waters;
   he restores my soul.

I shall dwell in the house of the LORD my whole life long.

◆ All stand and sing **Alleluia.**

GOSPEL
Mark 1:14–20

A reading from the holy Gospel according to Mark.

Now after John was arrested, Jesus came to Galilee proclaiming the good news of God and saying, "The time is fulfilled, and the kingdom of God has come near; repent, and believe in the good news."

As Jesus passed along the Sea of Galilee, he saw Simon and his brother Andrew casting a net into the sea, for they were fishers. And Jesus said to them, "Follow me and I will make you fishers of people." And immediately they left their nets and followed him. As he went a little farther, he saw James son of Zebedee and his brother John, who were in their boat mending the nets. Immediately he called them, and they left their father Zebedee in the boat with the hired men and followed him.

The Gospel of the Lord.

◆ All sit and observe silence.

FOR SILENT REFLECTION

Think about this silently in your heart. What is Jesus calling you to do?

CLOSING PRAYER

Let us pray to God for our needs and the needs of others: our family, neighborhood, and the world. For each need we say, "Lord, hear our prayer."

◆ All may add their own prayers here.

Let us pray: **Our Father . . . Amen.**

Lord Jesus,
you invite each of us to come to you.
Open our hearts and ears to hear you
   and respond by following you.
Who live and reign with God the Father,
in the unity of the Holy Spirit,
God, for ever and ever.

Amen.

✠ All make the sign of the cross.

PRAYER FOR MONDAY, JANUARY 22, 2024

OPENING

The presence of the Lord is accompanied by wind, earthquake, and fire. But these things only attract attention—the presence of God is not in them. The voice of the Lord is still and small, easy to miss if one is not listening. The presence of the Lord is unknowable, a mystery. Today we observe of a day of prayer for the unborn, and remember all those whose voices have never been heard on this earth.

✠ All make the sign of the cross.

In the name of the Father, and of the Son, and of the Holy Spirit. Amen.

PSALM

(For a longer psalm, see page xiii.)
Psalm 23:1–3a

I shall dwell in the house of the LORD my whole life long.

I shall dwell in the house of the LORD my whole life long.

The LORD is my shepherd; I shall not want.
   He makes me lie down in green pastures;
he leads me beside still waters;
   he restores my soul.

I shall dwell in the house of the LORD my whole life long.

READING

1 Kings 19:11–12, 13c–14c, 14f–g

A reading from the First Book of Kings.

The angel of the LORD said to Elijah, "Go out and stand on the mountain before the LORD, for the LORD is about to pass by." Now there was a great wind, so strong that it was splitting mountains and breaking rocks in pieces before the LORD, but the LORD was not in the wind, and after the wind an earthquake, but the LORD was not in the earthquake, and after the earthquake a fire, but the LORD was not in the fire, and after the fire a sound of sheer silence. Then there came a voice to him that said, "What are you doing here, Elijah?" He answered, "I have been very zealous for the LORD, the God of hosts, for the Israelites have forsaken your covenant. I alone am left, and they are seeking my life, to take it away."

The Word of the Lord.

◆ All observe silence.

FOR SILENT REFLECTION

Think about this silently in your heart. How do you listen for the voice of God?

CLOSING PRAYER

Let us pray to God for our needs and the needs of others: our family, neighborhood, and the world. For each need we say, "Lord, hear our prayer."

◆ All may add their own prayers here.

Let us pray: **Our Father . . . Amen.**

We give you thanks, O loving God,
for the gift of life.
We pray for all the unborn and those
   who need your protection.
Through Christ our Lord.

Amen.

✠ All make the sign of the cross.

PRAYER FOR
TUESDAY, JANUARY 23, 2024

OPENING

The Lord spoke to Moses in the fire, but as with Elijah, he was not in the fire. He spoke to Moses "face to face" and yet his presence did not have a face. The presence of the Lord is mysterious; it is as intimate as a close conversation and as intimidating as a burning bush. God appeared to Moses and the people of Israel on a mountain and in a bush. Today we remember St. Marianne Cope, who recognized the presence of the Lord in those afflicted with leprosy in Hawaii. She cared for them, and established a hospital and school for the people on Maui.

✚ All make the sign of the cross.

In the name of the Father, and of the Son, and of the Holy Spirit. Amen.

PSALM
(For a longer psalm, see page xiii.)
Psalm 23:1–3a

I shall dwell in the house of the LORD my whole life long.

I shall dwell in the house of the LORD my whole life long.

The LORD is my shepherd; I shall not want.
　He makes me lie down in green pastures;
he leads me beside still waters;
　he restores my soul.

I shall dwell in the house of the LORD my whole life long.

READING
Deuteronomy 5:1–5

A reading from the Book of Deuteronomy [doo-ter-AH-nuh-mee].

Moses convened all Israel and said to them: Hear, O Israel, the statutes and ordinances that I am addressing to you today; you shall learn them and observe them diligently. The LORD our God made a covenant with us at Horeb. Not with our ancestors did the LORD make this covenant but with us, who are all of us here alive today. The LORD spoke with you face to face at the mountain, out of the fire. (At that time I was standing between the LORD and you to declare to you the word of the LORD, for you were afraid because of the fire and did not go up the mountain.)

The Word of the Lord.

◆ All observe silence.

FOR SILENT REFLECTION

Think about this silently in your heart. When have you felt the presence of God?

CLOSING PRAYER

Let us pray to God for our needs and the needs of others: our family, neighborhood, and the world. For each need we say, "Lord, hear our prayer."

◆ All may add their own prayers here.

Let us pray: **Our Father . . . Amen.**

Holy God,
help us to follow your commandments
and live in service to you and others.
Through Christ our Lord.

Amen.

✚ All make the sign of the cross.

PRAYER FOR
WEDNESDAY, JANUARY 24, 2024

OPENING

Today we remember St. Francis de Sales (1567–1622), who was born into a French noble family and decided to become a priest. St. Francis believed that laypeople should have an active role in the church. He trained them to teach catechism classes.

✛ All make the sign of the cross.

In the name of the Father, and of the Son, and of the Holy Spirit. Amen.

PSALM
(For a longer psalm, see page xiii.)
Psalm 23:1–3a

I shall dwell in the house of the LORD my whole life long.

I shall dwell in the house of the LORD my whole life long.

The LORD is my shepherd; I shall not want.
　He makes me lie down in green pastures;
he leads me beside still waters;
　he restores my soul.

I shall dwell in the house of the LORD my whole life long.

◆ All stand and sing **Alleluia.**

GOSPEL
Mark 9:2–8

A reading from the holy Gospel according to Mark.

Six days later, Jesus took with him Peter and James and John and led them up a high mountain apart, by themselves. And he was transfigured before them, and his clothes became dazzling bright, such as no one on earth could brighten them. And there appeared to them Elijah with Moses, who were talking with Jesus. Then Peter said to Jesus, "Rabbi [RAB-Ī], it is good for us to be here; let us set up three tents: one for you, one for Moses, and one for Elijah." He did not know what to say, for they were terrified. Then a cloud overshadowed them, and from the cloud there came a voice, "This is my Son, the Beloved; listen to him!" Suddenly when they looked around, they saw no one with them anymore, but only Jesus.

The Gospel of the Lord.

◆ All sit and observe silence.

FOR SILENT REFLECTION

Think about this silently in your heart. What questions do you have about your faith? Bring them to prayer and to your teacher, parents, or priest.

CLOSING PRAYER

Let us pray to God for our needs and the needs of others: our family, neighborhood, and the world. For each need we say, "Lord, hear our prayer."

◆ All may add their own prayers here.

Let us pray: **Our Father . . . Amen.**

O Lord,
grant us wisdom to know the truth
　　and follow your will.
Through Christ our Lord.

Amen.

✛ All make the sign of the cross.

PRAYER FOR
THURSDAY, JANUARY 25, 2024

OPENING

Today is the feast of the conversion of St. Paul, who met the Lord in an unexpected fashion. A relentless persecutor of Christians, he was suddenly blinded on the way to Damascus. He immediately heeded the call of God and changed his life. St. Paul, the three disciples in today's Gospel, and all the saints share this in common: they heard the call of God and changed their lives to follow him.

✚ All make the sign of the cross.

In the name of the Father, and of the Son, and of the Holy Spirit. Amen.

PSALM

(For a longer psalm, see page xiii.)
Psalm 23:1–3a

I shall dwell in the house of the LORD my whole life long.

I shall dwell in the house of the LORD my whole life long.

The LORD is my shepherd; I shall not want.
   He makes me lie down in green pastures;
he leads me beside still waters;
   he restores my soul.

I shall dwell in the house of the LORD my whole life long.

◆ All stand and sing **Alleluia.**

GOSPEL

Mark 9:9–10, 30–32

A reading from the holy Gospel according to Mark.

As Peter, James, John, and Jesus were coming down the mountain, Jesus ordered them to tell no one about what they had seen, until after the Son of Man had risen from the dead. So they kept the matter to themselves, questioning what this rising from the dead could mean.

Jesus and his disciples went on from there and passed through Galilee. He did not want anyone to know it, for he was teaching his disciples, saying to them, "The Son of Man is to be betrayed into human hands, and they will kill him, and three days after being killed, he will rise again." But they did not understand what he was saying and were afraid to ask him.

The Gospel of the Lord.

◆ All sit and observe silence.

FOR SILENT REFLECTION

Think about this silently in your heart. How can you change your life in response to God?

CLOSING PRAYER

Let us pray to God for our needs and the needs of others: our family, neighborhood, and the world. For each need we say, "Lord, hear our prayer."

◆ All may add their own prayers here.

Let us pray: **Our Father . . . Amen.**

God of love and mercy,
you reveal yourself to us in varied ways.
May we follow you in faith and love.
Through Christ our Lord.

Amen.

✚ All make the sign of the cross.

PRAYER FOR
FRIDAY, JANUARY 26, 2024

OPENING

Jesus offered an important lesson to those who wish to follow him: to be his disciple is not to seek importance but to seek humility. Today we celebrate the feast of Sts. Timothy and Titus, companions and followers of St. Paul. They helped spread Jesus' teachings to the early Christian communities.

✢ All make the sign of the cross.

In the name of the Father, and of the Son, and of the Holy Spirit. Amen.

PSALM
(For a longer psalm, see page xiii.)
Psalm 23:1–3a

I shall dwell in the house of the LORD my whole life long.

I shall dwell in the house of the LORD my whole life long.

The LORD is my shepherd; I shall not want.
   He makes me lie down in green pastures;
he leads me beside still waters;
   he restores my soul.

I shall dwell in the house of the LORD my whole life long.

◆ All stand and sing **Alleluia**.

GOSPEL
Mark 9:33–37

A reading from the holy Gospel according to Mark.

Then Jesus and his disciples came to Capernaum [kuh-PER-nee-*m], and when he was in the house he asked them, "What were you arguing about on the way?'" But they were silent, for on the way they had argued with one another who was the greatest. Jesus sat down, called the twelve, and said to them, "Whoever wants to be first must be last of all and servant of all." Then he took a little child and put it among them, and taking it in his arms he said to them, "Whoever welcomes one such child in my name welcomes me, and whoever welcomes me welcomes not me but the one who sent me."

The Gospel of the Lord.

◆ All sit and observe silence.

FOR SILENT REFLECTION

Think about this silently in your heart. What does it mean to be humble?

CLOSING PRAYER

Let us pray to God for our needs and the needs of others: our family, neighborhood, and the world. For each need we say, "Lord, hear our prayer."

◆ All may add their own prayers here.

Let us pray: **Our Father . . . Amen.**

O God,
help us to know that putting others first
also means putting you first.
May we live as your obedient
   sons and daughters.
In Christ Jesus' name we pray.

Amen.

✢ All make the sign of the cross.

PRAYER FOR THE WEEK
WITH A READING FROM THE GOSPEL FOR **SUNDAY, JANUARY 28, 2024**

OPENING

A synagogue is the Jewish place of worship, instruction, and prayer. The Sabbath is the Jewish holy day of the week. The people in the synagogue were impressed that Jesus taught with authority, or with power.

✢ All make the sign of the cross.

In the name of the Father, and of the Son, and of the Holy Spirit. Amen.

PSALM

(For a longer psalm, see page xiii.)
Psalm 23:1–3a

I shall dwell in the house of the LORD my whole life long.

I shall dwell in the house of the LORD my whole life long.

The LORD is my shepherd; I shall not want.
   He makes me lie down in green pastures;
he leads me beside still waters;
   he restores my soul.

I shall dwell in the house of the LORD my whole life long.

◆ All stand and sing **Alleluia.**

GOSPEL

Mark 1:21–27

A reading from the holy Gospel according to Mark.

Jesus and his disciples went to Capernaum [kuh-PER-nee-*m], and when the Sabbath came, Jesus entered the synagogue and taught. They were astounded at his teaching, for he taught them as one having authority and not as the scribes. Just then there was in their synagogue a man with an unclean spirit, and he cried out, "What have you to do with us, Jesus of Nazareth? Have you come to destroy us? I know who you are, the Holy One of God." But Jesus rebuked him, saying, "Be quiet and come out of him!" And the unclean spirit, convulsing him and crying with a loud voice, came out of him. They were all amazed, and they kept on asking one another, "What is this? A new teaching—with authority! He commands even the unclean spirits, and they obey him."

The Gospel of the Lord.

◆ All sit and observe silence.

FOR SILENT REFLECTION

Think about this silently in your heart. How does Jesus amaze you?

CLOSING PRAYER

Let us pray to God for our needs and the needs of others: our family, neighborhood, and the world. For each need we say, "Lord, hear our prayer."

◆ All may add their own prayers here.

Let us pray: **Our Father . . . Amen.**

God our Father,
thank you for sending us Jesus.
May we glorify you and live by your will.
Through Christ our Lord.

Amen.

✢ All make the sign of the cross.

PRAYER FOR MONDAY, JANUARY 29, 2024

OPENING

In Jesus' day, the Jews did not like tax collectors because they were thought to be greedy and supporters of the Romans. But Jesus welcomed sinners and tax collectors—his ministry welcomed all into community with him. This was hard for some to understand.

✢ All make the sign of the cross.

In the name of the Father, and of the Son, and of the Holy Spirit. Amen.

PSALM

(For a longer psalm, see page xiii.)
Psalm 23:1–3a

I shall dwell in the house of the LORD my whole life long.

I shall dwell in the house of the LORD my whole life long.

The LORD is my shepherd; I shall not want.
 He makes me lie down in green pastures;
he leads me beside still waters;
 he restores my soul.

I shall dwell in the house of the LORD my whole life long.

◆ All stand and sing **Alleluia.**

GOSPEL

Mark 2:14–17

A reading from the holy Gospel according to Mark.

As Jesus was walking along, he saw Levi [LEE-vī] son of Alphaeus [AL-fee-uhs] sitting at the tax-collection station, and he said to him, "Follow me." And he got up and followed him. And as he sat at dinner in Levi's house, many tax collectors and sinners were also sitting with Jesus and his disciples, for there were many who followed him. When the scribes of the Pharisees [FAYR-uh-seez] saw that he was eating with sinners and tax collectors, they said to his disciples, "Why does he eat with tax collectors and sinners?" When Jesus heard this, he said to them, "Those who are well have no need of a physician but those who are sick; I have not come to call the righteous but sinners."

The Gospel of the Lord.

◆ All sit and observe silence.

FOR SILENT REFLECTION

Think about this silently in your heart. Why did Jesus call sinners to him?

CLOSING PRAYER

Let us pray to God for our needs and the needs of others: our family, neighborhood, and the world. For each need we say, "Lord, hear our prayer."

◆ All may add their own prayers here.

Let us pray: **Our Father . . . Amen.**

God of all that is good,
you welcome us all,
 though we are not perfect.
May we be as welcoming to others.
Through Christ our Lord.

Amen.

✢ All make the sign of the cross.

PRAYER FOR
TUESDAY, JANUARY 30, 2024

OPENING

Moses was instructed make a special, scented oil that would bestow holiness on those anointed. Anointing is a sacred action in the sacraments of baptism, confirmation, anointing of the sick, and holy orders. Anointing with the sacred chrism, a perfumed oil, bestows the gift of the Holy Spirit. The scent of chrism lingers, much as the presence of the Christ will linger in the person anointed, not for a day or two, but forever.

✢ All make the sign of the cross.

In the name of the Father, and of the Son, and of the Holy Spirit. Amen.

PSALM
(For a longer psalm, see page xiii.)
Psalm 23:1–3a

I shall dwell in the house of the LORD my whole life long.

I shall dwell in the house of the LORD my whole life long.

The LORD is my shepherd; I shall not want.
   He makes me lie down in green pastures;
he leads me beside still waters;
   he restores my soul.

I shall dwell in the house of the LORD my whole life long.

READING
Exodus 30:22, 23a, 24c–26, 29, 31–32

A reading from the Book of Exodus.

The LORD spoke to Moses, "Take the finest spices—measured by the sanctuary shekel [SHEK-*l]—and a hin of olive oil, and you shall make of these a sacred anointing oil blended as by the perfumer; it shall be a holy anointing oil. With it you shall anoint the tent of meeting and the ark of the covenant. You shall consecrate them, so that they may be most holy; whatever touches them will become holy. You shall say to the Israelites [IZ-ree-uh-lĪtz]: 'This shall be my holy anointing oil throughout your generations. It shall not be used in any ordinary anointing of the body, and you shall make no other like it in composition; it is holy, and it shall be holy to you.'"

The Word of the Lord.

◆ All observe silence.

FOR SILENT REFLECTION

Think about this silently in your heart. Have you ever witnessed anyone being anointed?

CLOSING PRAYER

Let us pray to God for our needs and the needs of others: our family, neighborhood, and the world. For each need we say, "Lord, hear our prayer."

◆ All may add their own prayers here.

Let us pray: **Our Father . . . Amen.**

Father,
you welcome us through the sacraments.
May we use your gifts to show others
   your love.
Through Christ our Lord.

Amen.

✢ All make the sign of the cross.

PRAYER FOR WEDNESDAY, JANUARY 31, 2024

OPENING

In today's reading, we hear about a prophetic mission: to bring good news to the poor, release to the captives, sight to the blind, and freedom to the oppressed. St. John Bosco (1815–88), whose feast day we celebrate today, truly embodied these prophetic virtues in his work as a teacher, reformer, and leader in faith. He is the patron saint of boys.

✢ All make the sign of the cross.

In the name of the Father, and of the Son, and of the Holy Spirit. Amen.

PSALM

(For a longer psalm, see page xiii.)
Psalm 23:1–3a

I shall dwell in the house of the Lord my whole life long.

I shall dwell in the house of the Lord my whole life long.

The Lord is my shepherd; I shall not want.
　He makes me lie down in green pastures;
he leads me beside still waters;
　he restores my soul.

I shall dwell in the house of the Lord my whole life long.

◆ All stand and sing **Alleluia.**

GOSPEL

Luke 4:16–19, 21

A reading from the holy Gospel according to Luke.

When Jesus came to Nazareth, where he had been brought up, he went to the synagogue on the Sabbath day, as was his custom. He stood up to read, and the scroll of the prophet Isaiah was given to him. He unrolled the scroll and found the place where it was written: "The Spirit of the Lord is upon me, because he has anointed me to bring good news to the poor. He has sent me to proclaim release to the captives and recovery of sight to the blind, to set free those who are oppressed, to proclaim the year of the Lord's favor." Then he began to say to them, "Today this scripture has been fulfilled in your hearing."

The Gospel of the Lord.

◆ All sit and observe silence.

FOR SILENT REFLECTION

Think about this silently in your heart. How do you share in Jesus' prophetic work?

CLOSING PRAYER

Let us pray to God for our needs and the needs of others: our family, neighborhood, and the world. For each need we say, "Lord, hear our prayer."

◆ All may add their own prayers here.

Let us pray: **Our Father . . . Amen.**

Lord God,
help us to be your voice in the world,
turning hearts to you.
Help us to follow the example of your Son,
　Jesus, our Master Teacher,
in whose name we pray.

Amen.

✢ All make the sign of the cross.

PRAYER FOR
THURSDAY, FEBRUARY 1, 2024

OPENING

The Spirit is conferred through one of the apostles or their representatives. Through generations of tradition, confirmation is now generally celebrated by a bishop, who is directly connected through the long line of apostolic succession to the twelve apostles. The bishop is the shepherd of his diocese, and confirmation strengthens the connection of the believer to the Church, the Body of Christ.

✚ All make the sign of the cross.

> In the name of the Father, and of the Son, and of the Holy Spirit. Amen.

PSALM
(For a longer psalm, see page xiii.)
Psalm 23:1–3a

I shall dwell in the house of the LORD my whole life long.

I shall dwell in the house of the LORD my whole life long.

The LORD is my shepherd; I shall not want.
 He makes me lie down in green pastures;
he leads me beside still waters;
 he restores my soul.

I shall dwell in the house of the LORD my whole life long.

READING
Acts 8:5–6, 14–17

A reading from the Acts of the Apostles.

Philip went down to the city of Samaria and proclaimed the Messiah to them. The crowds with one accord listened eagerly to what was said by Philip, hearing and seeing the signs that he did. Now when the apostles at Jerusalem heard that Samaria had accepted the word of God, they sent Peter and John to them. The two went down and prayed for them that they might receive the Holy Spirit (for as yet the Spirit had not come upon any of them; they had only been baptized in the name of the Lord Jesus). Then Peter and John laid their hands on them, and they received the Holy Spirit.

The Word of the Lord.

◆ All observe silence.

FOR SILENT REFLECTION

Think about this silently in your heart. What do you think it means to receive the Holy Spirit? How does receiving the Spirit change you?

CLOSING PRAYER

Let us pray to God for our needs and the needs of others: our family, neighborhood, and the world. For each need we say, "Lord, hear our prayer."

◆ All may add their own prayers here.

Let us pray: **Our Father . . . Amen.**

God our Father,
send down your Spirit upon us
that we might receive the many gifts of
 holiness that you can give to us.
Through Christ our Lord.

Amen.

✚ All make the sign of the cross.

PRAYER FOR FRIDAY, FEBRUARY 2, 2024

OPENING

Today is the feast of the Presentation of the Lord, popularly known as Candlemas. On this day, we bring candles to be blessed as a sign of the light we are all called to share. We hear that Paul sets a challenge before us: do not let your youth or station in life be an obstacle to sharing the good news of Christ. Be an example to everyone; let your life speak the goodness of God. Do not neglect the gift that has been given to you but put your faith into practice. This your challenge today.

✢ All make the sign of the cross.

In the name of the Father, and of the Son, and of the Holy Spirit. Amen.

PSALM

(For a longer psalm, see page xiii.)
Psalm 23:1–3a

I shall dwell in the house of the Lord my whole life long.

I shall dwell in the house of the Lord my whole life long.

The Lord is my shepherd; I shall not want.
   He makes me lie down in green pastures;
he leads me beside still waters;
   he restores my soul.

I shall dwell in the house of the Lord my whole life long.

READING

1 Timothy 4:11–16

A reading from the First Letter of Paul to Timothy.

Command and teach these things. Let no one despise your youth, but set the believers an example in speech and conduct, in love, in faith, in purity. Until I arrive, give attention to the public reading of scripture, to exhorting, to teaching. Do not neglect the gift that is in you, which was given to you through prophecy with the laying on of hands by the council of elders. Put these things into practice, devote yourself to them, so that all may see your progress. Pay close attention to yourself and to your teaching; continue in these things, for in doing this you will save both yourself and your hearers.

The Word of the Lord.

◆ All observe silence.

FOR SILENT REFLECTION

Think about this silently in your heart. How do you set an example for others?

CLOSING PRAYER

Let us pray to God for our needs and the needs of others: our family, neighborhood, and the world. For each need we say, "Lord, hear our prayer."

◆ All may add their own prayers here.

Let us pray: **Our Father . . . Amen.**

Lord,
you have blessed us with many good gifts.
Help us to use them to bring others to you
   through the example of our lives.
In Christ's name we pray.

Amen.

✢ All make the sign of the cross.

PRAYER FOR THE WEEK
WITH A READING FROM THE GOSPEL FOR **SUNDAY, FEBRUARY 4, 2024**

OPENING

Jesus healed many people of both physical and spiritual ills. Jesus' whole life was an example of incarnation, of God being physically present to his people. His care for all those afflicted was a sign of his power and his compassion for them, and for all of us.

✠ All make the sign of the cross.

In the name of the Father, and of the Son, and of the Holy Spirit. Amen.

PSALM
(For a longer psalm, see page xiii.)
Psalm 23:1–3a

I shall dwell in the house of the LORD my whole life long.

I shall dwell in the house of the LORD my whole life long.

The LORD is my shepherd; I shall not want.
  He makes me lie down in green pastures;
he leads me beside still waters;
  he restores my soul.

I shall dwell in the house of the LORD my whole life long.

◆ All stand and sing **Alleluia.**

GOSPEL
Mark 1:29–34

A reading from the holy Gospel according to Mark.

As soon as they left the synagogue, Jesus entered the house of Simon and Andrew, with James and John. Now Simon's mother-in-law was in bed with a fever, and they told him about her at once. He came and took her by the hand and lifted her up. Then the fever left her, and she began to serve them. That evening, at sunset, they brought to him all who were sick or possessed with demons. And the whole city was gathered around the door. And he cured many who were sick with various diseases and cast out many demons, and he would not permit the demons to speak, because they knew him.

The Gospel of the Lord.

◆ All sit and observe silence.

FOR SILENT REFLECTION

Think about this silently in your heart. What cure do you ask of Jesus? What sickness, sadness, loneliness, worry, or bad feeling can you lay before him? Pray to Jesus for healing.

CLOSING PRAYER

Let us pray to God for our needs and the needs of others: our family, neighborhood, and the world. For each need we say, "Lord, hear our prayer."

◆ All may add their own prayers here.

Let us pray: **Our Father . . . Amen.**

Lord Jesus,
you healed us body and spirit.
Be with us in our times of illness
  and suffering.
Who live and reign with God the Father,
in the unity of the Holy Spirit,
God, for ever and ever.

Amen.

✠ All make the sign of the cross.

PRAYER FOR MONDAY, FEBRUARY 5, 2024

OPENING

The Body of Christ is made beautiful by the varied ways we live out the same call to holiness, the call we have all received from the same Spirit. St. Agatha, whose feast day is today, is included in the Roman Canon of the Mass. She is honored for her courage and purity.

✢ All make the sign of the cross.

In the name of the Father, and of the Son, and of the Holy Spirit. Amen.

PSALM
(For a longer psalm, see page xiii.)
Psalm 23:1–3a

I shall dwell in the house of the LORD my whole life long.

I shall dwell in the house of the LORD my whole life long.

The LORD is my shepherd; I shall not want.
  He makes me lie down in green pastures;
he leads me beside still waters;
  he restores my soul.

I shall dwell in the house of the LORD my whole life long.

READING
1 Corinthians 12:4–11

A reading from the First Letter of Paul to the Corinthians [kohr-IN-thee-uhnz].

Now there are varieties of gifts but the same Spirit, and there are varieties of services but the same Lord, and there are varieties of activities, but it is the same God who activates all of them in everyone. To each is given the manifestation of the Spirit for the common good. To one is given through the Spirit the utterance of wisdom and to another the utterance of knowledge according to the same Spirit, to another faith by the same Spirit, to another gifts of healing by the one Spirit, to another the working of powerful deeds, to another prophecy, to another the discernment of spirits, to another various kinds of tongues, to another the interpretation of tongues. All these are activated by one and the same Spirit, who allots to each one individually just as the Spirit chooses.

The Word of the Lord.

◆ All observe silence.

FOR SILENT REFLECTION

Think about this silently in your heart. What gifts has the Spirit given to you?

CLOSING PRAYER

Let us pray to God for our needs and the needs of others: our family, neighborhood, and the world. For each need we say, "Lord, hear our prayer."

◆ All may add their own prayers here.

Let us pray: **Our Father . . . Amen.**

In your wisdom, O God,
you have given us various gifts.
May we honor you by using our talents
to serve you and others.
Through Christ our Lord.

Amen.

✢ All make the sign of the cross.

PRAYER FOR
TUESDAY, FEBRUARY 6, 2024

OPENING

Today we reflect on the unity of the Body in the Holy Spirit. No matter where we come from, our age, experience, or abilities, we are all united in Christ. It is the feast day of St. Paul Miki and Companions. St. Paul was a Japanese Jesuit and he and his companions were martyred for the faith.

✢ All make the sign of the cross.

In the name of the Father, and of the Son, and of the Holy Spirit. Amen.

PSALM

(For a longer psalm, see page xiii.)
Psalm 23:1–3a

I shall dwell in the house of the Lord my whole life long.

I shall dwell in the house of the Lord my whole life long.

The Lord is my shepherd; I shall not want.
    He makes me lie down in green pastures;
he leads me beside still waters;
    he restores my soul.

I shall dwell in the house of the Lord my whole life long.

READING

1 Corinthians 12:12–13; 10:31–33c

A reading from the First Letter of Paul to the Corinthians [kohr-IN-thee-uhnz].

For just as the body is one and has many members, and all the members of the body, though many, are one body, so it is with Christ. For in the one Spirit we were all baptized into one body—Jews or Greeks, slaves or free—and we were all made to drink of one Spirit. So, whether you eat or drink or whatever you do, do everything for the glory of God. Give no offense to Jews or to Greeks or to the church of God, just as I try to please everyone in everything I do, not seeking my own advantage, but that of many.

The Word of the Lord.

◆ All observe silence.

FOR SILENT REFLECTION

Think about this silently in your heart. How can you heal divisions in your community?

CLOSING PRAYER

Let us pray to God for our needs and the needs of others: our family, neighborhood, and the world. For each need we say, "Lord, hear our prayer."

◆ All may add their own prayers here.

Let us pray: **Our Father . . . Amen.**

Lord Jesus,
you made us into one Body.
Teach us to live together in peace and love,
so that all people may truly flourish.
Who live and reign with God the Father,
in the unity of the Holy Spirit,
God, for ever and ever.

Amen.

✢ All make the sign of the cross.

PRAYER FOR WEDNESDAY, FEBRUARY 7, 2024

OPENING

Have you ever been jealous of another person? It can be very hard not to compare ourselves to others, to envy what they can do or gifts they have been given. But as St. Paul made clear, the Body of Christ has many parts, each with its own purpose. We are each called to use our gifts to give glory to God in our own unique ways. The unity of the Body means that we are all a part of each other.

✚ All make the sign of the cross.

In the name of the Father, and of the Son, and of the Holy Spirit. Amen.

PSALM
(For a longer psalm, see page xiii.)
Psalm 23:1–3a

I shall dwell in the house of the LORD my whole life long.

I shall dwell in the house of the LORD my whole life long.

The LORD is my shepherd; I shall not want.
 He makes me lie down in green pastures;
he leads me beside still waters;
 he restores my soul.

I shall dwell in the house of the LORD my whole life long.

READING
1 Corinthians 12:14–17, 20, 26

A reading from the First Letter of Paul to the Corinthians [kohr-IN-thee-uhnz].

Indeed, the body does not consist of one member but of many. If the foot would say, "Because I am not a hand, I do not belong to the body," that would not make it any less a part of the body. And if the ear would say, "Because I am not an eye, I do not belong to the body," that would not make it any less a part of the body. If the whole body were an eye, where would the hearing be? If the whole body were hearing, where would the sense of smell be? As it is, there are many members yet one body. If one member suffers, all suffer together with it; if one member is honored, all rejoice together with it.

The Word of the Lord.

◆ All observe silence.

FOR SILENT REFLECTION

Think about this silently in your heart. How is the success of one the success of all? How is the suffering of one a tragedy for the whole body?

CLOSING PRAYER

Let us pray to God for our needs and the needs of others: our family, neighborhood, and the world. For each need we say, "Lord, hear our prayer."

◆ All may add their own prayers here.

Let us pray: **Our Father . . . Amen.**

O holy God,
we are all your sons and daughters.
May we celebrate our differences
 and be united by what we share.
We ask this in Christ Jesus' name.

Amen.

✚ All make the sign of the cross.

PRAYER FOR
THURSDAY, FEBRUARY 8, 2024

OPENING

St. Jerome Emiliani, whose memorial is today, was a good example of St. Paul's teaching about love as the most important spiritual gift. St. Jerome was born in Venice, Italy. The plague and famine of 1518 left many children orphans, and St. Jerome founded orphanages and hospitals that took care of the poor and the sick. Today we also remember St. Josephine Bakhita (c. 1868–1947), a former Sudanese slave who said, "Be good, love the Lord, pray for those who do not know him."

✚ All make the sign of the cross.

In the name of the Father, and of the Son, and of the Holy Spirit. Amen.

PSALM

(For a longer psalm, see page xiii.)
Psalm 23:1–3a

I shall dwell in the house of the LORD my whole life long.

I shall dwell in the house of the LORD my whole life long.

The LORD is my shepherd; I shall not want.
   He makes me lie down in green pastures;
he leads me beside still waters;
   he restores my soul.

I shall dwell in the house of the LORD my whole life long.

READING

1 Corinthians 13:1–2, 4–7

A reading from the First Letter of Paul to the Corinthians [kohr-IN-thee-uhnz].

If I speak in the tongues of mortals and of angels but do not have love, I am a noisy gong or a clanging cymbal. And if I have prophetic powers and understand all mysteries and all knowledge and if I have all faith so as to remove mountains but do not have love, I am nothing. Love is patient; love is kind; love is not envious or boastful or arrogant or rude. It does not insist on its own way; it is not irritable; it keeps no record of wrongs; it does not rejoice in wrongdoing but rejoices in the truth. It bears all things, believes all things, hopes all things, endures all things.

The Word of the Lord.

◆ All observe silence.

FOR SILENT REFLECTION

Think about this silently in your heart. Do you act with the kind of love that St. Paul described?

CLOSING PRAYER

Let us pray to God for our needs and the needs of others: our family, neighborhood, and the world. For each need we say, "Lord, hear our prayer."

◆ All may add their own prayers here.

Let us pray: **Our Father . . . Amen.**

Loving God,
help us to always act with love
   and compassion.
Through Christ our Lord,
who showed us how much he loves us.

Amen.

✚ All make the sign of the cross.

PRAYER FOR FRIDAY, FEBRUARY 9, 2024

OPENING

Clothes protect us from the elements: we wear coats and scarves to protect us from the cold winter air, shirts and caps to protect against the hot sun, and shoes to protect against the rough ground. According to St. Paul, we also put on virtues like a garment. These virtues not only protect against temptation and sin, but they also bind us together. Above all, we are called to wrap ourselves in love, which brings peace, harmony, gratitude, wisdom, and praise of God.

✚ All make the sign of the cross.

In the name of the Father, and of the Son, and of the Holy Spirit. Amen.

PSALM

(For a longer psalm, see page xiii.)
Psalm 23:1–3a

I shall dwell in the house of the LORD my whole life long.

I shall dwell in the house of the LORD my whole life long.

The LORD is my shepherd; I shall not want.
  He makes me lie down in green pastures;
he leads me beside still waters;
  he restores my soul.

I shall dwell in the house of the LORD my whole life long.

READING

Colossians 3:12–16

A reading from the Letter of Paul to the Colossians [kuh-LOSH-uhnz].

As God's chosen ones, holy and beloved, clothe yourselves with compassion, kindness, humility, meekness, and patience. Bear with one another and, if anyone has a complaint against another, forgive each other; just as the Lord has forgiven you, so you also must forgive. Above all, clothe yourselves with love, which binds everything together in perfect harmony. And let the peace of Christ rule in your hearts, to which indeed you were called in one body. And be thankful. Let the word of Christ dwell in you richly; teach and admonish one another in all wisdom; and with gratitude in your hearts sing psalms, hymns, and spiritual songs to God.

The Word of the Lord.

◆ All observe silence.

FOR SILENT REFLECTION

Think about this silently in your heart. What does it mean to put on love like a garment?

CLOSING PRAYER

Let us pray to God for our needs and the needs of others: our family, neighborhood, and the world. For each need we say, "Lord, hear our prayer."

◆ All may add their own prayers here.

Let us pray: **Our Father . . . Amen.**

Holy God,
give us the grace to live in your love
and share it with everyone we meet today.
Through Christ our Lord.

Amen.

✚ All make the sign of the cross.

PRAYER FOR THE WEEK
WITH A READING FROM THE GOSPEL FOR **SUNDAY, FEBRUARY 11, 2024**

OPENING

The man with leprosy came to Jesus in faith and humbly asked for healing. Jesus touched him and chose to make him clean. We know the Lord answers prayers (though many times he answers in unexpected ways), but it can be so hard to approach him with our needs.

✢ All make the sign of the cross.

In the name of the Father, and of the Son, and of the Holy Spirit. Amen.

PSALM
(For a longer psalm, see page xiii.)
Psalm 23:1–3a

I shall dwell in the house of the Lord my whole life long.

I shall dwell in the house of the Lord my whole life long.

The Lord is my shepherd; I shall not want.
   He makes me lie down in green pastures;
he leads me beside still waters;
   he restores my soul.

I shall dwell in the house of the Lord my whole life long.

◆ All stand and sing **Alleluia.**

GOSPEL
Mark 1:40–44a, 45

A reading from the holy Gospel according to Mark.

A man with a skin disease came to Jesus begging him, and kneeling he said to him, "If you are willing, you can make me clean." Moved with pity, Jesus stretched out his hand and touched him and said to him, "I am willing. Be made clean!" Immediately the skin disease left him, and he was made clean. After sternly warning him Jesus sent him away at once, saying to him, "See that you say nothing to anyone." But he went out and began to proclaim it freely and to spread the word, so that Jesus could no longer go into a town openly but stayed out in the country, and people came to him from every quarter.

The Gospel of the Lord.

◆ All sit and observe silence.

FOR SILENT REFLECTION

Think about this silently in your heart. Ask the Lord's healing for whatever you or others need.

CLOSING PRAYER

Let us pray to God for our needs and the needs of others: our family, neighborhood, and the world. For each need we say, "Lord, hear our prayer."

◆ All may add their own prayers here.

Let us pray: **Our Father . . . Amen.**

O Jesus,
you are always there for your people
   in times of trouble.
Heal us from our illnesses and hurts.
Who live and reign with God the Father,
in the unity of the Holy Spirit,
God for ever and ever.

Amen.

✢ All make the sign of the cross.

PRAYER FOR
MONDAY, FEBRUARY 12, 2024

OPENING

Jairus believed Jesus could heal his daughter even when she was at the point of death. His faith was in stark contrast to the crowd who scolded him for bothering Jesus over what they thought was a lost cause. As we see many times in his ministry, Jesus rewarded tremendous faith and performed a miracle, not just of healing, but of resurrection. This miracle is a sign for all of us: God sees our faith and rewards it.

✠ All make the sign of the cross.

In the name of the Father, and of the Son, and of the Holy Spirit. Amen.

PSALM
(For a longer psalm, see page xiii.)
Psalm 23:1–3a

I shall dwell in the house of the LORD my whole life long.

I shall dwell in the house of the LORD my whole life long.

The LORD is my shepherd; I shall not want.
　He makes me lie down in green pastures;
he leads me beside still waters;
　he restores my soul.

I shall dwell in the house of the LORD my whole life long.

◆ All stand and sing **Alleluia.**

GOSPEL
Mark 5:22–23, 35b–d, 36b, 39a, 39c, 40c–42a, 42c

A reading from the holy Gospel according to Mark.

Then one of the leaders of the synagogue, named Jairus, came and, when he saw Jesus, fell at his feet and pleaded with him repeatedly, "My little daughter is at the point of death. Come and lay your hands on her, so that she may be made well and live." Some people came from the synagogue leader's house to say, "Your daughter is dead. Why trouble the teacher any further?" Jesus said to the synagogue leader, "Do not be afraid; only believe." When Jesus had entered the house, he said to them, "The child is not dead but sleeping." Then he went in where the child was. Taking her by the hand, he said to her, "Little girl, get up!" And immediately the girl stood up and began to walk about.

The Gospel of the Lord.

◆ All sit and observe silence.

FOR SILENT REFLECTION

Think about this silently in your heart. How do you show your faith in God?

CLOSING PRAYER

Let us pray to God for our needs and the needs of others: our family, neighborhood, and the world. For each need we say, "Lord, hear our prayer."

◆ All may add their own prayers here.

Let us pray: **Our Father . . . Amen.**

Jesus,
help us to be faithful to you.
In your name we pray.

Amen.

✠ All make the sign of the cross.

PRAYER FOR
TUESDAY, FEBRUARY 13, 2024

OPENING

Jesus' enemies were so caught up in following the letter of the law that they neglected the spirit of it; namely, to love as God loves. It is easy to get so caught up in rules that we forget about the person in front of us. Jesus teaches us to love first, to act with love, and to love to the end.

✢ All make the sign of the cross.

In the name of the Father, and of the Son, and of the Holy Spirit. Amen.

PSALM

(For a longer psalm, see page xiii.)
Psalm 23:1–3a

I shall dwell in the house of the LORD my whole life long.

I shall dwell in the house of the LORD my whole life long.

The LORD is my shepherd; I shall not want.
   He makes me lie down in green pastures;
he leads me beside still waters;
   he restores my soul.

I shall dwell in the house of the LORD my whole life long.

◆ All stand and sing **Alleluia.**

GOSPEL
Mark 3:1–6

A reading from the holy Gospel according to Mark.

Again Jesus entered the synagogue, and a man was there who had a withered hand. They were watching him to see whether he would cure him on the Sabbath, so that they might accuse him. And he said to the man who had the withered hand, "Come forward." Then he said to them, "Is it lawful to do good or to do harm on the Sabbath, to save life or to kill?" But they were silent. He looked around at them with anger; he was grieved at their hardness of heart and said to the man, "Stretch out your hand." He stretched it out, and his hand was restored. The Pharisees went out and immediately conspired with the Herodians against him, how to destroy him.

The Gospel of the Lord.

◆ All sit and observe silence.

FOR SILENT REFLECTION

Think about this silently in your heart. How do you act with love first?

CLOSING PRAYER

Let us pray to God for our needs and the needs of others: our family, neighborhood, and the world. For each need we say, "Lord, hear our prayer."

◆ All may add their own prayers here.

Let us pray: **Our Father . . . Amen.**

Lord Jesus,
give us the heart to love one another
   without counting the cost.
Who live and reign with God the Father,
in the unity of the Holy Spirit,
God, for ever and ever.

Amen.

✢ All make the sign of the cross.

LENT

WEDNESDAY, FEBRUARY 14, 2024 — WEDNESDAY, MARCH 27, 2024

LENT

THE MEANING OF LENT

On Ash Wednesday the Church enters into her great retreat time called Lent. It is a time to reflect on how we are with God, with our neighbor, and with ourselves and to make some changes in our attitudes or speech or actions if we need to. We should do this often throughout the year, but we do it more consciously in Lent to prepare for the celebration of Easter when some people will be baptized and the rest of us will renew our baptismal promises.

We have six weeks to concentrate on this conversion of heart, this turning back to or moving closer to God. During this time we might ask ourselves a simple question: "What do I need to stop doing or start doing to be the very good person God made me?" If we find we have some bad habits or have hurt someone (even ourselves) or have neglected to do something we should, we can express our sincere regret and willingness to change in the Sacrament of Reconciliation.

The three Lenten disciplines can help us to train our hearts in love. We are called to pray, fast, and give alms. We pray more regularly and perhaps for longer periods of time. Praying is a conversation with God and a way to be closer to God.

We fast to remind ourselves that there is nothing more important than God and the needs of God's people. Perhaps we give up a certain food and give the money we save to the poor. We might give up playing video games and use the time to help around the house. Part of fasting is abstaining from meat on Fridays of Lent so we eat simply and sparingly as poor people must.

The third discipline is almsgiving. The word comes from the Greek meaning "compassion" and is associated with giving food, money, or clothing to the poor. The money we save by giving up a favorite food or activity might be used this way. We may have a toy, games, or clothes we no longer use very often that we could give to someone else.

Lent's purpose of preparing us to celebrate Easter becomes more focused as we enter into Holy Week. Lent ends with the Mass of the Lord's Supper on Holy Thursday evening. At that moment we enter the Triduum, the three holiest days of the Church year.

PREPARING TO CELEBRATE LENT IN THE CLASSROOM

SACRED SPACE

Remember that on Ash Wednesday, you will need to change your prayer tablecloth from green to purple. If you have a growing plant in the prayer space, remove it. Ask the children to bring in their family's dried palms from last year and put them in a simple vase. A clear bowl full of ashes would be appropriate. They are available through local religious goods stores. (Use the same bowl to hold water in Easter.)

MOVEMENT AND GESTURE

You may want to use some incense during some of the prayers. Ask the parish priest or deacon for some charcoal and incense. You'll also need a pot full of sand to place the charcoal in. An altar server can help you light the charcoal about ten minutes before the prayer. Then the leader can place just enough incense on the charcoal before the Scripture is proclaimed. Be sure to have open windows and let people know you are using the incense. Ask the children with allergies and asthma to stand in the back of the space in case the smoke bothers them. At the end of the prayer cover the charcoal with sand to stop it from smoking.

FESTIVITY IN SCHOOL AND HOME

Lent is a more solemn time. Festivity is kept to a minimum, although there may be special feasts such as St. Joseph's Day or St. Patrick's Day, when it is customary to celebrate and honor these saints. Because we are not in school during the three sacred days leading up to Easter, we have provided prayers the children can bring home. You will find Home Prayer pages to copy and send home so that families can keep Holy Thursday and Good Friday (pages 234–235). The Prayer Service for Ash Wednesday (pages 194–195) can be used for the classroom or for a larger group.

SACRED MUSIC

Lent is a more solemn time and our music reflects this. Our songs are more plaintive and contemplative. Children love to sing "Jesus, Remember Me," and "What Wondrous Love Is This?" Other songs for Lent are "Amazing Grace," the African American spiritual "Somebody's Knockin' at Your Door," and the Latin hymn "Ubi Caritas." We don't sing "Alleluia" during Lent. Tell the children we are saving all our Alleluia joy for Easter. For the Prayer for the Week, and during the week where there is a Gospel, we sing an acclamation, such as "Praise to you, Lord Jesus Christ" to whatever tune the parish is using.

PRAYERS FOR LENT

Lent is the perfect time to learn or to review an Act of Contrition. Psalm 51 is also a beautiful prayer for this season of penance and conversion.

A NOTE TO CATECHISTS

If any children in your group are preparing to celebrate the sacraments of initiation at the Easter Vigil, gather them to read the following three great accounts from the Gospel of John: (1) Jesus teaches the Woman at the Well who finally understands Jesus is the Messiah (John 4:5–15, 19b–26, 39a, 40–42); (2) Jesus cures the Man Born Blind of physical blindness and the man "sees" and follow him (John 9:1, 6–9, 13–17, 34–38); and (3) Jesus raises Lazarus from the dead (John 11:3–7, 17, 20–27, 33b–45). These are long passages and may require some time to read and discuss with your students, but fight the temptation to rush through them!

GRACE BEFORE MEALS
LENT

LEADER:
We adore you, O Christ, and we praise you

ALL: because by your holy Cross you have redeemed the world.

✛ All make the sign of the cross.

In the name of the Father, and of the Son, and of the Holy Spirit. Amen.

LEADER:
God of compassion,
we thank you for this meal
and for those who prepared it.
May we be nourished by this food
and by the love and friendship we share.
Help us to be mindful of people
in our community and other regions
who will remain hungry today.
May we become your true food for others
through gifts of your Spirit and our works
    of charity.
We ask this through Christ our Lord.

All: Amen.

✛ All make the sign of the cross.

In the name of the Father, and of the Son, and of the Holy Spirit. Amen.

PRAYER AT DAY'S END
LENT

LEADER:
Blessed be the Lord,

ALL: for he has heard the sound of my pleadings.

✢ All make the sign of the cross.

In the name of the Father, and of the Son, and of the Holy Spirit. Amen.

LEADER:
Merciful Lord,
sometimes we fail in what
we say or do.
As our school day ends,
help us to remember that
your mercy and love
are never-ending.
Guide us as we renew our commitment
to deepen our relationship with you
throughout this season of Lent.
We ask this in your name.

All: Amen.

✢ All make the sign of the cross.

In the name of the Father, and of the Son, and of the Holy Spirit. Amen.

HOME PRAYER
KEEPING LENT

Before you begin, place a candle, an empty bowl, and a jar with a slit cut into the lid (for coins to give to the poor) where the household will gather in prayer. Find the reading (Matthew 7:7–12) in your Bible, ask for a volunteer to read it and encourage him/her to practice reading it a few times. You may wish to begin with a simple song, such as "Jesus, Remember Me," or "Amen" (but not "Alleluia" during Lent). An older child or adult reads the leader parts.

LEADER:
Lent is a time of reflection
and of turning our hearts to God.
We turn our attention to
growing spiritually
so that we can fully cherish the joy of Easter.
Lent helps us to listen more and pray,
just as Jesus did in the desert.

✚ All make the sign of the cross.

In the name of the Father, and of the Son, and of the Holy Spirit. Amen.

LEADER: Psalm 37:5a, 3–4, 23–24, 27–28, 30–31
Let us repeat the Psalm Response:
Commit your way to the LORD.

ALL: Commit your way to the LORD.

Trust in the LORD, and do good;
    so you will live in the land, and
        enjoy security.
Take delight in the LORD,
    and he will give you the desires of
        your heart.

ALL: Commit your way to the LORD.

Our steps are made firm by the LORD,
    when he delights in our way;
though we stumble, we shall not fall
        headlong,
    for the LORD holds us by the hand.

ALL: Commit your way to the LORD.

◆ All stand and sing Praise to you, Lord Jesus Christ . . .

LEADER: Matthew 7:7–12
A reading from the holy Gospel according to Matthew

◆ Read the Gospel passage from the Bible.

The Gospel of the Lord.

◆ All sit and observe silence. An adult lights the candle.

LEADER:
Heavenly Father,
you sent your Son to us
to light the way back to you.
Guide us in this season of Lent
so that we can focus on you
and on others who may need our help.
We ask this through our Lord Jesus Christ,
your Son, who lives and reigns with you
in the unity of the Holy Spirit, one God,
forever and ever.

ALL: Amen.

LEADER:
Let us pray as Jesus taught us:
    Our Father . . . Amen.

✚ All make the sign of the cross.

PRAYER FOR
WEDNESDAY, FEBRUARY 14, 2024

OPENING

The Gospel reading for Ash Wednesday seems counter to the liturgical action of the day (the imposition of ashes). Jesus told his disciples to give alms, to fast, and to pray. But he also told them to pray in secret, to fast without looking sad, to give alms without fanfare. In other words, we need to enter into the spirit of Lent—to pray, fast, and give alms—in order to grow closer to God, not to perform for others.

✢ All make the sign of the cross.

In the name of the Father, and of the Son, and of the Holy Spirit. Amen.

PSALM
(For a longer psalm, see page xiv.)
Psalm 34:4–5

The LORD saves the crushed in spirit.

The LORD saves the crushed in spirit.

I sought the LORD, and he answered me
   and delivered me from all my fears.
Look to him, and be radiant,
   so your faces shall never be ashamed.

The LORD saves the crushed in spirit.

◆ All stand and sing **Praise to you, Lord Jesus Christ…**

GOSPEL
Matthew 6:2abe, 3–4, 5abce, 6

A reading from the holy Gospel according to Matthew.

So whenever you give alms, do not sound a trumpet before you, as the hypocrites do in the synagogues and in the streets. They have received their reward. But when you give alms, do not let your left hand know what your right hand is doing, so that your alms may be done in secret, and your Father who sees in secret will reward you.

And whenever you pray, do not be like the hypocrites, for they love to stand and pray in the synagogues and at the street corners, so that they may be seen by others. They have received their reward. But whenever you pray, go into your room and shut the door and pray to your Father who is in secret, and your Father who sees in secret will reward you.

The Gospel of the Lord.

◆ All sit and observe silence.

FOR SILENT REFLECTION

Think about this silently in your heart. How do you need to grow in this season of Lent?

CLOSING PRAYER

Let us pray to God for our needs and the needs of others: our family, neighborhood, and the world. For each need we say, "Lord, hear our prayer."

◆ All may add their own prayers here.

Let us pray: **Our Father . . . Amen.**

Father,
we humbly seek you.
During this time of preparation,
give us the faith and the will to forsake the
   things that keep us from your love.
Through Christ our Lord.

Amen.

✢ All make the sign of the cross.

PRAYER SERVICE
ASH WEDNESDAY

Prepare eight leaders for this service. Before you begin, prepare a long piece of butcher-block paper or cloth banner with the word "Alleluia" written on it. The inside of the first three letters, "A-l-l" should be colored in, but you should only be able to see an outline of the rest of the word's letters, "e-l-u-i-a." Hang this banner for all to see, but make it accessible so that an additional letter can be colored each week of Lent. On Fridays during Lent, you may want to incorporate coloring the additional letters when you do Prayer at Day's End for Lent, found on page 197.

The fifth and sixth leaders of this Prayer Service will need Bibles for the Scripture passages and may need help practicing them. You may wish to begin by singing "From Ashes to the Living Font" and end with "Soon and Very Soon." If the group will sing, prepare a song leader.

FIRST LEADER:

✢ All make the sign of the cross.

In the name of the Father, and of the Son, and of the Holy Spirit. Amen.

Today we embark together on a journey through Lent. It is a time for self-discovery as we remember how Jesus went into the desert for forty days and was tempted by the devil. During our Lenten experience, we pray more, eat less, and give to the poor to prepare ourselves for what is at the heart of our Christian faith—Christ's Resurrection at Easter! But we must make ready our hearts and minds, like an athlete trains for a key game or race. We need to strengthen our good habits as we remain God's sons and daughters through the waters of Baptism.

SECOND LEADER:
Each year, on Ash Wednesday, Catholics are marked with ashes in the sign of the cross as a reminder that we are entering into Lent. This ashen sign reminds us of our humanness, and that sometimes we fail. We need God's help to succeed. That's why prayer is so vital in our lives.

THIRD LEADER:
During Lent, we also fast from the word "Alleluia," which means "Praise the Lord" in Hebrew. We've prepared this banner with only three of the letters colored in. But you'll see that on this special day, we are *all* in this together! Lent can be a time for us *all* to get closer to Christ. Just like a team trains for a big game, we *all* can do this through prayer and sacrifice. So at the end of each week in Lent, we will color in one more letter to mark another week closer to our declaring this joyous word!

FOURTH LEADER:
Let us pray:
Almighty Father,
through the waters of Baptism,
you claimed us as
your sons and daughters.

You love us without condition.
May our prayers, fasting, and
works of charity deepen
our connection with you
as we better understand the suffering of
our brothers and sisters around the world.
May we remember how
Jesus was tempted in the desert
and that *all* of us need to make
you our priority
in word and deed.
We ask this through Christ our Lord.

ALL: Amen.

◆ All stand and sing **Praise to you, Lord Jesus Christ** . . .

FIFTH LEADER: Matthew 4:1–11
A reading from the holy Gospel according to Matthew.

◆ Read the Scripture passage from a Bible.

The Gospel of the Lord.

◆ All remain standing and observe silence.

SIXTH LEADER: Matthew 6:1–2
A reading from the holy Gospel according to Matthew.

◆ Read the Scripture passage from a Bible.

The Gospel of the Lord.

◆ All sit and observe silence.

SEVENTH LEADER:
Let us pray as Jesus taught us:

ALL: Our Father . . . Amen.

Lord God,
help us to be one with you
during this season of Lent.
Guide us as you led
Jesus through the
trying times in his life.
May we let go of
our negative habits and thoughts
that make us feel distant
from your loving presence.
We look forward to
the joy of Easter,
for our hope is Jesus
in this time of preparation.
We ask this through Christ our Lord.

ALL: Amen.

EIGHTH LEADER:
Let us offer to one another a sign of Christ's peace:

◆ All offer one another a sign of peace.

And may the Lord bless us,

✚ All make the sign of the cross.

protect us from all evil,
and bring us to everlasting life.

ALL: Amen.

PRAYER FOR
THURSDAY, FEBRUARY 15, 2024

OPENING

Why was Jesus so concerned that his disciples wash their faces? (And if that is a concern, why did we all have ashes smeared on our foreheads yesterday?) Jesus wasn't worried about hygiene as much as he was concerned with true faith. He didn't want his disciples to *perform* their faith for the benefit of others. He wanted them to live their faith in small simple ways. St. Thérèse of Lisieux called this the "Little Way" and she described it as doing little acts of holiness, not grandiose sacrifices to God. That Little Way is what we strive for during Lent.

✢ All make the sign of the cross.

In the name of the Father, and of the Son, and of the Holy Spirit. Amen.

PSALM
(For a longer psalm, see page xiv.)
Psalm 34:4–5

The LORD saves the crushed in spirit.

The LORD saves the crushed in spirit.

I sought the LORD, and he answered me
   and delivered me from all my fears.
Look to him, and be radiant,
   so your faces shall never be ashamed.

The LORD saves the crushed in spirit.

◆ All stand and sing **Praise to you, Lord Jesus Christ...**

GOSPEL
Matthew 6:7–8, 16–18

A reading from the holy Gospel according to Matthew.

When you are praying, do not heap up empty phrases as the gentiles do, for they think that they will be heard because of their many words. Do not be like them, for your Father knows what you need before you ask him.

And whenever you fast, do not look somber, like the hypocrites, for they mark their faces to show others that they are fasting. Truly I tell you, they have received their reward. But when you fast, put oil on your head and wash your face, so that your fasting may be seen not by others but by your Father who is in secret, and your Father who sees in secret will reward you.

The Gospel of the Lord.

◆ All sit and observe silence.

FOR SILENT REFLECTION

Think about this silently in your heart. What sacrifices can you make this Lent?

CLOSING PRAYER

Let us pray to God for our needs and the needs of others: our family, neighborhood, and the world. For each need we say, "Lord, hear our prayer."

◆ All may add their own prayers here.

Let us pray: **Our Father . . . Amen.**

Heavenly Father,
help us to grow in holiness every day,
in all that we do, large and small.
We ask this through Christ our Lord.

Amen.

✢ All make the sign of the cross.

PRAYER FOR FRIDAY, FEBRUARY 16, 2024

OPENING

The prophet Isaiah condemned the same issue we heard Jesus call out the last few days: hypocritical fasting. Fasting is not an end, but a means to an end. Fasting is not genuine if you don't reform yourself and your way of life. In Lent, we may fast from chocolate or french fries or screens, not because those things are bad, but because it is easy to value them too much. Lent is a time for us to re-form our desires, and remember that the desire for God should be first in our hearts.

✢ All make the sign of the cross.

In the name of the Father, and of the Son, and of the Holy Spirit. Amen.

PSALM

(For a longer psalm, see page xiv.)
Psalm 34:4–5

The LORD saves the crushed in spirit.

The LORD saves the crushed in spirit.

I sought the LORD, and he answered me
   and delivered me from all my fears.
Look to him, and be radiant,
   so your faces shall never be ashamed.

The LORD saves the crushed in spirit.

READING

Isaiah 58:5acde, 6–7, 8ab, 9ab

A reading from the Book of the prophet Isaiah.

Is such the fast that I choose, a day to humble oneself? And to lie in sackcloth and ashes? Will you call this a fast, a day acceptable to the LORD? Is not this the fast that I choose: to loose the bonds of injustice, to undo the straps of the yoke, to let the oppressed go free, and to break every yoke? Is it not to share your bread with the hungry and bring the homeless poor into your house; when you see the naked, to cover them and not to hide yourself from your own kin? Then your light shall break forth like the dawn, and your healing shall spring up quickly. Then you shall call, and the LORD will answer; you shall cry for help, and he will say, "Here I am."

The Word of the Lord.

◆ All observe silence.

FOR SILENT REFLECTION

Think about this silently in your heart. What is one way the prophet Isaiah says we may fast?

CLOSING PRAYER

Let us pray to God for our needs and the needs of others: our family, neighborhood, and the world. For each need we say, "Lord, hear our prayer."

◆ All may add their own prayers here.

Let us pray: **Our Father . . . Amen.**

Loving God,
we long for closeness with you.
Help us to remove the things that distract us
   that we might grow nearer to you.
We pray in the name of Jesus Christ
   our Lord.

Amen.

✢ All make the sign of the cross.

PRAYER FOR THE WEEK
WITH A READING FROM THE GOSPEL FOR **SUNDAY, FEBRUARY 18, 2024**

OPENING

Immediately after his baptism, Jesus was sent by the Spirit into the desert. The desert is the opposite of the Garden of Eden: it is spare and parched, whereas the Garden was lush and fruitful. And yet the desert bears some similarity to Eden as well: it is a place where a choice will be made between good and evil. In the desert, Jesus was both waited on by angels and menaced by wild beasts. In other Gospel accounts, we hear that Jesus was tempted by the devil to turn away from God. But unlike our human ancestors, Adam and Eve, Jesus remained steadfast and obedient to God the Father.

✢ All make the sign of the cross.

In the name of the Father, and of the Son, and of the Holy Spirit. Amen.

PSALM
(For a longer psalm, see page xiv.)
Psalm 34:4–5

The LORD saves the crushed in spirit.

The LORD saves the crushed in spirit.

I sought the LORD, and he answered me
   and delivered me from all my fears.
Look to him, and be radiant,
   so your faces shall never be ashamed.

The LORD saves the crushed in spirit.

◆ All stand and sing **Praise to you, Lord Jesus Christ...**

GOSPEL
Mark 1:12–15

A reading from the holy Gospel according to Mark.

And the Spirit immediately drove Jesus out into the wilderness. He was in the wilderness forty days, tested by Satan, and he was with the wild beasts, and the angels waited on him.

Now after John was arrested, Jesus came to Galilee proclaiming the good news of God and saying, "The time is fulfilled, and the kingdom of God has come near; repent, and believe in the good news."

The Gospel of the Lord.

◆ All sit and observe silence.

FOR SILENT REFLECTION

Think about this silently in your heart. Jesus was tempted for forty days. In what ways can you put God first during these forty days of Lent?

CLOSING PRAYER

Let us pray to God for our needs and the needs of others: our family, neighborhood, and the world. For each need we say, "Lord, hear our prayer."

◆ All may add their own prayers here.

Let us pray: **Our Father . . . Amen.**

Holy God,
give us the courage to choose you
over worldly temptations that we encounter.
May we especially commit ourselves
   to love and service,
in the name of Jesus Christ our Lord.

Amen.

✢ All make the sign of the cross.

PRAYER FOR MONDAY, FEBRUARY 19, 2024

OPENING

In order to truly love God, we are asked to love our neighbor as ourselves. And, in order for human love, service, and sacrifice to have meaning, we must put God before all else. Love of God and love of neighbor are forever linked. This week, we will be exploring forgiveness, a concrete way in which we act on our love for God, for neighbors, and for ourselves.

✚ All make the sign of the cross.

In the name of the Father, and of the Son, and of the Holy Spirit. Amen.

PSALM

(For a longer psalm, see page xiv.)
Psalm 34:4–5

The LORD saves the crushed in spirit.

The LORD saves the crushed in spirit.

I sought the LORD, and he answered me
   and delivered me from all my fears.
Look to him, and be radiant,
   so your faces shall never be ashamed.

The LORD saves the crushed in spirit.

◆ All stand and sing **Praise to you, Lord Jesus Christ…**

GOSPEL

Mark 12:28–31

A reading from the holy Gospel according to Mark.

One of the scribes came near and heard them disputing with one another, and seeing that Jesus answered them well he asked him, "Which commandment is the first of all?" Jesus answered, "The first is, 'Hear, O Israel: the Lord our God, the Lord is one; you shall love the Lord your God with all your heart and with all your soul and with all your mind and with all your strength.' The second is this, 'You shall love your neighbor as yourself.' There is no other commandment greater than these."

The Gospel of the Lord.

◆ All sit and observe silence.

FOR SILENT REFLECTION

Think about this silently in your heart. Do you truly follow Jesus' great commandment? What could you do better?

CLOSING PRAYER

Let us pray to God for our needs and the needs of others: our family, neighborhood, and the world. For each need we say, "Lord, hear our prayer."

◆ All may add their own prayers here.

Let us pray: **Our Father . . . Amen.**

O God,
we desire to love you with all our heart, soul,
   mind, and strength.
May we also love and care for everyone
   we meet with the same power of love.
Through Christ our Lord,

Amen.

✚ All make the sign of the cross.

PRAYER FOR
TUESDAY, FEBRUARY 20, 2024

OPENING

All of us have experienced the hurt of someone sinning against us by their hurtful actions or words. It can be hard to forgive, especially when we are deeply wounded or hurt again and again. But Jesus tells the disciples they must forgive not just once or twice, but an astronomical number of times. We are called to forgive as God does, abundantly and without reserve, loving the repentant sinner. We are called to do this over and over again in the course of a lifetime. Because we too are sinners in need of forgiveness.

✙ All make the sign of the cross.

In the name of the Father, and of the Son, and of the Holy Spirit. Amen.

PSALM

(For a longer psalm, see page xiv.)
Psalm 34:4–5

The LORD saves the crushed in spirit.

The LORD saves the crushed in spirit.

I sought the LORD, and he answered me
  and delivered me from all my fears.
Look to him, and be radiant,
  so your faces shall never be ashamed.

The LORD saves the crushed in spirit.

◆ All stand and sing **Praise to you, Lord Jesus Christ…**

GOSPEL

Matthew 18:15–16, 21–22

A reading from the holy Gospel according to Matthew.

Jesus said, "If your brother or sister sins against you, go and point out the fault when the two of you are alone. If you are listened to, you have regained that one. But if you are not listened to, take one or two others along with you, so that every word may be confirmed by the evidence of two or three witnesses."

Then Peter came and said to him, "Lord, if my brother or sister sins against me, how often should I forgive? As many as seven times?" Jesus said to him, "Not seven times, but, I tell you, seventy-seven times."

The Gospel of the Lord.

◆ All sit and observe silence.

FOR SILENT REFLECTION

Think about this silently in your heart. Is it hard for you to forgive? How can you open yourself to be able to forgive more readily?

CLOSING PRAYER

Let us pray to God for our needs and the needs of others: our family, neighborhood, and the world. For each need we say, "Lord, hear our prayer."

◆ All may add their own prayers here.

Let us pray: **Our Father . . . Amen.**

Merciful God,
may our hearts be open to the kind of love
  and compassion you always offer us.
Give us the grace to respond in love
  to those who hurt us.
Through Christ our Lord.
Amen.

✙ All make the sign of the cross.

PRAYER FOR WEDNESDAY, FEBRUARY 21, 2024

OPENING

In today's parable, the slave owes the lord a debt that is astronomical. His assurance to the lord that he will pay everything in full is laughable in the face of such a large debt. What we owe God is incalculable—the fullness of our lives, all the beauty and blessings and grace, the world we exist in—all has been given to us by God. And yet he does not count it as debt to be repaid, but as a gift of love. St. Peter Damian (988–1072), whose feast day we celebrate today, was a monk and bishop who lived a life of prayer and study of the Bible.

✢ All make the sign of the cross.

In the name of the Father, and of the Son, and of the Holy Spirit. Amen.

PSALM
(For a longer psalm, see page xiv.)
Psalm 34:4–5

The LORD saves the crushed in spirit.

The LORD saves the crushed in spirit.

I sought the LORD, and he answered me
   and delivered me from all my fears.
Look to him, and be radiant,
   so your faces shall never be ashamed.

The LORD saves the crushed in spirit.

◆ All stand and sing **Praise to you, Lord Jesus Christ…**

GOSPEL
Matthew 18:23–27

A reading from the holy Gospel according to Matthew.

Jesus said, "The kingdom of heaven may be compared to a king who wished to settle accounts with his slaves. When he began the reckoning, one who owed him ten thousand talents was brought to him, and, as he could not pay, his lord ordered him to be sold, together with his wife and children and all his possessions and payment to be made. So the slave fell on his knees before him, saying, 'Have patience with me, and I will pay you everything.' And out of pity for him, the lord of that slave released him and forgave him the debt."

The Gospel of the Lord.

◆ All sit and observe silence.

FOR SILENT REFLECTION

Think about this silently in your heart. How do you show God you are grateful for all that he has given you?

CLOSING PRAYER

Let us pray to God for our needs and the needs of others: our family, neighborhood, and the world. For each need we say, "Lord, hear our prayer."

◆ All may add their own prayers here.

Let us pray: **Our Father . . . Amen.**

Father in heaven,
thank you for loving us and giving us
   so much beauty, joy, and wonder.
Our whole lives are a gift of your love.
We praise you in Christ's name.

Amen.

✢ All make the sign of the cross.

PRAYER FOR
THURSDAY, FEBRUARY 22, 2024

OPENING

Today we celebrate a peculiar feast: the Chair of St. Peter. It is not about an actual piece of furniture, but the office it represents. Like St. Peter the apostle, who is the first pope, some of the occupants of the chair have stumbled (and some have failed). Yet the office of pope endures as a sign of our communion in the one Body of Christ, held together in love. We are called to do the opposite of the forgiven slave in today's Gospel.

✣ All make the sign of the cross.

In the name of the Father, and of the Son, and of the Holy Spirit. Amen.

PSALM
(For a longer psalm, see page xiv.)
Psalm 34:4–5

The Lord saves the crushed in spirit.

The Lord saves the crushed in spirit.

I sought the Lord, and he answered me
   and delivered me from all my fears.
Look to him, and be radiant,
   so your faces shall never be ashamed.

The Lord saves the crushed in spirit.

◆ All stand and sing **Praise to you, Lord Jesus Christ...**

GOSPEL
Matthew 18:28, 28c–33

A reading from the holy Gospel according to Matthew.

Jesus continued, "That same slave, as he went out, came upon one of his fellow-slaves who owed him a hundred denarii, and seizing him by the throat, he said, 'Pay what you owe.' Then his fellow-slave fell down and pleaded with him, 'Have patience with me, and I will pay you.' But he refused; then he went and threw him into prison until he should pay the debt. When his fellow-slaves saw what had happened, they were greatly distressed, and they went and reported to their lord all that had taken place. Then his lord summoned him and said to him, 'You wicked slave! I forgave you all that debt because you pleaded with me. Should you not have had mercy on your fellow-slave, as I had mercy on you?'"

The Gospel of the Lord.

◆ All sit and observe silence.

FOR SILENT REFLECTION

Think about this silently in your heart. How do you share God's love and forgiveness?

CLOSING PRAYER

Let us pray to God for our needs and the needs of others: our family, neighborhood, and the world. For each need we say, "Lord, hear our prayer."

◆ All may add their own prayers here.

Let us pray: **Our Father . . . Amen.**

Merciful Father,
teach us to forgive others
   as you have forgiven us.
Through Christ our Lord.

Amen.

✣ All make the sign of the cross.

PRAYER FOR
FRIDAY, FEBRUARY 23, 2024

OPENING

Today is the feast of St. Polycarp, an early Christian martyr and Bishop of Smyrna. The account of his death is considered the most reliable account of an early martyr. In the Gospel passage, Jesus compares himself to a vine, and the people of God to the branches. The vine of Christ's church grows and spreads with each new believer, and those believers are connected to the same one vine. We bear fruit by abiding in God.

✠ All make the sign of the cross.

In the name of the Father, and of the Son, and of the Holy Spirit. Amen.

PSALM
(For a longer psalm, see page xiv.)
Psalm 34:4–5

The Lord saves the crushed in spirit.

The Lord saves the crushed in spirit.

I sought the Lord, and he answered me
   and delivered me from all my fears.
Look to him, and be radiant,
   so your faces shall never be ashamed.

The Lord saves the crushed in spirit.

◆ All stand and sing **Praise to you, Lord Jesus Christ...**

GOSPEL
John 15:1–2a, 4–7

A reading from the holy Gospel according to John.

Jesus said, "I am the true vine, and my Father is the vinegrower. He removes every branch in me that bears no fruit. Abide in me as I abide in you. Just as the branch cannot bear fruit by itself unless it abides in the vine, neither can you unless you abide in me. I am the vine; you are the branches. Those who abide in me and I in them bear much fruit, because apart from me you can do nothing. Whoever does not abide in me is thrown away like a branch and withers; such branches are gathered, thrown into the fire, and burned. If you abide in me and my words abide in you, ask for whatever you wish, and it will be done or you."

The Gospel of the Lord.

◆ All sit and observe silence.

FOR SILENT REFLECTION

Think about this silently in your heart. How does your life produce fruit for God?

CLOSING PRAYER

Let us pray to God for our needs and the needs of others: our family, neighborhood, and the world. For each need we say, "Lord, hear our prayer."

◆ All may add their own prayers here.

Let us pray: **Our Father . . . Amen.**

Heavenly Father,
you abide in each of us.
Help us to live truly as branches
   of the one true vine,
gathered together in love and mutual care
   to produce good fruit
in the name of Christ our Lord.

Amen.

✠ All make the sign of the cross.

PRAYER FOR THE WEEK
WITH A READING FROM THE GOSPEL FOR SUNDAY, FEBRUARY 25, 2024

OPENING

The mystery of the transfiguration did not stop with Jesus. The disciples, too, were changed when they went up the mountain. We are called to experience this same change. But we won't encounter God if we don't first accept the invitation to travel alongside him like the disciples, to journey through life with him. He will lead us, like them, to joy and insight and wonder and mystery.

✢ All make the sign of the cross.

In the name of the Father, and of the Son, and of the Holy Spirit. Amen.

PSALM
(For a longer psalm, see page xiv.)
Psalm 34:4–5

The LORD saves the crushed in spirit.

The LORD saves the crushed in spirit.

I sought the LORD, and he answered me
   and delivered me from all my fears.
Look to him, and be radiant,
   so your faces shall never be ashamed.

The LORD saves the crushed in spirit.

◆ All stand and sing **Praise to you, Lord Jesus Christ…**

GOSPEL
Mark 9:2–4, 7–10a

A reading from the holy Gospel according to Mark.

Six days later, Jesus took with him Peter and James and John and led them up a high mountain apart, by themselves. And he was transfigured before them, and his clothes became dazzling bright, such as no one on earth could brighten them. And there appeared to them Elijah with Moses, who were talking with Jesus. Then a cloud overshadowed them, and from the cloud there came a voice, "This is my Son, the Beloved; listen to him!" Suddenly when they looked around, they saw no one with them any more, but only Jesus.

As they were coming down the mountain, he ordered them to tell no one about what they had seen. So they kept the matter to themselves.

The Gospel of the Lord.

◆ All sit and observe silence.

FOR SILENT REFLECTION

Think about this silently in your heart. Where has God called you to go?

CLOSING PRAYER

Let us pray to God for our needs and the needs of others: our family, neighborhood, and the world. For each need we say, "Lord, hear our prayer."

◆ All may add their own prayers here.

Let us pray: **Our Father . . . Amen.**

Lord Jesus,
help us to see you as you truly are
and to follow you always.
Who live and reign with God the Father,
in the unity of the Holy Spirit,
God, for ever and ever.

Amen.

✢ All make the sign of the cross.

PRAYER FOR MONDAY, FEBRUARY 26, 2024

OPENING

This week our readings focus on the particular love God has for those who are lost and then come back to God. In the Parable of the Lost Sheep, Jesus compared himself to a shepherd who refuses to lose even one sheep out of one hundred. And when he finds his lost sheep, he rejoices. God welcomes each of us back into his kingdom in this same way: with rejoicing and with enduring love.

✚ All make the sign of the cross.

In the name of the Father, and of the Son, and of the Holy Spirit. Amen.

PSALM
(For a longer psalm, see page xiv.)
Psalm 34:4–5

The L<small>ORD</small> saves the crushed in spirit.

The L<small>ORD</small> saves the crushed in spirit.

I sought the L<small>ORD</small>, and he answered me
   and delivered me from all my fears.
Look to him, and be radiant,
   so your faces shall never be ashamed.

The L<small>ORD</small> saves the crushed in spirit.

◆ All stand and sing **Praise to you, Lord Jesus Christ…**

GOSPEL
Luke 15:2–7

A reading from the holy Gospel according to Luke.

The Pharisees [FAYR-uh-seez] and the scribes were grumbling and saying, "This fellow welcomes sinners and eats with them." So Jesus told them this parable: "Which one of you, having a hundred sheep and losing one of them, does not leave the ninety-nine in the wilderness and go after the one that is lost until he finds it? When he has found it, he lays it on his shoulders and rejoices. And when he comes home, he calls together his friends and neighbors, saying to them, 'Rejoice with me, for I have found my lost sheep.' Just so, I tell you, there will be more joy in heaven over one sinner who repents than over ninety-nine righteous persons who need no repentance."

The Gospel of the Lord.

◆ All sit and observe silence.

FOR SILENT REFLECTION

Think about this silently in your heart. Why would the heavens rejoice when one person returns to God?

CLOSING PRAYER

Let us pray to God for our needs and the needs of others: our family, neighborhood, and the world. For each need we say, "Lord, hear our prayer."

◆ All may add their own prayers here.

Let us pray: **Our Father . . . Amen.**

Good Shepherd,
thank you for tender care and welcome,
especially when we become lost.
Who live and reign with God the Father,
in the unity of the Holy Spirit,
God, for ever and ever.

Amen.

✚ All make the sign of the cross.

PRAYER FOR
TUESDAY, FEBRUARY 27, 2024

OPENING

The woman in today's parable searches carefully for her lost coin, and when it is found, rejoices with all of her friends and neighbors. Jesus makes it clear that there is nothing that will permanently separate us from God. If we truly repent and desire to live in God again, not only will that desire be granted, there will also be a celebration among the angels in heaven!

✢ All make the sign of the cross.

> **In the name of the Father, and of the Son, and of the Holy Spirit. Amen.**

PSALM

(For a longer psalm, see page xiv.)
Psalm 34:4–5

The LORD saves the crushed in spirit.

The LORD saves the crushed in spirit.

I sought the LORD, and he answered me
 and delivered me from all my fears.
Look to him, and be radiant,
 so your faces shall never be ashamed.

The LORD saves the crushed in spirit.

◆ All stand and sing **Praise to you, Lord Jesus Christ…**

GOSPEL

Luke 15:1–3, 8–10

A reading from the holy Gospel according to Luke.

Now all the tax collectors and sinners were coming near to listen to Jesus. And the Pharisees and the scribes were grumbling and saying, "This fellow welcomes sinners and eats with them." So he told them this parable: "What woman having ten silver coins, if she loses one of them, does not light a lamp, sweep the house, and search carefully until she finds it? And when she has found it, she calls together her friends and neighbors, saying, 'Rejoice with me, for I have found the coin that I had lost.' Just so, I tell you, there is joy in the presence of the angels of God over one sinner who repents."

The Gospel of the Lord.

◆ All sit and observe silence.

FOR SILENT REFLECTION

Think about this silently in your heart. How may the sacrament of reconciliation help you come back to God?

CLOSING PRAYER

Let us pray to God for our needs and the needs of others: our family, neighborhood, and the world. For each need we say, "Lord, hear our prayer."

◆ All may add their own prayers here.

Let us pray: **Our Father . . . Amen.**

Kind Father,
you have taught us how to forgive
 through your own vast and loving
 mercy.
Help us to accept your love and mercy
 and live always in your light.
Through Jesus Christ our Lord.

Amen.

✢ All make the sign of the cross.

PRAYER FOR WEDNESDAY, FEBRUARY 28, 2024

OPENING

The younger son in the Parable of the Prodigal Son wanted for nothing in his father's home. But he was prideful and desired to possess all that he could, demanding his inheritance and leaving his home. He squandered all of these good gifts, and then found he was left with nothing. God has given us many blessings: our families and homes, food to eat, gifts of intelligence and joy, simple pleasures, this entire beautiful world.

✚ All make the sign of the cross.

In the name of the Father, and of the Son, and of the Holy Spirit. Amen.

PSALM
(For a longer psalm, see page xiv.)
Psalm 34:4–5

The Lord saves the crushed in spirit.

The Lord saves the crushed in spirit.

I sought the Lord, and he answered me
   and delivered me from all my fears.
Look to him, and be radiant,
   so your faces shall never be ashamed.

The Lord saves the crushed in spirit.

◆ All stand and sing **Praise to you, Lord Jesus Christ…**

GOSPEL
Luke 15:11–13a, 14ac, 15–16a, 17a, 18ab, 19a

A reading from the holy Gospel according to Luke.

Then Jesus said, "There was a man who had two sons. The younger of them said to his father, 'Father, give me the share of the wealth that will belong to me.' So he divided his assets between them. A few days later the younger son gathered all he had and traveled to a distant region. When he had spent everything, he began to be in need. So he went and hired himself out to one of the citizens of that region, who sent him to his fields to feed the pigs. He would gladly have filled his stomach with the pods that the pigs were eating. But when he came to his senses he said, 'I will get up and go to my father, and I will say to him, "I am no longer worthy to be called your son."'"

The Gospel of the Lord.

◆ All sit and observe silence.

FOR SILENT REFLECTION

Think about this silently in your heart. How do you treat the gifts God has given to you?

CLOSING PRAYER

Let us pray to God for our needs and the needs of others: our family, neighborhood, and the world. For each need we say, "Lord, hear our prayer."

◆ All may add their own prayers here.

Let us pray: **Our Father . . . Amen.**

Father in heaven,
you are the source of all that is good.
We praise you and thank you
   for all that we have,
and all that you have in store for us.
Through Christ our Lord.

Amen.

✚ All make the sign of the cross.

PRAYER FOR THURSDAY, FEBRUARY 29, 2024

OPENING

When the younger son came home, he begged his father to treat him as a servant, believing himself no longer worthy to be called a son. But his father rejoiced at his son's return. He does not hold a grudge, and he is not interested in making his son pay for his mistakes. He sees his beloved and feels pure joy and love. Our heavenly Father is just as merciful. His love extends far beyond anything we can imagine, and is much stronger than anything we can do to offend. All we need to do is return to him.

✚ All make the sign of the cross.

In the name of the Father, and of the Son, and of the Holy Spirit. Amen.

PSALM

(For a longer psalm, see page xiv.)
Psalm 34:4–5

The LORD saves the crushed in spirit.

The LORD saves the crushed in spirit.

I sought the LORD, and he answered me
   and delivered me from all my fears.
Look to him, and be radiant,
   so your faces shall never be ashamed.

The LORD saves the crushed in spirit.

◆ All stand and sing **Praise to you, Lord Jesus Christ...**

GOSPEL

Luke 15:20–24

A reading from the holy Gospel according to Luke.

Jesus continued, "So the younger son set off and went to his father. But while he was still far off, his father saw him and was filled with compassion; he ran and put his arms around him and kissed him. Then the son said to him, 'Father, I have sinned against heaven and before you; I am no longer worthy to be called your son.' But the father said to his slaves, 'Quickly, bring out a robe—the best one—and put it on him; put a ring on his finger and sandals on his feet. And get the fatted calf and kill it, and let us eat and celebrate, for this son of mine was dead and is alive again; he was lost and is found!' And they began to celebrate."

The Gospel of the Lord.

◆ All sit and observe silence.

FOR SILENT REFLECTION

Think about this silently in your heart. How do you feel about the father's reaction to the return of his younger son?

CLOSING PRAYER

Let us pray to God for our needs and the needs of others: our family, neighborhood, and the world. For each need we say, "Lord, hear our prayer."

◆ All may add their own prayers here.

Let us pray: **Our Father . . . Amen.**

O compassionate God,
give us the courage to return to you,
again and again, in humility.
Through Christ our Lord.

Amen.

✚ All make the sign of the cross.

PRAYER FOR
FRIDAY, MARCH 1, 2024

OPENING

In the conclusion of the Parable of the Prodigal Son, the older brother was furious that his brother did not pay for his mistakes. But the love of the father for both of his sons is infinite and unchanging, as is the love of our heavenly Father. He rejoices in each of his children without reserve, giving all of his love to each one of us.

✠ All make the sign of the cross.

In the name of the Father, and of the Son, and of the Holy Spirit. Amen.

PSALM
(For a longer psalm, see page xiv.)
Psalm 34:4–5

The Lord saves the crushed in spirit.

The Lord saves the crushed in spirit.

I sought the Lord, and he answered me
    and delivered me from all my fears.
Look to him, and be radiant,
    so your faces shall never be ashamed.

The Lord saves the crushed in spirit.

◆ All stand and sing **Praise to you, Lord Jesus Christ…**

GOSPEL
Luke 15:25–29acd, 30–32ac

A reading from the holy Gospel according to Luke.

Jesus continued, "Now his elder son was in the field, and when he came and approached the house, he heard music and dancing. He called one of the slaves and asked what was going on. He replied, 'Your brother has come, and your father has killed the fatted calf because he has got him back safe and sound.' Then he became angry and refused to go in. His father came out and began to plead with him. But he answered his father, 'Listen! You have never given me even a young goat so that I might celebrate with my friends. But when this son of yours came back, who has devoured your property with prostitutes, you killed the fatted calf for him!' Then the father said to him, 'Son, you are always with me, and all that is mine is yours. But we had to celebrate and rejoice, he was lost and has been found.'"

The Gospel of the Lord.

◆ All sit and observe silence.

FOR SILENT REFLECTION

Think about this silently in your heart. Have you ever felt jealous like the older brother in today's Gospel? How might you overcome feelings of envy?

CLOSING PRAYER

Let us pray to God for our needs and the needs of others: our family, neighborhood, and the world. For each need we say, "Lord, hear our prayer."

◆ All may add their own prayers here.

Let us pray: **Our Father . . . Amen.**

Heavenly Father,
cleanse our hearts of jealousy and anger.
Through Christ our Lord.

Amen.

✠ All make the sign of the cross.

PRAYER FOR THE WEEK
WITH A READING FROM THE GOSPEL FOR SUNDAY, MARCH 3, 2024

OPENING

The scene of Jesus flipping tables and driving livestock out of the temple is startling. Jesus flipped those tables to signify a new worship symbolized by his presence, one cleansed of the excesses and false practice that had overtaken the house of Israel. His actions continue to be a sign for all of us to cleanse our worship of the trappings of power or the performance of faith, to cling fast to the core of faith. Namely, to a person: Jesus Christ.

✢ All make the sign of the cross.

In the name of the Father, and of the Son, and of the Holy Spirit. Amen.

PSALM
(For a longer psalm, see page xiv.)
Psalm 34:4–5

The LORD saves the crushed in spirit.

The LORD saves the crushed in spirit.

I sought the LORD, and he answered me
   and delivered me from all my fears.
Look to him, and be radiant,
   so your faces shall never be ashamed.

The LORD saves the crushed in spirit.

◆ All stand and sing **Praise to you, Lord Jesus Christ...**

GOSPEL
John 2:13–17

A reading from the holy Gospel according to John.

The Passover of the Jews was near, and Jesus went up to Jerusalem. In the temple he found people selling cattle, sheep, and doves and the money changers seated at their tables. Making a whip of cords, he drove all of them out of the temple, with the sheep and the cattle. He also poured out the coins of the money changers and overturned their tables. He told those who were selling the doves, "Take these things out of here! Stop making my Father's house a marketplace!" His disciples remembered that it was written, "Zeal for your house will consume me."

The Gospel of the Lord.

◆ All sit and observe silence.

FOR SILENT REFLECTION

Think about this silently in your heart. Have you ever been distracted from true worship of God? How can you root out what holds you back from true prayer and worship?

CLOSING PRAYER

Let us pray to God for our needs and the needs of others: our family, neighborhood, and the world. For each need we say, "Lord, hear our prayer."

◆ All may add their own prayers here.

Let us pray: **Our Father . . . Amen.**

Lord Jesus,
you are at the center of our worship.
Help us to hold on to our faith in you
   as a gift beyond price.
Who live and reign with God the Father,
in the unity of the Holy Spirit,
God, for ever and ever.

Amen.

✢ All make the sign of the cross.

PRAYER FOR MONDAY, MARCH 4, 2024

OPENING

St. James describes a good life as one lived in gentleness, peace, and mercy, without jealousy or resentment. Today, we remember St. Casimir, patron of Poland, Lithuania, and Russia. Though wealthy and powerful, the young prince lived a simple life, sleeping on the hard ground, praying, and choosing lifelong celibacy. When his father desired to make war, Casimir committed himself to peace, and stood firm against much pressure. Casimir truly lived a good life of gentleness, peace, and wisdom.

✣ All make the sign of the cross.

In the name of the Father, and of the Son, and of the Holy Spirit. Amen.

PSALM

(For a longer psalm, see page xiv.)
Psalm 34:4–5

The LORD saves the crushed in spirit.

The LORD saves the crushed in spirit.

I sought the LORD, and he answered me
 and delivered me from all my fears.
Look to him, and be radiant,
 so your faces shall never be ashamed.

The LORD saves the crushed in spirit.

READING

James 3:13, 16–18

A reading from the Letter of James.

Who is wise and knowledgeable among you? Show by your good life that your works are done with gentleness born of wisdom. For where there is envy and selfish ambition, there will also be disorder and wickedness of every kind. But the wisdom from above is first pure, then peaceable, gentle, willing to yield, full of mercy and good fruits, without a trace of partiality or hypocrisy. And the fruit of righteousness is sown in peace for those who make peace.

The Word of the Lord.

◆ All observe silence.

FOR SILENT REFLECTION

Think about this silently in your heart. What does it mean to live a good life? How can you sow peace in your life?

CLOSING PRAYER

Let us pray to God for our needs and the needs of others: our family, neighborhood, and the world. For each need we say, "Lord, hear our prayer."

◆ All may add their own prayers here.

Let us pray: **Our Father . . . Amen.**

O God,
give us the grace to seek a good life,
to turn away from jealousy and ambition
and toward gentleness and peace.
Through Christ our Lord.

Amen.

✣ All make the sign of the cross.

PRAYER FOR
TUESDAY, MARCH 5, 2024

OPENING

It seems easy to avoid breaking the fifth commandment, "You shall not kill." However, Jesus broadened the commandment to mean not only actual murder, but also insult or anger against a brother or sister. Jesus challenges us to do more than the bare minimum, but also to follow the spirit of the law. Let us not offend our brothers or sisters in any way; let us refrain from harming with words or actions. In doing so, we truly follow Jesus.

✙ All make the sign of the cross.

In the name of the Father, and of the Son, and of the Holy Spirit. Amen.

PSALM
(For a longer psalm, see page xiv.)
Psalm 34:4–5

The L ORD saves the crushed in spirit.

The L ORD saves the crushed in spirit.

I sought the L ORD, and he answered me
   and delivered me from all my fears.
Look to him, and be radiant,
   so your faces shall never be ashamed.

The L ORD saves the crushed in spirit.

◆ All stand and sing **Praise to you, Lord Jesus Christ…**

GOSPEL
Matthew 5:21–24

A reading from the holy Gospel according to Matthew.

Jesus said, "You have heard that it was said to those of ancient times, 'You shall not murder'; and 'whoever murders shall be liable to judgment.' But I say to you that if you are angry with a brother or sister, you will be liable to judgment, and if you insult a brother or sister, you will be liable to the council, and if you say, 'You fool,' you will be liable to the hell of fire. So when you are offering your gift at the altar, if you remember that your brother or sister has something against you, leave your gift there before the altar and go; first be reconciled to your brother or sister, and then come and offer your gift."

The Gospel of the Lord.

◆ All sit and observe silence.

FOR SILENT REFLECTION

Think about this silently in your heart. Have you hurt someone recently? How can you reconcile with that person?

CLOSING PRAYER

Let us pray to God for our needs and the needs of others: our family, neighborhood, and the world. For each need we say, "Lord, hear our prayer."

◆ All may add their own prayers here.

Let us pray: **Our Father . . . Amen.**

Merciful God,
help us to see how anger affects
   our relationship with others.
May we ask for forgiveness
   and reconcile with them and with you.
We pray in Christ's name.
Amen.

✙ All make the sign of the cross.

PRAYER FOR
WEDNESDAY, MARCH 6, 2024

OPENING

This part of the Sermon on the Plain is perhaps one of the most challenging teachings of Jesus. After all, it is possible not to retaliate when someone harms you. But to bless them? To do good for them? to love them? Those actions seem too hard, and frankly, too extreme. But we are called not to tolerance, but to *love*, just as Jesus does. The hardest people to love are those who don't love you, those who hurt you and set themselves against you.

✚ All make the sign of the cross.

In the name of the Father, and of the Son, and of the Holy Spirit. Amen.

PSALM
(For a longer psalm, see page xiv.)
Psalm 34:4–5

The Lord saves the crushed in spirit.

The Lord saves the crushed in spirit.

I sought the Lord, and he answered me
   and delivered me from all my fears.
Look to him, and be radiant,
   so your faces shall never be ashamed.

The Lord saves the crushed in spirit.

◆ All stand and sing **Praise to you, Lord Jesus Christ...**

GOSPEL
Luke 6:27b–32, 35a

A reading from the holy Gospel according to Luke.

Jesus said, "Love your enemies; do good to those who hate you; bless those who curse you; pray for those who mistreat you. If anyone strikes you on the cheek, offer the other also, and from anyone who takes away your coat do not withhold even your shirt. Give to everyone who asks of you, and if anyone takes away what is yours, do not ask for it back again. Do to others as you would have them do to you. If you love those who love you, what credit is that to you? For even sinners love those who love them. Instead, love your enemies, do good, and lend, expecting nothing in return."

The Gospel of the Lord.

◆ All sit and observe silence.

FOR SILENT REFLECTION

Think about this silently in your heart. Think about someone who has hurt you and pray for that person today.

CLOSING PRAYER

Let us pray to God for our needs and the needs of others: our family, neighborhood, and the world. For each need we say, "Lord, hear our prayer."

◆ All may add their own prayers here.

Let us pray: **Our Father . . . Amen.**

Father in heaven,
may we be kinder and more forgiving,
especially during this holy season of Lent.
Through Christ our Lord.

Amen.

✚ All make the sign of the cross.

PRAYER FOR
THURSDAY, MARCH 7, 2024

OPENING

Today, we will hear Jesus condemn hypocrisy. Jesus does not want followers in name only—he wants us to be willing to show our faith by the way we live. He also wants us to refrain from judgement, knowing that each of us have faults and failings too. We need to be concerned with our own lives and hearts before we worry about others. We honor Sts. Perpetua and Felicity today, respectively a noblewoman and a slave. Both were young mothers martyred together in the third century. Their faith sustained them even in the face of persecution and death.

✤ All make the sign of the cross.

In the name of the Father, and of the Son, and of the Holy Spirit. Amen.

PSALM
(For a longer psalm, see page xiv.)
Psalm 34:4–5

The LORD saves the crushed in spirit.

The LORD saves the crushed in spirit.

I sought the LORD, and he answered me
   and delivered me from all my fears.
Look to him, and be radiant,
   so your faces shall never be ashamed.

The LORD saves the crushed in spirit.

◆ All stand and sing **Praise to you, Lord Jesus Christ...**

GOSPEL
Luke 6:37–38A, 41–42

A reading from the holy Gospel according to Luke.

Jesus said, "Do not judge, and you will not be judged; do not condemn, and you will not be condemned. Forgive, and you will be forgiven; give, and it will be given to you. Why do you see the speck in your neighbor's eye but do not notice the log in your own eye? Or how can you say to your neighbor, 'Friend, let me take out the speck in your eye,' when you yourself do not see the log in your own eye? You hypocrite, first take the log out of your own eye, and then you will see clearly to take the speck out of your neighbor's eye."

The Gospel of the Lord.

◆ All sit and observe silence.

FOR SILENT REFLECTION

Think about this silently in your heart. What do you need to change in your life? How can you be less judgmental of others?

CLOSING PRAYER

Let us pray to God for our needs and the needs of others: our family, neighborhood, and the world. For each need we say, "Lord, hear our prayer."

◆ All may add their own prayers here.

Let us pray: **Our Father . . . Amen.**

God of love,
give us the courage to look deeply
   into our own hearts
and make changes to follow you
   more closely.
Through Christ our Lord.

Amen.

✤ All make the sign of the cross.

PRAYER FOR FRIDAY, MARCH 8, 2024

OPENING

St. John of God (1495–1550) was an ex-soldier who desired to repent of his former sinful life. He first sought physical repentance, beating himself publicly. Eventually he was advised to redirect his energies to the needs of others. St. John devoted the rest of his life to tending to the poor and the sick. He lived the words we hear today about the Final Judgment: giving food and drink and welcoming the stranger.

✢ All make the sign of the cross.

In the name of the Father, and of the Son, and of the Holy Spirit. Amen.

PSALM
(For a longer psalm, see page xiv.)
Psalm 34:4–5

The Lord saves the crushed in spirit.

The Lord saves the crushed in spirit.

I sought the Lord, and he answered me
   and delivered me from all my fears.
Look to him, and be radiant,
   so your faces shall never be ashamed.

The Lord saves the crushed in spirit.

◆ All stand and sing **Praise to you, Lord Jesus Christ…**

GOSPEL
Matthew 25:34–35, 37–38A, 40

A reading from the holy Gospel according to Matthew.

Then the king will say to those at his right hand, "Come, you that are blessed by my Father, inherit the kingdom prepared for you from the foundation of the world, for I was hungry and you gave me food, I was thirsty and you gave me something to drink, I was a stranger and you welcomed me." Then the righteous will answer him, "Lord, when was it that we saw you hungry and gave you food or thirsty and gave you something to drink? And when was it that we saw you a stranger and welcomed you?" And the king will answer them, "Truly I tell you, just as you did it to one of the least of these brothers and sisters of mine, you did it to me."

The Gospel of the Lord.

◆ All sit and observe silence.

FOR SILENT REFLECTION

Think about this silently in your heart. How do you care for others, especially those most in need of help?

CLOSING PRAYER

Let us pray to God for our needs and the needs of others: our family, neighborhood, and the world. For each need we say, "Lord, hear our prayer."

◆ All may add their own prayers here.

Let us pray: **Our Father . . . Amen.**

Compassionate God,
in caring for the sick and poor,
   we honor you.
By the intercession of St. John,
may we respond to those who suffer.
Through Christ our Lord.

Amen.

✢ All make the sign of the cross.

PRAYER FOR THE WEEK
WITH A READING FROM THE GOSPEL FOR **SUNDAY, MARCH 10, 2024**

OPENING

Today is Laetare Sunday, and we rejoice in the midst of Lent! Jesus came into the world for salvation, not for judgment. He came to lead people out of the darkness of sin and selfishness into the light of love and truth. We are free to choose evil instead of good, hate instead of love, self instead of others. May each of us choose to walk as children of the light and live in truth, honesty, and goodness.

✚ All make the sign of the cross.

In the name of the Father, and of the Son, and of the Holy Spirit. Amen.

PSALM
(For a longer psalm, see page xiv.)
Psalm 34:4–5

The LORD saves the crushed in spirit.

The LORD saves the crushed in spirit.

I sought the LORD, and he answered me
 and delivered me from all my fears.
Look to him, and be radiant,
 so your faces shall never be ashamed.

The LORD saves the crushed in spirit.

◆ All stand and sing **Praise to you, Lord Jesus Christ…**

GOSPEL
John 3:16–18a, 19–21

A reading from the holy Gospel according to John.

For God so loved the world that he gave his only Son, so that everyone who believes in him may not perish but may have eternal life. Indeed, God did not send the Son into the world to condemn the world but in order that the world might be saved through him. Those who believe in him are not condemned. And this is the judgment, that the light has come into the world, and people loved darkness rather than light because their deeds were evil. For all who do evil hate the light and do not come to the light, so that their deeds may not be exposed. But those who do what is true come to the light, so that it may be clearly seen that their deeds have been done in God.

The Gospel of the Lord.

◆ All sit and observe silence.

FOR SILENT REFLECTION

Think about this silently in your heart. We are each faced with choices every day. How can you choose to live in the light today and every day?

CLOSING PRAYER

Let us pray to God for our needs and the needs of others: our family, neighborhood, and the world. For each need we say, "Lord, hear our prayer."

◆ All may add their own prayers here.

Let us pray: **Our Father . . . Amen.**

O God,
may your love that
creates, redeems, and sustains us
be with us always, until the end of time.
We pray in Christ's name.

Amen.

✚ All make the sign of the cross.

PRAYER FOR MONDAY, MARCH 11, 2024

OPENING

Jesus told the Samaritan woman that he would give her living water, a water that would end thirst and lead to eternal life. When we drink from the spring of earthly pleasure, we still thirst for more beauty, more truth, more justice, more peace, more joy. To drink of the living water, to be consumed by it, to be enveloped in the waterfall of grace is to thirst no more: this is the water of eternal life.

✚ All make the sign of the cross.

In the name of the Father, and of the Son, and of the Holy Spirit. Amen.

PSALM
(For a longer psalm, see page xiv.)
Psalm 34:4–5

The Lord saves the crushed in spirit.

The Lord saves the crushed in spirit.

I sought the Lord, and he answered me
   and delivered me from all my fears.
Look to him, and be radiant,
   so your faces shall never be ashamed.

The Lord saves the crushed in spirit.

◆ All stand and sing **Praise to you, Lord Jesus Christ...**

GOSPEL
John 4:5a, 6a, 7, 9a, 10–11ac, 13aC, 14

A reading from the holy Gospel according to John.

So Jesus came to a Samaritan [suh-MAYR-uh-tuhn] city called Sychar [SĪ-kahr]. Jacob's well was there. A Samaritan woman came to draw water, and Jesus said to her, "Give me a drink." The Samaritan woman said to him, "How is it that you, a Jew, ask a drink of me, a woman of Samaria?" Jesus answered her, "If you knew the gift of God and who it is that is saying to you, 'Give me a drink,' you would have asked him, and he would have given you living water." The woman said to him, "Sir, where do you get that living water? Jesus said to her, "Those who drink of the water that I will give them will never be thirsty. The water that I will give will become in them a spring of water gushing up to eternal life."

The Gospel of the Lord.

◆ All sit and observe silence.

FOR SILENT REFLECTION

Think about this silently in your heart. What do you think the living water is like? How does it change a person?

CLOSING PRAYER

Let us pray to God for our needs and the needs of others: our family, neighborhood, and the world. For each need we say, "Lord, hear our prayer."

◆ All may add their own prayers here.

Let us pray: **Our Father . . . Amen.**

We thank you and praise you, O God,
for the thirst of our souls is quenched
by the Living Water that is Christ Jesus,
in whose name we pray.

Amen.

✚ All make the sign of the cross.

PRAYER FOR
TUESDAY, MARCH 12, 2024

OPENING

Jesus is the light of the world. He gave sight to the man born blind so that others might see clearly. And yet there were still those who willfully refused to see Jesus for what and who he was. The Pharisees questioned the man born blind and even his parents, trying to find evidence to discredit Jesus. They refused to believe the evidence before them. They refused to see the light.

✢ All make the sign of the cross.

In the name of the Father, and of the Son, and of the Holy Spirit. Amen.

PSALM
(For a longer psalm, see page xiv.)
Psalm 34:4–5

The LORD saves the crushed in spirit.

The LORD saves the crushed in spirit.

I sought the LORD, and he answered me
    and delivered me from all my fears.
Look to him, and be radiant,
    so your faces shall never be ashamed.

The LORD saves the crushed in spirit.

◆ All stand and sing **Praise to you, Lord Jesus Christ...**

GOSPEL
John 9:1b, 5, 7ac, 15, 17e, 35c, 36a, 37, 38a

A reading from the holy Gospel according to John.

Jesus saw a man blind from birth [and said,] "As long as I am in the world, I am the light of the world. Go, wash in the pool of Siloam." Then he went and washed and came back able to see. Then the Pharisees also began to ask him how he had received his sight. He said to them, "Jesus put mud on my eyes. Then I washed, and now I see. He is a prophet." Jesus said to one born blind, "Do you believe in the Son of Man?" He answered, "And who is he, sir?" Jesus said to him, "You have seen him, and the one speaking with you is he." He said, "Lord, I believe."

The Gospel of the Lord.

◆ All sit and observe silence.

FOR SILENT REFLECTION

Think about this silently in your heart. Open your eyes to God and say with the man born blind, "Lord, I believe."

CLOSING PRAYER

Let us pray to God for our needs and the needs of others: our family, neighborhood, and the world. For each need we say, "Lord, hear our prayer."

◆ All may add their own prayers here.

Let us pray: **Our Father . . . Amen.**

O Jesus, Light of the World,
help us to be a light in the darkness.
May we be a healing presence to those who are in pain and who are suffering.
Who live and reign with God the Father,
in the unity of the Holy Spirit,
God, for ever and ever.

Amen.

✢ All make the sign of the cross.

PRAYER FOR WEDNESDAY, MARCH 13, 2024

OPENING

Lazarus' sister Martha went to Jesus and professed her faith in him and his saving grace. And out of her faith, Jesus performed a miracle, calling her dead brother back to life. If we believe Jesus is the Son of God, then we also believe he is the resurrection, the kingdom come, the fulfillment of hope. And we will have new life in him.

✦ All make the sign of the cross.

In the name of the Father, and of the Son, and of the Holy Spirit. Amen.

PSALM
(For a longer psalm, see page xiv.)
Psalm 34:4–5

The LORD saves the crushed in spirit.

The LORD saves the crushed in spirit.

I sought the LORD, and he answered me
   and delivered me from all my fears.
Look to him, and be radiant,
   so your faces shall never be ashamed.

The LORD saves the crushed in spirit.

◆ All stand and sing **Praise to you, Lord Jesus Christ…**

GOSPEL
John 11:1ab, 3, 17, 21–25ab, 27ab, 43b, 44a

A reading from the holy Gospel according to John.

Now a certain man was ill, Lazarus of Bethany. So the sisters sent a message to Jesus, "Lord, he whom you love is ill." When Jesus arrived, he found Lazarus had already been in the tomb four days. Martha said to Jesus, "Lord, if you had been here, my brother would not have died. But even now I know that God will give you whatever you ask of him." Jesus said to her, "Your brother will rise again." Martha said to him, "I know that he will rise again in the resurrection on the last day." Jesus said to her, "I am the resurrection and the life." Martha said to him, "Yes Lord, I believe you are the Messiah." Jesus cried with a loud voice, "Lazarus, come out!" The dead man came out.

The Gospel of the Lord.

◆ All sit and observe silence.

FOR SILENT REFLECTION

Think about this silently in your heart. Do you believe in Jesus as fervently as Martha did?

CLOSING PRAYER

Let us pray to God for our needs and the needs of others: our family, neighborhood, and the world. For each need we say, "Lord, hear our prayer."

◆ All may add their own prayers here.

Let us pray: **Our Father . . . Amen.**

Lord Jesus,
you have set us free from sin and given us
   everlasting life.
We thank you and love you!
Who live and reign with God the Father,
in the unity of the Holy Spirit,
God, for ever and ever.

Amen.

✦ All make the sign of the cross.

PRAYER FOR
THURSDAY, MARCH 14, 2024

OPENING

St. Paul says that to be an imitator of God, we must speak truth, not let our anger lead us to sin, give to others, use words for building up and not breaking down, put away bitterness and wrath and scheming and malice. Why are we called to do these things? Because we are all "members of each other." Each person you meet is part of you, because we are all part of God.

✚ All make the sign of the cross.

In the name of the Father, and of the Son, and of the Holy Spirit. Amen.

PSALM

(For a longer psalm, see page xiv.)
Psalm 34:4–5

The LORD saves the crushed in spirit.

The LORD saves the crushed in spirit.

I sought the LORD, and he answered me
   and delivered me from all my fears.
Look to him, and be radiant,
   so your faces shall never be ashamed.

The LORD saves the crushed in spirit.

READING

Ephesians 4:25–26, 28ac, 29ab, 31–32; 5:1–2b

A reading from the Letter of Paul to the Ephesians [ee-FEE-zhuhnz].

So then, putting away falsehood, let each of you speak the truth with your neighbor, for we are members of one another. Be angry but do not sin; do not let the sun go down on your anger. Those who steal must give up stealing, so as to have something to share with the needy. Let no evil talk come out of your mouths but only what is good for building up. Put away from you all bitterness and wrath and anger and wrangling and slander, together with all malice. Be kind to one another, tenderhearted, forgiving one another, as God in Christ has forgiven you. Therefore be imitators of God, as beloved children, and walk in love, as Christ loved us and gave himself up for us.

The Word of the Lord.

◆ All observe silence.

FOR SILENT REFLECTION

Think about this silently in your heart. How can you be kinder and more forgiving to others?

CLOSING PRAYER

Let us pray to God for our needs and the needs of others: our family, neighborhood, and the world. For each need we say, "Lord, hear our prayer."

◆ All may add their own prayers here.

Let us pray: **Our Father . . . Amen.**

O Christ Jesus,
help us learn from your example,
so that we may be kinder,
forgive others easily,
and love as you love.
Who live and reign with God the Father,
in the unity of the Holy Spirit,
God, for ever and ever.

Amen.

✚ All make the sign of the cross.

PRAYER FOR FRIDAY, MARCH 15, 2024

OPENING

In God, "there is no darkness at all," but there is darkness in ourselves. There is sin, anger, jealousy, fear, hatred, pride, avarice, cruelty. God's light has the power to banish the darkness in each of us, if we let it. In moments of anger, pray for calm. In moments of pride, pray for humility. In moments of hatred, pray for love. In moments of jealousy, pray for generosity.

✢ All make the sign of the cross.

In the name of the Father, and of the Son, and of the Holy Spirit. Amen.

PSALM
(For a longer psalm, see page xiv.)
Psalm 34:4–5

The LORD saves the crushed in spirit.

The LORD saves the crushed in spirit.

I sought the LORD, and he answered me
   and delivered me from all my fears.
Look to him, and be radiant,
   so your faces shall never be ashamed.

The LORD saves the crushed in spirit.

READING
1 John 1:5; 2:9–11ac, 12, 14c

A reading from the First Book of John.

This is the message we have heard from him and proclaim to you, that God is light and in him there is no darkness at all.

Whoever says, "I am in the light," while hating a brother or sister, is still in the darkness. Whoever loves a brother or sister abides in the light, and in such a person there is no cause for stumbling. But whoever hates a brother or sister is in the darkness, and does not know the way to go, because the darkness has brought on blindness. I am writing to you, little children, because your sins are forgiven on account of his name. I write to you, young people, because you are strong and the word of God abides in you, and you have overcome the evil one.

The Word of the Lord.

◆ All observe silence.

FOR SILENT REFLECTION

Think about this silently in your heart. With God's light, we can vanquish sin. With God's help, we can dedicate our lives to virtue, and walk in the light instead of stumbling in the darkness.

CLOSING PRAYER

Let us pray to God for our needs and the needs of others: our family, neighborhood, and the world. For each need we say, "Lord, hear our prayer."

◆ All may add their own prayers here.

Let us pray: **Our Father . . . Amen.**

O God,
as we continue on our Lenten journey,
may we be faithful to your commands.
By our fasting, prayer, and almsgiving,
may we be bearers of Christ's light.
Through Christ our Lord.

Amen.

✢ All make the sign of the cross.

PRAYER FOR THE WEEK
WITH A READING FROM THE GOSPEL FOR **SUNDAY, MARCH 17, 2024**

OPENING

We are approaching the time of Christ's death and meditating on it with him. As the cold days alternate with glimpses of warmth, as seeds slumber under the ground and buds grow on the trees, as birds tentatively begin to awaken and call, we may see Jesus in the seeds. They have lain on the ground, covered up by dead leaves and soil, seemingly dead. But in time, they will burst forth with life. Christ, our light, was laid in the dark tomb, but rose again, glorified. And even in all the dark, wintry, painful, sad days of our lives, God will give us new life and light.

✣ All make the sign of the cross.

In the name of the Father, and of the Son, and of the Holy Spirit. Amen.

PSALM
(For a longer psalm, see page xiv.)
Psalm 34:4–5

The LORD saves the crushed in spirit.

The LORD saves the crushed in spirit.

I sought the LORD, and he answered me
   and delivered me from all my fears.
Look to him, and be radiant,
   so your faces shall never be ashamed.

The LORD saves the crushed in spirit.

◆ All stand and sing **Praise to you, Lord Jesus Christ...**

GOSPEL
John 12:23–26

A reading from the holy Gospel according to John.

Jesus answered them, "The hour has come for the Son of Man to be glorified. Very truly, I tell you, unless a grain of wheat falls into the earth and dies, it remains just a single grain, but if it dies it bears much fruit. Those who love their life lose it, and those who hate their life in this world will keep it for eternal life. Whoever serves me must follow me, and where I am, there will my servant be also. Whoever serves me, the Father will honor."

The Gospel of the Lord.

◆ All sit and observe silence.

FOR SILENT REFLECTION

Think about this silently in your heart. Have you ever experienced new life or hope after a hard time?

CLOSING PRAYER

Let us pray to God for our needs and the needs of others: our family, neighborhood, and the world. For each need we say, "Lord, hear our prayer."

◆ All may add their own prayers here.

Let us pray: **Our Father . . . Amen.**

Jesus,
as Good Friday draws closer,
may we reflect on your suffering
   and sacrifice.
Let them fill us with meekness
   and consideration.
Who live and reign with God the Father,
in the unity of the Holy Spirit,
God, for ever and ever.

Amen.

✣ All make the sign of the cross.

PRAYER FOR
MONDAY, MARCH 18, 2024

OPENING

We call Jesus' entry into Jerusalem triumphant, but that would have been laughable to the authorities of the time. A Roman general returning home in honor would be feted with large crowds, priests burning incense, and a military parade. And yet Jesus' humility is the triumph. By the manner of his entry, Jesus provides an alternative to the aggressive, prideful, war-mongering leaders of his time. He is the Messiah, but he comes not in a show of power and glory, but in peace.

✢ All make the sign of the cross.

In the name of the Father, and of the Son, and of the Holy Spirit. Amen.

PSALM
(For a longer psalm, see page xiv.)
Psalm 34:4–5

The LORD saves the crushed in spirit.

The LORD saves the crushed in spirit.

I sought the LORD, and he answered me
    and delivered me from all my fears.
Look to him, and be radiant,
    so your faces shall never be ashamed.

The LORD saves the crushed in spirit.

◆ All stand and sing **Praise to you, Lord Jesus Christ...**

GOSPEL
Mark 11:1a, 1c–2, 7–10

A reading from the holy Gospel according to Mark.

When they were approaching Jerusalem, Jesus sent two of his disciples and said to them, "Go into the village ahead of you, and immediately as you enter it you will find tied there a colt that has never been ridden; untie it and bring it." Then they brought the colt to Jesus and threw their cloaks on it, and he sat on it. Many people spread their cloaks on the road, and others spread leafy branches that they had cut in the fields. Then those who went ahead and those who followed were shouting, "Hosanna! Blessed is the one who comes in the name of the Lord! Blessed is the coming kingdom of our ancestor David! Hosanna in the highest heaven!"

The Gospel of the Lord.

◆ All sit and observe silence.

FOR SILENT REFLECTION

Think about this silently in your heart. How do you express your joy or praise Jesus?

CLOSING PRAYER

Let us pray to God for our needs and the needs of others: our family, neighborhood, and the world. For each need we say, "Lord, hear our prayer."

◆ All may add their own prayers here.

Let us pray: **Our Father . . . Amen.**

O Jesus,
you come in triumph, peace, and humility.
Let us walk with you in your journey.
Who live and reign with God the Father,
in the unity of the Holy Spirit,
God, for ever and ever.

Amen.

✢ All make the sign of the cross.

PRAYER SERVICE
SOLEMNITY OF ST. JOSEPH

Prepare six leaders for this service. The third leader will need a Bible for the passage from Matthew. Take time to help the third leader practice the readings. You may wish to sing "You Are the Light of the World," "Blest Are They," or "We Are Called," as opening or closing songs. If the group will sing, prepare someone to lead.

FIRST LEADER:
Today we remember St. Joseph, the husband of Mary and the foster father of Jesus here on earth. At several key times in his life, St. Joseph listened and followed special messengers that God directed to this humble carpenter. St. Joseph's faith led him to marry his fiancée, even though she became pregnant in a divinely inspired way. He courageously took them to Egypt to escape Herod's wrath. And St. Joseph raised Jesus as his own son, guiding his growth.

✢ All make the sign of the cross.

In the name of the Father, and of the Son, and of the Holy Spirit. Amen.

Let us remember St. Joseph as we begin by singing the opening song.

SONG LEADER:

◆ Gesture for all to stand, and lead the first few verses of the song.

SECOND LEADER:
Let us pray:
Almighty Father,
may we look to St. Joseph as our guide
as he responded to your call to be
a devoted husband and father.

We pray with him to your Son Jesus,
our Lord and Savior,
in union with the Holy Spirit.

Amen.

- Remain standing and sing **Praise to you, Lord Jesus Christ . . .**

THIRD LEADER: Matthew 2:13–15

A reading from the holy Gospel according to Matthew.

- Read the Gospel passage from the Bible.

The Gospel of the Lord.

- All remain standing and observe silence.

FOURTH LEADER:

Let us bring our hopes and needs to God as we pray, Lord, hear our prayer.

For the courage to live our faith
through word and action
as St. Joseph did throughout his days,
we pray to the Lord.

For all who are struggling with
tough decisions in life,
may they look to St. Joseph as
a brave friend,
we pray to the Lord.

For all married couples,
may they continue to be an example
of the love and devotion that
St. Joseph and Mary shared,
we pray to the Lord.

For all fathers
and those who nurture others.
Help us to respect and protect life
from conception until natural death,
we pray to the Lord.
May we have the conviction
to lead the way, as St. Joseph did
to hope and the promise
of new life through Jesus Christ,
we pray to the Lord.

FIFTH LEADER:

Let us pray as Jesus taught us:

Our Father . . . Amen.

- Pause, and then say:

Let us offer one another the sign of Christ's peace.

- All offer one another a sign of peace.

SIXTH LEADER:

Let us pray:
Heavenly Father,
your servant St. Joseph
was a man of great faith.
He listened to you in prayer
and to angels whom you sent
in dreams.
He is a symbol for courage
in following God's will.
May we look to him
in times of trouble or doubt.
We ask this through Christ our Lord.

ALL: Amen.

- All make the sign of the cross.

PRAYER FOR
TUESDAY, MARCH 19, 2024

OPENING

We will hear how Judas' heart was full of darkness in this moment, perhaps seething with jealousy or bitterness or anger or greed. And it is scary, because we may have experienced those feelings. As a counter to Judas' dark actions, today we also celebrate the feast of St. Joseph, the adoptive father of Jesus. Joseph, when faced with darkness, chose the light. He accepted his young fiancée and her pregnancy; he believed in her and in the promises of God.

✢ All make the sign of the cross.

In the name of the Father, and of the Son, and of the Holy Spirit. Amen.

PSALM
(For a longer psalm, see page xiv.)
Psalm 34:4–5

The LORD saves the crushed in spirit.

The LORD saves the crushed in spirit.

I sought the LORD, and he answered me
   and delivered me from all my fears.
Look to him, and be radiant,
   so your faces shall never be ashamed.

The LORD saves the crushed in spirit.

◆ All stand and sing **Praise to you, Lord Jesus Christ...**

GOSPEL
Mark 14:1–2, 10–11

A reading from the holy Gospel according to Mark.

It was two days before the Passover and the Festival of Unleavened Bread. The chief priests and the scribes were looking for a way to arrest Jesus by stealth and kill him, for they said, "Not during the festival, or there may be a riot among the people." Then Judas Iscariot [JOO-duhs ih-SKAYR-ee-uht], who was one of the twelve, went to the chief priests in order to betray Jesus to them. When they heard it, they were greatly pleased and promised to give him money. So he began to look for an opportunity to betray Jesus.

The Gospel of the Lord.

◆ All sit and observe silence.

FOR SILENT REFLECTION

Think about this silently in your heart. Have you ever hurt a loved one? How could you have chosen differently?

CLOSING PRAYER

Let us pray to God for our needs and the needs of others: our family, neighborhood, and the world. For each need we say, "Lord, hear our prayer."

◆ All may add their own prayers here.

Let us pray: **Our Father . . . Amen.**

Christ Jesus,
   help us to resist temptations to evil.
Fill our hearts with your love, compassion,
   and mercy.
Who live and reign with God the Father,
in the unity of the Holy Spirit,
God, for ever and ever.,

Amen.

✢ All make the sign of the cross.

PRAYER FOR
WEDNESDAY, MARCH 20, 2024

OPENING

We can only imagine the confusion and fear the apostles felt as Jesus told them that one of them would betray him. Did they look at one another with suspicion? Did they search their hearts for a hint of betrayal? Today, we are called to search our own hearts.

✚ All make the sign of the cross.

In the name of the Father, and of the Son, and of the Holy Spirit. Amen.

PSALM
(For a longer psalm, see page xiv.)
Psalm 34:4–5

The LORD saves the crushed in spirit.

The LORD saves the crushed in spirit.

I sought the LORD, and he answered me
   and delivered me from all my fears.
Look to him, and be radiant,
   so your faces shall never be ashamed.

The LORD saves the crushed in spirit.

◆ All stand and sing **Praise to you, Lord Jesus Christ...**

GOSPEL
Mark 14:12a–b, 13a, 15c–20

A reading from the holy Gospel according to Mark.

On the first day of Unleavened Bread, when the Passover lamb is sacrificed, Jesus sent two of his disciples, saying to them, "Go into the city, and make preparations for us there." So the disciples set out and went to the city and found everything as he had told them, and they prepared the Passover meal. When it was evening, Jesus came with the twelve. And when they had taken their places and were eating, Jesus said, "Truly I tell you, one of you will betray me, one who is eating with me." They began to be distressed and to say to him one after another, "Surely, not I?" He said to them, "It is one of the twelve, one who is dipping bread into the bowl with me."

The Gospel of the Lord.

◆ All sit and observe silence.

FOR SILENT REFLECTION

Think about this silently in your heart. Search your own heart and pray that you may always stay true to Jesus.

CLOSING PRAYER

Let us pray to God for our needs and the needs of others: our family, neighborhood, and the world. For each need we say, "Lord, hear our prayer."

◆ All may add their own prayers here.

Let us pray: **Our Father . . . Amen.**

Lord Jesus,
help us to forgive those
   who have offended us,
as you have forgiven those who have hurt
   and betrayed you.
Who live and reign with God the Father,
in the unity of the Holy Spirit,
God, for ever and ever.

Amen.

✚ All make the sign of the cross.

PRAYER FOR
THURSDAY, MARCH 21, 2024

OPENING

Not long after Jesus told the apostles that one of them would betray him, he shared the first Eucharistic meal with them, sealing his promise in bread and wine. He extends his covenant to us too, and we share in the promise of the kingdom of God each time we partake in his Body and Blood. We come to Jesus as we are: imperfect, hurting, broken. And he shares his whole self with us so that we might grow in love, grace, and wisdom.

✠ All make the sign of the cross.

In the name of the Father, and of the Son, and of the Holy Spirit. Amen.

PSALM
(For a longer psalm, see page xiv.)
Psalm 34:4–5

The Lord saves the crushed in spirit.

The Lord saves the crushed in spirit.

I sought the Lord, and he answered me
   and delivered me from all my fears.
Look to him, and be radiant,
   so your faces shall never be ashamed.

The Lord saves the crushed in spirit.

◆ All stand and sing **Praise to you, Lord Jesus Christ...**

GOSPEL
Mark 14:22–25

A reading from the holy Gospel according to Mark.

While they were eating, Jesus took a loaf of bread, and after blessing it he broke it, gave it to them, and said, "Take; this is my body." Then he took a cup, and after giving thanks he gave it to them, and all of them drank from it. He said to them, "This is my blood of the covenant, which is poured out for many. Truly I tell you, I will never again drink of the fruit of the vine until that day when I drink it new in the kingdom of God."

The Gospel of the Lord.

◆ All sit and observe silence.

FOR SILENT REFLECTION

Think about this silently in your heart. What does the Eucharist mean to you?

CLOSING PRAYER

Let us pray to God for our needs and the needs of others: our family, neighborhood, and the world. For each need we say, "Lord, hear our prayer."

◆ All may add their own prayers here.

Let us pray: **Our Father . . . Amen.**

O Jesus,
you give us the great gift of yourself
   in the Eucharist.
Thank you for nourishing our body, mind,
   and spirit
so that we might live with you always.
Who live and reign with God the Father,
in the unity of the Holy Spirit,
God, for ever and ever.

Amen.

✠ All make the sign of the cross.

PRAYER FOR FRIDAY, MARCH 22, 2024

OPENING

After the Passover meal, Jesus went to pray and asked his friends to stay with him as he did. Jesus sought God's comfort in the face of his upcoming ordeal. Over the next week, we too will be asked to stay with Jesus, to walk with him on the road from the table to the garden, to the cross, to pray with him.

✚ All make the sign of the cross.

In the name of the Father, and of the Son, and of the Holy Spirit. Amen.

PSALM
(For a longer psalm, see page xiv.)
Psalm 34:4–5

The Lord saves the crushed in spirit.

The Lord saves the crushed in spirit.

I sought the Lord, and he answered me
 and delivered me from all my fears.
Look to him, and be radiant,
 so your faces shall never be ashamed.

The Lord saves the crushed in spirit.

◆ All stand and sing **Praise to you, Lord Jesus Christ…**

GOSPEL
Mark 14:32, 43b–46, 48–50

A reading from the holy Gospel according to Mark.

After the Passover meal, Jesus and his disciples went to a place called Gethsemane [gehth-SEM-uh-nee], and he said to his disciples, "Sit here while I pray." Judas, one of the twelve, arrived, and with him there was a crowd with swords and clubs, from the chief priests, the scribes, and the elders. Now the betrayer had given them a sign, saying, "The one I will kiss is the man; arrest him and lead him away under guard." So when he came, he went up to him at once and said, "Rabbi! [RAB-ī]" and kissed him. Then they laid hands on him and arrested him. Then Jesus said to them, "Have you come out with swords and clubs to arrest me as though I were a rebel? Day after day I was with you in the temple teaching, and you did not arrest me. But let the scriptures be fulfilled."

The Gospel of the Lord.

◆ All sit and observe silence.

FOR SILENT REFLECTION

Think about this silently in your heart. How can you watch and pray with Jesus as we enter Holy Week?

CLOSING PRAYER

Let us pray to God for our needs and the needs of others: our family, neighborhood, and the world. For each need we say, "Lord, hear our prayer."

◆ All may add their own prayers here.

Let us pray: **Our Father . . . Amen.**

Jesus our Lord,
may we be true friends to you and to others.
Who live and reign with God the Father,
in the unity of the Holy Spirit,
God, for ever and ever.

Amen.

✚ All make the sign of the cross.

PRAYER FOR THE WEEK
WITH A READING FROM THE GOSPEL FOR **SUNDAY, MARCH 24, 2024**

OPENING

At Mass today, the liturgy begins with a reading from the Gospel: the account of Jesus' triumphal entry into Jerusalem. *Hosanna* was a common jubilant shout of joy in God's saving power. *Blessed is he who comes in the name of the Lord* comes from Psalm 118, a psalm of thanksgiving. The people were joyfully proclaiming their belief that Jesus is the Messiah, bringing his saving power to the people of God. We sing these same words every time we go to Mass, as we proclaim our belief in the mystery of God's salvation.

✦ All make the sign of the cross.

In the name of the Father, and of the Son, and of the Holy Spirit. Amen.

PSALM
(For a longer psalm, see page xiv.)
Psalm 34:4–5

The LORD saves the crushed in spirit.

The LORD saves the crushed in spirit.

I sought the LORD, and he answered me
   and delivered me from all my fears.
Look to him, and be radiant,
   so your faces shall never be ashamed.

The LORD saves the crushed in spirit.

◆ All stand and sing **Praise to you, Lord Jesus Christ…**

GOSPEL
John 12:12–16

A reading from the holy Gospel according to John.

The next day the great crowd that had come to the festival heard that Jesus was coming to Jerusalem. So they took branches of palm trees and went out to meet him, shouting, "Hosanna! Blessed is the one who comes in the name of the Lord—the King of Israel!" Jesus found a young donkey and sat on it, as it is written: "Do not be afraid, daughter of Zion. Look, your king is coming, sitting on a donkey's colt!" His disciples did not understand these things at first, but when Jesus was glorified, then they remembered that these things had been written of him and had been done to him.

The Gospel of the Lord.

◆ All sit and observe silence.

FOR SILENT REFLECTION

Think about this silently in your heart. What do you thank God for this week?

CLOSING PRAYER

Let us pray to God for our needs and the needs of others: our family, neighborhood, and the world. For each need we say, "Lord, hear our prayer."

◆ All may add their own prayers here.

Let us pray: **Our Father . . . Amen.**

Hosanna! Blessed be the name of the Lord!
We sing your praises, O God,
and proclaim your saving power
   to all the earth!
Through Christ our Lord.

Amen.

✦ All make the sign of the cross.

PRAYER FOR MONDAY, MARCH 25, 2024

OPENING

Peter had been so steadfast in his faith that Jesus called him a rock. And yet soon after Jesus was arrested, Peter found himself denying Jesus, over and over again. Worse, Jesus himself had told Peter this would happen. How do you think Peter felt when he heard that rooster crow? But even though Peter failed, he was one of the first to whom Jesus appeared after he rose again. Peter was a leader of the early church. Even when we fail to love, we are always invited to come back to God.

✚ All make the sign of the cross.

In the name of the Father, and of the Son, and of the Holy Spirit. Amen.

PSALM

(For a longer psalm, see page xiv.)
Psalm 34:4–5

The LORD saves the crushed in spirit.

The LORD saves the crushed in spirit.

I sought the LORD, and he answered me
   and delivered me from all my fears.
Look to him, and be radiant,
   so your faces shall never be ashamed.

The LORD saves the crushed in spirit.

◆ All stand and sing **Praise to you, Lord Jesus Christ…**

GOSPEL

Mark 14:66, 67b, 68a–b, 68d, 69a, 69c–72

A reading from the holy Gospel according to Mark.

While Peter was below in the courtyard, one of the female servants of the high priest came by and said, "You also were with Jesus." But he denied it, saying, "I do not know or understand what you are talking about." Then the cock crowed. And the female servant began again to say to the bystanders, "This man is one of them." But again he denied it. Then after a little while the bystanders again said to Peter, "Certainly you are one of them, for you are a Galilean [gal-ih-LEE-uhn]." But he began to curse, and he swore an oath, "I do not know this man you are talking about." At that moment the cock crowed for the second time. Then Peter remembered that Jesus had said to him, "Before the cock crows twice, you will deny me three times." And he broke down and wept.

The Gospel of the Lord.

◆ All sit and observe silence.

FOR SILENT REFLECTION

Think about this silently in your heart. Pray about a time you failed to love Jesus.

CLOSING PRAYER

Let us pray to God for our needs and the needs of others: our family, neighborhood, and the world. For each need we say, "Lord, hear our prayer."

◆ All may add their own prayers here.

Let us pray: **Our Father . . . Amen.**

O God,
help us to repent and return to you.
Through Christ our Lord.

Amen.

✚ All make the sign of the cross.

PRAYER FOR
TUESDAY, MARCH 26, 2024

OPENING

Today we hear a difficult moment of the passion narrative, in which the crowd so despises Jesus that they choose to release a known murderer and crucify Jesus instead.

✚ All make the sign of the cross.

In the name of the Father, and of the Son, and of the Holy Spirit. Amen.

PSALM

(For a longer psalm, see page xiv.)
Psalm 34:4–5

The LORD saves the crushed in spirit.

The LORD saves the crushed in spirit.

I sought the LORD, and he answered me
   and delivered me from all my fears.
Look to him, and be radiant,
   so your faces shall never be ashamed.

The LORD saves the crushed in spirit.

◆ All stand and sing **Praise to you, Lord Jesus Christ...**

GOSPEL

Mark 15:1c–e, 3, 6–7, 9–10, 11–13, 15

A reading from the holy Gospel according to Mark.

The soldiers bound Jesus, led him away, and handed him over to Pilate. Then the chief priests accused him of many things.

Now at the festival Pilate used to release a prisoner for them, anyone for whom they asked. Now a man called Barabbas [buh-RAB-uhs] was in prison with the insurrectionists who had committed murder during the insurrection. "Do you want me to release for you the King of the Jews?" But the chief priests stirred up the crowd to have him release Barabbas for them instead. Pilate spoke to them again, "Then what do you wish me to do with the man you call the King of the Jews?" They shouted back, "Crucify him!" So Pilate, wishing to satisfy the crowd, released Barabbas for them, and after flogging Jesus he handed him over to be crucified.

The Gospel of the Lord.

◆ All sit and observe silence.

FOR SILENT REFLECTION

Think about this silently in your heart. Let us strive to be people of peace, of forgiveness, and of love.

CLOSING PRAYER

Let us pray to God for our needs and the needs of others: our family, neighborhood, and the world. For each need we say, "Lord, hear our prayer."

◆ All may add their own prayers here.

Let us pray: **Our Father . . . Amen.**

Lord Jesus,
your heart broke at the taunts of your people.
Help us to stand up for you.
Who live and reign with God the Father,
in the unity of the Holy Spirit,
God, for ever and ever.

Amen.

✚ All make the sign of the cross.

PRAYER FOR WEDNESDAY, MARCH 27, 2024

OPENING

As we listen to the final moments of Jesus' Passion, we hear how Jesus was tortured, mocked, and crucified by the Romans. As he was a political threat to the Romans as well as a threat to the Jewish leaders, they charged and addressed him as "The King of the Jews." Jesus was brought to a hill called Golgotha [GAWL-guh-thuh], also known as Calvary, outside the walls of Jerusalem to be crucified.

✚ All make the sign of the cross.

In the name of the Father, and of the Son, and of the Holy Spirit. Amen.

PSALM
(For a longer psalm, see page xiv.)
Psalm 34:4–5

The LORD saves the crushed in spirit.

The LORD saves the crushed in spirit.

I sought the LORD, and he answered me
  and delivered me from all my fears.
Look to him, and be radiant,
  so your faces shall never be ashamed.

The LORD saves the crushed in spirit.

◆ All stand and sing **Praise to you, Lord Jesus Christ…**

GOSPEL
Mark 15:16a, 17–18, 20–21d, 22a, 23–25

A reading from the holy Gospel according to Mark.

Then the soldiers led Jesus into the courtyard of the palace. And they clothed him in a purple cloak, and after twisting some thorns into a crown they put it on him. And they began saluting him, "Hail, King of the Jews!" After mocking him, they stripped him of the purple cloak and put his own clothes on him. Then they led him out to crucify him.

They compelled a passer-by, who was coming in from the country, to carry his cross; it was Simon of Cyrene [sī-REEN]. Then they brought Jesus to the place called Golgotha [GAWL-guh-thuh]. And they offered him wine mixed with myrrh, but he did not take it. And they crucified him and divided his clothes among them, casting lots to decide what each should take. It was nine o'clock in the morning when they crucified him.

The Gospel of the Lord.

◆ All sit and observe silence.

FOR SILENT REFLECTION

Think about this silently in your heart. How can you help others carry their burdens, just as Simon of Cyrene helped Jesus carry his cross?

CLOSING PRAYER

Let us pray to God for our needs and the needs of others: our family, neighborhood, and the world. For each need we say, "Lord, hear our prayer."

◆ All may add their own prayers here.

Let us pray: **Our Father . . . Amen.**

Loving and merciful God,
we thank you for the gift of your Son Jesus.
We ask you to hear our prayers in his name.

Amen.

✚ All make the sign of the cross.

HOME PRAYER
HOLY THURSDAY

Before you begin, find the reading (John 13:3–5) in your Bible, ask for a volunteer to read it, and help the reader to practice reading it a few times. You could begin with a simple song, such as "Jesus, Remember Me," or "Amen." (We don't sing "Alleluia" until the Easter Vigil.) An older child or adult reads the leader parts.

LEADER
Today is Holy Thursday, and this evening we will remember two important things that Jesus did for his disciples and for us. On this night of the Last Supper, Jesus offered himself in the form of bread and wine and said, "This is my Body. . . . This is my Blood. Do this in memory of me." Later, he washed the feet of his followers, teaching them by example how we must be a servant for all.

✙ All make the sign of the cross.

In the name of the Father, and of the Son, and of the Holy Spirit. Amen.

LEADER: *Psalm 27:1, 4, 11, 13–14*
Let us repeat the Psalm Response:
Teach me your way, O Lord.

ALL: Teach me your way, O Lord.

The Lord is my light and my salvation;
  whom shall I fear?
The Lord is the stronghold of my life;
  of whom shall I be afraid?

ALL: Teach me your way, O Lord.

One thing I asked of the Lord,
  that will I seek after:
to live in the house of the Lord
  all the days of my life,
to behold the beauty of the Lord,
  and to inquire in his temple.

ALL: Teach me your way, O Lord.

I believe that I shall see the goodness
    of the Lord
  in the land of the living.
Wait for the Lord;
  be strong, and let your heart take courage;
  wait for the Lord!

ALL: Teach me your way, O Lord.

◆ All stand and sing **Praise to you, Lord Jesus Christ** . . .

LEADER: *John 13:3–5*
A reading from the holy Gospel according to John.

◆ Read the Gospel passage from the Bible.

The Gospel of the Lord.

◆ All sit and observe silence.

FOR SILENT REFLECTION
Why did Jesus, the disciples' leader, wish to be their servant?

LEADER:
Let us pray as Jesus taught us:

Our Father . . . Amen.

LEADER:
Almighty God,
we remember Jesus'
act of service of washing his friends' feet.
May we honor you with
our acts of love and service today and always.
We ask this through Christ our Lord.

ALL: Amen.

✙ All make the sign of the cross.

HOME PRAYER
GOOD FRIDAY

Before you begin, find the reading (John 18:33–37) in your Bible, ask for a volunteer to read it, and help the reader to practice it a few times. You could begin with a simple song, such as "Jesus, Remember Me," or "Amen." (We don't sing "Alleluia" until the Easter Vigil.) An older child or adult reads the leader parts.

LEADER:
Today we remember Jesus' anguish and Death on the Cross. It is a sad time we don't understand. But Good Friday is also a day that we recall the goodness of God's Son who chose to die so that he could save us from sin and death. This day gives us so much hope because of the promise of new life!

✝ All make the sign of the cross.

In the name of the Father, and of the Son, and of the Holy Spirit. Amen.

LEADER: *Psalm 31:1, 2, 5a, 21*
Let us repeat the Psalm Response:
Into your hand I commit my spirit.

ALL: Into your hand I commit my spirit.

In you, O LORD, I seek refuge;
   do not let me ever be put to shame;
   in your righteousness deliver me.
Incline your ear to me;
   rescue me speedily.
Be a rock of refuge for me,
   a strong fortress to save me.

ALL: Into your hand I commit my spirit.

Blessed be the LORD,
   for he has wondrously shown his steadfast love to me
when I was beset as a city under siege.

ALL: Into your hand I commit my spirit.

◆ All stand and sing **Praise to you, Lord Jesus Christ** . . .

LEADER: *John 18:33–37*
A reading from the holy Gospel according to John.

◆ Read the Gospel passage from the Bible.

The Gospel of the Lord.

◆ All sit and observe silence.

LEADER:
As I reflect on Jesus' love for me, how can I thank him?

LEADER:
Let us pray as Jesus taught us:

Our Father . . . Amen.

LEADER:
Today we remember Jesus' great love.
Help us to honor him with our lives.
We ask this in the name of the Father, the Son, and the Holy Spirit.

ALL: Amen.

EASTER TIME

SUNDAY, MARCH 31, 2024 — FRIDAY, MAY 19, 2024

EASTER TIME

THE MEANING OF EASTER

The heart of Easter lies in the word *covenant*. A covenant is an agreement or contract between two parties. The history of salvation is the story of God's covenant with his people—God's promise to provide and care for humankind and humankind's response to return God's love and follow God's teachings to care for one another and all creation. In the Old Testament, God made covenants with Noah, Abraham, and Moses. In the New Testament, Jesus is the new covenant: "Whoever believes in me will never be thirsty" (John 6:35). With the resurrection, God promises that the covenant of love will extend to all peoples for all time.

The Prayer for the Week will reflect the Sunday Gospels but during the week we will again "walk through the Bible." Scripture stories tell us of people throughout history from King David, to the Israelites, to the people of Jesus' time, to Paul and the early Christians who believed that faith and trust in God helped them to live joyfully in spite of difficulties.

As we read the stories of Jesus' appearances to his disciples after the resurrection, we can reflect on how Jesus is always present in our lives. We will read stories of St. Paul and the early Christians who carried Jesus' teachings to people in many lands. Easter Time ends with the wonderful celebration of Pentecost. After Jesus died, his disciples were filled with fear and confusion. Jesus promised that he would send the Spirit to strengthen them. On Pentecost, we celebrate the Spirit that strengthened the disciples. This same Spirit fills us with wisdom, knowledge, courage, and love. These gifts make our lives and the world a better place for all God's creation.

PREPARING TO CELEBRATE EASTER IN THE CLASSROOM

SACRED SPACE

The liturgical color for Easter Time is white, so your prayer table cloth will need to change once more. You may want to add to your prayer table a vase of fresh daisies or lilies and a small glass bowl with a little water in it. When you introduce the water to your students you may say, "Jesus said, 'Let anyone who is thirsty come to me, and let the one who believes in me drink'" (John 7:37b–38a). Have children process in single file to the prayer table, carrying and placing the white cloth, a small white pillar candle, the flowers, and the bowl of water. Make sure you dim the lights before you begin. Then after all the objects have been placed on the prayer table, light the white pillar and chant the following phrase and response three times:

LEADER: The Light of Christ!

ALL: Thanks be to God!

Perhaps one of your students, or someone they know, received the sacrament of baptism at the Holy Saturday celebration of the Easter Vigil. If so, while standing before the water, you could explain that the water of baptism recalls the great flood that Noah had to pass through to reach God's promise of peace, the Red Sea that Moses and the Israelites had to pass through to reach freedom, and the death that Jesus had to pass through to reach the life of the resurrection. When we pass through (are baptized with) the water in the baptismal font, we enter into that same new life of the resurrected Christ.

Easter Time ends with the Solemnity of Pentecost. When you celebrate Pentecost as a group, make sure you exchange your white prayer table cloth for a red one.

MOVEMENT AND GESTURE

Children love this expanded form of the Easter procession. After you have changed the color of the prayer cloth to white, carried in the white pillar candle, placed the objects on the prayer table, and lit the candle, sing "The Light of Christ" on one note. When you are finished singing, read a Gospel account of the resurrection (such as John 20:11–18). Sing Alleluia and then announce the following: "Jesus has risen from the dead; Jesus, the Light of the World, has destroyed death. The light of the Risen Christ will never go out, for he shares his light and life with each of us. Not only that, but his light can spread and grow. Jesus shares his new life with each of us." Then call each child by name, one at a time, inviting them to come forward. For each child, light a small votive candle from the large pillar. As you give it to the child, say, "The risen Christ shares his light with (child's name)." The child will then put the votive candle on the prayer table and sit down. Don't rush. Wait until the child is seated before you call the next child's name. If you are worried about fire, allow each child to hold his or her votive holder briefly, then you can place the candle on the table beside the lit pillar. Make sure you light a votive candle for yourself. When all the small candles are lit, sit in silence with the children and enjoy the beauty of the light. End your celebration by singing all the Alleluias that you know!

FESTIVITY IN SCHOOL AND HOME

You might want to engage some of the older children in making an Easter candle like the one that stands beside the altar in church. Use a tall white pillar candle. The Easter, or Paschal, candle has three symbols: a central cross identifies it as the Christ candle, and its flame burns despite the death Christ endured. The letters alpha and omega, which begin and end the Greek alphabet, signify that God is the beginning and the ending of all things. The current year indicates that God is present not just at the beginning and the end of time, but throughout history and among those gathered here and now around the candle. You can stand this candle on a candle holder beside the table in your prayer corner at school or at home.

In this book you will find special prayer services that may be used in the classroom or with a larger group. There is the service for Easter, pages 242–243; for the Ascension, pages 282–283; and for Pentecost, pages 290–291. There is also a special prayer service to honor May as the month of Mary, pages 272–273. In May, you might add pictures of Mary and fresh spring flowers to your prayer table. Invite children who know the Rosary to say a decade as part of your daily prayer.

SACRED MUSIC

Here are some Easter songs that children love: "Jesus Christ Is Risen Today," "What Wondrous Love Is This," "Alleluia, Sing to Jesus," "Come Down, O Love Divine," and "O Sons and Daughters." For Pentecost you might enjoy singing "Come, Holy Ghost" or "Veni Sancte Spiritus," or "Spirit of the Living God."

PRAYERS FOR EASTER

The following prayer is a beautiful psalm from the Easter Vigil:

Psalm 42:1–2, 43:3–4

As a deer longs for flowing streams,
   so my soul longs for you, O God.
My soul thirsts for God
   for the living God.
When shall I come and behold
   the face of God?
O send out your light and your truth;
   let them lead me;
let them bring me to your holy hill
   and to your dwelling.
Then I will go to the altar of God
   to God my exceeding joy;
and I will praise you with the harp,
   O God, my God.

A NOTE TO CATECHISTS

You may wish to study the prayers of baptism with your students. The prayer of Blessing the Waters of Baptism is particularly rich in symbolism. You can recall with the children baptisms they remember seeing as well as stories and pictures of their own baptisms. You can find the Baptismal Rite online or ask your parish priest for a copy.

GRACE BEFORE MEALS
EASTER TIME

LEADER:
Jesus Christ is risen! He is truly risen!

ALL: Alleluia! Alleluia!

✚ All make the sign of the cross.

In the name of the Father, and of the Son, and of the Holy Spirit. Amen.

LEADER:
God, our Creator,
we are thankful for the
air we breathe and the
nourishment you offer
in our every moment on earth.
We are grateful for the meal
we are about to share,
for its nutrients sustain us and
give us energy for
working and playing for the glory
of Christ our Savior.
We ask this in his name.

ALL: Amen.

✚ All make the sign of the cross.

In the name of the Father, and of the Son, and of the Holy Spirit. Amen.

PRAYER AT DAY'S END
EASTER TIME

LEADER:
All the ends of the earth have seen

ALL: the victory of our God.

✚ All make the sign of the cross.

In the name of the Father, and of the Son, and of the Holy Spirit. Amen.

LEADER:
Heavenly Father,
we are grateful for
what we've learned today.
We thank you for our
teachers, assistants, coaches,
and friends who guide us
along our path.
Help us through the remainder of this day
as we are renewed by your Spirit
and the promise of an
eternal Easter.
We ask this through Christ our Lord.

ALL: Amen.

✚ All make the sign of the cross.

In the name of the Father, and of the Son, and of the Holy Spirit. Amen.

PRAYER SERVICE
EASTER

Prepare seven leaders for this prayer service. The third and fourth leaders will need Bibles for the Scripture passages and may need help finding them and practicing. You may wish to begin by singing "Jesus Christ Is Risen Today" and end with "Alleluia, Sing to Jesus." If there will be singing, prepare a song leader.

FIRST LEADER:
The grace, peace, and light of the Risen Christ be with us all.

ALL: Amen.

FIRST LEADER:
Today we celebrate Easter, the holiest, most important *solemnity* [suh-LEM-nuh-tee] of the Church, when we remember the resurrection of Jesus Christ. Jesus won a great victory over death! He rose from death to new life and he will never die again! We can follow him and we too can rise from the dead and live forever with him. Easter is so important to us that one day could never contain all our joy, so we celebrate Easter for fifty days!

SECOND LEADER:

✢ All make the sign of the cross.

In the name of the Father, and of the Son, and of the Holy Spirit. Amen.

Let us pray:
Heavenly Father,
our hearts are filled with thankfulness
    and praise
as we think about Jesus' great love for us,
the sacrifice he made,

and the never-ending life he lives and shares
	with us now.
May we always thank you for the gift your
	Son has given to us.
We ask this through the same Jesus Christ
	our Lord.

ALL: Amen.

THIRD LEADER: Isaiah 42:10–12
A reading from the Book of the prophet Isaiah.

◆ Read the Scripture passage from the Bible.

The Word of the Lord.

◆ All observe silence. Then all stand and sing **Alleluia.**

FOURTH LEADER: John 20:11–18
A reading from the holy Gospel according to John.

◆ Read the Gospel passage from the Bible.

The Gospel of the Lord.

◆ All sit and observe silence.

FIFTH LEADER:
Let us stand and bring our hopes and needs to God as we pray, "Lord, hear our prayer."

For all who live in fear or worry, may the power of the Resurrection give them new hope, we pray to the Lord.

For an end to hatred, divisions, and war, we pray to the Lord.

For all who are unable to see the hand of God at work in their lives, may God open their eyes, we pray to the Lord.

For those who are sick and for those who have died, we pray to the Lord.

SIXTH LEADER:
Let us pray as Jesus taught us.

ALL: Our Father . . . Amen.

◆ Pause, and then say the following.

Let us offer one another a sign of Christ's peace.

◆ All offer one another a sign of peace.

SEVENTH LEADER:
Let us pray:
Lord God almighty,
in the death and resurrection of your Son,
	Jesus Christ,
you have created a new heaven and
	a new earth.
Bring the light and life of the resurrection
into our hearts so that we too may be
	renewed in holiness.
We ask this through our Lord Jesus Christ,
	your Son, who lives and reigns with
	you in the unity of the Holy Spirit,
	one God, for ever and ever.

ALL: Amen.

✚ All make the sign of the cross.

PRAYER FOR THE WEEK
WITH A READING FROM THE GOSPEL FOR **SUNDAY, MARCH 31, 2024**

OPENING

Christ is risen! With Mary Magdalene, Peter and John, we wonder at the displaced stone and the discarded burial cloths. What a mystery. What a gift. Alleluia! We will continue to celebrate Christ's resurrection over the next fifty days.

✛ All make the sign of the cross.

In the name of the Father, and of the Son, and of the Holy Spirit. Amen.

PSALM
(For a longer psalm, see page xiv.)
Psalm 105:1–2

Let the hearts of those who seek the Lord rejoice.

Let the hearts of those who seek the Lord rejoice.

O give thanks to the Lord, call on his name,
　make known his deeds among the peoples.
Sing to him, sing praises to him;
　tell of all his wonderful works.

Let the hearts of those who seek the Lord rejoice.

◆ All stand and sing **Alleluia.**

GOSPEL
John 20:1–3, 4B, 5B–8ACD

A reading from the holy Gospel according to John.

Early on the first day of the week, while it was still dark, Mary Magdalene came to the tomb and saw that the stone had been removed from the tomb. So she ran and went to Simon Peter and the other disciple, the one whom Jesus loved, and said to them, "They have taken the Lord out of the tomb, and we do not know where they have laid him." Then Peter and the other disciple set out and went toward the tomb. The other disciple outran Peter and reached the tomb first. But he did not go in. Then Simon Peter came, and went into the tomb. He saw the linen wrappings lying there, and the cloth that had been on Jesus's head, not lying with the linen wrappings but rolled up in a place by itself. Then the other disciple also went in, and he saw and believed.

The Gospel of the Lord.

◆ All sit and observe silence.

FOR SILENT REFLECTION

Think about this silently in your heart. How can you share Easter joy?

CLOSING PRAYER

Let us pray to God for our needs and the needs of others: our family, neighborhood, and the world. For each need we say, "Lord, hear our prayer."

◆ All may add their own prayers here.

Let us pray: **Our Father . . . Amen.**

Alleluia, Christ is risen!
We praise God's holy name,
　now and for ever!
Through Jesus Christ our risen Lord.

Amen.

✛ All make the sign of the cross.

PRAYER FOR MONDAY, APRIL 1, 2024

OPENING

The Lord is our rock of refuge. He is a place of shelter; he is as protective as a strong fortress. When we call upon the Lord, he hears us, and he keeps his promises. In the joy of Easter, Jesus has kept his promise. He will be an eternal refuge for all who call upon him. He shelters us from the powers of sin, death, and destruction. He lives, and we live, eternally. Blessed be the Lord!

✛ All make the sign of the cross.

In the name of the Father, and of the Son, and of the Holy Spirit. Amen.

PSALM
(For a longer psalm, see page xiv.)
Psalm 105:1–2

Let the hearts of those who seek the LORD rejoice.

Let the hearts of those who seek the LORD rejoice.

O give thanks to the LORD; call on his name;
　make known his deeds among the peoples.
Sing to him, sing praises to him;
　tell of all his wonderful works.

Let the hearts of those who seek the LORD rejoice.

READING
2 Samuel 22:2ac, 3b–g, 4ab, 7c, 31bc, 32, 47

A reading from the Second Book of the prophet Samuel.

David said: The LORD is my rock and my deliverer, my God, my rock in whom I take refuge, my shield and the horn of my salvation, my stronghold and my refuge, my savior. I call upon the LORD, who is worthy to be praised. From his temple he heard my voice. The promise of the LORD proves true; he is a shield for all who take refuge in him. For who is God but the LORD? And who is a rock except our God? The LORD lives! Blessed be my rock, and exalted be my God, the rock of my salvation.

The Word of the Lord.

◆ All observe silence.

FOR SILENT REFLECTION

Think about this silently in your heart. In what ways does God shelter, protect, and save you?

CLOSING PRAYER

Let us pray to God for our needs and the needs of others: our family, neighborhood, and the world. For each need we say, "Lord, hear our prayer."

◆ All may add their own prayers here.

Let us pray: **Our Father . . . Amen.**

Eternal God,
you have been a refuge from one generation
　to the next.
Keep your people gathered here safe
　within your embrace.
Through Christ our Lord.

Amen.

✛ All make the sign of the cross.

PRAYER FOR
TUESDAY, APRIL 2, 2024

OPENING

Today we will hear God call us "precious" and "honored." *I love you*, he says. During Easter Time, we celebrate God's love for us, a love so great that he sent his Son as a Savior for his beloved people, to lead them from death into life. He did not do this for himself, but purely and freely out of love for his precious ones—that includes you!

✚ All make the sign of the cross.

In the name of the Father, and of the Son, and of the Holy Spirit. Amen.

PSALM
(For a longer psalm, see page xiv.)
Psalm 105:1–2

Let the hearts of those who seek the Lord rejoice.

Let the hearts of those who seek the Lord rejoice.

O give thanks to the Lord; call on his name;
  make known his deeds among the peoples.
Sing to him, sing praises to him;
  tell of all his wonderful works.

Let the hearts of those who seek the Lord rejoice.

READING
Isaiah 43:1acde, 3a, 4ab, 5a, 10ab, 11–12ac

A reading from the Book of the prophet Isaiah.

But now thus says the Lord, Do not fear, for I have redeemed you; I have called you by name, you are mine. For I am the Lord your God, the Holy One of Israel, your Savior. Because you are precious in my sight and honored and I love you, I give people in return for you, nations in exchange for your life. Do not fear, for I am with you; You are my witnesses, says the Lord, and my servant whom I have chosen. I, I am the Lord, and besides me there is no savior. I declared and saved and proclaimed, you are my witnesses, says the Lord.

The Word of the Lord.

◆ All observe silence.

FOR SILENT REFLECTION

Think about this silently in your heart. How has God shown his love for you?

CLOSING PRAYER

Let us pray to God for our needs and the needs of others: our family, neighborhood, and the world. For each need we say, "Lord, hear our prayer."

◆ All may add their own prayers here.

Let us pray: **Our Father . . . Amen.**

Jesus our Savior,
give us the eyes to see our neighbors
and ourselves as you do,
as something holy and precious in your sight.
Who live and reign with God the Father,
in the unity of the Holy Spirit,
God, for ever and ever.

Amen.

✚ All make the sign of the cross.

PRAYER FOR WEDNESDAY, APRIL 3, 2024

OPENING

A few weeks ago, we heard the story of the Samaritan woman at the well. Today we will hear how it ends. Many of the woman's friends sought Jesus after experiencing the power of her witness. We, too, are called to be witnesses to the saving power of God, to invite others into relationship with him, just as the Samaritan woman did.

✢ All make the sign of the cross.

In the name of the Father, and of the Son, and of the Holy Spirit. Amen.

PSALM
(For a longer psalm, see page xiv.)
Psalm 105:1–2

Let the hearts of those who seek the Lord rejoice.

Let the hearts of those who seek the Lord rejoice.

O give thanks to the Lord; call on his name;
  make known his deeds among the peoples.
Sing to him, sing praises to him;
  tell of all his wonderful works.

Let the hearts of those who seek the Lord rejoice.

◆ All stand and sing **Alleluia.**

GOSPEL
John 4:25ab, 26, 28–30, 39a, 40–42ad

A reading from the holy Gospel according to John.

The woman said to Jesus, "I know that Messiah is coming" (who is called Christ). Jesus said to her, "I am he, the one who is speaking to you." Then the woman left her water jar and went back to the city. She said to the people, "Come and see a man who told me everything I have ever done! He cannot be the Messiah, can he?" They left the city and were on their way to him. Many Samaritans from that city believed in him because of the woman's testimony. So when the Samaritans came to him, they asked him to stay with them, and he stayed there two days. And many more believed because of his word. They said to the woman, "We know that this is truly the Savior of the world."

The Gospel of the Lord.

◆ All sit and observe silence.

FOR SILENT REFLECTION

Think about this silently in your heart. How can you invite others to come to know Jesus?

CLOSING PRAYER

Let us pray to God for our needs and the needs of others: our family, neighborhood, and the world. For each need we say, "Lord, hear our prayer."

◆ All may add their own prayers here.

Let us pray: **Our Father . . . Amen.**

Lord Jesus,
you are the Truth that we all need to hear.
May we bring others to know you more.
Who live and reign with God the Father,
in the unity of the Holy Spirit,
God, for ever and ever.

Amen.

✢ All make the sign of the cross.

PRAYER FOR
THURSDAY, APRIL 4, 2024

OPENING

Timothy was a favored associate and follower of St. Paul, and in two letters, we hear Paul exhorting Timothy in faith and discipleship. In today's reading, Paul tells his friend that he should be faithful in how he teaches and in his life as a whole and to look to God alone for salvation. In the end, he is told to set an example for believers, despite his youth.

✚ All make the sign of the cross.

In the name of the Father, and of the Son, and of the Holy Spirit. Amen.

PSALM
(For a longer psalm, see page xiv.)
Psalm 105:1–2

Let the hearts of those who seek the LORD rejoice.

Let the hearts of those who seek the LORD rejoice.

O give thanks to the LORD; call on his name;
  make known his deeds among the peoples.
Sing to him, sing praises to him;
  tell of all his wonderful works.

Let the hearts of those who seek the LORD rejoice.

READING
1 Timothy 4:6, 7b–8, 10–12

A reading from the First Letter to Timothy.

If you put these instructions before the brothers and sisters, you will be a good servant of Christ Jesus, nourished on the words of the faith and of the sound teaching that you have followed. Train yourself in godliness, for, while physical training is of some value, godliness is valuable in every way, holding promise for both the present life and the life to come. For to this end we toil and suffer reproach, because we have our hope set on the living God, who is the Savior of all people, especially of those who believe. Command and teach these things. Let no one despise your youth, but set the believers an example in speech and conduct, in love, in faith, in purity.

The Word of the Lord.

◆ All observe silence.

FOR SILENT REFLECTION

Think about this silently in your heart. Do you set an example for others in your life? How?

CLOSING PRAYER

Let us pray to God for our needs and the needs of others: our family, neighborhood, and the world. For each need we say, "Lord, hear our prayer."

◆ All may add their own prayers here.

Let us pray: **Our Father . . . Amen.**

Christ Jesus,
give us the faith to overcome any obstacles
that might be in our way
and truly spread the Good News of your
life, death, and resurrection to all we meet.
Who live and reign with God the Father,
in the unity of the Holy Spirit,
God, for ever and ever.

Amen.

✚ All make the sign of the cross.

PRAYER FOR
FRIDAY, APRIL 5, 2024

OPENING

How can we achieve life in God? The answer is simple: through love. God is Love. God loved us so much, he sent us his only Son. He loved us so much, he suffered and died to give us eternal life. If we are to live in God, we must love the way God does: loving not just our families or people we like, but also people we don't like or know. We will see God in one another.

✚ All make the sign of the cross.

In the name of the Father, and of the Son, and of the Holy Spirit. Amen.

PSALM
(For a longer psalm, see page xiv.)
Psalm 105:1–2

Let the hearts of those who seek the LORD rejoice.

Let the hearts of those who seek the LORD rejoice.

O give thanks to the LORD; call on his name;
   make known his deeds among the peoples.
Sing to him, sing praises to him;
   tell of all his wonderful works.

Let the hearts of those who seek the LORD rejoice.

READING
1 John 4:7, 9, 11–12, 14, 16bcd

A reading from the First Letter of John.

Beloved, let us love one another, because love is from God; everyone who loves is born of God and knows God. God's love was revealed among us in this way: God sent his only Son into the world so that we might live through him. Beloved, since God loved us so much, we also ought to love one another. No one has ever seen God; if we love one another, God lives in us, and his love is perfected in us. And we have seen and do testify that the Father has sent his Son as the Savior of the world. God is love, and those who abide in love abide in God, and God abides in them.

The Word of the Lord.

◆ All observe silence.

FOR SILENT REFLECTION

Think about this silently in your heart. What are some ways you can love others this week? Think about family, friends, and your community or neighborhood.

CLOSING PRAYER

Let us pray to God for our needs and the needs of others: our family, neighborhood, and the world. For each need we say, "Lord, hear our prayer."

◆ All may add their own prayers here.

Let us pray: **Our Father . . . Amen.**

Father in heaven,
you have lovingly given everything we have.
Pour forth your love into our hearts
and teach us to love as you do
that we might live in your love eternally.
Through Christ our risen Lord.

Amen.

✚ All make the sign of the cross.

PRAYER FOR THE WEEK
WITH A READING FROM THE GOSPEL FOR **SUNDAY, APRIL 7, 2024**

OPENING

After the events of Jesus' passion, most of the disciples hid together and locked the doors. They were terrified that they would be punished too. Into this tense environment, Jesus came and said, "Peace be with you." In the midst of their fear, he breathed hope, the very breath of the Holy Spirit, and sent them out to spread the good news. We might feel paralyzed by fear or anxiety, but Jesus comes and breathes the same blessing and mission upon each of us.

✚ All make the sign of the cross.

In the name of the Father, and of the Son, and of the Holy Spirit. Amen.

PSALM

(For a longer psalm, see page xiv.)
Psalm 105:1–2

Let the hearts of those who seek the LORD rejoice.

Let the hearts of those who seek the LORD rejoice.

O give thanks to the LORD; call on his name;
  make known his deeds among the peoples.
Sing to him, sing praises to him;
  tell of all his wonderful works.

Let the hearts of those who seek the LORD rejoice.

◆ All stand and sing **Alleluia.**

GOSPEL

John 20:19–22

A reading from the holy Gospel according to John.

When it was evening on that day, the first day of the week, and the doors were locked where the disciples were, for fear of the Jews, Jesus came and stood among them and said, "Peace be with you." After he said this, he showed them his hands and his side. Then the disciples rejoiced when they saw the Lord. Jesus said to them again, "Peace be with you. As the Father has sent me, so I send you." When he had said this, he breathed on them and said to them, "Receive the Holy Spirit."

The Gospel of the Lord.

◆ All sit and observe silence.

FOR SILENT REFLECTION

Think about this silently in your heart. How do you share peace in the world?

CLOSING PRAYER

Let us pray to God for our needs and the needs of others: our family, neighborhood, and the world. For each need we say, "Lord, hear our prayer."

◆ All may add their own prayers here.

Let us pray: **Our Father . . . Amen.**

Spirit of God,
banish fear and anxiety
    and breathe new life on us,
that we might spread
    your message of hope everywhere.
Through Christ our risen Lord.

Amen.

✚ All make the sign of the cross.

PRAYER FOR MONDAY, APRIL 8, 2024

OPENING

Today we celebrate the Solemnity of the Annunciation of the Lord, and we marvel at the dual gift of God's grace and Mary's yes. God did great things for Mary and for the world, but Mary had to say yes to God's plan of salvation. After Christ's resurrection, the disciples also said yes to an angelic visitor, believing that all they had been told was true: that Jesus had been raised from the dead; that he was truly the Son of God. Today and every day, we are asked to say yes to God.

✛ All make the sign of the cross.

In the name of the Father, and of the Son, and of the Holy Spirit. Amen.

PSALM

(For a longer psalm, see page xiv.)
Psalm 105:1–2

Let the hearts of those who seek the LORD rejoice.

Let the hearts of those who seek the LORD rejoice.

O give thanks to the LORD; call on his name;
　make known his deeds among the peoples.
Sing to him, sing praises to him;
　tell of all his wonderful works.

Let the hearts of those who seek the LORD rejoice.

◆ All stand and sing **Alleluia.**

GOSPEL

Mark 16:1, 2c, 4–7

A reading from the holy Gospel according to Mark.

When the Sabbath was over, Mary Magdalene and Mary the mother of James and Salome [suh-LOH-mee] bought spices, so that they might go and anoint Jesus. They went to the tomb. When they looked up, they saw that the stone, which was very large, had already been rolled back. As they entered the tomb, they saw a young man dressed in a white robe sitting on the right side, and they were alarmed. But he said to them, "Do not be alarmed; you are looking for Jesus of Nazareth, who was crucified. He has been raised; he is not here. Look, there is the place they laid him. But go, tell his disciples and Peter that he is going ahead of you to Galilee; there you will see him, just as he told you."

The Gospel of the Lord.

◆ All sit and observe silence.

FOR SILENT REFLECTION

Think about this silently in your heart. How often have you said yes to God?

CLOSING PRAYER

Let us pray to God for our needs and the needs of others: our family, neighborhood, and the world. For each need we say, "Lord, hear our prayer."

◆ All may add their own prayers here.

Let us pray: **Our Father . . . Amen.**

We rejoice at your resurrection, O Lord.
We rejoice that you have conquered death.
Alleluia, Alleluia, Alleluia!

Amen.

✛ All make the sign of the cross.

PRAYER FOR
TUESDAY, APRIL 9, 2024

OPENING

The disciples in today's reading were downhearted and sad. We can imagine that their faith in Jesus was shaken. Their hope had been nailed to the cross. Even though they had heard the story that he was still alive, they still doubted. They lost hope. Listen to what happens next.

✢ All make the sign of the cross.

In the name of the Father, and of the Son, and of the Holy Spirit. Amen.

PSALM

(For a longer psalm, see page xiv.)
Psalm 105:1–2

Let the hearts of those who seek the Lord rejoice.

Let the hearts of those who seek the Lord rejoice.

O give thanks to the Lord; call on his name;
   make known his deeds among the peoples.
Sing to him, sing praises to him;
   tell of all his wonderful works.

Let the hearts of those who seek the Lord rejoice.

◆ All stand and sing **Alleluia.**

GOSPEL

Luke 24:13a, 15b–18A, 19b, 20, 22–23

A reading from the holy Gospel according to Luke.

Two of Jesus' disciples were going to a village called Emmaus [eh-MAY-uhs]. Jesus himself came near and went with them, but their eyes were kept from recognizing him. And he said to them, "What are you discussing?" They stood still, looking sad. Then one of them, whose name was Cleopas, answered him, "The things about Jesus of Nazareth, and how our chief priests and leaders handed him over to be condemned to death and crucified him. Moreover, some women of our group were at the tomb early this morning, and when they did not find his body there they came back and told us that they had indeed seen a vision of angels who said that he was alive."

The Gospel of the Lord.

◆ All sit and observe silence.

FOR SILENT REFLECTION

Think about this silently in your heart. Have you ever doubted God?

CLOSING PRAYER

Let us pray to God for our needs and the needs of others: our family, neighborhood, and the world. For each need we say, "Lord, hear our prayer."

◆ All may add their own prayers here.

Let us pray: **Our Father . . . Amen.**

Lord,
be with those who find it hard
   to believe and hope in you,
and help all of us to be signs of hope
   for everyone.
Who live and reign with God the Father,
in the unity of the Holy Spirit,
God, for ever and ever.

Amen.

✢ All make the sign of the cross.

PRAYER FOR WEDNESDAY, APRIL 10, 2024

OPENING

Though the disciples on the road to Emmaus had lost faith, Jesus did not lose faith in them. He came to them and he comes to us too. Maybe, like the disciples, we do not recognize him at first. Maybe he is disguised in a friend or a kind stranger, or is invisibly present in a solitary moment. And we may also recognize him in the Eucharist.

✢ All make the sign of the cross.

In the name of the Father, and of the Son, and of the Holy Spirit. Amen.

PSALM

(For a longer psalm, see page xiv.)
Psalm 105:1–2

Let the hearts of those who seek the Lord rejoice.

Let the hearts of those who seek the Lord rejoice.

O give thanks to the Lord; call on his name;
 make known his deeds among the peoples.
Sing to him, sing praises to him;
 tell of all his wonderful works.

Let the hearts of those who seek the Lord rejoice.

◆ All stand and sing **Alleluia.**

GOSPEL

Luke 24:28–31, 33, 35

A reading from the holy Gospel according to Luke.

As they came near the village to which they were going, Jesus walked ahead as if he were going on. But they urged him strongly, saying, "Stay with us, because it is almost evening." So he went in to stay with them. When he was at the table with them, he took bread, blessed and broke it, and gave it to them. Then their eyes were opened, and they recognized him, and he vanished from their sight. That same hour they got up and returned to Jerusalem, and they found the eleven and their companions gathered together. Then they told what had happened on the road and how Jesus had been made known to them in the breaking of the bread.

The Gospel of the Lord.

◆ All sit and observe silence.

FOR SILENT REFLECTION

Think about this silently in your heart. Jesus always comes to us to offer comfort, understanding, and hope.

CLOSING PRAYER

Let us pray to God for our needs and the needs of others: our family, neighborhood, and the world. For each need we say, "Lord, hear our prayer."

◆ All may add their own prayers here.

Let us pray: **Our Father . . . Amen.**

O God,
thank you for the witness of the two disciples on the road to Emmaus.
You remind us that, despite doubts,
 you remain faithful to your promises.
We pray in the risen Christ's name.

Amen.

✢ All make the sign of the cross.

PRAYER FOR THURSDAY, APRIL 11, 2024

OPENING

The disciples of Jesus who remained in Jerusalem after his death were worried. But into their fear and worry, Jesus came, and he showed them who he was. And slowly, the disciples came to believe in him. We remember St. Stanislaus, bishop and patron saint of Poland. He was martyred for opposing the king's unjust government.

✢ All make the sign of the cross.

In the name of the Father, and of the Son, and of the Holy Spirit. Amen.

PSALM

(For a longer psalm, see page xiv.)
Psalm 105:1–2

Let the hearts of those who seek the LORD rejoice.

Let the hearts of those who seek the LORD rejoice.

O give thanks to the LORD; call on his name;
  make known his deeds among the peoples.
Sing to him, sing praises to him;
  tell of all his wonderful works.

Let the hearts of those who seek the LORD rejoice.

◆ All stand and sing **Alleluia.**

GOSPEL

Luke 24:36–39c, 40–43

A reading from the holy Gospel according to Luke.

While the disciples were talking about Jesus' death and disappearance from the tomb, Jesus himself stood among them and said to them, "Peace be with you." They were startled and terrified and thought that they were seeing a ghost. He said to them, "Why are you frightened, and why do doubts arise in your hearts? Look at my hands and my feet; see that it is I myself. Touch me and see." And when he had said this, he showed them his hands and his feet. Yet for all their joy they were disbelieving and still wondering, he said to them, "Have you anything here to eat?" They gave him a piece of broiled fish, and he took it and ate in their presence.

The Gospel of the Lord.

◆ All sit and observe silence.

FOR SILENT REFLECTION

Think about this silently in your heart. How has Jesus revealed himself to you?

CLOSING PRAYER

Let us pray to God for our needs and the needs of others: our family, neighborhood, and the world. For each need we say, "Lord, hear our prayer."

◆ All may add their own prayers here.

Let us pray: **Our Father . . . Amen.**

Lord Jesus,
help us to believe the evidence of eyes, ears,
  and hearts
to believe in you and your truth.
Who live and reign with God the Father,
in the unity of the Holy Spirit,
God, for ever and ever.

Amen.

✢ All make the sign of the cross.

PRAYER FOR FRIDAY, APRIL 12, 2024

OPENING

Christ's resurrection was real. Jesus was not raised as a spirit or ghost. His whole physical body was raised from the dead and glorified. Even the marks of his suffering, the nail holes, and the wound in his side were not erased but glorified. Jesus promises that we too will be raised, body and soul. This is the faith that we share, the faith given to Peter and the twelve, to the five hundred, to the whole early church, and all the generations that come after.

✢ All make the sign of the cross.

In the name of the Father, and of the Son, and of the Holy Spirit. Amen.

PSALM

(For a longer psalm, see page xiv.)
Psalm 105:1–2

Let the hearts of those who seek the Lord rejoice.

Let the hearts of those who seek the Lord rejoice.

O give thanks to the Lord; call on his name;
  make known his deeds among the peoples.
Sing to him, sing praises to him;
  tell of all his wonderful works.

Let the hearts of those who seek the Lord rejoice.

READING

1 Corinthians 15:1a, 3b–7

A reading from First Letter of Paul to the Corinthians [kohr-IN-thee-uhnz].

Now I want you to understand, brothers and sisters, the good news that I proclaimed to you: that Christ died for our sins in accordance with the scriptures, and that he was buried and that he was raised on the third day in accordance with the scriptures, and that he appeared to Cephas [SEE-fuhs], then to the twelve. Then he appeared to more than five hundred brothers and sisters at one time, most of whom are still alive, though some have died. Then he appeared to James, then to all the apostles.

The Word of the Lord.

◆ All observe silence.

FOR SILENT REFLECTION

Think about this silently in your heart. Who has passed this faith on to you?

CLOSING PRAYER

Let us pray to God for our needs and the needs of others: our family, neighborhood, and the world. For each need we say, "Lord, hear our prayer."

◆ All may add their own prayers here.

Let us pray: **Our Father . . . Amen.**

Lord,
we hope in your resurrection
and in the glory of the Father's kingdom.
May we be ready and willing to share
  the Gospel message every day.
Who live and reign with God the Father,
in the unity of the Holy Spirit,
God, for ever and ever.

Amen.

✢ All make the sign of the cross.

PRAYER FOR THE WEEK
WITH A READING FROM THE GOSPEL FOR **SUNDAY, APRIL 14, 2024**

OPENING

On this third Sunday of Easter, we hear another post-resurrection appearance by Jesus: he opens the minds of the disciples so that they might fully understand the Scriptures. He reminds them that repentance and forgiveness are both central to his message.

✚ All make the sign of the cross.

In the name of the Father, and of the Son, and of the Holy Spirit. Amen.

PSALM
(For a longer psalm, see page xiv.)
Psalm 105:1–2

Let the hearts of those who seek the Lord rejoice.

Let the hearts of those who seek the Lord rejoice.

O give thanks to the Lord; call on his name;
　make known his deeds among the peoples.
Sing to him, sing praises to him;
　tell of all his wonderful works.

Let the hearts of those who seek the Lord rejoice.

◆ All stand and sing **Alleluia.**

GOSPEL
Luke 24:36–38a, 39b–d, 45–48

A reading from the holy Gospel according to Luke.

While the disciples were talking about this, Jesus himself stood among them and said to them, "Peace be with you." They were startled and terrified, and thought that they were seeing a ghost. He said to them, "Why are you frightened? See that it is I myself. Touch me and see; for a ghost does not have flesh and bones as you see that I have." Then he opened their minds to understand the scriptures, and he said to them, "Thus it is written, that the Messiah is to suffer and to rise from the dead on the third day and that repentance and forgiveness of sins is to be proclaimed in his name to all nations, beginning from Jerusalem. You are witnesses of these things."

The Gospel of the Lord.

◆ All sit and observe silence.

FOR SILENT REFLECTION

Think about this silently in your heart. How can you tell others about repentance and forgiveness?

CLOSING PRAYER

Let us pray to God for our needs and the needs of others: our family, neighborhood, and the world. For each need we say, "Lord, hear our prayer."

◆ All may add their own prayers here.

Let us pray: **Our Father . . . Amen.**

Lord Jesus,
help us to make you known in all times
　　and places,
to follow in your ways and bear witness to
　　your ministry on earth.
Who live and reign with God the Father,
in the unity of the Holy Spirit,
God, for ever and ever.

Amen.

✚ All make the sign of the cross.

PRAYER FOR MONDAY, APRIL 15, 2024

OPENING

We will focus this week on the earliest Christian believers. Baptism is the sacrament of belief: those in the early church who came to believe in Jesus were told to repent and be baptized so that they might receive the gift of the Holy Spirit. We believe that baptism confers an indelible mark upon the believer, a mark that can never be erased or destroyed.

✛ All make the sign of the cross.

In the name of the Father, and of the Son, and of the Holy Spirit. Amen.

PSALM
(For a longer psalm, see page xiv.)
Psalm 105:1–2

Let the hearts of those who seek the LORD rejoice.

Let the hearts of those who seek the LORD rejoice.

O give thanks to the LORD; call on his name;
   make known his deeds among the peoples.
Sing to him, sing praises to him;
   tell of all his wonderful works.

Let the hearts of those who seek the LORD rejoice.

READING
Acts 2:14ac, 22c, 23ac, 32, 37–38, 41

A reading from the Acts of the Apostles.

But Peter raised his voice and addressed them, "Jesus of Nazareth, a man attested to you by God with deeds of power, wonders, and signs, this man, you crucified and killed by the hands of those outside the law. This Jesus God raised up, and of that all of us are witnesses." Now when they heard this, they were cut to the heart and said to Peter and to the other apostles, "Brothers, what should we do?" Peter said to them, "Repent and be baptized every one of you in the name of Jesus Christ so that your sins may be forgiven, and you will receive the gift of the Holy Spirit." So those who welcomed his message were baptized, and that day about three thousand persons were added.

The Word of the Lord.

◆ All observe silence.

FOR SILENT REFLECTION

Think about this silently in your heart. We have been changed by baptism, changed into Christ by the power of the Holy Spirit.

CLOSING PRAYER

Let us pray to God for our needs and the needs of others: our family, neighborhood, and the world. For each need we say, "Lord, hear our prayer."

◆ All may add their own prayers here.

Let us pray: **Our Father . . . Amen.**

Praise be to you, O God!
You have marked us as your own people
   through the sacrament of baptism.
By the wondrous example
   of your early Church,
help us to do your work in the world.
Through Christ our risen Lord.

Amen.

✛ All make the sign of the cross.

PRAYER FOR
TUESDAY, APRIL 16, 2024

OPENING

In today's reading, we will hear a description of what life was like within the early Church community. Our lives look very different today than those of the earliest disciples, but we should learn from them not to put too much weight on personal possessions. We should give to those in need. We should dedicate ourselves to worshipping together, to breaking the bread of the Eucharist regularly. We should cultivate a spirit of gratitude and praise.

✢ All make the sign of the cross.

In the name of the Father, and of the Son, and of the Holy Spirit. Amen.

PSALM
(For a longer psalm, see page xiv.)
Psalm 105:1–2

Let the hearts of those who seek the Lord rejoice.

Let the hearts of those who seek the Lord rejoice.

O give thanks to the Lord; call on his name;
  make known his deeds among the peoples.
Sing to him, sing praises to him;
  tell of all his wonderful works.

Let the hearts of those who seek the Lord rejoice.

READING
Acts 2:42–47

A reading from the Acts of the Apostles.

They devoted themselves to the apostles' teaching and fellowship, to the breaking of bread and the prayers. Awe came upon everyone because many wonders and signs were being done through the apostles. All who believed were together and had all things in common; they would sell their possessions and goods and distribute the proceeds to all, as any had need. Day by day, as they spent much time together in the temple, they broke bread at home and ate their food with glad and generous hearts, praising God and having the goodwill of all the people. And day by day the Lord added to their number those who were being saved.

The Word of the Lord.

◆ All observe silence.

FOR SILENT REFLECTION

Think about this silently in your heart. How can you be a leader in your church or school community?

CLOSING PRAYER

Let us pray to God for our needs and the needs of others: our family, neighborhood, and the world. For each need we say, "Lord, hear our prayer."

◆ All may add their own prayers here.

Let us pray: **Our Father . . . Amen.**

We praise you, God,
for all the goodness you have shown to us
    today and every day.
Give us hearts for service in the name of
Jesus Christ our Lord.

Amen.

✢ All make the sign of the cross.

PRAYER FOR WEDNESDAY, APRIL 17, 2024

OPENING

The earliest Christian believers witnessed to a kind of unity by sharing all goods in common. No one among their community was in need. Sadly, we cannot always make the same claim about the Church today.

✛ All make the sign of the cross.

In the name of the Father, and of the Son, and of the Holy Spirit. Amen.

PSALM

(For a longer psalm, see page xiv.)
Psalm 105:1–2

Let the hearts of those who seek the L<small>ORD</small> rejoice.

Let the hearts of those who seek the L<small>ORD</small> rejoice.

O give thanks to the L<small>ORD</small>; call on his name;
 make known his deeds among the peoples.
Sing to him, sing praises to him;
 tell of all his wonderful works.

Let the hearts of those who seek the L<small>ORD</small> rejoice.

READING

Acts 4:32–37

A reading from the Acts of the Apostles.

Now the whole group of those who believed were of one heart and soul, and no one claimed private ownership of any possessions, but everything they owned was held in common. With great power the apostles gave their testimony to the resurrection of the Lord Jesus, and great grace was upon them all. There was not a needy person among them, for as many as owned lands or houses sold them and brought the proceeds of what was sold. They laid it at the apostles' feet, and it was distributed to each as any had need. There was a Levite from Cyprus, Joseph, to whom the apostles gave the name Barnabas (which means "son of encouragement"). He sold a field that belonged to him, then brought the money and laid it at the apostles' feet.

The Word of the Lord.

◆ All observe silence.

FOR SILENT REFLECTION

Think about this silently in your heart. How can you help those in need in your community?

CLOSING PRAYER

Let us pray to God for our needs and the needs of others: our family, neighborhood, and the world. For each need we say, "Lord, hear our prayer."

◆ All may add their own prayers here.

Let us pray: **Our Father . . . Amen.**

Lord,
we trust in you and depend on you
 in all things.
You inspired your followers
 to give generously.
Help us to live in that same spirit of love.
Who live and reign with God the Father,
in the unity of the Holy Spirit,
God, for ever and ever.

Amen.

✛ All make the sign of the cross.

PRAYER FOR
THURSDAY, APRIL 18, 2024

OPENING

The Jewish authorities arrested the apostles several times in an attempt to stop the spread of their faith. In the end, a Pharisee convinced the authorities not to kill the apostles, saying that it is likely the followers of Jesus would scatter and come to nothing. But if they are of God, then he will not let them be destroyed. The faith of these apostles spread quickly and powerfully to many nations and around the world.

✝ All make the sign of the cross.

In the name of the Father, and of the Son, and of the Holy Spirit. Amen.

PSALM
(For a longer psalm, see page xiv.)
Psalm 105:1–2

Let the hearts of those who seek the LORD rejoice.

Let the hearts of those who seek the LORD rejoice.

O give thanks to the LORD; call on his name;
　make known his deeds among the peoples.
Sing to him, sing praises to him;
　tell of all his wonderful works.

Let the hearts of those who seek the LORD rejoice.

READING
Acts 5:17bd, 18, 27c, 28a, 29a, 33b, 35, 38b, 39c

A reading from the Acts of the Apostles.

The high priest and all who were with him, being filled with jealousy, arrested the apostles and put them in the public prison. The high priest questioned them, saying, "We gave you strict orders not to teach in this name." But Peter and the apostles answered, "We must obey God rather than any human authority." They were enraged and wanted to kill them. Then Gamaliel [guh-MAY-lee-uhl] said to them, "Fellow Israelites, I tell you, keep away from these men and let them alone."

The Word of the Lord.

◆ All observe silence.

FOR SILENT REFLECTION

Think about this silently in your heart. How do you think the apostles felt as they faced arrest and execution?

CLOSING PRAYER

Let us pray to God for our needs and the needs of others: our family, neighborhood, and the world. For each need we say, "Lord, hear our prayer."

◆ All may add their own prayers here.

Let us pray: **Our Father . . . Amen.**

Praise and glory to you, O God!
Though your people are plagued by sin,
your Holy Spirit sustains your Church.
Help us to be faithful followers and witnesses
　　to your great love.
Through Christ our risen Lord.

Amen.

✝ All make the sign of the cross.

PRAYER FOR FRIDAY, APRIL 19, 2024

OPENING

In Antioch [AN-tee-ahk], gentiles were successfully introduced into the community of believers for the first time. So the followers of Christ came to be known as "Christians" to more clearly express their unity in Christ. We profess a belief in one, holy, catholic, and apostolic Church. *Catholic* means "universal"—our faith is not limited to a certain group of people, but is open to everyone in all times and all places.

✢ All make the sign of the cross.

In the name of the Father, and of the Son, and of the Holy Spirit. Amen.

PSALM
(For a longer psalm, see page xiv.)
Psalm 105:1–2

Let the hearts of those who seek the Lord rejoice.

Let the hearts of those who seek the Lord rejoice.

O give thanks to the Lord; call on his name;
  make known his deeds among the peoples.
Sing to him, sing praises to him;
  tell of all his wonderful works.

Let the hearts of those who seek the Lord rejoice.

READING
Acts 11:20, 22–26

A reading from the Acts of the Apostles.

But among them were some men of Cyprus [SI-pruhs] and Cyrene [si-REEN] who, on coming to Antioch [AN-tee-ahk], spoke to the Hellenists also, proclaiming the Lord Jesus. News of this came to the ears of the church in Jerusalem, and they sent Barnabas to Antioch. When he came and saw the grace of God, he rejoiced, and he exhorted them all to remain faithful to the Lord with steadfast devotion, for he was a good man, full of the Holy Spirit and of faith. And a great many people were brought to the Lord. Then Barnabas went to Tarsus to look for Saul, and when he had found him he brought him to Antioch. So it was that for an entire year they met with the church and taught a great many people, and it was in Antioch that the disciples were first called "Christians."

The Word of the Lord.

◆ All observe silence.

FOR SILENT REFLECTION

Think about this silently in your heart. How do you demonstrate steadfast devotion to Jesus?

CLOSING PRAYER

Let us pray to God for our needs and the needs of others: our family, neighborhood, and the world. For each need we say, "Lord, hear our prayer."

◆ All may add their own prayers here.

Let us pray: **Our Father . . . Amen.**

Loving God,
help us to be good Christians.
We ask this in the name of Christ our Lord.

Amen.

✢ All make the sign of the cross.

PRAYER FOR THE WEEK
WITH A READING FROM THE GOSPEL FOR **SUNDAY, APRIL 21, 2024**

OPENING

Jesus is the Good Shepherd, and we are the sheep of his flock. His sheep come in a variety of sizes, shapes, and colors. They come from different sheepfolds, but they all listen to the voice of the Shepherd, who doesn't fail us. He saves us from the specter of death. He lays down his life for us. The shepherd loves us. May we return his love.

✜ All make the sign of the cross.

In the name of the Father, and of the Son, and of the Holy Spirit. Amen.

PSALM
(For a longer psalm, see page xiv.)
Psalm 105:1–2

Let the hearts of those who seek the LORD rejoice.

Let the hearts of those who seek the LORD rejoice.

O give thanks to the LORD; call on his name;
  make known his deeds among the peoples.
Sing to him, sing praises to him;
  tell of all his wonderful works.

Let the hearts of those who seek the LORD rejoice.

◆ All stand and sing **Alleluia.**

GOSPEL
John 10:11–12, 14, 15b–18b

A reading from the holy Gospel according to John.

Jesus said, "I am the good shepherd. The good shepherd lays down his life for the sheep. The hired hand, who is not the shepherd and does not own the sheep, sees the wolf coming and leaves the sheep and runs away, and the wolf snatches them and scatters them. I am the good shepherd. I know my own, and my own know me. And I lay down my life for the sheep. I have other sheep that do not belong to this fold. I must bring them also, and they will listen to my voice. So there will be one flock, one shepherd. For this reason the Father loves me, because I lay down my life in order to take it up again. No one takes it from me, but I lay it down of my own accord."

The Gospel of the Lord.

◆ All sit and observe silence.

FOR SILENT REFLECTION

Think about this silently in your heart. How has God protected and loved you?

CLOSING PRAYER

Let us pray to God for our needs and the needs of others: our family, neighborhood, and the world. For each need we say, "Lord, hear our prayer."

◆ All may add their own prayers here.

Let us pray: **Our Father . . . Amen.**

Lord Jesus, our Good Shepherd,
may we always be close to you
and hear your voice above all others.
Who live and reign with God the Father,
in the unity of the Holy Spirit,
God, for ever and ever.

Amen.

✜ All make the sign of the cross.

PRAYER FOR MONDAY, APRIL 22, 2024

OPENING

This week, we will be reflecting on the titles of Jesus. In our reading today, we hear Isaiah's prophecy of a child named Immanuel, which came to symbolize a messiah for the people of Israel. *Immanuel* means "God with us." We believe that Jesus is the fulfillment of the prophecy, that God came to earth and was born, that he took on human life in every way except in sin, that he even suffered and died to bring us eternal life.

✣ All make the sign of the cross.

In the name of the Father, and of the Son, and of the Holy Spirit. Amen.

PSALM

(For a longer psalm, see page xiv.)
Psalm 105:1–2

Let the hearts of those who seek the LORD rejoice.

Let the hearts of those who seek the LORD rejoice.

O give thanks to the LORD; call on his name;
    make known his deeds among the peoples.
Sing to him, sing praises to him;
    tell of all his wonderful works.

Let the hearts of those who seek the LORD rejoice.

READING

Isaiah 7:3ab, 4ab, 10–14

A reading from the Book of the prophet Isaiah.

Then the LORD said to Isaiah, "Go out to meet Ahaz [AY-haz], and say to him: Take heed, be quiet, do not fear." Again the LORD spoke to Ahaz, saying, "Ask a sign of the LORD your God; let it be deep as Sheol [SHAY-ohl] or high as heaven." But Ahaz said, "I will not ask, and I will not put the LORD to the test." Then Isaiah said: "Hear then, O house of David! Is it too little for you to weary mortals that you weary my God also? Therefore the Lord himself will give you a sign. Look, the young woman is with child and shall bear a son, and shall name him Immanuel [ihm-MAN-yoo-el]."

The Word of the Lord.

◆ All observe silence.

FOR SILENT REFLECTION

Think about this silently in your heart. How is God with you today?

CLOSING PRAYER

Let us pray to God for our needs and the needs of others: our family, neighborhood, and the world. For each need we say, "Lord, hear our prayer."

◆ All may add their own prayers here.

Let us pray: **Our Father . . . Amen.**

Lord God,
thank you for humbling yourself
    to take on our flesh.
Be with us today and every day
as we strive to live and love as you do.
Who live and reign with God the Father,
in the unity of the Holy Spirit,
God, for ever and ever.

Amen.

✣ All make the sign of the cross.

PRAYER FOR
TUESDAY, APRIL 23, 2024

OPENING

Jesus brings the light of life to all who are trapped in the darkness of sin. Today we remember two saints, one of whom is a beloved saint of England, St. George. Because he is popularly believed to have slain a dragon, he is one of the better-known military saints. We also honor St. Adalbert, martyr and bishop of Prague in the seventh century.

✦ All make the sign of the cross.

In the name of the Father, and of the Son, and of the Holy Spirit. Amen.

PSALM
(For a longer psalm, see page xiv.)
Psalm 105:1–2

Let the hearts of those who seek the LORD rejoice.

Let the hearts of those who seek the LORD rejoice.

O give thanks to the LORD; call on his name;
   make known his deeds among the peoples.
Sing to him, sing praises to him;
   tell of all his wonderful works.

Let the hearts of those who seek the LORD rejoice.

◆ All stand and sing **Alleluia.**

GOSPEL
John 8:12–14a, 18–19

A reading from the holy Gospel according to John.

Again Jesus spoke to them, saying, "I am the light of the world. Whoever follows me will never walk in darkness but will have the light of life." Then the Pharisees [FAYR-uh-seez] said to him, "You are testifying on your own behalf; your testimony is not valid." Jesus answered, "Even if I testify on my own behalf, my testimony is valid because I know where I have come from and where I am going. I testify on my own behalf, and the Father who sent me testifies on my behalf." Then they said to him, "Where is your Father?" Jesus answered, "You know neither me nor my Father. If you knew me, you would know my Father also."

The Gospel of the Lord.

◆ All sit and observe silence.

FOR SILENT REFLECTION

Think about this silently in your heart. Those who follow Jesus walk in the light.

CLOSING PRAYER

Let us pray to God for our needs and the needs of others: our family, neighborhood, and the world. For each need we say, "Lord, hear our prayer."

◆ All may add their own prayers here.

Let us pray: **Our Father . . . Amen.**

Light of the World,
give us the courage to walk
   in your light always.
Who live and reign with God the Father,
in the unity of the Holy Spirit,
God, for ever and ever.

Amen.

✦ All make the sign of the cross.

PRAYER FOR WEDNESDAY, APRIL 24, 2024

OPENING

Those who minister to God's people follow in the footsteps of Jesus. But all of us are anointed to be "priest, prophet, and king" in baptism. We worship at Mass with the ordained priests, and we offer ourselves, our gifts and sacrifices, to God. Today we honor St. Fidelis of Sigmaringen [zihg-MAHR-ing-*n] (1577–1622), who was martyred when he refused to renounce his faith.

✚ All make the sign of the cross.

In the name of the Father, and of the Son, and of the Holy Spirit. Amen.

PSALM
(For a longer psalm, see page xiv.)
Psalm 105:1–2

Let the hearts of those who seek the LORD rejoice.

Let the hearts of those who seek the LORD rejoice.

O give thanks to the LORD; call on his name;
  make known his deeds among the peoples.
Sing to him, sing praises to him;
  tell of all his wonderful works.

Let the hearts of those who seek the LORD rejoice.

READING
Hebrews 5:1–6

A reading from the Book of Hebrews.

Every high priest chosen from among mortals is put in charge of things pertaining to God on their behalf, to offer gifts and sacrifices for sins. He is able to deal gently with the ignorant and wayward, since he himself is subject to weakness, and because of this he must offer sacrifice for his own sins as well as for those of the people. And one does not presume to take this honor but takes it only when called by God, just as Aaron was. So also Christ did not glorify himself in becoming a high priest but was appointed by the one who said to him, "You are my Son; today I have begotten you"; as he says also in another place, "You are a priest forever, according to the order of Melchizedek [mehl-KEEZ-uh-dehk]."

The Word of the Lord.

◆ All observe silence.

FOR SILENT REFLECTION

Think about this silently in your heart. What do you offer to God this week?

CLOSING PRAYER

Let us pray to God for our needs and the needs of others: our family, neighborhood, and the world. For each need we say, "Lord, hear our prayer."

◆ All may add their own prayers here.

Let us pray: **Our Father . . . Amen.**

Lord,
you have called us to share in
  your priesthood.
Give us the humility to offer all that we have
  to you.
Who live and reign with God the Father for
  ever and ever.

Amen.

✚ All make the sign of the cross.

PRAYER FOR
THURSDAY, APRIL 25, 2024

OPENING

We see evidence of war and violence, jealousy, pride, materialism, and selfishness in this world. Our Savior, by the power of his love, helps us to break from the grip of sin. He even died so that death would have no more power over us. Jesus is truly the Savior of the world. Today is the feast of St. Mark the Evangelist. Countless generations have come to know the good news of Jesus Christ and his saving love.

✜ All make the sign of the cross.

In the name of the Father, and of the Son, and of the Holy Spirit. Amen.

PSALM
(For a longer psalm, see page xiv.)
Psalm 105:1–2

Let the hearts of those who seek the LORD rejoice.

Let the hearts of those who seek the LORD rejoice.

O give thanks to the LORD; call on his name;
 make known his deeds among the peoples.
Sing to him, sing praises to him;
 tell of all his wonderful works.

Let the hearts of those who seek the LORD rejoice.

READING
Acts 4:18–20; 5:27b, 28a, 29–31

A reading from the Acts of the Apostles.

So the Council called the apostles and ordered them not to speak or teach at all in the name of Jesus. But Peter and John answered them, "Whether it is right in God's sight to listen to you rather than to God, you must judge; for we cannot keep from speaking about what we have seen and heard." The high priest questioned them, saying, "We gave you strict orders not to teach in this name." But Peter and the apostles answered, "We must obey God rather than any human authority. The God of our ancestors raised up Jesus, whom you had killed by hanging him on a tree. God exalted him at his right hand as Leader and Savior that he might give repentance to Israel and forgiveness of sins."

The Word of the Lord.

◆ All observe silence.

FOR SILENT REFLECTION

Think about this silently in your heart. Ask Jesus for the strength to eradicate, little by little, sin in the world.

CLOSING PRAYER

Let us pray to God for our needs and the needs of others: our family, neighborhood, and the world. For each need we say, "Lord, hear our prayer."

◆ All may add their own prayers here.

Let us pray: **Our Father . . . Amen.**

Savior of the world,
help us to live as a people redeemed.
Who live and reign with God the Father,
in the unity of the Holy Spirit,
God, for ever and ever.

Amen.

✜ All make the sign of the cross.

PRAYER FOR FRIDAY, APRIL 26, 2024

OPENING

Alpha and omega are the first and last letters of the Greek alphabet. We call Jesus the Alpha and the Omega because he is the first and the last, "the Beginning and the End." While we have some knowledge of the beginning of the world, the end is shrouded in mystery. But what we do know is that the end of this earthly life is not the end of life altogether. Christ promised us that we would be with him eternally. This is our hope.

✦ All make the sign of the cross.

In the name of the Father, and of the Son, and of the Holy Spirit. Amen.

PSALM

(For a longer psalm, see page xiv.)
Psalm 105:1–2

Let the hearts of those who seek the LORD rejoice.

Let the hearts of those who seek the LORD rejoice.

O give thanks to the LORD; call on his name;
  make known his deeds among the peoples.
Sing to him, sing praises to him;
  tell of all his wonderful works.

Let the hearts of those who seek the LORD rejoice.

READING

Revelation 20:11a; 21:2ac, 3ab, 4, 5ab, 6ab

A reading from the Book of Revelation.

Then I saw a great white throne and the one who sat on it. And I saw the holy city, the new Jerusalem, coming down out of heaven from God. And I heard a loud voice from the throne saying, "See, the home of God is among mortals. He will wipe every tear from their eyes. Death will be no more; mourning and crying and pain will be no more, for the first things have passed away." And the one who was seated on the throne said, "See, I am making all things new." Then he said to me, "I am the Alpha and the Omega, the Beginning and the End."

The Word of the Lord.

◆ All observe silence.

FOR SILENT REFLECTION

Think about this silently in your heart. This week, you have heard many names for Jesus. What others do you know?

CLOSING PRAYER

Let us pray to God for our needs and the needs of others: our family, neighborhood, and the world. For each need we say, "Lord, hear our prayer."

◆ All may add their own prayers here.

Let us pray: **Our Father . . . Amen.**

Almighty God,
you make all things new.
May we be made ready for when Christ is
  all in all.
In his name we pray.

Amen.

✦ All make the sign of the cross.

PRAYER FOR THE WEEK
WITH A READING FROM THE GOSPEL FOR SUNDAY, APRIL 28, 2024

OPENING

All of us are called to bear the fruit of faith. We are called to bring love, kindness, faith, patience, peace, and every kind of virtue into the world. But we cannot bear fruit apart from the true vine, Jesus Christ. He sustains us and gives us all that is good.

✣ All make the sign of the cross.

In the name of the Father, and of the Son, and of the Holy Spirit. Amen.

PSALM
(For a longer psalm, see page xv.)
Psalm 118:1–2, 4

The stone that the builders rejected has become the chief cornerstone.

The stone that the builders rejected has become the chief cornerstone.

O give thanks to the LORD, for he is good;
  his steadfast love endures forever!
Let Israel say,
  "His steadfast love endures forever."
Let those who fear the Lord say,
  "His steadfast love endures forever."

The stone that the builders rejected has become the chief cornerstone.

◆ All stand and sing **Alleluia.**

GOSPEL
John 15:1–2a, 4–7

A reading from the holy Gospel according to John.

Jesus said to his disciples, "I am the true vine, and my Father is the vinegrower. He removes every branch in me that bears no fruit. Abide in me as I abide in you. Just as the branch cannot bear fruit by itself unless it abides in the vine, neither can you unless you abide in me. I am the vine; you are the branches. Those who abide in me and I in them bear much fruit, because apart from me you can do nothing. Whoever does not abide in me is thrown away like a branch and withers; such branches are gathered, thrown into the fire, and burned. If you abide in me, and my words abide in you, ask for whatever you wish, and it will be done for you."

The Gospel of the Lord.

◆ All sit and observe silence.

FOR SILENT REFLECTION

Think about this silently in your heart. Does your life bear fruit? What kind?

CLOSING PRAYER

Let us pray to God for our needs and the needs of others: our family, neighborhood, and the world. For each need we say, "Lord, hear our prayer."

◆ All may add their own prayers here.

Let us pray: **Our Father . . . Amen.**

O Jesus the True Vine,
thank you for sustaining us
and giving all that we need to bear your fruit
    in the world.
Who live and reign with God the Father,
in the unity of the Holy Spirit,
God, for ever and ever.

Amen.

✣ All make the sign of the cross.

PRAYER FOR MONDAY, APRIL 29, 2024

OPENING

Today we remember St. Catherine of Siena (1347–1380), one of many patron saints of Italy and a theologian and philosopher. She is one of four female Doctors of the Church. Although she devoted herself to holiness, she advocated strongly for reform in the Church. Catherine trusted in the Good Shepherd alone to care for his flock.

✙ All make the sign of the cross.

In the name of the Father, and of the Son, and of the Holy Spirit. Amen.

PSALM

(For a longer psalm, see page xv.)
Psalm 118:1–2, 4

The stone that the builders rejected has become the chief cornerstone.

The stone that the builders rejected has become the chief cornerstone.

O give thanks to the LORD, for he is good;
 his steadfast love endures forever!
Let Israel say,
 "His steadfast love endures forever."
Let those who fear the Lord say,
 "His steadfast love endures forever."

The stone that the builders rejected has become the chief cornerstone.

◆ All stand and sing **Alleluia.**

GOSPEL
John 10:9–15a

A reading from the holy Gospel according to John.

I am the gate. Whoever enters by me will be saved and will come in and go out and find pasture. The thief comes only to steal and kill and destroy. I came that they may have life and have it abundantly. I am the good shepherd. The good shepherd lays down his life for the sheep. The hired hand, who is not the shepherd and does not own the sheep, sees the wolf coming and leaves the sheep and runs away, and the wolf snatches them and scatters them. The hired hand runs away because a hired hand does not care for the sheep. I am the good shepherd. I know my own and my own know me, just as the Father knows me and I know the Father.

The Gospel of the Lord.

◆ All sit and observe silence.

FOR SILENT REFLECTION

Think about this silently in your heart. Who is the "hired hand" who leads but does not care for us? How can we distinguish between false voices and the voice of the Good Shepherd?

CLOSING PRAYER

Let us pray to God for our needs and the needs of others: our family, neighborhood, and the world. For each need we say, "Lord, hear our prayer."

◆ All may add their own prayers here.

Let us pray: **Our Father . . . Amen.**

Father in heaven,
thank you for your care and leadership.
Through Christ our risen Lord.

Amen.

✙ All make the sign of the cross.

PRAYER FOR TUESDAY, APRIL 30, 2024

OPENING

We have been invited into the love of God, the love that binds together Father, Son, and Holy Spirit. Because we are loved so completely, we are also called to share this love as God does, without counting the cost. Our saint today, Pope Pius V, was elected pope in the 1500s, during great upheaval following the Reformation and the Council of Trent. He led the Church into a new age of renewal.

✚ All make the sign of the cross.

In the name of the Father, and of the Son, and of the Holy Spirit. Amen.

PSALM

(For a longer psalm, see page xv.)
Psalm 118:1–2, 4

The stone that the builders rejected has become the chief cornerstone.

The stone that the builders rejected has become the chief cornerstone.

O give thanks to the Lord, for he is good;
  his steadfast love endures forever!
Let Israel say,
  "His steadfast love endures forever."
Let those who fear the Lord say,
  "His steadfast love endures forever."

The stone that the builders rejected has become the chief cornerstone.

◆ All stand and sing **Alleluia.**

GOSPEL

John 15:9–12

A reading from the holy Gospel according to John.

As the Father has loved me, so I have loved you; abide in my love. If you keep my commandments, you will abide in my love, just as I have kept my Father's commandments and abide in his love. I have said these things to you so that my joy may be in you, and that your joy may be complete. This is my commandment, that you love one another as I have loved you.

The Gospel of the Lord.

◆ All sit and observe silence.

FOR SILENT REFLECTION

Think about this silently in your heart. How do you share the love of God with others?

CLOSING PRAYER

Let us pray to God for our needs and the needs of others: our family, neighborhood, and the world. For each need we say, "Lord, hear our prayer."

◆ All may add their own prayers here.

Let us pray: **Our Father . . . Amen.**

Heavenly Father,
you love us with an everlasting love.
Help us to keep your commandments
    and abide in your love.
Through Christ our Lord.

Amen.

✚ All make the sign of the cross.

PRAYER FOR WEDNESDAY, MAY 1, 2024

OPENING

Jesus told his disciples that he would prepare a place for them and they would know the way there. They were confused and a little panicked because they did not know the way. But Jesus assured them (and all of us) that he is the Way, the Truth, and the Life.

✣ All make the sign of the cross.

In the name of the Father, and of the Son, and of the Holy Spirit. Amen.

PSALM

(For a longer psalm, see page xv.)
Psalm 118:1–2, 4

The stone that the builders rejected has become the chief cornerstone.

The stone that the builders rejected has become the chief cornerstone.

O give thanks to the LORD, for he is good;
  his steadfast love endures forever!
Let Israel say,
  "His steadfast love endures forever."
Let those who fear the Lord say,
  "His steadfast love endures forever."

The stone that the builders rejected has become the chief cornerstone.

◆ All stand and sing **Alleluia.**

GOSPEL

John 14:6–7a, 8–9d, 10b–c, 11

A reading from the holy Gospel according to John.

Jesus said to Philip, "I am the way and the truth and the life. No one comes to the Father except through me. If you know me, you will know my Father also." Philip said to him, "Lord, show us the Father, and we will be satisfied." Jesus said to him, "Have I been with you all this time, Philip, and you still do not know me? Whoever has seen me has seen the Father. How can you say, 'Show us the Father'? Do you not believe that I am in the Father and the Father is in me? The words that I say to you I do not speak on my own, but the Father who dwells in me does his works. Believe me that I am in the Father and the Father is in me, but if you do not, then believe me because of the works themselves."

The Gospel of the Lord.

◆ All sit and observe silence.

FOR SILENT REFLECTION

Think about this silently in your heart. If we know Jesus, he will take us on the Way to the Father, to the Truth, to the fullness of Life.

CLOSING PRAYER

Let us pray to God for our needs and the needs of others: our family, neighborhood, and the world. For each need we say, "Lord, hear our prayer."

◆ All may add their own prayers here.

Let us pray: **Our Father . . . Amen.**

Lord Jesus,
lead us to the fullness of life with God.
Who live and reign with God the Father,
in the unity of the Holy Spirit,
God, for ever and ever.

Amen.

✣ All make the sign of the cross.

PRAYER SERVICE
TO HONOR MARY IN MAY

Add an image or statue of Mary, flowers, and candles to the sacred space. Prepare six leaders for this service. The third leader will need a Bible for the passages from Luke. Take time to help the lector practice the readings. You may wish to sing "Sing of Mary" as the opening song. If the group will sing, prepare someone to lead it.

FIRST LEADER:

Throughout the month of May, we remember Mary, the Mother of our Lord Jesus. She was a life-giving caregiver for our Savior, and she remains so for us today. She represents the fullness of holiness, for she was conceived without sin and was assumed into heaven because of her special role in our salvation. She serves as an example for all of us to say "yes" in practical ways to God's Spirit of goodness. Many Catholics turn to this beloved first disciple of Christ for inspiration and for prayer, particularly as the events of Jesus' life unfold in Scripture during the Church year.

SONG LEADER:

◆ Gesture for all to stand, and lead the first few verses of the song.

SECOND LEADER:

✚ All make the sign of the cross.

In the name of the Father, and of the Son, and of the Holy Spirit. Amen.

Let us pray:
Almighty Father,
we honor Mary as our Mother
because you chose her to be
the human vessel for
your Son Jesus,
who was both human and divine.

Help us to be open to
the same Spirit
who appeared to Mary,
guiding her throughout her
challenging life with
the Savior of our world.
We ask this through Christ our Lord.

Amen.

◆ Remain standing and sing **Alleluia.**

THIRD LEADER: Luke 1:26–38
A reading from the holy Gospel according
to Luke.

◆ Read the Gospel passage from the Bible.

The Gospel of the Lord.

◆ All sit and observe silence.

FOURTH LEADER:

◆ Gesture for all to stand.

Let us bring our hopes and needs to God as
we respond, "Lord, hear our prayer."
For all mothers
and those who nurture others
throughout life.
May they be open to
God's creative Spirit to bring
new life into the world,

we pray to the Lord . . .

For those facing difficult decisions.
May they look to Mary
for guidance
in following God's plan,

we pray to the Lord . . .

For all married couples.
May they remain devoted
to God, to each other,
and to their sacrament of marriage,

we pray to the Lord . . .

For the sick and the abandoned.
For those who have passed
to the other side of life.
May they feel the loving arms
of Mary with Jesus,

we pray to the Lord . . .

FIFTH LEADER:
Let us pray the Hail Mary:

ALL: Hail Mary, full of grace . . .

◆ Pause, and then say:

Let us offer one another a sign of
Christ's peace.

◆ All offer one another a sign of peace.

SIXTH LEADER:
Let us pray Mary's special prayer,
the Magnificat:
"My soul magnifies the Lord,
  and my spirit rejoices in God my Savior,
for he has looked with favor on the lowliness
    of his servant.
  Surely, from now on all generations will
    call me blessed;
for the Mighty One has done great things
    for me,
and holy is his name."

✢ All make the sign of the cross.

**In the name of the Father, and of the
Son, and of the Holy Spirit. Amen.**

PRAYER FOR
THURSDAY, MAY 2, 2024

OPENING

Jesus tells his disciples to love him by keeping his words. Today's saint, St. Athanasius [ath-uh-NAY-shuhs], was a third-century bishop and theologian who dedicated his life to fighting heresy. Though he suffered and was exiled for it, he was steadfast in keeping the words of Christ.

✝ All make the sign of the cross.

In the name of the Father, and of the Son, and of the Holy Spirit. Amen.

PSALM

(For a longer psalm, see page xv.)
Psalm 118:1–2, 4

The stone that the builders rejected has become the chief cornerstone.

The stone that the builders rejected has become the chief cornerstone.

O give thanks to the LORD, for he is good;
   his steadfast love endures forever!
Let Israel say,
   "His steadfast love endures forever."
Let those who fear the Lord say,
   "His steadfast love endures forever."

The stone that the builders rejected has become the chief cornerstone.

◆ All stand and sing **Alleluia.**

GOSPEL
John 14:23–27

A reading from the holy Gospel according to John.

Jesus answered Peter, "Those who love me will keep my word, and my Father will love them, and we will come to them and make our home with them. Whoever does not love me does not keep my words, and the word that you hear is not mine but is from the Father who sent me. I have said these things to you while I am still with you. But the Advocate, the Holy Spirit, whom the Father will send in my name, will teach you everything, and remind you of all that I have said to you. Peace I leave with you; my peace I give to you. I do not give to you as the world gives. Do not let your hearts be troubled, and do not let them be afraid."

The Gospel of the Lord.

◆ All sit and observe silence.

FOR SILENT REFLECTION

Think about this silently in your heart. How do you keep the words of Jesus?

CLOSING PRAYER

Let us pray to God for our needs and the needs of others: our family, neighborhood, and the world. For each need we say, "Lord, hear our prayer."

◆ All may add their own prayers here.

Let us pray: **Our Father . . . Amen.**

Christ Jesus,
help us to keep your words by the way we live
      and love our neighbors.
Who live and reign with God the Father,
in the unity of the Holy Spirit,
God, for ever and ever.

Amen.

✝ All make the sign of the cross.

PRAYER FOR FRIDAY, MAY 3, 2024

OPENING

Today is the feast of the apostles Philip and James. They (along with all the apostles) were slow to recognize the true identity of Jesus. At one point, Philip even asked Jesus to show them the Father, perhaps desiring a burning bush of his own, a big flashy sign. But Jesus offered them only himself, the light of the world. He offered the example of his life, that we might see the Father in him.

✛ All make the sign of the cross.

In the name of the Father, and of the Son, and of the Holy Spirit. Amen.

PSALM

(For a longer psalm, see page xv.)
Psalm 118:1–2, 4

The stone that the builders rejected has become the chief cornerstone.

The stone that the builders rejected has become the chief cornerstone.

O give thanks to the Lord, for he is good;
　his steadfast love endures forever!
Let Israel say,
　"His steadfast love endures forever."
Let those who fear the Lord say,
　"His steadfast love endures forever."

The stone that the builders rejected has become the chief cornerstone.

◆ All stand and sing **Alleluia.**

GOSPEL

John 12:44–46, 49–50

A reading from the holy Gospel according to John.

Then Jesus cried aloud: "Whoever believes in me believes not in me but in him who sent me. And whoever sees me sees him who sent me. I have come as light into the world, so that everyone who believes in me should not remain in the darkness. I have not spoken on my own, but the Father who sent me has himself given me a commandment about what to say and what to speak. And I know that his commandment is eternal life. What I speak, therefore, I speak just as the Father has told me."

The Gospel of the Lord.

◆ All sit and observe silence.

FOR SILENT REFLECTION

Think about this silently in your heart. How does Jesus reveal the Father to us?

CLOSING PRAYER

Let us pray to God for our needs and the needs of others: our family, neighborhood, and the world. For each need we say, "Lord, hear our prayer."

◆ All may add their own prayers here.

Let us pray: **Our Father . . . Amen.**

O God our Father,
thank you for sending us your Son
so that we might know you in him.
We are sometimes slow in understanding
　　your will; guide us with your wisdom.
Through Christ our Lord.

Amen.

✛ All make the sign of the cross.

PRAYER FOR THE WEEK
WITH A READING FROM THE GOSPEL FOR **SUNDAY, MAY 5, 2024**

OPENING

All of us will be faced with a choice at some point between our beloved and possessions, reputation, power, or even our own desires. Jesus teaches us that true love is not selfish or grasping.

✚ All make the sign of the cross.

In the name of the Father, and of the Son, and of the Holy Spirit. Amen.

PSALM

(For a longer psalm, see page xv.)
Psalm 118:1–2, 4

The stone that the builders rejected has become the chief cornerstone.

The stone that the builders rejected has become the chief cornerstone.

O give thanks to the Lord, for he is good;
 his steadfast love endures forever!
Let Israel say,
 "His steadfast love endures forever."
Let those who fear the Lord say,
 "His steadfast love endures forever."

The stone that the builders rejected has become the chief cornerstone.

◆ All stand and sing **Alleluia.**

GOSPEL

John 15:9–10, 12–14a, 15c–16ac, 17

A reading from the holy Gospel according to John.

Jesus said, "As the Father has loved me, so I have loved you; abide in my love. If you keep my commandments, you will abide in my love, just as I have kept my Father's commandments and abide in his love. This is my commandment, that you love one another as I have loved you. No one has greater love than this, to lay down one's life for one's friends. You are my friends if you do what I command you. I have called you friends, because I have made known to you everything that I have heard from my Father. You did not choose me, but I chose you. And I appointed you to go and bear fruit, fruit that will last. I am giving you these commands so that you may love one another."

The Gospel of the Lord.

◆ All sit and observe silence.

FOR SILENT REFLECTION

Think about this silently in your heart. How does serving others connect with what Jesus is saying?

CLOSING PRAYER

Let us pray to God for our needs and the needs of others: our family, neighborhood, and the world. For each need we say, "Lord, hear our prayer."

◆ All may add their own prayers here.

Let us pray: **Our Father . . . Amen.**

Thank you for your love, O God,
which helps us strengthen our connection
to you and to others.
Please give us the grace we need to follow
your commandments.
Through Christ our risen Lord.
Amen.

✚ All make the sign of the cross.

PRAYER FOR
MONDAY, MAY 6, 2024

OPENING

This week we will explore the conversion of St. Paul. Paul was formerly known as Saul. Like many of his forefathers (Abraham, Jacob), his name changed after he received a call from God. When we meet Saul, he is overseeing the torture and death of St. Stephen, the first martyr.

✢ All make the sign of the cross.

In the name of the Father, and of the Son, and of the Holy Spirit. Amen.

PSALM
(For a longer psalm, see page xv.)
Psalm 118:1–2, 4

The stone that the builders rejected has become the chief cornerstone.

The stone that the builders rejected has become the chief cornerstone.

O give thanks to the LORD, for he is good;
  his steadfast love endures forever!
Let Israel say,
  "His steadfast love endures forever."
Let those who fear the Lord say,
  "His steadfast love endures forever."

The stone that the builders rejected has become the chief cornerstone.

READING
Acts 6:8–9ac, 10–11; 7:54, 58–59, 60c; 8:1a

A reading from the Acts of the Apostles.

Stephen, full of grace and power, did great wonders and signs among the people. Then some of those who belonged to the synagogue of the Freedmen stood up and argued with Stephen. But they could not withstand the wisdom and the Spirit with which he spoke. Then they secretly instigated some men to say, "We have heard him speak blasphemous words against Moses and God." When the Council heard these things, they became enraged and ground their teeth at Stephen. Then they dragged him out of the city and began to stone him, and the witnesses laid their coats at the feet of a young man named Saul. While they were stoning Stephen, he prayed, "Lord Jesus, receive my spirit." When he had said this, he died. And Saul approved of their killing him.

The Word of the Lord.

◆ All observe silence.

FOR SILENT REFLECTION

Think about this silently in your heart. Have you ever stood by while someone was hurt, like Saul? How did you feel?

CLOSING PRAYER

Let us pray to God for our needs and the needs of others: our family, neighborhood, and the world. For each need we say, "Lord, hear our prayer."

◆ All may add their own prayers here.

Let us pray: **Our Father . . . Amen.**

Lord God,
help us stay true to our faith,
as St. Stephen did.
Through Christ our Lord.

Amen.

✢ All make the sign of the cross.

PRAYER FOR
TUESDAY, MAY 7, 2024

OPENING

Saul led a reign of terror persecuting Christians, and he sought to imprison and bring any followers of Jesus to Jerusalem for punishment. Saul was entrenched in sin. It would take a lot for him to see another way forward.

✛ All make the sign of the cross.

In the name of the Father, and of the Son, and of the Holy Spirit. Amen.

PSALM

(For a longer psalm, see page xv.)
Psalm 118:1–2, 4

The stone that the builders rejected has become the chief cornerstone.

The stone that the builders rejected has become the chief cornerstone.

O give thanks to the LORD, for he is good;
   his steadfast love endures forever!
Let Israel say,
   "His steadfast love endures forever."
Let those who fear the Lord say,
   "His steadfast love endures forever."

The stone that the builders rejected has become the chief cornerstone.

READING

Acts 8:1,3; 9:1–2

A reading from the Acts of the Apostles.

That day [when Stephen was stoned to death] a severe persecution began against the church in Jerusalem, and all except the apostles were scattered throughout the countryside of Judea [joo-DEE-uh] and Samaria [suh-MAYR-ee-uh]. But Saul was ravaging the church by entering house after house; dragging off both men and women, he committed them to prison. Meanwhile Saul, still breathing threats and murder against the disciples of the Lord, went to the high priest and asked him for letters to the synagogues [SIN-uh-gogs] at Damascus [duh-MAS-kuhs], so that if he found any who belonged to the Way, men or women, he might bring them bound to Jerusalem.

The Word of the Lord.

◆ All observe silence.

FOR SILENT REFLECTION

Think about this silently in your heart. Have you ever been caught up in something you knew was wrong and couldn't break free? What did it feel like?

CLOSING PRAYER

Let us pray to God for our needs and the needs of others: our family, neighborhood, and the world. For each need we say, "Lord, hear our prayer."

◆ All may add their own prayers here.

Let us pray: **Our Father . . . Amen.**

Heavenly Father,
when we sin and turn away from you,
help us find our way back to you.
Through Christ our Lord

Amen.

✛ All make the sign of the cross.

PRAYER FOR
WEDNESDAY, MAY 8, 2024

OPENING

Saul was so wrapped up in sin and death that the Lord needed to do something big to get his attention. As Saul traveled to Damascus, he was blinded by a flash of light from heaven. Saul, powerful and in the prime of his life, was rendered helpless in an instant. He, who had been suffering from spiritual blindness, unable to see the truth of the Good News the Christians proclaimed, was now physically blind.

✣ All make the sign of the cross.

In the name of the Father, and of the Son, and of the Holy Spirit. Amen.

PSALM
(For a longer psalm, see page xv.)
Psalm 118:1–2, 4

The stone that the builders rejected has become the chief cornerstone.

The stone that the builders rejected has become the chief cornerstone.

O give thanks to the Lord, for he is good;
  his steadfast love endures forever!
Let Israel say,
  "His steadfast love endures forever."
Let those who fear the Lord say,
  "His steadfast love endures forever."

The stone that the builders rejected has become the chief cornerstone.

READING
Acts 9:3–6, 8–9

A reading from the Acts of the Apostles.

Now as Saul was going along and approaching Damascus [duh-MAS-kuhs], suddenly a light from heaven flashed around him. He fell to the ground and heard a voice saying to him, "Saul, Saul, why do you persecute me?" He asked, "Who are you, Lord?" The reply came, "I am Jesus, whom you are persecuting. But get up and enter the city, and you will be told what you are to do." Saul got up from the ground, and though his eyes were open, he could see nothing; so they led him by the hand and brought him into Damascus. For three days he was without sight and neither ate nor drank.

The Word of the Lord.

◆ All observe silence.

FOR SILENT REFLECTION

Think about this silently in your heart. Have you ever had a sign from God?

CLOSING PRAYER

Let us pray to God for our needs and the needs of others: our family, neighborhood, and the world. For each need we say, "Lord, hear our prayer."

◆ All may add their own prayers here.

Let us pray: **Our Father . . . Amen.**

Lord Jesus,
you come to us in many different ways.
Let us be attentive to your voice.
Who live and reign with God the Father,
in the unity of the Holy Spirit,
God, for ever and ever.

Amen.

✣ All make the sign of the cross.

PRAYER FOR
THURSDAY, MAY 9, 2024

OPENING

The Lord sent Ananias, a Christian, to Saul to lay hands on him and restore his sight. In several sacraments the laying of hands is a gesture that calls down the Holy Spirit. The Holy Spirit filled Saul and inspired him to change his life. The Holy Spirit fills each of us as well, urging us to live virtuous lives, to be loving, peaceful, and merciful, to follow Jesus.

✢ All make the sign of the cross.

In the name of the Father, and of the Son, and of the Holy Spirit. Amen.

PSALM

(For a longer psalm, see page xv.)
Psalm 118:1–2, 4

The stone that the builders rejected has become the chief cornerstone.

The stone that the builders rejected has become the chief cornerstone.

O give thanks to the LORD, for he is good;
  his steadfast love endures forever!
Let Israel say,
  "His steadfast love endures forever."
Let those who fear the Lord say,
  "His steadfast love endures forever."

The stone that the builders rejected has become the chief cornerstone.

READING

Acts 9:10a, 11–12, 16, 17abce, 18

A reading from the Acts of the Apostles.

Now there was a disciple in Damascus [duh-MAS-kuhs] named Ananias [a-nuh-NĪ-uhs]. The Lord said to him, "Get up and go to the street called Straight, and at the house of Judas look for a man of Tarsus named Saul. At this moment he is praying, and he has seen in a vision a man named Ananias come in and lay his hands on him so that he might regain his sight. I myself will show him how much he must suffer for the sake of my name." So Ananias went and entered the house. He laid his hands on Saul and said, "Brother Saul, the Lord Jesus has sent me so that you may regain your sight and be filled with the Holy Spirit." And immediately something like scales fell from his eyes, and his sight was restored. Then he got up and was baptized.

The Word of the Lord.

◆ All observe silence.

FOR SILENT REFLECTION

Think about this silently in your heart. How does the Holy Spirit help you "see"?

CLOSING PRAYER

Let us pray to God for our needs and the needs of others: our family, neighborhood, and the world. For each need we say, "Lord, hear our prayer."

◆ All may add their own prayers here.

Let us pray: **Our Father . . . Amen.**

Spirit of truth,
inspire us to walk uprightly
    and live in the light.
Through Christ our Lord.

Amen.

✢ All make the sign of the cross.

PRAYER FOR FRIDAY, MAY 10, 2024

OPENING

Today is the feast day of St. Damien (1840–1889), a Belgian priest. He went on mission to the Kingdom of Hawaii and introduced the Catholic faith to the indigenous people. After receiving the gift of the Holy Spirit, Saul's life changed. He used his gifts of persuasion and leadership to convince many of the truth of Jesus Christ. He organized the early believers and helped to unite the church. St. Paul is one of the Church's greatest saints.

✢ All make the sign of the cross.

In the name of the Father, and of the Son, and of the Holy Spirit. Amen.

PSALM
(For a longer psalm, see page xv.)
Psalm 118:1–2, 4

The stone that the builders rejected has become the chief cornerstone.

The stone that the builders rejected has become the chief cornerstone.

O give thanks to the Lord, for he is good;
  his steadfast love endures forever!
Let Israel say,
  "His steadfast love endures forever."
Let those who fear the Lord say,
  "His steadfast love endures forever."

The stone that the builders rejected has become the chief cornerstone.

READING
Acts 9:19–21a, 22–23, 24b–25

A reading from the Acts of the Apostles. After taking some food, Saul regained his strength. For several days he was with the disciples in Damascus, and immediately he began to proclaim Jesus in the synagogues, saying, "He is the Son of God." All who heard him were amazed and said, "Is not this the man who made havoc in Jerusalem among those who invoked this name?" Saul became increasingly more powerful and confounded the Jews who lived in Damascus by proving that Jesus was the Messiah. After some time had passed, the Jews plotted to kill him. They were watching the gates day and night so that they might kill him, but his disciples took him by night and let him down through an opening in the wall, lowering him in a basket.

The Word of the Lord.

◆ All observe silence.

FOR SILENT REFLECTION

Think about this silently in your heart. How can you be a leader in faith like St. Paul?

CLOSING PRAYER

Let us pray to God for our needs and the needs of others: our family, neighborhood, and the world. For each need we say, "Lord, hear our prayer."

◆ All may add their own prayers here.

Let us pray: **Our Father . . . Amen.**

Lord God,
send your Spirit to open the hearts of those
  who don't yet know you.
Through Christ our Lord.

Amen.

✢ All make the sign of the cross.

PRAYER SERVICE
ASCENSION

Prepare six leaders and a song leader for this service. The second and third leaders will need Bibles to read the Scripture passages and may need help finding and practicing them. You may wish to begin by singing "All Will Be Well" and end with "Sing Out, Earth and Skies." Help the song leader prepare to lead the singing.

SONG LEADER:
Please stand and join in singing our opening song.

FIRST LEADER:
So if you have been raised with Christ, seek the things that are above, where Christ is, seated at the right hand of God.

ALL: Amen.

FIRST LEADER:
Today we celebrate the Solemnity of the Ascension of the Lord. We are joyful on this fortieth day of Easter because Jesus Christ returned to his Father in heaven, and he promised that we could experience his Presence in Spirit forever.

✙ All make the sign of the cross.

In the name of the Father, and of the Son, and of the Holy Spirit. Amen.

Let us pray:
Almighty God,
you fulfilled your promise
of sending a Savior
to redeem the world.
Now he sits at your right hand
and your Spirit guides us
with holy Presence.
Help us to listen and act according to your will

so that we can enter into
your kingdom too.
We ask this through Christ our Lord.

ALL: Amen.

◆ Gesture for all to sit.

SECOND LEADER: Colossians 3:2–4
A reading from the Letter of Paul to the Colossians.

◆ Read the Scripture passage from the Bible.

The Word of the Lord.

◆ All observe silence.

THIRD LEADER: Acts 1:6–11
A reading from the Acts of the Apostles.

◆ Read the Scripture passage from the Bible.

The Word of the Lord.

◆ All observe silence.

FOURTH LEADER:
Let us stand and bring our hopes and needs to God as we pray, "Lord, hear our prayer."

For our brothers and sisters around the world
who do not know Christ.
May they experience
our Risen Lord in eternity,

we pray to the Lord . . .

For our parents and family members
who care for us.
May we remain grateful for their
acts of sacrificial love
that are a reflection of
God's abundant love for us,

we pray to the Lord . . .

For the teachers, school assistants,
and coaches who
guide us in our school activities.
May they continue to
teach us about God
through their
kindness and generosity,

we pray to the Lord . . .

For those who suffer from
illness, hunger, or political strife.
For those who have died,

we pray to the Lord . . .

FIFTH LEADER:
Let us pray the prayer that Jesus taught us:
Our Father . . . Amen.

◆ Pause and then say the following:

Let us offer one another a sign of
Christ's peace.

◆ All offer one another a sign of peace.

SIXTH LEADER:
Let us pray:
Lord our God,
your immense love for us
shines for all to see
in the glory of your resurrection
and in your return to God.
We praise you for your Spirit
of truth and light
and the promise of your
return again.
We ask this through Christ our Lord.

ALL: Amen.

PRAYER FOR THE WEEK

WITH A READING FROM THE GOSPEL FOR **SUNDAY, MAY 12, 2024**

OPENING

Jesus was taken into heaven to sit at the right hand of God. His glorified body ascended to the Father as a sign that our human bodies, too, are destined for heaven.

✝ All make the sign of the cross.

In the name of the Father, and of the Son, and of the Holy Spirit. Amen.

PSALM

(For a longer psalm, see page xv.)
Psalm 118:1–2, 4

The stone that the builders rejected has become the chief cornerstone.

The stone that the builders rejected has become the chief cornerstone.

O give thanks to the Lord, for he is good;
   his steadfast love endures forever!
Let Israel say,
   "His steadfast love endures forever."
Let those who fear the Lord say,
   "His steadfast love endures forever."

The stone that the builders rejected has become the chief cornerstone.

◆ All stand and sing **Alleluia.**

GOSPEL

Mark 16:15–20

A reading from the holy Gospel according to Mark.

And Jesus said to the disciples, "Go into all the world and proclaim the good news to the whole creation. The one who believes and is baptized will be saved, but the one who does not believe will be condemned. And these signs will accompany those who believe: by using my name they will cast out demons; they will speak in new tongues; they will pick up snakes, and if they drink any deadly thing, it will not hurt them; they will lay their hands on the sick, and they will recover."

So then the Lord Jesus, after he had spoken to them, was taken up into heaven and sat down at the right hand of God. And they went out and proclaimed the good news everywhere, while the Lord worked with them and confirmed the message by the signs that accompanied it.

The Gospel of the Lord.

◆ All sit and observe silence.

FOR SILENT REFLECTION

Think about this silently in your heart. What might a glimpse of heaven look like?

CLOSING PRAYER

Let us pray to God for our needs and the needs of others: our family, neighborhood, and the world. For each need we say, "Lord, hear our prayer."

◆ All may add their own prayers here.

Let us pray: **Our Father . . . Amen.**

Lord,
let your glory shine on us forever.
Who live and reign with God the Father,
in the unity of the Holy Spirit,
God, for ever and ever.

Amen.

✝ All make the sign of the cross.

PRAYER FOR
MONDAY, MAY 13, 2024

OPENING

Today we remember the apparitions of Mary received by three children in Fatima, Portugal, in 1917. Mary's message to the children was simple: Pray. This week, we will hear about apparitions of a different kind, the post-resurrection appearances of Jesus.

✢ All make the sign of the cross.

In the name of the Father, and of the Son, and of the Holy Spirit. Amen.

PSALM
(For a longer psalm, see page xv.)
Psalm 118:1–2, 4

The stone that the builders rejected has become the chief cornerstone.

The stone that the builders rejected has become the chief cornerstone.

O give thanks to the LORD, for he is good;
 his steadfast love endures forever!
Let Israel say,
 "His steadfast love endures forever."
Let those who fear the Lord say,
 "His steadfast love endures forever."

The stone that the builders rejected has become the chief cornerstone.

◆ All stand and sing **Alleluia.**

GOSPEL
Mark 16:9–14

A reading from the holy Gospel according to Mark.

Now after Jesus rose early on the first day of the week, he appeared first to Mary Magdalene, from whom he had cast out seven demons. She went out and told those who had been with him, while they were mourning and weeping. But when they heard that he was alive and had been seen by her, they would not believe it.

After this he appeared in another form to two of them, as they were walking into the country. And they went back and told the rest, but they did not believe them.

Later he appeared to the eleven themselves as they were sitting at the table, and he upbraided them for their lack of faith and stubbornness, because they had not believed those who saw him after he had risen.

The Gospel of the Lord.

◆ All sit and observe silence.

FOR SILENT REFLECTION

Think about this silently in your heart. His friends needed to see Jesus to believe. Do you believe without seeing?

CLOSING PRAYER

Let us pray to God for our needs and the needs of others: our family, neighborhood, and the world. For each need we say, "Lord, hear our prayer."

◆ All may add their own prayers here.

Let us pray: **Our Father . . . Amen.**

Lord God,
give us faith to see with our hearts.
Through Christ our Lord.

Amen.

✢ All make the sign of the cross.

PRAYER FOR
TUESDAY, MAY 14, 2024

OPENING

Thomas has gone down in history as the doubter, but he was no different from the other apostles. Peter and John did not believe the women, and the other apostles did not believe Peter and John, or the two on the road to Emmaus. Although Thomas doubted, he also exclaimed in great faith and trust as soon as he saw the Lord.

✢ All make the sign of the cross.

In the name of the Father, and of the Son, and of the Holy Spirit. Amen.

PSALM

(For a longer psalm, see page xv.)
Psalm 118:1–2, 4

The stone that the builders rejected has become the chief cornerstone.

The stone that the builders rejected has become the chief cornerstone.

O give thanks to the LORD, for he is good;
   his steadfast love endures forever!
Let Israel say,
   "His steadfast love endures forever."
Let those who fear the Lord say,
   "His steadfast love endures forever."

The stone that the builders rejected has become the chief cornerstone.

◆ All stand and sing **Alleluia.**

GOSPEL   John 20:19d, 24acd, 25abd, 26ad, 27abc, 28b, 29b

A reading from the holy Gospel according to John.

Jesus came and stood among the apostles and said, "Peace be with you." But Thomas was not with them when Jesus came. So the other disciples told him, "We have seen the Lord." But he said to them, "Unless I see the mark of the nails in his hands, I will not believe." A week later Jesus' disciples were again in the house, and Thomas was with them. Jesus came and stood among them and said, "Peace be with you." Then he said to Thomas, "Put your finger here and see my hands. Reach out your hand and put it in my side." Thomas answered him, "My Lord and my God!" Jesus said to him, "Blessed are those who have not seen and yet have come to believe."

The Gospel of the Lord.

◆ All sit and observe silence.

FOR SILENT REFLECTION

Think about this silently in your heart. Why did the apostles find it hard to believe in the resurrection? Would you have doubted?

CLOSING PRAYER

Let us pray to God for our needs and the needs of others: our family, neighborhood, and the world. For each need we say, "Lord, hear our prayer."

◆ All may add their own prayers here.

Let us pray: **Our Father . . . Amen.**

O God,
help us overcome our fears and doubt,
and to put our complete trust
   and faith in you.
Through Christ our Lord.

Amen.

✢ All make the sign of the cross.

PRAYER FOR WEDNESDAY, MAY 15, 2024

OPENING

Jesus gave his followers a mission: to proclaim the Good News to the whole creation. We share this mission with generations of believers. St. Isidore the Farmer was a simple laborer who lived and worked in Spain in the twelfth century. Prayer was the center of each day. He gave to the poor out of his own meager supply. His life proclaimed the Good News.

✦ All make the sign of the cross.

In the name of the Father, and of the Son, and of the Holy Spirit. Amen.

PSALM
(For a longer psalm, see page xv.)
Psalm 118:1–2, 4

The stone that the builders rejected has become the chief cornerstone.

The stone that the builders rejected has become the chief cornerstone.

O give thanks to the LORD, for he is good;
 his steadfast love endures forever!
Let Israel say,
 "His steadfast love endures forever."
Let those who fear the Lord say,
 "His steadfast love endures forever."

The stone that the builders rejected has become the chief cornerstone.

◆ All stand and sing **Alleluia.**

GOSPEL
Mark 16:15, 17, 19ac, 20

A reading from the holy Gospel according to Mark.

Jesus said to them, "Go into all the world and proclaim the good news to the whole creation. And these signs will accompany those who believe: by using my name they will cast out demons; they will speak in new tongues." So then the Lord Jesus was taken up into heaven and sat down at the right hand of God. And they went out and proclaimed the good news everywhere, while the Lord worked with them and confirmed their message by the signs that accompanied it.

The Gospel of the Lord.

◆ All sit and observe silence.

FOR SILENT REFLECTION

Think about this silently in your heart. How can you spread the Good News?

CLOSING PRAYER

Let us pray to God for our needs and the needs of others: our family, neighborhood, and the world. For each need we say, "Lord, hear our prayer."

◆ All may add their own prayers here.

Let us pray: **Our Father . . . Amen.**

Lord,
thank you for your presence,
 now and to the end of the age.
Give us the grace to proclaim your goodness
 in everything we do.
May prayer be at the heart of each of our days,
as it was for St. Isidore,
 whose prayer we ask for today.

Through Christ our Lord.

Amen.

✦ All make the sign of the cross.

PRAYER FOR
THURSDAY, MAY 16, 2024

OPENING

In today's reading, we find a summary of the events of Jesus' death and resurrection, with a particular emphasis on those who had witnessed his presence after his resurrection. In this letter, Paul seeks to convince the Corinthians that Jesus is truly God, and the witnesses to his resurrection are part of that argument. Those eyewitnesses passed their faith to others, who also passed it on through the ages, and down to us today.

✛ All make the sign of the cross.

In the name of the Father, and of the Son, and of the Holy Spirit. Amen.

PSALM

(For a longer psalm, see page xv.)
Psalm 118:1–2, 4

The stone that the builders rejected has become the chief cornerstone.

The stone that the builders rejected has become the chief cornerstone.

O give thanks to the LORD, for he is good;
　his steadfast love endures forever!
Let Israel say,
　"His steadfast love endures forever."
Let those who fear the Lord say,
　"His steadfast love endures forever."

The stone that the builders rejected has become the chief cornerstone.

READING

1 Corinthians 15:1ab, 2a, 3–6ab, 7–8ac

A reading from the First Letter to the Corinthians.

Now I, Paul, want you to understand, brothers and sisters, the good news that I proclaimed to you, through which also you are being saved. For I handed on to you as of first importance what I in turn had received: that Christ died for our sins in accordance with the scriptures and that he was buried and that he was raised on the third day in accordance with the scriptures, and that he appeared to Cephas [SEE-fuhs], then to the twelve. Then he appeared to more than five hundred brothers and sisters at one time, most of whom are still alive. Then he appeared to James, then to all the apostles. Last of all, he appeared also to me.

The Word of the Lord.

◆ All observe silence.

FOR SILENT REFLECTION

Think about this silently in your heart. How can you pass your faith to others?

CLOSING PRAYER

Let us pray to God for our needs and the needs of others: our family, neighborhood, and the world. For each need we say, "Lord, hear our prayer."

◆ All may add their own prayers here.

Let us pray: **Our Father . . . Amen.**

O loving God,
give us the courage to witness to you and
　　your amazing deeds of love.
Through Christ our Lord.

Amen.

✛ All make the sign of the cross.

PRAYER FOR FRIDAY, MAY 17, 2024

OPENING

There is much to fear in the world, but Jesus reassures us that there's nothing to be afraid of. We do not fear because we know God has our lives—indeed the whole world—in the palm of his hand. And he has proven, from the beginning to the end, that he acts out of love. Jesus is the ultimate proof of this love, poured out even unto death, and yet not destroyed. We do not fear because we know that love triumphs.

✛ All make the sign of the cross.

In the name of the Father, and of the Son, and of the Holy Spirit. Amen.

PSALM

(For a longer psalm, see page xv.)
Psalm 118:1–2, 4

The stone that the builders rejected has become the chief cornerstone.

The stone that the builders rejected has become the chief cornerstone.

O give thanks to the LORD, for he is good;
  his steadfast love endures forever!
Let Israel say,
  "His steadfast love endures forever."
Let those who fear the Lord say,
  "His steadfast love endures forever."

The stone that the builders rejected has become the chief cornerstone.

READING

Revelation 1:9ac, 10b, 12–13, 17–18abc

A reading from the Book of Revelation.

I, John, was on the island called Patmos because of the word of God and the testimony of Jesus. I heard behind me a loud voice like a trumpet. Then I turned to see whose voice it was that spoke to me, and on turning I saw seven golden lampstands, and in the midst of the lampstands I saw one like the Son of Man, clothed with a long robe and with a golden sash across his chest. When I saw him, I fell at his feet as though dead. But he placed his right hand on me, saying, "Do not be afraid; I am the First and the Last and the Living One. I was dead, and see, I am alive for ever and ever."

The Word of the Lord.

◆ All observe silence.

FOR SILENT REFLECTION

Think about this silently in your heart. Bring your fears and worries to God.

CLOSING PRAYER

Let us pray to God for our needs and the needs of others: our family, neighborhood, and the world. For each need we say, "Lord, hear our prayer."

◆ All may add their own prayers here.

Let us pray: **Our Father . . . Amen.**

Heavenly Father,
your love triumphs over fear.
May we reflect the light of your love and
    truth to others in all that we
    say and do.
Through Christ our risen Lord.

Amen.

✛ All make the sign of the cross.

PRAYER SERVICE
PENTECOST

Prepare a simple environment with a table covered with a red cloth. Leave a Bible and candle off to the side until the entrance procession. If possible, ring wind chimes during the procession. "Come, Holy Ghost," may be sung. Prepare the three leaders, the reader, and the three processors. The processors get in place: chimer, candle bearer, and lector with Bible. As the song begins they move slowly to the table in a solemn manner with chimes ringing gently. At the table the chimer moves to the side, the candle bearer places the candle, and the lector places the Bible. Then the chimes are silenced and the processors move away. When the song ends:

✚ All make the sign of the cross.

FIRST LEADER:

In the name of the Father and of the Son and of the Holy Spirit. Amen.

ALL: Amen.

FIRST LEADER:
God came to us in the Person of Jesus
    to let us know
        how much we are loved and forgiven.
Jesus promised the disciples that when he
    ascended into heaven
        they would not be left alone.
God the Holy Spirit would be with them
    always.
That promise was for us, too.

Let us pray:
We call on you, Holy Spirit,
   to give us wisdom in everything we do
   and courage to always do the right thing.
   We ask for the gift of wonder and awe
   so we will always know the beauty of
      God's world.
   We ask this through Christ our Lord.

◆ Gesture for all to sit.

LECTOR: Acts 1:8–9; 2:1–4

A reading from the Acts of the Apostles.

◆ Read the passage from the Bible.

The Word of the Lord.

FOR SILENT REFLECTION

FIRST LEADER:

What gifts of the Holy Spirit do we see in our friends?

◆ All observe silence.

SECOND LEADER:

Let us stand. (pause)

◆ All stand.

We say together, "Come, Holy Spirit, come!"

ALL: Come, Holy Spirit, come!

SECOND LEADER:

Come, Holy Spirit, come!
And from your celestial home
   Shed a ray of light divine!
Come, Father of the poor!
Come, source of all our store!
We say together:

ALL: Come . . .

Heal our wounds, our strength renew;
On our dryness pour your dew;
   Wash the stains of guilt away:
Bend the stubborn heart and will;
Melt the frozen, warm the chill;
   Guide the steps that go astray.
We say together:

ALL: Come . . .

On the faithful, who adore
And confess you, evermore
   In your sevenfold gift descend;
Give them virtue's sure reward;
Give them your salvation, Lord;
   Give them joys that never end. Amen.
We say together:

ALL: Come . . .

THIRD LEADER:

Let us pray:
Holy Spirit, strengthen us with your many
   good gifts.
Help us become more and more
   a part of the Holy Trinity's life of love.
We ask this through Jesus Christ our Lord.

ALL: Amen.

✠ All make the sign of the cross.

THIRD LEADER:

In the name of the Father and of the Son and of the Holy Spirit. Amen.

Let us offer one another a sign of Christ's peace.

◆ All exchange a sign of peace.

PRAYER FOR THE WEEK
WITH A READING FROM THE GOSPEL FOR SUNDAY, MAY 19, 2024

OPENING

The Holy Spirit is the Spirit of Truth, bringing the Good News. It is the Spirit of Light, illuminating the dark. It is the Spirit of Justice, doing God's will. It is the Spirit of Joy, bringing light to the world. It is the Spirit of Mercy, redeeming hearts. It is the Spirit of Wisdom, filling minds with the knowledge of good and evil. It is the Spirit of Love, overflowing in our hearts and lives.

✢ All make the sign of the cross.

In the name of the Father, and of the Son, and of the Holy Spirit. Amen.

PSALM
(For a longer psalm, see page xv.)
Psalm 118:1–2, 4

The stone that the builders rejected has become the chief cornerstone.

The stone that the builders rejected has become the chief cornerstone.

O give thanks to the Lord, for he is good;
   his steadfast love endures forever!
Let Israel say,
   "His steadfast love endures forever."
Let those who fear the Lord say,
   "His steadfast love endures forever."

The stone that the builders rejected has become the chief cornerstone.

◆ All stand and sing **Alleluia.**

GOSPEL
John 15:26–27; 16:12–15a

A reading from the holy Gospel according to John.

Jesus said, "When the Advocate comes, whom I will send to you from the Father, the Spirit of truth who comes from the Father, he will testify on my behalf. You also are to testify because you have been with me from the beginning. I still have many things to say to you, but you cannot bear them now. When the Spirit of truth comes, he will guide you into all the truth; for he will not speak on his own, but will speak what he hears, and he will declare to you the things that are to come. He will glorify me, because he will take what is mine and declare it to you. All that the Father has is mine."

The Gospel of the Lord.

◆ All sit and observe silence.

FOR SILENT REFLECTION

Think about this silently in your heart. How has the Holy Spirit worked in your life?

CLOSING PRAYER

Let us pray to God for our needs and the needs of others: our family, neighborhood, and the world. For each need we say, "Lord, hear our prayer."

◆ All may add their own prayers here.

Let us pray: **Our Father . . . Amen.**

Come, Holy Spirit,
renew the hearts of your faithful gathered here.
Through Christ our risen Lord.

Amen.

✢ All make the sign of the cross.

ORDINARY TIME SUMMER

MONDAY, MAY 20, 2024 — FRIDAY, JUNE 28, 2024

SUMMER ORDINARY TIME

THE MEANING OF ORDINARY TIME

We just celebrated the great feasts of Easter and Pentecost and now move back to Ordinary Time—the ordered time when each week has a number. The Prayers for the Week will reflect the Sunday Gospels but during the week we will again "walk through the Bible."

On Pentecost, the Spirit descended upon Jesus' disciples, strengthening them with wisdom and courage. Passages from the Acts of the Apostles and the letters of St. Paul tell stories of the travels of Jesus' disciples to spread his teachings to love God and to love one another.

We will read several stories of Jesus' miracles. Jesus used two languages in his preaching: one was words, particularly the parables, and another was signs, particularly the miracles. Miracles consist of an observable action. But with Jesus' touch or presence something very unusual and unexpected happens: a stormy sea is calmed, a boy is healed from epilepsy. Like the parables, the miracle stories contain more than what appears to us at first glance. As "signs," they carry a deeper meaning about the kingdom of God—a time when there will be no suffering, hunger or death. The miracles are an announcement of hope—they are points of light that help us "see" what the kingdom of God is like.

As we end this school year, our focus is mission and being family to one another. The Scripture passages tell us that Jesus told his disciples to go out and proclaim the kingdom of God and they did. As we prepare for summer vacation, it is a good time to remind ourselves that we are Christ's disciples and our mission is also to proclaim God's love through our words and our actions.

During these weeks of Ordinary Time, we celebrate the Solemnities of the Most Holy Trinity and the Most Sacred Heart of Jesus. A solemnity is a very high celebration in the Church calendar.

PREPARING TO CELEBRATE ORDINARY TIME IN THE CLASSROOM

This will be your last time changing the prayer tablecloth this year. Even if you haven't had a procession each time the cloth changes, try to have one now. As the school year winds down, it is good to bring the students' focus squarely on the prayer life of your classroom community. You may wish to invite the students to choose something to carry in the procession that helped their spiritual growth this year. Clear an area near the prayer table, spread it with a green cloth, and let the children place their objects there. As a final project, ask them to write a short essay or poem about the significance of the object they chose. Suggest that they illustrate their work. Invite them to share their writings aloud during one of your final prayer times together. (Some students might feel uncomfortable sharing private thoughts in front of a group. Don't force them to participate in this aspect of your celebration.) You might even consider collecting all the papers into a booklet, which you can photocopy for each student to keep as a memento of the year.

SACRED SPACE

Bring your potted plant back to the prayer table. You may want to discuss how it might be different from how it looked when you first placed it on the prayer table. Some plants, such as spider plants, send out shoots with new plants on them. If your spider plant is sufficiently mature, you may even have enough "spider babies" to clip and give to each of your students in a paper cup with a little soil in it. Or you may like to keep the table adorned with fresh flowers from a spring garden. Children love to bring flowers from their parents' or grandparents' gardens.

SACRED MUSIC

If you have been singing with your students all year, they will probably be quite comfortable with at least one or two of their favorite hymns. Consider scheduling a visit to one of the other classrooms to offer a small concert or sing-along (an older classroom could visit a younger grade; smaller children could sing for the "big kids"). If your students are particularly confident, you may even suggest that they volunteer to sing for an all-school Mass or end-of-the-year prayer service. If you invite parents to the class for one of your final sessions, don't be shy about including them in your prayer. And by all means, sing for them! Some songs that work well in this season are "Christ for the World We Sing," "Lord, I Want to Be a Christian," and "Spirit of the Living God."

PRAYERS FOR ORDINARY TIME

There are only a few precious places in the Gospel where we have the chance to listen to Jesus as he prays to his Father in heaven. In these moments, we can see clearly what it is Jesus wants for the world. The following prayer, taken from the Gospel according to John, shows how much Jesus wants us to abide in his love and to live with each other in the love and peace shared by the Father, Son, and Holy Spirit.

"As you, Father, are in me and I am in you, may my followers also be in us, so that the world may believe that you have sent me. The glory that you have given me I have given them, so that they may be one, as we are one, I in them and you in me, that they may become completely one, so that the world may know that you have sent me and have loved them even as you have loved me" (John 17:21b–23).

A NOTE TO CATECHISTS

You may wish to write the names of your students into your personal calendar during the summer months, so that you will remember to pray for them even when your group is no longer meeting. Prayer is the most useful and effective way we have to be of service to those about whom we care.

GRACE BEFORE MEALS
ORDINARY TIME • SUMMER

LEADER:
O give thanks to the Lord, for he is good;

ALL: for his steadfast love endures forever.

✝ All make the sign of the cross.

In the name of the Father, and of the Son, and of the Holy Spirit. Amen.

LEADER:
God of abundance,
your grace fills the hearts of
all those who call you Lord,
and even those who may not
know you yet.
Thank you for the gift of this meal
and the nourishment it will provide.
We are grateful for this time to
share it with each other.
May we work together to fill the plates
of those in our community and around the
world who may experience
extreme hunger or thirst today.
We ask this through Christ our Lord.

ALL: Amen.

✝ All make the sign of the cross.

In the name of the Father, and of the Son, and of the Holy Spirit. Amen.

PRAYER AT DAY'S END
ORDINARY TIME • SUMMER

LEADER:
See what love the Father has given us,

ALL: that we should be called children of God.

✙ All make the sign of the cross.

In the name of the Father, and of the Son, and of the Holy Spirit. Amen.

LEADER:
Almighty Father,
you created us in your image
of goodness and light.
Grant that we may offer you
all that we are in thanksgiving,
here at the end of our school day,
and this night, when we close our eyes
for restful sleep.
May the peace of Christ remain with us
now and forever.
We ask this in Christ's name.

ALL: Amen.

✙ All make the sign of the cross.

In the name of the Father, and of the Son, and of the Holy Spirit. Amen.

PRAYER FOR MONDAY, MAY 20, 2024

OPENING

Filled with the Holy Spirit, the disciples began to speak in many languages so that each person in the crowd heard and understood the Good News. Today is the memorial of St. Bernardine of Siena (1380–1444), an Italian priest who preached using themes from the everyday lives of the people. Jesus had the same approach to preaching.

✣ All make the sign of the cross.

In the name of the Father, and of the Son, and of the Holy Spirit. Amen.

PSALM

(For a longer psalm, see page xv.)
Psalm 118:1–2, 4

The stone that the builders rejected has become the chief cornerstone.

The stone that the builders rejected has become the chief cornerstone.

O give thanks to the LORD, for he is good;
  his steadfast love endures forever!
Let Israel say,
  "His steadfast love endures forever."
Let those who fear the Lord say,
  "His steadfast love endures forever."

The stone that the builders rejected has become the chief cornerstone.

READING

Acts 2:1–2a, 3–7a, 8, 11b

A reading from the Acts of the Apostles.

When the day of Pentecost had come, the disciples were all together in one place. And suddenly from heaven there came a sound like the rush of a violent wind. Divided tongues, as of fire, appeared among them, and a tongue rested on each of them. All of them were filled with the Holy Spirit and began to speak in other languages, as the Spirit gave them ability. Now there were devout Jews from every people under heaven living in Jerusalem. And at this sound the crowd gathered and was bewildered, because each one heard them speaking in the native language of each. Amazed and astonished, they asked, "And how is it that we hear, each of us, in our own native language? In our own languages we hear them speaking about God's deeds of power."

The Word of the Lord.

◆ All observe silence.

FOR SILENT REFLECTION

Think about this silently in your heart. How can you be a voice of God's love for others?

CLOSING PRAYER

Let us pray to God for our needs and the needs of others: our family, neighborhood, and the world. For each need we say, "Lord, hear our prayer."

◆ All may add their own prayers here.

Let us pray: **Our Father . . . Amen.**

Holy Spirit,
inspire us to speak with wisdom and love.
Through Christ our Lord.

Amen.

✣ All make the sign of the cross.

PRAYER FOR TUESDAY, MAY 21, 2024

OPENING

Today we remember a group of twentieth-century Mexican martyrs. Living under a very anti-Catholic government, St. Christopher Magallanes (1869–1927) did not compromise his faith and spread the Good News. The strength of his and his companions' faith helped them face persecution.

✢ All make the sign of the cross.

In the name of the Father, and of the Son, and of the Holy Spirit. Amen.

PSALM

(For a longer psalm, see page xv.)
Psalm 118:1–2, 4

The stone that the builders rejected has become the chief cornerstone.

The stone that the builders rejected has become the chief cornerstone.

O give thanks to the Lord, for he is good;
   his steadfast love endures forever!
Let Israel say,
   "His steadfast love endures forever."
Let those who fear the Lord say,
   "His steadfast love endures forever."

The stone that the builders rejected has become the chief cornerstone.

READING

Acts 3:1–2a, 3, 6–9, 10b

A reading from the Acts of the Apostles.

One day Peter and John were going up to the temple at the hour of prayer, at three o'clock in the afternoon. And a man lame from birth was being carried in. When he saw Peter and John about to go into the temple, he asked them for alms. Peter said, "I have no silver or gold, but what I have I give you; in the name of Jesus Christ of Nazareth, stand up and walk." And he took him by the right hand and raised him up, and immediately his feet and ankles were made strong. Jumping up, he stood and began to walk, and he entered the temple with them, walking and leaping and praising God. And they were filled with wonder and astonishment at what had happened to him.

The Word of the Lord.

◆ All observe silence.

FOR SILENT REFLECTION

Think about this silently in your heart. How has faith made you strong?

CLOSING PRAYER

Let us pray to God for our needs and the needs of others: our family, neighborhood, and the world. For each need we say, "Lord, hear our prayer."

◆ All may add their own prayers here.

Let us pray: **Our Father . . . Amen.**

Heavenly Father,
we thank you for the gift of faith
that helps us believe in your many
marvelous deeds.
In Christ's name, we pray.

Amen.

✢ All make the sign of the cross.

PRAYER FOR
WEDNESDAY, MAY 22, 2024

OPENING

Today is the feast day of St. Rita of Cascia (1381–1457). On Good Friday, 1441, St. Rita was praying before a crucifix and a wound opened on her forehead, appearing like a puncture from a crown of thorns. For fifteen years it caused her daily pain but she viewed her stigmata as a share in Christ's suffering. We hear today that if we suffer with Christ "we may also be glorified with him."

✚ All make the sign of the cross.

In the name of the Father, and of the Son, and of the Holy Spirit. Amen.

PSALM
(For a longer psalm, see page xv.)
Psalm 118:1–2, 4

The stone that the builders rejected has become the chief cornerstone.

The stone that the builders rejected has become the chief cornerstone.

O give thanks to the LORD, for he is good;
 his steadfast love endures forever!
Let Israel say,
 "His steadfast love endures forever."
Let those who fear the Lord say,
 "His steadfast love endures forever."

The stone that the builders rejected has become the chief cornerstone.

READING
Romans 8:14, 15b–17, 26–27

A reading from the Letter to the Romans.

For all who are led by the Spirit of God are children of God. You received a spirit of adoption. When we cry, "Abba! Father!" it is that very Spirit bearing witness with our spirit that we are children of God, and if children, then heirs: heirs of God and joint heirs with Christ, if we in fact suffer with him so that we may also be glorified with him. Likewise the Spirit helps us in our weakness, for we do not know how to pray as we ought, but that very Spirit intercedes with groanings too deep for words. And God, who searches hearts, knows what is the mind of the Spirit, because the Spirit intercedes for the saints according to the will of God.

The Word of the Lord.

◆ All observe silence.

FOR SILENT REFLECTION

Think about this silently in your heart. How has the Holy Spirit interceded for you?

CLOSING PRAYER

Let us pray to God for our needs and the needs of others: our family, neighborhood, and the world. For each need we say, "Lord, hear our prayer."

◆ All may add their own prayers here.

Let us pray: **Our Father . . . Amen.**

Holy Spirit,
you know our hearts better than we do.
Help us to live in spirit and truth.
Through Christ our Lord.

Amen.

✚ All make the sign of the cross.

PRAYER FOR THURSDAY, MAY 23, 2024

OPENING

St. Paul tells us how to live rightly, justly, and lovingly with one another. He teaches that love—genuine love of our neighbor—is how we follow and fulfill Jesus' work and commandments.

✠ All make the sign of the cross.

In the name of the Father, and of the Son, and of the Holy Spirit. Amen.

PSALM

(For a longer psalm, see page xv.)
Psalm 118:1–2, 4

The stone that the builders rejected has become the chief cornerstone.

The stone that the builders rejected has become the chief cornerstone.

O give thanks to the LORD, for he is good;
  his steadfast love endures forever!
Let Israel say,
  "His steadfast love endures forever."
Let those who fear the Lord say,
  "His steadfast love endures forever."

The stone that the builders rejected has become the chief cornerstone.

READING

Romans 12:9–10; 13:8–10

A reading from the Letter to the Romans.

Let love be genuine; hate what is evil; hold fast to what is good; love one another with mutual affection; outdo one another in showing honor. Owe no one anything, except to love one another, for the one who loves another has fulfilled the law. The commandments, "You shall not commit adultery; you shall not murder; you shall not steal; you shall not covet," and any other commandment, are summed up in this word, "You shall love your neighbor as yourself." Love does no wrong to a neighbor; therefore, love is the fulfilling of the law.

The Word of the Lord.

◆ All observe silence.

FOR SILENT REFLECTION

Think about this silently in your heart. Do you truly love your neighbor well? What are some concrete acts of love you can do today?

CLOSING PRAYER

Let us pray to God for our needs and the needs of others: our family, neighborhood, and the world. For each need we say, "Lord, hear our prayer."

◆ All may add their own prayers here.

Let us pray: **Our Father . . . Amen.**

God of love,
help us to love our neighbors, our enemies,
and strangers as much as ourselves,
our friends, and our family.
Help us to love others as you have loved us.
We pray in the name of Jesus Christ,
    our Lord.

Amen.

✠ All make the sign of the cross.

PRAYER FOR
FRIDAY, MAY 24, 2024

OPENING

God created us to be free, and Jesus restored our freedom by destroying the shackles of sin. But freedom isn't a license to be selfish. Through Christ, God revealed that we are most free and most joyful when we spend our lives in love and service for others, not in competition with one another. In these free and loving acts of service, we may begin to taste the fullness of joy, love, and peace.

✜ All make the sign of the cross.

In the name of the Father, and of the Son, and of the Holy Spirit. Amen.

PSALM
(For a longer psalm, see page xv.)
Psalm 118:1–2, 4

The stone that the builders rejected has become the chief cornerstone.

The stone that the builders rejected has become the chief cornerstone.

O give thanks to the LORD, for he is good;
   his steadfast love endures forever!
Let Israel say,
   "His steadfast love endures forever."
Let those who fear the Lord say,
   "His steadfast love endures forever."

The stone that the builders rejected has become the chief cornerstone.

READING
Galatians 5:13–14, 22–23b, 25–26

A reading from the Letter to the Galatians [guh-LAY-shuhnz].

For you were called to freedom, brothers and sisters, only do not use your freedom as an opportunity for self-indulgence, but through love become enslaved to one another. For the whole law is summed up in a single commandment, "You shall love your neighbor as yourself." By contrast, the fruit of the Spirit is love, joy, peace, patience, kindness, generosity, faithfulness, gentleness, and self-control. If we live by the Spirit, let us also be guided by the Spirit. Let us not become conceited, competing against one another, envying one another.

The Word of the Lord.

◆ All observe silence.

FOR SILENT REFLECTION

Think about this silently in your heart. How do you feel when you help others? How might you help someone else this week?

CLOSING PRAYER

Let us pray to God for our needs and the needs of others: our family, neighborhood, and the world. For each need we say, "Lord, hear our prayer."

◆ All may add their own prayers here.

Let us pray: **Our Father . . . Amen.**

Loving Father,
thank you for the gift of a free will.
Help us to use this freedom always in the
   service of love.
We make this prayer in Jesus' name.

Amen.

✜ All make the sign of the cross.

PRAYER FOR THE WEEK

WITH A READING FROM THE GOSPEL FOR **SUNDAY, MAY 26, 2024**

OPENING

The week after Pentecost, we celebrate the Holy Trinity—God the Father, our Creator; Jesus the Son, our redeemer; and the Holy Spirit, the one who sustains us. The Father, Son, and Holy Spirit are three Persons in one God.

✢ All make the sign of the cross.

In the name of the Father, and of the Son, and of the Holy Spirit. Amen.

PSALM
(For a longer psalm, see page xv.)
Psalm 85:8–9

The LORD speaks of peace to his people.

The LORD speaks of peace to his people.

Let me hear what God the LORD will speak,
   for he will speak peace to his people,
   to his faithful, to those who turn to him
      in their hearts.
Surely his salvation is at hand for those
   who fear him,
   that his glory may dwell in our land.

The LORD speaks of peace to his people.

◆ All stand and sing **Alleluia.**

GOSPEL
matthew 28:16–20

A reading from the holy Gospel according to Matthew.

Now the eleven disciples went to Galilee, to the mountain to which Jesus had directed them. When they saw him, they worshiped him, but they doubted. And Jesus came and said to them, "All authority in heaven and on earth has been given to me. Go therefore and make disciples of all nations, baptizing them in the name of the Father and of the Son and of the Holy Spirit and teaching them to obey everything that I have commanded you. And remember, I am with you always, to the end of the age."

The Gospel of the Lord.

◆ All sit and observe silence.

FOR SILENT REFLECTION

Think about this silently in your heart. Have you ever experienced doubt? What did it feel like?

CLOSING PRAYER

Let us pray to God for our needs and the needs of others: our family, neighborhood, and the world. For each need we say, "Lord, hear our prayer."

◆ All may add their own prayers here.

Let us pray: **Our Father . . . Amen.**

O God,
you are love,
and through that love,
you gave us your Son, Jesus Christ,
who poured upon us your Spirit.
May your love that
creates, redeems, and sustains us
be with us always, until the end of time.
We pray in Christ's name.

Amen.

✢ All make the sign of the cross.

PRAYER FOR
MONDAY, MAY 27, 2024

OPENING

Throughout the ages, beautiful holy spaces were set aside dedicated to the worship of God. The ancient Israelites built their temple. Christians worship in cathedrals and basilicas of stunning beauty. Today is the feast day of St. Augustine (c. early sixth century). He was a monk who became the first Archbishop of Canterbury, England, and consecrated a holy space that eventually became the great Canterbury Cathedral.

✢ All make the sign of the cross.

In the name of the Father, and of the Son, and of the Holy Spirit. Amen.

PSALM
(For a longer psalm, see page xv.)
Psalm 85:8–9

The Lord speaks of peace to his people.

The Lord speaks of peace to his people.

Let me hear what God the Lord will speak,
 for he will speak peace to his people,
 to his faithful, to those who turn to him in their hearts.
Surely his salvation is at hand for those who fear him,
 that his glory may dwell in our land.

The Lord speaks of peace to his people.

READING
Exodus 25:1a, 8, 10–11a, 23–24; 26:1, 7

A reading from the Book of Exodus.

The Lord said to Moses: the Israelites [IZ-ree-uh-līts] shall make me a sanctuary [SANGK-choo-ayr-ee] so that I may dwell among them. They shall make an ark of acacia wood; it shall be two and a half cubits long, a cubit and a half wide, and a cubit and a half high. You shall overlay it with pure gold, inside and outside, a molding of gold upon it all around. You shall make a table of acacia wood, two cubits long, one cubit wide, and a cubit and a half high. You shall overlay it with pure gold and make a molding of gold around it. The tabernacle [TAB-uhr-nak-*l] itself you shall make with ten curtains of fine twisted linen and blue, purple, and crimson yarns; you shall make them with cherubim skillfully worked into them. You shall also make curtains of goats' hair for a tent over the tabernacle; you shall make eleven curtains.

The Word of the Lord.

◆ All observe silence.

FOR SILENT REFLECTION

Think about this silently in your heart. What are some sacred spaces you go to for prayer?

CLOSING PRAYER

Let us pray to God for our needs and the needs of others: our family, neighborhood, and the world. For each need we say, "Lord, hear our prayer."

◆ All may add their own prayers here.

Let us pray: **Our Father . . . Amen.**

Holy God,
you have made the world good and beautiful.
We praise you through Christ our Lord.

Amen.

✢ All make the sign of the cross.

PRAYER FOR
TUESDAY, MAY 28, 2024

OPENING

Today we will hear about the aftermath of the Maccabean [mak-uh-BE-uhn] revolt: a group of faithful Jews took back their land and Jerusalem from the Greek empire. After they entered Jerusalem, the Maccabees [MAK-uh-beez] cleansed and rededicated the temple. They needed a holy place to worship the Lord, where they could celebrate their victory and give thanks to God.

✢ All make the sign of the cross.

In the name of the Father, and of the Son, and of the Holy Spirit. Amen.

PSALM
(For a longer psalm, see page xv.)
Psalm 85:8–9

The Lord speaks of peace to his people.

The Lord speaks of peace to his people.

Let me hear what God the Lord will speak,
　for he will speak peace to his people,
　to his faithful, to those who turn to him in
　　their hearts.
Surely his salvation is at hand for those who
　　fear him,
　that his glory may dwell in our land.

The Lord speaks of peace to his people.

READING
1 Maccabees 4:36–38b, 43a, 47b–51

A reading from the First Book of Maccabees.

Judas and his brothers said, "See, our enemies are crushed; let us go up to cleanse the sanctuary [SANGK-choo-ayr-ee] and dedicate it." So all the army assembled and went up to Mount Zion [ZI-uhn]. There they saw the sanctuary desolate, the altar profaned, and the gates burned. They rebuilt the sanctuary and the interior of the temple and consecrated the courts. They made new holy vessels and brought the lampstand, the altar of incense, and the table into the temple. Then they offered incense on the altar and lit the lamps on the lampstand, and these gave light in the temple. Then they offered incense on the altar and lit the lamps on the lampstand, and these gave light in the temple. They placed the bread on the table and hung up the curtains. Thus they finished all the work they had undertaken.

The Word of the Lord.

◆ All observe silence.

FOR SILENT REFLECTION

Think about this silently in your heart. Have you ever seen a holy object or place treated without respect? How did it make you feel?

CLOSING PRAYER

Let us pray to God for our needs and the needs of others: our family, neighborhood, and the world. For each need we say, "Lord, hear our prayer."

◆ All may add their own prayers here.

Let us pray: **Our Father . . . Amen.**

O God,
help us to keep spaces holy to offer you
　worship and praise in Christ's name.

Amen.

✢ All make the sign of the cross.

PRAYER FOR
WEDNESDAY, MAY 29, 2024

OPENING

The Maccabees [MAK-uh-beez] celebrated and praised the Lord for eight days with great joy. Those eight days are remembered every year in Hannukah.

✝ All make the sign of the cross.

In the name of the Father, and of the Son, and of the Holy Spirit. Amen.

PSALM
(For a longer psalm, see page xv.)
Psalm 85:8–9

The Lord speaks of peace to his people.

The Lord speaks of peace to his people.

Let me hear what God the Lord will speak,
　for he will speak peace to his people,
　to his faithful, to those who turn to him in their hearts.
Surely his salvation is at hand for those who fear him,
　that his glory may dwell in our land.

The Lord speaks of peace to his people.

READING
1 Maccabees 4:52a, 53, 54b–56b, 57a–b, 58–59a

A reading from the First Book of Maccabees.

Early in the morning on the twenty-fifth day of the ninth month, the Hebrew people rose and offered sacrifice, as the law directs, on the new altar of burnt offering that they had built. It was dedicated with songs and harps and lutes and cymbals. All the people fell on their faces and worshiped and blessed heaven, who had prospered them. So they celebrated the dedication of the altar for eight days. They decorated the front of the temple with golden crowns and small shields; they restored the gates and the chambers for the priests. There was very great joy among the people, and the disgrace brought by the nations was removed. Then Judas and his brothers and all the assembly of Israel determined that every year at that season the days of dedication of the altar should be observed with joy and gladness for eight days.

The Word of the Lord.

◆ All observe silence.

FOR SILENT REFLECTION

Think about this silently in your heart. What are some of the decorations in your church? What makes your church a holy place?

CLOSING PRAYER

Let us pray to God for our needs and the needs of others: our family, neighborhood, and the world. For each need we say, "Lord, hear our prayer."

◆ All may add their own prayers here.

Let us pray: **Our Father . . . Amen.**

God of love,
thank you for giving us special places
　　dedicated to praising
　　and worshipping you.
We praise you through Christ our Lord.
Amen.

✝ All make the sign of the cross.

PRAYER FOR THURSDAY, MAY 30, 2024

OPENING

"You enter these gates to worship the LORD." Do we think about this as we enter the church for Mass? Do we come inside with a peaceful, prayerful state of mind? We believe the church is the dwelling place of the Lord, a holy place, a place that inspires us to amend our ways, to love others.

✛ All make the sign of the cross.

In the name of the Father, and of the Son, and of the Holy Spirit. Amen.

PSALM

(For a longer psalm, see page xv.)
Psalm 85:8–9

The LORD speaks of peace to his people.

The LORD speaks of peace to his people.

Let me hear what God the LORD will speak,
　for he will speak peace to his people,
　to his faithful, to those who turn to him in their hearts.
Surely his salvation is at hand for those who fear him,
　that his glory may dwell in our land.

The LORD speaks of peace to his people.

READING

Jeremiah 7:1–2ce, 3b, 5–7a, 9a–d, 10acd, 11c

A reading from the Book of the prophet Jeremiah [jayr-uh-MĪ-uh].

The word that came to Jeremiah from the LORD: Stand in the gate of the LORD's house, and proclaim there this word, and say, Hear the word of the LORD, you that enter these gates to worship the LORD. Amend your ways and your doings. For if you truly amend your ways and your doings, if you truly act justly one with another, if you do not oppress the alien, the orphan, and the widow or shed innocent blood in this place, and if you do not go after other gods to your own hurt, then I will dwell with you in this place. Will you steal, murder, commit adultery, swear falsely, and then come and stand before me in this house, and say, "We are safe!"—only to go on doing all these abominations [uh-baw-muh-NAY-sh*nz]? I, too, am watching, says the LORD.

The Word of the Lord.

◆ All observe silence.

FOR SILENT REFLECTION

Think about this silently in your heart. How do you prepare to meet the Lord at Mass?

CLOSING PRAYER

Let us pray to God for our needs and the needs of others: our family, neighborhood, and the world. For each need we say, "Lord, hear our prayer."

◆ All may add their own prayers here.

Let us pray: **Our Father . . . Amen.**

Lord,
you come to dwell with us in the sacred space
　of our hearts.
Make us worthy to receive you.
In Christ's name we pray.

Amen.

✛ All make the sign of the cross.

PRAYER FOR
FRIDAY, MAY 31, 2024

OPENING

Today St. Paul describes the people of faith as a structure, as part of a house. This house is built on the foundation of the apostles, with Christ as the cornerstone. Christ holds this house of God, this Church, together and makes it holy. Today is the feast of the Visitation of Mary to her cousin Elizabeth; they both rejoiced in the presence of God growing within Mary.

✙ All make the sign of the cross.

In the name of the Father, and of the Son, and of the Holy Spirit. Amen.

PSALM
(For a longer psalm, see page xv.)
Psalm 85:8–9

The LORD speaks of peace to his people.

The LORD speaks of peace to his people.

Let me hear what God the LORD will speak,
  for he will speak peace to his people,
  to his faithful, to those who turn to him in their hearts.
Surely his salvation is at hand for those who fear him,
  that his glory may dwell in our land.

The LORD speaks of peace to his people.

READING
Ephesians 2:11a, 13–14, 19–22

A reading from First Letter of Paul to the Ephesians [ee-FEE-zhuhnz].

Remember that at one time you gentiles now in Christ Jesus you who once were far off have been brought near by the blood of Christ. For he is our peace; in his flesh he has made both Jews and gentiles into one and has broken down the dividing wall, that is, the hostility between us. So then, you are no longer strangers and aliens, but you are fellow citizens with the saints and also members of the household of God, built upon the foundation of the apostles and prophets, with Christ Jesus himself as the cornerstone; in him the whole structure is joined together and grows into a holy temple in the Lord, in whom you also are built together spiritually into a dwelling-place for God.

The Word of the Lord.

◆ All observe silence.

FOR SILENT REFLECTION

Think about this silently in your heart. How can you be a holy dwelling place for God?

CLOSING PRAYER

Let us pray to God for our needs and the needs of others: our family, neighborhood, and the world. For each need we say, "Lord, hear our prayer."

◆ All may add their own prayers here.

Let us pray: **Our Father . . . Amen.**

Heavenly Father,
every member in the Body of Christ is
  equally important to you.
May the we live together in perfect unity.
In your Son Jesus' name we pray.

Amen.

✙ All make the sign of the cross.

PRAYER FOR THE WEEK
WITH A READING FROM THE GOSPEL FOR **SUNDAY, JUNE 2, 2024**

OPENING

Today is the Solemnity of the Most Holy Body and Blood of Christ. We celebrate the real presence of Christ in the Eucharist. We eat of Jesus' Body and drink of his Blood, and receive the gift of his presence. Today, we give thanks for this great gift through prayers, songs, and processions. We give thanks that we can become what we receive in the Eucharist.

✠ All make the sign of the cross.

In the name of the Father, and of the Son, and of the Holy Spirit. Amen.

PSALM
(For a longer psalm, see page xv.)
Psalm 85:8–9

The LORD speaks of peace to his people.

The LORD speaks of peace to his people.

Let me hear what God the LORD will speak,
   for he will speak peace to his people,
   to his faithful, to those who turn to him in
      their hearts.
Surely his salvation is at hand for those who
      fear him,
   that his glory may dwell in our land.

The LORD speaks of peace to his people.

◆ All stand and sing **Alleluia.**

GOSPEL
Mark 14:12A, 16C, 22–26

A reading from the holy Gospel according to Mark.

On the first day of Unleavened Bread, when the Passover lamb is sacrificed, Jesus' disciples prepared the Passover meal. While they were eating, he took a loaf of bread, and after blessing it he broke it, gave it to them, and said, "Take; this is my body." Then he took a cup, and after giving thanks he gave it to them, and all of them drank from it. He said to them, "This is my blood of covenant, which is poured out for many. Truly I tell you, I will never again drink of the fruit of the vine until that day when I drink it new in the kingdom of God." When they had sung the hymn, they went out to the Mount of Olives.

The Gospel of the Lord.

◆ All sit and observe silence.

FOR SILENT REFLECTION

Think about this silently in your heart. When we partake of the Body and Blood of Christ, we allow Christ to fill and transform us.

CLOSING PRAYER

Let us pray to God for our needs and the needs of others: our family, neighborhood, and the world. For each need we say, "Lord, hear our prayer."

◆ All may add their own prayers here.

Let us pray: **Our Father . . . Amen.**

Heavenly Father,
thank you for sending us your Son Jesus.
Help us to satisfy the needs of others.
Through Christ our Lord.

Amen.

✠ All make the sign of the cross.

PRAYER FOR MONDAY, JUNE 3, 2024

OPENING

It is easy to get wrapped up in the power and majesty of God, to want to find the perfect words of prayer, the perfect time to pray. But God wants to be a friend to each of us. God doesn't want perfect; he just wants our presence, like any friend would. Today is the memorial for St. Charles Lwanga and friends. St. Charles lived in the Kingdom of Buganda, which is in part of Uganda today. He and many other Christian converts were martyred for refusing to give up their new faith.

✛ All make the sign of the cross.

In the name of the Father, and of the Son, and of the Holy Spirit. Amen.

PSALM

(For a longer psalm, see page xv.)
Psalm 85:8–9

The LORD speaks of peace to his people.

The LORD speaks of peace to his people.

Let me hear what God the LORD will speak,
  for he will speak peace to his people,
  to his faithful, to those who turn to him in their hearts.
Surely his salvation is at hand for those who fear him,
  that his glory may dwell in our land.

The LORD speaks of peace to his people.

READING

Exodus 33:7a, 9–11b

A reading from the Book of Exodus.

Now Moses used to take the tent and pitch it outside the camp, far off from the camp; he called it the tent of meeting. When Moses entered the tent, the pillar of cloud would descend and stand at the entrance of the tent, and the LORD would speak with Moses. When all the people saw the pillar of cloud standing at the entrance of the tent, all the people would rise and bow down, all of them, at the entrance of the tent. Thus the LORD used to speak to Moses face to face, as one speaks to a friend.

The Word of the Lord.

◆ All observe silence.

FOR SILENT REFLECTION

Think about this silently in your heart. How do you talk to God like a friend?

CLOSING PRAYER

Let us pray to God for our needs and the needs of others: our family, neighborhood, and the world. For each need we say, "Lord, hear our prayer."

◆ All may add their own prayers here.

Let us pray: **Our Father . . . Amen.**

O God,
you spoke to Moses as a friend.
May we, too, approach you
    in friendship and love.
Through Christ our Lord.

Amen.

✛ All make the sign of the cross.

PRAYER FOR TUESDAY, JUNE 4, 2024

OPENING

Wisdom is worth more than wealth, health, or beauty. She is brighter than light and renews all things. Wisdom makes us friends of God. We acquire wisdom when we realize we don't know the world as well as God does, when we acknowledge our own limitations, and trust in the love and mercy of God's friendship.

◆ All make the sign of the cross.

In the name of the Father, and of the Son, and of the Holy Spirit. Amen.

PSALM
(For a longer psalm, see page xv.)
Psalm 85:8–9

The LORD speaks of peace to his people.

The LORD speaks of peace to his people.

Let me hear what God the LORD will speak,
 for he will speak peace to his people,
 to his faithful, to those who turn to him in their hearts.
Surely his salvation is at hand for those who fear him,
 that his glory may dwell in our land.

The LORD speaks of peace to his people.

READING
Wisdom 7:7–9b, 10, 27d–e

A reading from the Book of Wisdom.

Therefore I prayed, and understanding was given me; I called on God, and the spirit of wisdom came to me. I preferred her to scepters and thrones, and I accounted wealth as nothing in comparison with her. Neither did I liken to her any priceless gem, because all gold is but a little sand in her sight. I loved her more than health and beauty, and I chose to have her rather than light because her radiance never ceases. She renews all things; in every generation she passes into holy souls and makes them friends of God and prophets.

The Word of the Lord.

◆ All observe silence.

FOR SILENT REFLECTION

Think about this silently in your heart. What do you think Wisdom consists of? How can you grow in Wisdom?

CLOSING PRAYER

Let us pray to God for our needs and the needs of others: our family, neighborhood, and the world. For each need we say, "Lord, hear our prayer."

◆ All may add their own prayers here.

Let us pray: **Our Father . . . Amen.**

Holy Spirit,
inspire us with the Spirit of Wisdom
to know you better and love you more.
We make this prayer
 through Christ our Lord.

Amen.

✚ All make the sign of the cross.

PRAYER FOR
WEDNESDAY, JUNE 5, 2024

OPENING

Like any good friend, Jesus felt the pain his friend had felt, and he wept at being separated from him. Jesus is a friend to you too. He is there with you in your most difficult days, and he hurts when he is separated from you. Today is the feast day of St. Boniface (675–754), the patron saint of Germany. St. Boniface, whose name means "a man who does good deeds," spread Christianity throughout Germany.

✦ All make the sign of the cross.

In the name of the Father, and of the Son, and of the Holy Spirit. Amen.

PSALM

(For a longer psalm, see page xv.)
Psalm 85:8–9

The Lord speaks of peace to his people.

The Lord speaks of peace to his people.

Let me hear what God the Lord will speak,
　for he will speak peace to his people,
　to his faithful, to those who turn to him in
　　their hearts.
Surely his salvation is at hand for those who
　fear him,
　that his glory may dwell in our land.

The Lord speaks of peace to his people.

◆ All stand and sing **Alleluia.**

GOSPEL
John 11:1, 3–4b, 11b, 17, 32, 35–36

A reading from the holy Gospel according to John.

Now a certain man was ill, Lazarus of Bethany, the village of Mary and her sister Martha. So the sisters sent a message to Jesus, "Lord, he whom you love is ill." But when Jesus heard it, he said, "This illness does not lead to death. Our friend Lazarus has fallen asleep, but I am going there to awaken him."

When Jesus arrived, he found that Lazarus had already been in the tomb four days. When Mary came where Jesus was and saw him, she knelt at his feet and said to him, "Lord, if you had been here, my brother would not have died." Jesus began to weep. So, the Jews said, "See how he loved him!"

The Gospel of the Lord.

◆ All sit and observe silence.

FOR SILENT REFLECTION

Think about this silently in your heart. How are you a friend to Jesus? How has he been a friend to you?

CLOSING PRAYER

Let us pray to God for our needs and the needs of others: our family, neighborhood, and the world. For each need we say, "Lord, hear our prayer."

◆ All may add their own prayers here.

Let us pray: **Our Father . . . Amen.**

Heavenly Father,
you desire that we have life here on earth
and someday with you in heaven.
For this we give you thanks and praise,
Through Christ our Lord.

Amen.

✦ All make the sign of the cross.

PRAYER FOR
THURSDAY, JUNE 6, 2024

OPENING

Jesus has called us friends, showing his love by laying down his life for each of us. What do you need to lay down for him? Maybe you need to lay down pride and rely on him more. Maybe you need to lay down your electronic devices to spend more time with him in prayer. Maybe you need to lay down envy and nurture gratitude for what you have been given. Maybe you need to lay down resentment and foster joy and contentment. Today is the feast day of St. Norbert (d. 1134), who praised God for success in converting, energizing, and reconciling people to the faith.

✠ All make the sign of the cross.

In the name of the Father, and of the Son, and of the Holy Spirit. Amen.

PSALM
(For a longer psalm, see page xv.)
Psalm 85:8–9

The Lord speaks of peace to his people.

The Lord speaks of peace to his people.

Let me hear what God the Lord will speak,
    for he will speak peace to his people,
    to his faithful, to those who turn to him in their hearts.
Surely his salvation is at hand for those who fear him,
    that his glory may dwell in our land.

The Lord speaks of peace to his people.

◆ All stand and sing **Alleluia.**

GOSPEL
John 15:12–15, 17

A reading from the holy Gospel according to John.

Jesus said, "This is my commandment, that you love one another as I have loved you. No one has greater love than this, to lay down one's life for one's friends. You are my friends if you do what I command you. I do not call you servants any longer, because the servant does not know what the master is doing, but I have called you friends, because I have made known to you everything that I have heard from my Father. I am giving you these commands so that you may love one another."

The Gospel of the Lord.

◆ All sit and observe silence.

FOR SILENT REFLECTION

Think about this silently in your heart. What is getting in the way of friendship with Jesus?

CLOSING PRAYER

Let us pray to God for our needs and the needs of others: our family, neighborhood, and the world. For each need we say, "Lord, hear our prayer."

◆ All may add their own prayers here.

Let us pray: **Our Father . . . Amen.**

Lord Jesus,
you perpetually show your love for us.
May your Spirit of love flow through
    each of us to others.
Who live and reign with God the Father,
in the unity of the Holy Spirit,
God, for ever and ever.

Amen.

✠ All make the sign of the cross.

PRAYER FOR
FRIDAY, JUNE 7, 2024

OPENING

Today is the Solemnity of the Most Sacred Heart of Jesus, when we are reminded that we must devote our hearts—our human thoughts, feelings, and desires—to God. Jesus had a perfectly loving heart that was united to the will of the Father. Let us devote ourselves anew to making our own hearts loving, patient, pure, and obedient like his.

✣ All make the sign of the cross.

In the name of the Father, and of the Son, and of the Holy Spirit. Amen.

PSALM
(For a longer psalm, see page xv.)
Psalm 85:8–9

The LORD speaks of peace to his people.

The LORD speaks of peace to his people.

Let me hear what God the LORD will speak,
   for he will speak peace to his people,
   to his faithful, to those who turn to him in
     their hearts.
Surely his salvation is at hand for those who
   fear him,
   that his glory may dwell in our land.

The LORD speaks of peace to his people.

READING
3 John 1:1–6a

A reading from the Third Letter of John.

To the beloved Gaius, whom I love in truth.

Beloved, I pray that all may go well with you and that you may be in good health, just as it is well with your soul. For I was overjoyed when some brothers and sisters arrived and testified to your faithfulness to the truth, how you walk in the truth. I have no greater joy than this, to hear that my children are walking in the truth. Beloved, you do faithfully whatever you do for the brothers and sisters, even though they are strangers to you; they have testified to your love before the church.

The Word of the Lord.

◆ All observe silence.

FOR SILENT REFLECTION

Think about this silently in your heart. How can you better unite your heart to Jesus?

CLOSING PRAYER

Let us pray to God for our needs and the needs of others: our family, neighborhood, and the world. For each need we say, "Lord, hear our prayer."

◆ All may add their own prayers here.

Let us pray: **Our Father . . . Amen.**

O most Sacred Heart of Jesus,
thank you for your great love.
Help us to be humble, patient,
and obedient disciples,
open to following you
and bringing others to know you
and love you, too.
In your holy name we pray.

Amen.

✣ All make the sign of the cross.

PRAYER FOR THE WEEK
WITH A READING FROM THE GOSPEL FOR **SUNDAY, JUNE 9, 2024**

OPENING

When you first hear today's Gospel reading, it may seem like Jesus is dismissing or disowning his mother. However, upon closer inspection, he is actually issuing an invitation to all of his followers. The most important question is not whether he is disowning his family, but whether *we* are a part of his family. And how do we become part of his family? By doing the will of God.

✚ All make the sign of the cross.

In the name of the Father, and of the Son, and of the Holy Spirit. Amen.

PSALM
(For a longer psalm, see page xv.)
Psalm 85:8–9

The Lord speaks of peace to his people.

The Lord speaks of peace to his people.

Let me hear what God the Lord will speak,
   for he will speak peace to his people,
   to his faithful, to those who turn to him in their hearts.
Surely his salvation is at hand for those who fear him,
   that his glory may dwell in our land.

The Lord speaks of peace to his people.

◆ All stand and sing **Alleluia.**

GOSPEL
Mark 3:31–35

A reading from the holy Gospel according to Mark.

Jesus' mother and his brothers came, and standing outside they sent to him and called him. A crowd was sitting around him, and they said to Jesus, "Your mother and your brothers are outside, asking for you." And he replied, "Who are my mother and my brothers?" And looking at those who sat around him, he said, "Here are my mother and my brothers! Whoever does the will of God is my brother and sister and mother."

The Gospel of the Lord.

◆ All sit and observe silence.

FOR SILENT REFLECTION

Think about this silently in your heart. How do you do the will of God?

CLOSING PRAYER

Let us pray to God for our needs and the needs of others: our family, neighborhood, and the world. For each need we say, "Lord, hear our prayer."

◆ All may add their own prayers here.

Let us pray: **Our Father . . . Amen.**

Lord Jesus,
you invite us to be as close to you as family.
Send down your spirit of wisdom and
   obedience on us
that we might follow where you lead.
Who live and reign with God the Father,
in the unity of the Holy Spirit,
God, for ever and ever.

Amen.

✚ All make the sign of the cross.

PRAYER FOR MONDAY, JUNE 10, 2024

OPENING

A miracle is a surprising and welcome event that cannot be explained through natural laws. Throughout salvation history, God has worked miracles as a sign and covenant of his love for his people. Today we remember how the Lord brought his people out of slavery in Egypt. God keeps his promises.

✤ All make the sign of the cross.

In the name of the Father, and of the Son, and of the Holy Spirit. Amen.

PSALM

(For a longer psalm, see page xv.)
Psalm 85:8–9

The LORD speaks of peace to his people.

The LORD speaks of peace to his people.

Let me hear what God the LORD will speak,
   for he will speak peace to his people,
  to his faithful, to those who turn to him in their hearts.
Surely his salvation is at hand for those who fear him,
  that his glory may dwell in our land.

The LORD speaks of peace to his people.

READING

Deuteronomy 6:1ac, 3, 20–21, 24a, 24Acd

A reading from the Book of Deuteronomy [doo-ter-AH-nuh-mee].

Now this is the commandment that the LORD your God charged me to teach you to observe in the land that you are about to cross into and occupy. Hear therefore, O Israel, and observe them diligently, so that it may go well with you and so that you may multiply greatly in a land flowing with milk and honey, as the Lord, the God of your ancestors, has promised you. When your children ask you in time to come, 'What is the meaning of the decrees and the statutes and the ordinances that the LORD our God has commanded you?' then you shall say to your children, "We were Pharaoh's [FAYR-ohz] slaves in Egypt, but the LORD brought us out of Egypt with a mighty hand. Then the LORD commanded us to observe all these statutes, for our lasting good, so as to keep us alive, as is now the case."

The Word of the Lord.

◆ All observe silence.

FOR SILENT REFLECTION

Think about this silently in your heart. Have you ever witnessed a miracle?

CLOSING PRAYER

Let us pray to God for our needs and the needs of others: our family, neighborhood, and the world. For each need we say, "Lord, hear our prayer."

◆ All may add their own prayers here.

Let us pray: **Our Father . . . Amen.**

Almighty God,
throughout history, you have brought
   freedom to your people.
May we observe your commandments
   faithfully.
We ask this through Christ our Lord.

Amen.

✤ All make the sign of the cross.

PRAYER FOR TUESDAY, JUNE 11, 2024

OPENING

Sometimes, we may feel like we are on the verge of being swamped by the wild storms of life. Jesus' miracle reminds us to have faith in God alone. Today we remember St. Barnabas, who was a friend of St. Paul and apostle to the gentiles in Antioch.

✚ All make the sign of the cross.

In the name of the Father, and of the Son, and of the Holy Spirit. Amen.

PSALM
(For a longer psalm, see page xv.)
Psalm 85:8–9

The LORD speaks of peace to his people.

The LORD speaks of peace to his people.

Let me hear what God the LORD will speak,
   for he will speak peace to his people,
   to his faithful, to those who turn to him in
   their hearts.
Surely his salvation is at hand for those who
   fear him,
   that his glory may dwell in our land.

The LORD speaks of peace to his people.

◆ All stand and sing **Alleluia.**

GOSPEL
Mark 4:35b–36a, 37–38, 39B–41

A reading from the holy Gospel according to Mark.

When evening had come, Jesus said to them, "Let us go across to the other side." And leaving the crowd behind, they took him with them in the boat. A great windstorm arose, and the waves beat into the boat, so that the boat was already being swamped. But Jesus was in the stern, asleep on the cushion, and they woke him up and said to him, "Teacher, do you not care that we are perishing?" He rebuked the wind, and said to the sea, "Be silent! Be still!" Then the wind ceased, and there was a dead calm. He said to them, "Why are you afraid? Have you still no faith?" And they were filled with great fear and said to one another, "Who then is this, that even the wind and the sea obey him?"

The Gospel of the Lord.

◆ All sit and observe silence.

FOR SILENT REFLECTION

Think about this silently in your heart. Have you ever felt overwhelmed and scared? How has your faith in Jesus calmed you?

CLOSING PRAYER

Let us pray to God for our needs and the needs of others: our family, neighborhood, and the world. For each need we say, "Lord, hear our prayer."

◆ All may add their own prayers here.

Let us pray: **Our Father . . . Amen.**

O Father,
may we rest in your arms
and give ourselves to your calming ways.
Bring us peace in our hearts.
Through Christ our Lord.

Amen.

✚ All make the sign of the cross.

PRAYER FOR
WEDNESDAY, JUNE 12, 2024

OPENING

Even after witnessing Jesus' miracles, the apostles did not understand. Perhaps they were afraid to believe. We, too, are not perfect. We might miss the signs Jesus is showing us, the miracles he is performing in our own lives. And yet, even when we lack faith, Jesus says to us, "It is I; do not be afraid."

✚ All make the sign of the cross.

In the name of the Father, and of the Son, and of the Holy Spirit. Amen.

PSALM

(For a longer psalm, see page xv.)
Psalm 85:8–9

The LORD speaks of peace to his people.

The LORD speaks of peace to his people.

Let me hear what God the LORD will speak,
  for he will speak peace to his people,
  to his faithful, to those who turn to him in their hearts.
Surely his salvation is at hand for those who fear him,
  that his glory may dwell in our land.

The LORD speaks of peace to his people.

◆ All stand and sing **Alleluia.**

GOSPEL

Mark 6:45–51

A reading from the holy Gospel according to Mark.

Immediately Jesus made his disciples get into the boat and go on ahead to the other side, to Bethsaida [beth-SAY-uh-duh], while he dismissed the crowd. After saying farewell to them, he went up on the mountain to pray. When evening came, the boat was out on the sea, and he was alone on the land. When he saw that they were straining at the oars against an adverse wind, he came toward them early in the morning, walking on the sea. He intended to pass them by. But when they saw him walking on the sea, they thought it was a ghost and cried out, for they all saw him and were terrified. But immediately he spoke to them and said, "Take heart, it is I; do not be afraid." Then he got into the boat with them and the wind ceased. And they were utterly astounded.

The Gospel of the Lord.

◆ All sit and observe silence.

FOR SILENT REFLECTION

Think about this silently in your heart. How has God shown his power and love to you?

CLOSING PRAYER

Let us pray to God for our needs and the needs of others: our family, neighborhood, and the world. For each need we say, "Lord, hear our prayer."

◆ All may add their own prayers here.

Let us pray: **Our Father . . . Amen.**

Almighty God,
help us to trust and have faith in you,
so that we may have the courage to face
    any storm.
Through Christ our Lord.,
Amen.

✚ All make the sign of the cross.

PRAYER FOR
THURSDAY, JUNE 13, 2024

OPENING

Today is the memorial of St. Anthony of Padua, Portugal (1195–1231). He is the patron saint of finding lost things. According to legend, he once began to preach to the water off the coast of Italy. A huge school of fish gathered around him to listen. St. Anthony said that the fish were more eager to listen to him than the people. Today's reading is about a group who was listening to Philip.

✦ All make the sign of the cross.

In the name of the Father, and of the Son, and of the Holy Spirit. Amen.

PSALM
(For a longer psalm, see page xv.)
Psalm 85:8–9

The LORD speaks of peace to his people.

The LORD speaks of peace to his people.

Let me hear what God the LORD will speak,
    for he will speak peace to his people,
    to his faithful, to those who turn to him in their hearts.
Surely his salvation is at hand for those who fear him,
    that his glory may dwell in our land.

The LORD speaks of peace to his people.

READING
Acts 8:5–6, 9, 12–13

A reading from the Acts of the Apostles.

Philip went down to the city of Samaria and proclaimed the Messiah to them. The crowds with one accord listened eagerly to what was said by Philip, hearing and seeing the signs that he did. Now a certain man named Simon had previously practiced magic in the city and amazed the people of Samaria, saying that he was someone great. But when they believed Philip, who was proclaiming the good news about the kingdom of God and the name of Jesus Christ, they were baptized, both men and women. Even Simon himself believed. After being baptized, he stayed constantly with Philip and was amazed when he saw the signs and great miracles that took place.

The Word of the Lord.

◆ All observe silence.

FOR SILENT REFLECTION

Think about this silently in your heart. Have you seen God working in your life?

CLOSING PRAYER

Let us pray to God for our needs and the needs of others: our family, neighborhood, and the world. For each need we say, "Lord, hear our prayer."

◆ All may add their own prayers here.

Let us pray: **Our Father . . . Amen.**

Dear God,
you give us true signs that point to you.
Help us come to a deeper understanding that Jesus is the Christ.
We ask this in his name.

Amen.

✦ All make the sign of the cross.

PRAYER FOR
FRIDAY, JUNE 14, 2024

OPENING

A mustard seed is tiny. It is a speck, but when planted, it grows into a mighty tree. Today, we hear Jesus tell his disciples that if they had even a tiny speck of faith—the size of the mustard seed—then something mighty would grow. They would be able to move mountains and perform miracles.

✤ All make the sign of the cross.

In the name of the Father, and of the Son, and of the Holy Spirit. Amen.

PSALM
(For a longer psalm, see page xv.)
Psalm 85:8–9

The LORD speaks of peace to his people.

The LORD speaks of peace to his people.

Let me hear what God the LORD will speak,
　for he will speak peace to his people,
　to his faithful, to those who turn to him in their hearts.
Surely his salvation is at hand for those who fear him,
　that his glory may dwell in our land.

The LORD speaks of peace to his people.

◆ All stand and sing **Alleluia.**

GOSPEL
Matthew 17:14–16, 17c–21

A reading from the holy Gospel according to Matthew.

When they came to the crowd, a man came to Jesus, knelt before him, and said, "Lord, have mercy on my son, for he has epilepsy and suffers terribly; he often falls into the fire and often into the water. And I brought him to your disciples, but they could not cure him." Jesus answered, "Bring him here to me." And Jesus rebuked the demon, and it came out of him, and the boy was cured from that moment. Then the disciples came to Jesus privately and said, "Why could we not cast it out?" He said to them, "Because of your little faith. For truly I tell you, if you have faith the size of a mustard seed, you will say to this mountain, 'Move from here to there', and it will move; and nothing will be impossible for you."

The Gospel of the Lord.

◆ All sit and observe silence.

FOR SILENT REFLECTION

Think about this silently in your heart. How do you nurture your faith?

CLOSING PRAYER

Let us pray to God for our needs and the needs of others: our family, neighborhood, and the world. For each need we say, "Lord, hear our prayer."

◆ All may add their own prayers here.

Let us pray: **Our Father . . . Amen.**

May we have enough faith, O God,
to build your kingdom here on earth.
Through Christ our Lord.

Amen.

✤ All make the sign of the cross.

PRAYER FOR THE WEEK
WITH A READING FROM THE GOSPEL FOR **SUNDAY, JUNE 16, 2024**

OPENING

Jesus often used imagery from everyday life to teach about the kingdom of God. Many of his followers were farmers and could understand how the smallest of seeds could grow into a magnificent creation.

✚ All make the sign of the cross.

In the name of the Father, and of the Son, and of the Holy Spirit. Amen.

PSALM
(For a longer psalm, see page xv.)
Psalm 85:8–9

The Lord speaks of peace to his people.

The Lord speaks of peace to his people.

Let me hear what God the Lord will speak,
   for he will speak peace to his people,
   to his faithful, to those who turn to him in their hearts.
Surely his salvation is at hand for those who fear him,
   that his glory may dwell in our land.

The Lord speaks of peace to his people.

◆ All stand and sing **Alleluia.**

GOSPEL
Mark 4:26–32

A reading from the holy Gospel according to Mark.

Jesus said, "The kingdom of God is as if someone would scatter seed on the ground, and would sleep and rise night and day, and the seed would sprout and grow, he does not know how. The earth produces of itself first the stalk, then the head, then the full grain in the head. But when the grain is ripe, at once he goes in with his sickle because the harvest has come."

He also said, "With what can we compare the kingdom of God, or what parable will we use for it? It is like a mustard seed, which, when sown upon the ground, is the smallest of all the seeds on earth, yet when it is sown it grows up and becomes the greatest of all shrubs and puts forth large branches, so that the birds of the air can make nests in its shade."

The Gospel of the Lord.

◆ All sit and observe silence.

FOR SILENT REFLECTION

Think about this silently in your heart. What helps a small amount of faith grow into a lifetime of service to God?

CLOSING PRAYER

Let us pray to God for our needs and the needs of others: our family, neighborhood, and the world. For each need we say, "Lord, hear our prayer."

◆ All may add their own prayers here.

Let us pray: **Our Father . . . Amen.**

Creator God,
thank you for the mystery of life.
May we continue to grow in love and faith.
Through Christ our Lord.

Amen.

✚ All make the sign of the cross.

PRAYER FOR
MONDAY, JUNE 17, 2024

OPENING

In today's reading, we will hear of the first missionary trip of the Twelve. Jesus prepares them to spread the good news, to teach and heal in his name. Every Christian shares in this mission. We are called to reach out to others with Christ's message of love and peace. We are called to live simply and in community. We are called to share our blessings with each other. In this way, we build up the kingdom of God.

✚ All make the sign of the cross.

In the name of the Father, and of the Son, and of the Holy Spirit. Amen.

PSALM
(For a longer psalm, see page xv.)
Psalm 85:8–9

The LORD speaks of peace to his people.

The LORD speaks of peace to his people.

Let me hear what God the LORD will speak,
   for he will speak peace to his people,
   to his faithful, to those who turn to him in their hearts.
Surely his salvation is at hand for those who fear him,
   that his glory may dwell in our land.

The LORD speaks of peace to his people.

◆ All stand and sing **Alleluia.**

GOSPEL
Mark 6:7–13

A reading from the holy Gospel according to Mark.

Jesus called the twelve and began to send them out two by two and gave them authority over the unclean spirits. He ordered them to take nothing for their journey except a staff: no bread, no bag, no money in their belts, but to wear sandals and not to put on two tunics. He said to them, "Wherever you enter a house, stay there until you leave the place. If any place will not welcome you and they refuse to hear you, as you leave, shake off the dust that is on your feet as a testimony against them." So they went out and proclaimed that all should repent. They cast out many demons and anointed with oil many who were sick and cured them.

The Gospel of the Lord.

◆ All sit and observe silence.

FOR SILENT REFLECTION

Think about this silently in your heart. What do you tell others about your faith?

CLOSING PRAYER

Let us pray to God for our needs and the needs of others: our family, neighborhood, and the world. For each need we say, "Lord, hear our prayer."

◆ All may add their own prayers here.

Let us pray: **Our Father . . . Amen.**

Dear God,
may we be messengers of your Good News.
May we continue the work of the Twelve so that others will know of your saving love.
We ask this through Christ our Lord.

Amen.

✚ All make the sign of the cross.

PRAYER FOR TUESDAY, JUNE 18, 2024

OPENING

In waters of baptism, we have been reborn into Christ's Body. And as part of that Body, we live for and with one another. We live in a community. Together, the apostles saw and believed in the resurrection of Christ. Together, they went out into the world to proclaim the Good News.

✤ All make the sign of the cross.

In the name of the Father, and of the Son, and of the Holy Spirit. Amen.

PSALM

(For a longer psalm, see page xv.)
Psalm 85:8–9

The LORD speaks of peace to his people.

The LORD speaks of peace to his people.

Let me hear what God the LORD will speak,
   for he will speak peace to his people,
   to his faithful, to those who turn to him in their hearts.
Surely his salvation is at hand for those who fear him,
   that his glory may dwell in our land.

The LORD speaks of peace to his people.

◆ All stand and sing **Alleluia.**

GOSPEL

Mark 16:12–16a, 19–20a

A reading from the holy Gospel according to Mark.

Jesus appeared in another form to two of them, as they were walking into the country. And they went back and told the rest, but they did not believe them.

Later he appeared to the eleven themselves as they were sitting at the table, and he upbraided them for their lack of faith and stubbornness, because they had not believed those who saw him after he had risen. And he said to them, "Go into all the world and proclaim the good news to the whole creation. The one who believes and is baptized will be saved."

So then the Lord Jesus, after he had spoken to them, was taken up into heaven and sat down at the right hand of God. And they went out and proclaimed the good news everywhere.

The Gospel of the Lord.

◆ All sit and observe silence.

FOR SILENT REFLECTION

Think about this silently in your heart. We, too, gather together and proclaim the goodness of God and share in the mission of love.

CLOSING PRAYER

Let us pray to God for our needs and the needs of others: our family, neighborhood, and the world. For each need we say, "Lord, hear our prayer."

◆ All may add their own prayers here.

Let us pray: **Our Father . . . Amen.**

May we continue the work of the Twelve,
   O God,
so that others will know of your saving love.
We ask this through Christ our Lord.

Amen.

✤ All make the sign of the cross.

PRAYER FOR
WEDNESDAY, JUNE 19, 2024

OPENING

Jesus was born a child of Israel, but he came to spread his light over all the earth. He did not come only for the holy, or the clean, or the perfect. He came for the sinner, the tax collector, the Samaritan. In the early church, this universal mission was rejected by many Jews, who viewed the inclusion of gentiles as unholy. But the apostles persisted in their missionary work to bring salvation to the ends of the earth.

✢ All make the sign of the cross.

In the name of the Father, and of the Son, and of the Holy Spirit. Amen.

PSALM

(For a longer psalm, see page xv.)
Psalm 85:8–9

The LORD speaks of peace to his people.

The LORD speaks of peace to his people.

Let me hear what God the LORD will speak,
    for he will speak peace to his people,
    to his faithful, to those who turn to him in their hearts.
Surely his salvation is at hand for those who fear him,
    that his glory may dwell in our land.

The LORD speaks of peace to his people.

READING

ACTS 13:43b–47

A reading from the Acts of the Apostles.

Many Jews and devout converts to Judaism [JOO-dee-ihz-*m] followed Paul and Barnabas, who spoke to them and urged them to continue in the grace of God. The next Sabbath almost the whole city gathered to hear the word of the Lord. But when the Jews saw the crowds, they were filled with jealousy, and blaspheming, they contradicted what was spoken by Paul. Then both Paul and Barnabas spoke out boldly, saying, "It was necessary that the word of God should be spoken first to you. Since you reject it and judge yourselves to be unworthy of eternal life, we are now turning to the gentiles [JEN-tīls]. For so the Lord has commanded us, saying, 'I have set you to be a light for the gentiles, so that you may bring salvation to the ends of the earth.'"

The Word of the Lord.

◆ All observe silence.

FOR SILENT REFLECTION

Think about this silently in your heart. Do you include others? What does it mean for the church to be universal today?

CLOSING PRAYER

Let us pray to God for our needs and the needs of others: our family, neighborhood, and the world. For each need we say, "Lord, hear our prayer."

◆ All may add their own prayers here.

Let us pray: **Our Father . . . Amen.**

Thank you, O God, for the generations of
    disciples who have built your
    kingdom on earth.
Through Christ our Lord.

Amen.

✢ All make the sign of the cross.

PRAYER FOR THURSDAY, JUNE 20, 2024

OPENING

After Christ's resurrection, the apostles began to build a structure for their fledgling faith, appointing elders to continue the mission of the apostles, who themselves carried out the mission of Christ. In this way, faith has passed from generation to generation. We are all heirs of this mission.

✠ All make the sign of the cross.

In the name of the Father, and of the Son, and of the Holy Spirit. Amen.

PSALM

(For a longer psalm, see page xv.)
Psalm 85:8–9

The Lord speaks of peace to his people.

The Lord speaks of peace to his people.

Let me hear what God the Lord will speak,
    for he will speak peace to his people,
    to his faithful, to those who turn to him in their hearts.
Surely his salvation is at hand for those who fear him,
    that his glory may dwell in our land.

The Lord speaks of peace to his people.

READING

ACTS 14:21–22a, 23–25, 26a, 27

A reading from the Acts of the Apostles.

After they had proclaimed the good news to that city and had made many disciples, they returned to Lystra [LIS-truh], then on to Iconium [ī-KOH-nee-uhm] and Antioch [AN-tee-ahk]. There they strengthened the souls of the disciples and encouraged them to continue in the faith. And after they had appointed elders for them in each church, with prayer and fasting they entrusted them to the Lord in whom they had come to believe. Then they passed through Pisidia [pih-SID-ee-uh] and came to Pamphylia [pam-FIL-ee-uh]. When they had spoken the word in Perga, they went down to Attalia [at-uh-LĪ-uh]. From there they sailed back to Antioch. When they arrived, they called the church together and related all that God had done with them and how he had opened a door of faith for the gentiles [JEN-tīls].

The Word of the Lord.

◆ All observe silence.

FOR SILENT REFLECTION

Think about this silently in your heart. Thank God for all the people who work to keep your Church community strong.

CLOSING PRAYER

Let us pray to God for our needs and the needs of others: our family, neighborhood, and the world. For each need we say, "Lord, hear our prayer."

◆ All may add their own prayers here.

Let us pray: **Our Father . . . Amen.**

May we be encouraging to others in their own faith journey, O God,
so that we all grow together in prayer and love.
We pray in Christ's name.

Amen.

✠ All make the sign of the cross.

PRAYER FOR FRIDAY, JUNE 21, 2024

OPENING

We are ambassadors for Christ. This is what St. Paul tells the church in Corinth, and perhaps this is what we need to hear today. Today we remember St. Aloysius Gonzaga [al-oh-WISH-uhs guhn-ZAHG-uh] (1568–1591), the patron saint of youth. Though born of a princely family, he became a priest. He spent his short life caring for the less fortunate and vulnerable members of society.

✠ All make the sign of the cross.

In the name of the Father, and of the Son, and of the Holy Spirit. Amen.

PSALM

(For a longer psalm, see page xv.)
Psalm 85:8–9

The LORD speaks of peace to his people.

The LORD speaks of peace to his people.

Let me hear what God the LORD will speak,
  for he will speak peace to his people,
  to his faithful, to those who turn to him in their hearts.
Surely his salvation is at hand for those who fear him,
  that his glory may dwell in our land.

The LORD speaks of peace to his people.

READING

2 Corinthians 1:1b–2; 5:17, 20; 6:1–2

A reading from the Second Letter to the Corinthians [kohr-IN-thee-uhnz].

To the church of God that is in Corinth [KOHR-ihnth], together with all the saints throughout Achaia [uh-KAY-yuh]: Grace to you and peace from God our Father and the Lord Jesus Christ. So if anyone is in Christ, there is a new creation: everything old has passed away; look, new things have come into being! So we are ambassadors for Christ, since God is making his appeal through us; we entreat you on behalf of Christ: be reconciled to God.

As we work together with him, we entreat you also not to accept the grace of God in vain. For he says, "At an acceptable time I have listened to you, and on a day of salvation I have helped you." Look, now is the acceptable time; look, now is the day of salvation!

The Word of the Lord.

◆ All observe silence.

FOR SILENT REFLECTION

Think about this silently in your heart. How can you be an ambassador for Christ?

CLOSING PRAYER

Let us pray to God for our needs and the needs of others: our family, neighborhood, and the world. For each need we say, "Lord, hear our prayer."

◆ All may add their own prayers here.

Let us pray: **Our Father . . . Amen.**

Dear God,
help us to be leaders in our faith
and to spread Jesus' love, forgiveness,
and grace to others.
We ask this through Christ our Lord.

Amen.

✠ All make the sign of the cross.

PRAYER FOR THE WEEK
WITH A READING FROM THE GOSPEL FOR **SUNDAY, JUNE 23, 2024**

OPENING

Have you ever felt overwhelmed? Maybe you felt stressed about school, or were in trouble with your parents, or in a fight with a friend. All of us go through tough times. But Jesus is there in the storm with us. We believe in a God who holds the entire world in his hand.

✙ All make the sign of the cross.

In the name of the Father, and of the Son, and of the Holy Spirit. Amen.

PSALM
(For a longer psalm, see page xv.)
Psalm 85:8–9

The Lord speaks of peace to his people.

The Lord speaks of peace to his people.

Let me hear what God the Lord will speak,
　for he will speak peace to his people,
　　to his faithful, to those who turn to him in their hearts.
Surely his salvation is at hand for those who fear him,
　that his glory may dwell in our land.

The Lord speaks of peace to his people.

◆ All stand and sing **Alleluia.**

GOSPEL
MARK 4:35–36a, 37–41

A reading from the holy Gospel according to Mark.

On that day, when evening had come, Jesus said to them, "Let us go across to the other side." And leaving the crowd behind, they took him with them in the boat, just as he was. A great windstorm arose, and the waves beat into the boat, so that the boat was already being swamped. But he was in the stern, asleep on the cushion, and they woke him up and said to him, "Teacher, do you not care that we are perishing?" He rebuked the wind and said to the sea, "Be silent! Be still!" Then the wind ceased, and there was a dead calm. He said to them, "Why are you afraid? Have you still no faith?" And they were filled with great fear and said to one another, "Who then is this, that even the wind and the sea obey him?"

The Gospel of the Lord.

◆ All sit and observe silence.

FOR SILENT REFLECTION

Think about this silently in your heart. Jesus is also known as the Prince of Peace. Calm your mind, heart, and body to the peace of Jesus.

CLOSING PRAYER

Let us pray to God for our needs and the needs of others: our family, neighborhood, and the world. For each need we say, "Lord, hear our prayer."

◆ All may add their own prayers here.

Let us pray: **Our Father . . . Amen.**

Father in heaven,
you encourage our faith when the storms of
　　life seem overwhelming.
Help us to live in total dependence on you.
Through Christ our Lord.

Amen.

✙ All make the sign of the cross.

PRAYER FOR
MONDAY, JUNE 24, 2024

OPENING

Today we celebrate the Nativity, or birth, of John the Baptist. John prepared the way for Jesus. He lived his life in humility, always pointing toward the Light that surpassed his own. John was also Jesus' cousin, a member of his own family. We are called to be part of this family as well. We are adopted brothers and sisters of Jesus, sons and daughters of the Father. We are called to do the will of the Father. Like John, our whole lives should point toward Jesus.

✚ All make the sign of the cross.

In the name of the Father, and of the Son, and of the Holy Spirit. Amen.

PSALM
(For a longer psalm, see page xv.)
Psalm 85:8–9

The LORD speaks of peace to his people.

The LORD speaks of peace to his people.

Let me hear what God the LORD will speak,
    for he will speak peace to his people,
    to his faithful, to those who turn to him in their hearts.
Surely his salvation is at hand for those who fear him,
    that his glory may dwell in our land.

The LORD speaks of peace to his people.

◆ All stand and sing **Alleluia.**

GOSPEL
Mark 3:31–35

A reading from the holy Gospel according to Mark.

Then Jesus' mother and his brothers came, and standing outside they sent to him and called him. A crowd was sitting around him, and they said to him, "Your mother and your brothers and sisters are outside, asking for you." And he replied, "Who are my mother and my brothers?" And looking at those who sat around him, he said, "Here are my mother and my brothers! Whoever does the will of God is my brother and sister and mother."

The Gospel of the Lord.

◆ All sit and observe silence.

FOR SILENT REFLECTION

Think about this silently in your heart. How do you point your life toward God?

CLOSING PRAYER

Let us pray to God for our needs and the needs of others: our family, neighborhood, and the world. For each need we say, "Lord, hear our prayer."

◆ All may add their own prayers here.

Let us pray: **Our Father . . . Amen.**

Dear God,
thank you for including us in your family.
May we see all those around us as our
    brothers and sisters in Christ,
in whose name we pray.

Amen.

✚ All make the sign of the cross.

PRAYER FOR TUESDAY, JUNE 25, 2024

OPENING

The community of believers first came together in awe. This community worshipped together. They broke bread together. They lived together. They ate together. They shared all things, and praised God with glad and generous hearts. This community was attractive to others—they lived together in love and cooperation. The community grew and grew.

✠ All make the sign of the cross.

In the name of the Father, and of the Son, and of the Holy Spirit. Amen.

PSALM

(For a longer psalm, see page xv.)
Psalm 85:8–9

The LORD speaks of peace to his people.

The LORD speaks of peace to his people.

Let me hear what God the LORD will speak,
  for he will speak peace to his people,
  to his faithful, to those who turn to him in their hearts.
Surely his salvation is at hand for those who fear him,
  that his glory may dwell in our land.

The LORD speaks of peace to his people.

READING

Acts 2:38, 43–47

A reading from the Acts of the Apostles.

Peter said to them, "Repent and be baptized every one of you in the name of Jesus Christ so that your sins may be forgiven, and you will receive the gift of the Holy Spirit."

Awe came upon everyone because many wonders and signs were being done through the apostles. All who believed were together and had all things in common; they would sell their possessions and goods and distribute the proceeds to all, as any had need. Day by day, as they spent much time together in the temple, they broke bread at home and ate their food with glad and generous hearts, praising God and having the goodwill of all the people. And day by day the Lord added to their number those who were being saved.

The Word of the Lord.

◆ All observe silence.

FOR SILENT REFLECTION

Think about this silently in your heart. How do you follow Jesus and live by his example?

CLOSING PRAYER

Let us pray to God for our needs and the needs of others: our family, neighborhood, and the world. For each need we say, "Lord, hear our prayer."

◆ All may add their own prayers here.

Let us pray: **Our Father . . . Amen.**

Holy Spirit,
you enlivened the early Church.
Inspire us with the same zeal and love
we experience in a family of faith.
Through Christ our Lord.

Amen.

✠ All make the sign of the cross.

PRAYER FOR
WEDNESDAY, JUNE 26, 2024

OPENING

Ritual sacrifice was part of many ancient religions, including Judaism in Jesus' day. But St. Paul told the Romans to offer their own bodies as a sacrifice. In other words, we must sacrifice our bodies out of love for one another. We are called not just to pray for our neighbor, but to be there with them in the unseen and unglamorous daily tasks. We are called to sacrifice our time and energy in service to one another.

✚ All make the sign of the cross.

In the name of the Father, and of the Son, and of the Holy Spirit. Amen.

PSALM
(For a longer psalm, see page xv.)
Psalm 85:8–9

The Lord speaks of peace to his people.

The Lord speaks of peace to his people.

Let me hear what God the Lord will speak,
    for he will speak peace to his people,
    to his faithful, to those who turn to him in their hearts.
Surely his salvation is at hand for those who fear him,
    that his glory may dwell in our land.

The Lord speaks of peace to his people.

READING
Romans 12:1a–c, 9–10; 13:9

A reading from the Letter to the Romans.

I appeal to you therefore, brothers and sisters, on the basis of God's mercy, to present your bodies as a living sacrifice, holy and acceptable to God.

Let love be genuine; hate what is evil, hold fast to what is good; love one another with mutual affection; outdo one another in showing honor.

The commandments, "You shall not commit adultery; you shall not murder; you shall not steal; you shall not covet," and any other commandment, are summed up in this word, "You shall love your neighbor as yourself."

The Word of the Lord.

◆ All observe silence.

FOR SILENT REFLECTION

Think about this silently in your heart. In what way can you serve others this week?

CLOSING PRAYER

Let us pray to God for our needs and the needs of others: our family, neighborhood, and the world. For each need we say, "Lord, hear our prayer."

◆ All may add their own prayers here.

Let us pray: **Our Father . . . Amen.**

Loving Father,
you gave us a commandment to
    love one another.
May we show Christ's love
    to all whom we meet today.
Through Christ our Lord.

Amen.

✚ All make the sign of the cross.

PRAYER FOR THURSDAY, JUNE 27, 2024

OPENING

Today we remember fifth-century archbishop St. Cyril of Alexandria, Egypt. He was a champion of the faith's doctrine and fought heresy. Words have power. They can lift up spirits, or tear someone down to the ground. In today's reading we will hear St. Paul caution us to be careful with our words, to use them only for building up and giving grace to others.

✠ All make the sign of the cross.

In the name of the Father, and of the Son, and of the Holy Spirit. Amen.

PSALM

(For a longer psalm, see page xv.)
Psalm 85:8–9

The LORD speaks of peace to his people.

The LORD speaks of peace to his people.

Let me hear what God the LORD will speak,
  for he will speak peace to his people,
  to his faithful, to those who turn to him in
    their hearts.
Surely his salvation is at hand for those who
    fear him,
  that his glory may dwell in our land.

The LORD speaks of peace to his people.

READING

Ephesians 4:25–27, 29–32

A reading from the Letter to the Ephesians [ee-FEE-zhuhnz].

So then, putting away falsehood, let each of you speak the truth with your neighbor, for we are members of one another. Be angry but do not sin; do not let the sun go down on your anger, and do not make room for the devil. Let no evil talk come out of your mouths but only what is good for building up, as there is need, so that your words may give grace to those who hear. And do not grieve the Holy Spirit of God, with which you were marked with a seal for the day of redemption. Put away from you all bitterness and wrath and anger and wrangling and slander, together with all malice. Be kind to one another, tenderhearted, forgiving one another, as God in Christ has forgiven you.

The Word of the Lord.

◆ All observe silence.

FOR SILENT REFLECTION

Think about this silently in your heart. Do you take care with your words? How can you use them to build people up?

CLOSING PRAYER

Let us pray to God for our needs and the needs of others: our family, neighborhood, and the world. For each need we say, "Lord, hear our prayer."

◆ All may add their own prayers here.

Let us pray: **Our Father . . . Amen.**

O God,
we ask for the strength to encourage one
  another in the faith.
Help us to forgive those who hurt us,
and rid our hearts of anger and pain.
In Christ's name we pray.

Amen.

✠ All make the sign of the cross.

PRAYER FOR FRIDAY, JUNE 28, 2024

OPENING

Today we remember St. Irenaeus [eer-uh-NAY-uhs], a second-century Greek bishop who passed on Church teaching as it was handed down from St. Peter and the apostles. In today's letter, St. Paul encourages the Philippians—and us—to be loving, gentle, and peaceful. Strive to be a child of God, and the joy of the Lord will be yours.

✛ All make the sign of the cross.

In the name of the Father, and of the Son, and of the Holy Spirit. Amen.

PSALM

(For a longer psalm, see page xv.)
Psalm 85:8–9

The LORD speaks of peace to his people.

The LORD speaks of peace to his people.

Let me hear what God the LORD will speak,
 for he will speak peace to his people,
 to his faithful, to those who turn to him in
  their hearts.
Surely his salvation is at hand for those who
  fear him,
 that his glory may dwell in our land.

The LORD speaks of peace to his people.

READING

Philippians 4:1, 4–5a, 7–9

A reading from the Letter to the Philippians [fih-LIP-ee-uhnz].
Therefore, my brothers and sisters, whom I love and long for, my joy and crown, stand firm in the Lord in this way, my beloved. Rejoice in the Lord always; again I will say, Rejoice. Let your gentleness be known to everyone. And the peace of God, which surpasses all understanding, will guard your hearts and your minds in Christ Jesus. Finally, brothers and sisters, whatever is true, whatever is honorable, whatever is just, whatever is pure, whatever is pleasing, whatever is commendable, if there is any excellence and if there is anything worthy of praise, think about these things. As for the things that you have learned and received and heard and noticed in me, do them, and the God of peace will be with you.

The Word of the Lord.

◆ All observe silence.

FOR SILENT REFLECTION

Think about this silently in your heart. Where do you find joy? Do you strive to live a virtuous life?

CLOSING PRAYER

Let us pray to God for our needs and the needs of others: our family, neighborhood, and the world. For each need we say, "Lord, hear our prayer."

◆ All may add their own prayers here.

Let us pray: **Our Father . . . Amen.**

God of love and peace,
we rejoice in you!
Thank you for all you have given and taught
  us this year.
Watch over us during these summer months,
and may we continue our journey of faith.
Through Christ our Lord.

Amen.

✛ All make the sign of the cross.

BLESSING FOR BIRTHDAYS

✚ All make the sign of the cross.

ALL: In the name of the Father, and of the Son, and of the Holy Spirit. Amen.

LEADER:
Loving God,
you created all the people of the world,
and you know each of us by name.
We thank you for N., who today
    celebrates his/her birthday.
Bless him/her with your love and friendship
that he/she may grow in wisdom, knowledge,
    and grace.
May he/she love his/her family always
and be faithful to his/her friends.
Grant this through Christ our Lord.

ALL: Amen.

LEADER:
Let us bow our heads and pray for N.

◆ All observe silence.

LEADER:
May God, in whose presence our ancestors walked, bless you.

ALL: Amen.

LEADER:
May God, who has been your shepherd from birth until now, keep you.

ALL: Amen.

LEADER:
May God, who saves you from all harm, give you peace.

ALL: Amen.

✚ All make the sign of the cross.

In the name of the Father, and of the Son, and of the Holy Spirit. Amen.

PRAYER SERVICE
LAST DAY OF SCHOOL

Prepare eight leaders for this service. The fourth leader will need a Bible for the Scripture passage and may need help practicing the reading. You may wish to begin by singing "In the Lord I'll Be Ever Thankful" and end with "Send Forth Your Spirit, O Lord." If the group will sing, prepare a song leader.

FIRST LEADER:
Our school year is drawing to a close, and we can see in ourselves so much growth! With each passing day, God worked through each person to make a new creation. Together, let us thank our Creator for the many blessed memories we've shared in our time together.

SECOND LEADER:

✦ All make the sign of the cross.

In the name of the Father, and of the Son, and of the Holy Spirit. Amen.

Let us pray:
God of all creation,
we are blessed to be with one another
in this time and place.
We are excited to start our break,
yet we may feel sad as we
think about friends
we may not see for a while.
In these times of change,
help us to stay
connected with you, Lord,
for you desire happiness and peace
for all your brothers and sisters.
We ask this through Jesus Christ our Lord.

ALL: Amen.

THIRD LEADER: Psalm 119:1–3, 10–11, 41–42, 89–90, 105
Let us repeat the Psalm Response: Your word is a lamp to my feet and a light to my path.

ALL: Your word is a lamp to my feet and a light to my path.

Happy are those whose way is blameless,
   who walk in the law of the Lord.
Happy are those who keep his decrees,
   who seek him with their whole heart,
who also do no wrong,
   but walk in his ways.

ALL: Your word is a lamp to my feet and a light to my path.

With my whole heart I seek you;
   do not let me stray from your
      commandments.
I treasure your word in my heart,
   so that I may not sin against you.

ALL: Your word is a lamp to my feet and a light to my path.

Let your steadfast love come to me, O Lord,
   your salvation according to your promise.
Then I shall have an answer for those who
     taunt me,
   for I trust in your word.

ALL: Your word is a lamp to my feet and a light to my path.

The Lord exists forever;
   your word is firmly fixed in heaven.
Your faithfulness endures to all generations;
   you have established the earth, and it
      stands fast.

ALL: Your word is a lamp to my feet and a light to my path.

FOURTH LEADER: Romans 12:9–18
A reading from the Letter of Paul to the Romans.

- Read the Scripture passage from the Bible.

The Word of the Lord.

- All observe silence.

FIFTH LEADER:
Let us bring our hopes and needs to God as we pray, "Lord, hear our prayer."
For our teachers, administrators,
volunteers, coaches, and school staff
who worked hard to produce our
quality learning time together,

we pray to the Lord . . .

For our parents, grandparents,
and family members who helped us
with homework and other tasks
throughout the year,

we pray to the Lord . . .

For the friends we've made
and those on the horizon,
may they reflect the warmth and compassion
that Jesus feels for us,

we pray to the Lord . . .

For those who are dealing with sickness,
job loss, or other difficulties in life,
for those who have gone before us
to the other side of life,
may they experience the peace of Christ,

we pray to the Lord . . .

SIXTH LEADER:
Lord Jesus,
your gentle Spirit has
nudged and guided us
these past several months.
May we continue to seek your wisdom
as we daily pray to you,
ever mindful of
how much you care for us.
We ask this in your name.

Amen.

SEVENTH LEADER:
Let us offer to one another a sign of
Christ's peace:

- All offer one another a sign of peace.

EIGHTH LEADER:
Let us pray:
Creator God,
you are Lord of all things,
and you are always with us.
May we embrace
all our new experiences
in our break from school.
Help us to listen to you,
source of all truth,
and go forth to
new adventures,
cherishing the love that
we've shared this year.

ALL: Amen.

✢ All make the sign of the cross.

PRAYER SERVICE
FOR SAD DAYS

The following prayer can be used when there is a sad or tragic event in the school community. This may be an illness or death of a student, faculty, or staff member, or a parent of a student. It may also be used at a time of a local or national crisis when the school gathers to pray. For this prayer, an adult should take the part of the leader as it is important to offer a few words that describe the particular need or concern.

✠ All make the sign of the cross.

ALL: In the name of the Father, and of the Son, and of the Holy Spirit. Amen.

LEADER:
We gather today to pray for [name the person or concern].
We trust, O God, that you hear us.
We trust that you understand the suffering and pain of your people.
We trust that you are with all those in need.
Let us listen to the Word of God.

READER: Matthew 11:28–30
A reading from the holy Gospel according to Matthew.

"Come to me, all you that are weary and are carrying heavy burdens, and I will give you rest. Take my yoke upon you, and learn from me; for I am gentle and humble in heart, and you will find rest for your souls. For my yoke is easy, and my burden is light."

LEADER:
Let us take a few moments to pray in our hearts for [name the person or concern].

LEADER:
Let us pray:
God of all,
help us to remember that your son Jesus suffered, died, and rose so that we might know of your great love.

He invites us to bring our cares and concerns to you in prayer, and so we ask you to be with [name the persons]. Give them courage and peace.

We ask you also to be with us during this time of difficulty. Help us to trust that you are always with us.

◆ [If appropriate, invite spontaneous prayers from those gathered.]

LEADER:
Assured of your great love, we pray:
Our Father . . . Amen.

◆ Pause and say:

As we conclude our prayer, let us offer one another the sign of Christ's peace.

◆ All offer one another a sign of peace.

LEADER:
May God the Creator bless us:

✠ All make the sign of the cross.

In the name of the Father, and of the Son, and of the Holy Spirit. Amen.

PSALMS AND CANTICLES

PSALMS

PSALM 23

This psalm is appropriate during all liturgical seasons. It may be prayed in times of difficulty or stress, when comfort is needed, or to meditate on Christ's presence in the sacraments.

The Lord is my shepherd, I shall not want.
    He makes me lie down in green pastures;
he leads me beside still waters;
    he restores my soul.
He leads me in right paths
    for his name's sake.

Even though I walk through the darkest valley,
    I fear no evil;
for you are with me;
    your rod and your staff—
    they comfort me.

You prepare a table before me
    in the presence of my enemies;
you anoint my head with oil;
    my cup overflows.
Surely goodness and mercy shall follow me
    all the days of my life,
and I shall dwell in the house of the Lord
    my whole life long.

PSALM 27

Psalm 27:1, 4–5, 7–9, 13–14

Use this psalm during times of darkness, anxiety, or uncertainty. This psalm is also an affirmation of God's goodness at any moment in life.

The LORD is my light and my salvation;
   whom shall I fear?
The LORD is the stronghold of my life;
   of whom shall I be afraid?

One thing I asked of the LORD,
   that will I seek after:
to live in the house of the LORD
   all the days of my life,
to behold the beauty of the LORD,
   and to inquire in his temple.

For he will hide me in his shelter
   in the day of trouble;
he will conceal me under the cover of his tent;
   he will set me high on a rock.

Hear, O LORD, when I cry aloud,
   be gracious to me and answer me!
"Come," my heart says, "seek his face!"
   Your face, LORD do I seek.
   Do not hide your face from me.

I believe that I shall see the goodness of the LORD
   in the land of the living.
Wait for the LORD;
   be strong, and let your heart take courage;
   wait for the LORD!

PSALMS

PSALM 34

Psalm 34:1–8

This psalm of trust in God's power may be prayed by anyone seeking to wonder and rejoice in Christ's presence in the Eucharist. It is especially appropriate for those preparing to celebrate first Communion.

I will bless the Lord at all times;
   his praise shall continually be in my mouth.
My soul makes its boast in the Lord;
   let the humble hear and be glad.
O magnify the Lord with me,
   and let us exalt his name together.

I sought the Lord, and he answered me,
   and delivered me from all my fears.
Look to him, and be radiant;
   so your faces shall never be ashamed.
This poor soul cried, and was heard by the Lord,
   and was saved from every trouble.
The angel of the Lord encamps
   around those who fear him, and delivers them.
O taste and see that the Lord is good;
   happy are those who take refuge in him.

PSALMS

PSALM 46

Psalm 46:1–5

This psalm may be used during times of suffering, confusion, or fear. Its offer of comfort and renewal will give cause for hope in any extremity.

God is our refuge and strength,
   a very present help in trouble.
Therefore we will not fear, though the earth should change,
   though the mountains shake in the heart of the sea;
though its waters roar and foam,
   though the mountains tremble with its tumult.

There is a river whose streams make glad the city of God,
   the holy habitation of the Most High.
God is in the midst of the city; it shall not be moved;
   God will help it when the morning dawns.

PSALMS

PSALM 51

Psalm 51:1–2, 6, 10, 12, 15

This is a penitential psalm that is especially appropriate during a communal celebration of the sacrament of reconciliation. It can also be incorporated into any Lenten prayer service.

Have mercy on me, O God,
    according to your steadfast love;
according to your abundant mercy
    blot out my transgressions.
Wash me thoroughly from my iniquity,
    and cleanse me from my sin.

You desire truth in the inward being;
    therefore teach me wisdom in my secret heart.

Create in me a clean heart, O God,
    and put a new and right spirit within me.
Restore to me the joy of your salvation,
    and sustain in me a willing spirit.

O Lord, open my lips,
    and my mouth will declare your praise.

PSALMS

PSALM 100

This is a joyful psalm of thanksgiving that helps orient the heart to God.

Make a joyful noise to the LORD, all the earth.
    Worship the LORD with gladness;
    come into his presence with singing.
Know that the LORD is God.
    It is he that made us, and we are his;
    we are his people, and the sheep of his pasture.
Enter his gates with thanksgiving,
    and his courts with praise.
    Give thanks to him, bless his name.
For the LORD is good;
    his steadfast love endures forever,
    and his faithfulness to all generations.

PSALMS

PSALM 103

Psalm 103:1–5, 19–22

This is a deeply meditative psalm of grateful acknowledgment of God's gifts and God's mercy.

Bless the LORD, O my soul,
   and all that is within me,
   bless his holy name.
Bless the LORD, O my soul,
   and do not forget all his benefits—
who forgives all your iniquity,
   who heals all your diseases,
who redeems your life from the Pit,
   who crowns you with steadfast love and mercy,
who satisfies you with good as long as you live
   so that your youth is renewed like the eagle's.

The LORD has established his throne in the heavens,
   and his kingdom rules over all.
Bless the LORD, O you his angels,
   you mighty ones who do his bidding,
   obedient to his spoken word.
Bless the LORD, all his works,
   in all places of his dominion.
Bless the LORD, O my soul.

PSALMS

PSALM 139

Psalm 139:1–6, 13–16

This psalm expresses the wonder and awe of our mysterious relationship to the God who knows us intimately and loves us completely.

O Lord, you have searched me and known me.
You know when I sit down and when I rise up;
   you discern my thoughts from far away.
You search out my path and my lying down,
   and are acquainted with all my ways.
Even before a word is on my tongue,
   O Lord, you know it completely.
You hem me in, behind and before,
   and lay your hand upon me.
Such knowledge is too wonderful for me;
   it is so high that I cannot attain it.

For it was you who formed my inward parts;
   you knit me together in my mother's womb.
I praise you, for I am fearfully and wonderfully made.
   Wonderful are your works;
that I know very well.
   My frame was not hidden from you,
when I was being made in secret,
   intricately woven in the depths of the earth.
Your eyes beheld my unformed substance.
In your book were written
all the days that were formed for me,
   when none of them as yet existed.

PSALMS

PSALM 148

Psalm 148:1-4; 7-13

This is a psalm praising God for the glory of creation. It is a good prayer to use especially during the weeks in which the Scripture readings focus on creation of the earth.

Praise the Lord!
Praise the Lord from the heavens; praise him in the heights!
Praise him, all his angels; praise him all his host!

Praise him, sun and moon; praise him, all you shining stars!
Praise him, you highest heavens, and your waters below the heavens!

Praise the Lord from the earth,
    you sea monsters and all deeps,
fire and hail, snow and frost, stormy wind fulfilling his command!

Mountains and all hills, fruit trees and all cedars!
Wild animals and all cattle, creeping things and flying birds!

Kings of the earth and all peoples,
    Princes and all rulers of the earth1
Young men and women alike, old and young together.

Let them praise the name of the Lord,
    For his name alone is exalted;
His glory is above earth and heaven.

PSALMS

PSALM 150

Psalm 150

This psalm praises God, suggesting that we use all sorts of musical instruments to offer our praise. It is a song of great joy and rejoicing.

Praise the LORD!
Praise God in his sanctuary; praise him in his mighty firmament!
Praise him for his mighty deeds; praise him
    according to his surpassing greatness!

Praise him with trumpet sound; praise him with lute and harp!
Praise him with tambourine and dance;
    praise him with strings and pipe!
    Praise him with clanging cymbals;
        Praise him with loud clashing cymbals!
    Let everything that breathes praise the LORD!
    Praise the LORD!

CANTICLES

THE MAGNIFICAT OF MARY

Luke 1:46–55

Mary prayed with these words when she visited her relative, Elizabeth, after Elizabeth declared, "Blessed are you among women and blessed is the fruit of your womb!" For centuries, this beautiful song of praise and trust has been the Church's evening prayer.

And Mary said,
"My soul magnifies the Lord,
    and my spirit rejoices in God my savior,
for he has looked with favor on the lowliness of his servant.
    Surely, from now on all generations will call me blessed;
for the Mighty One has done great things for me,
    and holy is his name.
His mercy is for those who fear him
    from generation to generation.
He has shown strength with his arm;
    he has scattered the proud in the thoughts of their hearts.
He has brought down the powerful from their thrones,
    and lifted up the lowly;
he has filled the hungry with good things,
    and sent the rich away empty.
He has helped his servant Israel,
    in remembrance of his mercy,
according to the promise he made to our ancestors,
    to Abraham and to his descendants forever."

CANTICLES

THE BENEDICTUS OF ZECHARIAH

Luke 1:68–79

Zechariah had been struck mute during the pregnancy of his wife, Elizabeth. After their baby was born, on the day when they gave him his name, Zechariah's voice was restored and he spoke these prophetic words over his child, John the Baptist. His prophecy is part of the Church's traditional morning prayer.

"Blessed be the Lord God of Israel,
  for he has looked favorably on his people and redeemed them.
He has raised up a mighty savior for us
  in the house of his servant David,
as he spoke through the mouth of his holy prophets from of old,
  that we would be saved from our enemies and from the hand
    of all who hate us.
Thus he has shown the mercy promised to our ancestors,
  and has remembered his holy covenant,
the oath that he swore to our ancestor Abraham,
  to grant us that we, being rescued from the hands
    of our enemies,
might serve him without fear, in holiness and righteousness,
  before him all our days.
And you, child, will be called the prophet of the Most High;
  for you will go before the Lord to prepare his ways,
to give knowledge of salvation to his people
  by the forgiveness of their sins.
By the tender mercy of our God,
  the dawn from on high will break upon us,
to give light to those who sit in darkness and in the shadow
    of death,
  to guide our feet into the way of peace."

RESOURCES FOR PRAYING WITH CHILDREN

In addition to *Children's Daily Prayer*, teachers, principals, and catechists may find these LTP resources to be helpful in their work of developing prayer services and preparing children for Mass and reception of the sacraments.

PREPARING MASSES WITH CHILDREN: 15 EASY STEPS

A resource to assist teachers and catechists in preparing children to participate fully in the Mass.

FROM MASS TO MISSION

A small guide that explains the significance of the Mass for living a Christian life. There is a guide for children and a guide for teens; each has a leader's guide to accompany the book.

THE YEAR OF GRACE LITURGICAL CALENDAR

This annual circular calendar displays the liturgical year. It highlights the color for each liturgical season and provides a visual guide to the major feasts and saints' days throughout the year. Each year, the calendar has beautiful art to illustrate a particular theme or liturgical focus.

CHILDREN'S LITURGY OF THE WORD

An annual publication that offers a guide to help prepare a Liturgy of the Word for children on Sundays and Holydays of Obligation.

BLESSINGS AND PRAYERS THROUGH THE YEAR: A RESOURCE FOR SCHOOL AND PARISH

This is an illustrated collection of prayers and blessings and prayer services, which includes two CD-ROMS of music with vocal instruction and musical accompaniment to facilitate singing.

COMPANION TO THE CALENDAR: A GUIDE TO THE SAINTS, SEASONS, AND HOLIDAYS OF THE YEAR.

An invaluable resource for learning more about the particular saint or feast of the day. This book could be used to help children learn more about their patron saint or saints of special interest.

SCHOOL YEAR, CHURCH YEAR: CUSTOMS AND DECORATIONS FOR THE CLASSROOM

Teachers and catechists who wish to create an environment in the classroom that reflects the liturgical season will find many creative and doable ideas in this book.